Robert M. Turner

with the cordial regards of

F. W. Taussig

[illegible]. 1913

Principles of Economics

Volume I.

F. W. Taussig

Simon Publications, Inc.
2003

Published in 1916 by the Macmillan Company, New York, London

Library of Congress Card Number: 15010737

ISBN: 1-932512-06-3

Published by Simon Publications, Inc. P. O. Box 910455, San Diego, CA 92191-0455

PATRI • DILECTO
FILIVS • GRATVS

PREFACE

I HAVE tried in this book to state the principles of economics in such form that they shall be comprehensible to an educated and intelligent person who has not before made any systematic study of the subject. Though designed in this sense for beginners, the book does not gloss over difficulties or avoid severe reasoning. No one can understand economic phenomena or prepare himself to deal with economic problems who is unwilling to follow trains of reasoning which call for sustained attention. I have done my best to be clear, and to state with care the grounds on which my conclusions rest, as well as the conclusions themselves, but have made no vain pretense of simplifying all things.

The order of the topics has been determined more by convenience for exposition than by any strict regard for system. In general, a subject has been entered on only when the main conclusions relating to it could be followed to the end. Yet so close is the connection between the different parts of economics that it has been necessary sometimes to go part way in the consideration of matters on which the final word had to be reserved for a later stage. Taxation has offered, as regards its place in the arrangement, perhaps the greatest difficulties. It is so closely connected with economics that some consideration of it seemed essential; whereas public finance in the stricter sense, whose problems are political quite as much as economic, has been omitted. Yet a suitable place for taxation was not easy to find. I concluded finally to put the chapters on this subject at the very close, even though they may have the effect of an anticlimax, coming as they do after those on socialism.

The book deals chiefly with the industrial conditions of modern countries, and most of all with those of the United States. Economic history and economic development are not considered in any set chapters, being touched only as they happen to illustrate one or another of the problems of contemporary society. Some topics to which economists give much attention in discussion among themselves receive scant attention or none at all. I have omitted entirely the usual chapters or sections on definition, methodology, and history of dogma; and have said little on such a topic as the subjective theory of value, which in my judgment is of less service for explaining the phenomena of the real world than is supposed by its votaries. These matters and others of the same sort are best left to the professional literature of the subject. I hope this book is not undeserving the attention of specialists; but it is meant to be read by others than specialists.

Though not written on the usual model of textbooks, and not planned primarily to meet the needs of teachers and students, the book will prove of service, I hope, in institutions which offer substantial courses in economics. The fact that it is addressed to mature persons, not to the immature, should be an argument in favor of such use rather than against it. Being neither an encyclopedic treatise nor a textbook of the familiar sort, it offers no voluminous footnotes and no detailed directions for collateral reading. When facts and figures not of common knowledge have been cited, my sources of information have been stated. At the close of each of the eight Books into which the whole is divided, I have given suggestions for further reading and study, mentioning the really important books and papers.

I have expressed in the text, as occasion arose, my obligations to the contemporary thinkers from whom I have derived most stimulus. For great aid in revising the manuscript and proof, on matters both of form and substance, I am indebted to my colleagues Drs. R. F. Foerster and E. E. Day of Harvard University.

F. W. TAUSSIG.

HARVARD UNIVERSITY,
March, 1911.

CONTENTS

BOOK I

THE ORGANIZATION OF PRODUCTION

BOOK III

MONEY AND THE MECHANISM OF EXCHANGE

CHAPTER 17

CHAPTER 18

CHAPTER 19

BOOK IV

INTERNATIONAL TRADE

CHAPTER 32

CHAPTER 33

VOLUME II

BOOK V

THE DISTRIBUTION OF WEALTH

CHAPTER 47

CHAPTER 48

CHAPTER 49

CHAPTER 54

BOOK VI

PROBLEMS OF LABOR

CHAPTER 55

CHAPTER 69

CHAPTER 70

BOOK I

THE ORGANIZATION OF PRODUCTION

CHAPTER 1

Of Wealth and Labor

§ 1. To define with accuracy the scope and contents of economics is not of importance in the earlier stages of its study. The precise demarcation of its subject matter, and its relation to other branches of knowledge, can be understood only when something is known of its main conclusions. It suffices at the outset to indicate by an example what is the nature of the problems dealt with. A good example is found in the economic position of one of the most familiar articles of use, — water.

In a thinly settled community, where springs and streams are abundant, water is free to all. No question can arise as to its ownership or as to the mode in which the community should deal with it. Every one is fortunate in having an unlimited supply. No one can gain advantage by taking possession of part of it, or devoting labor to procuring it.

Water under such conditions is said to be a "free" good, not an "economic" good. It is not an economic good, in the sense that no economic problems arise regarding it. Every one has all he wants, and thereby is prospered; what more is there to say?

A stage may come very early when some labor will be given to making the water conveniently available, and when it will be no longer strictly a free good; and when yet no economic questions of any complexity arise. The individual may dig a well, or pipe the water from a spring or stream to his dwelling. The very first economic problem, that which may even be considered the fundamental problem, then emerges: How much effort is it worth while to give to the supply of this convenience?

But the problem remains a very simple one, so long as the individual exerts himself to satisfy his own wants only. There is no dealing with others, no sale, no question of price. If men were to work solely for the satisfaction of their own wants, the difficult economic questions would not arise at all.

A more complex stage is reached when water is brought in by some individuals and sold to others. In Oriental towns the water carrier, with his runlet or skin, is still a familiar figure. In our own cities private individuals sometimes sell carboys of spring water or distilled water. Here questions of sale and price arise. What settles the terms on which water is sold? What settles the earnings of those who supply it? Are they in a position of advantage or not? Here are matters less simple.

Still another stage (not necessarily a later stage) is reached when common action is taken to procure the water. Here the problem may remain comparatively simple, or it may become one of the troublesome problems of modern communities. The traveler in Italy sees the village fountain, supplied by its aqueduct; even in larger towns, through some parts of Europe, the public fountain has remained until very recently the chief source of supply. The water is no longer strictly a "free" good, since effort and expense were required to bring it where wanted. But the effort was made long ago, does not need to be renewed (there are no expenses of upkeep), and there is so much water that it can be used *ad libitum*. In the modern city, however, the case has become different. There are great reservoirs, elaborate pumping stations, mains, and pipes. Water is supplied abundantly and conveniently to every household. There is not only a vast initial outlay for the plant, but a continuing cost of upkeep. The questions arise, Who shall make the outlay and manage the supply? Shall there be public or private ownership? And, whether under public or private ownership, what are to be the conditions of sale? Conceivably the water, if under public management, may still be supplied gratuitously to all, as it is at the village fountain; or payment may be required of the users. The questions of profit arise, of sound public policy, of possible monopoly gains, of conflict between financial and hygienic considerations. The really complex problems of economics arise full-fledged.

§ 2. To designate these different sorts of conditions, some quasi-technical terms are often used: "free goods," "economic goods," "public goods," "wealth."

What are free goods and what are economic goods has just been indicated. Fresh air, climate, sunshine, are the obvious cases of free goods; so is water under the simplest conditions, or standing timber in a thinly settled and well-wooded country.

Scarcity is the earmark of an economic good, — scarcity, that is, relatively to the demand. Water becomes an economic good when effort is needed to obtain it in the quantity desired, at the place of use. It is conceivable that in the future fresh air may become, for considerable parts of mankind, an economic good. It is so already when many persons are gathered in a large room or hall. Fans, conduits, engines, are installed; it becomes a question how the needful efforts shall be best directed, who shall bear the expense. With the concentration of population in great cities, and the multiplication of agencies that pollute the air in them, it is possible that elaborate means will have to be taken for keeping it healthful. Then the same complex problems will present themselves as in the case of water; all resting on the relative scarcity of the thing in question.

"Public goods" are economic goods supplied gratuitously to individuals, yet involving effort and consequent expense to some one. Though free to the users, they are not free goods. Such is water at the public fountain; such are public education, parks, museums, free concerts, bridges, and highways. What goods shall be public, and by whom the expense of providing them shall be met, — whether by levy on all persons, or on some only, — these are the problems as to public functions and as to taxation for defraying their expense; among the most difficult and far-reaching that the economist has to deal with.

It was common in the older books on our subject to define political economy (a phrase replaced in modern times by the simpler "economics") as the "science of wealth." In this usage, "wealth" meant all the economic goods, including the public goods. Either term — wealth or economic goods — serves to describe the subject matter with which economics has to deal; those things which men want, which are not free, and which present the problems of effort, of satisfaction through effort, of the organization of industry.

Evidently a community is the better off, the more free goods it has and the less the range of things that come within the category of "wealth." Where unlimited pure water and fresh air are at every one's disposal, the conditions of life are eased by so much. A mild and equable climate relieves the people of some favored spots from much labor that must be given elsewhere to protection from heat or cold. It may be said, with an appearance of paradox, that the more things in the nature of wealth a community has, the less prosperous it is. The paradox is easily solved. The wealth of a community is not the sum total of things on which its welfare depends, — these include its free goods as well as its economic goods. The more things are free, the easier are the conditions of living. The more things are economic, the wider is the range of commodities concerning which the economic problems arise, and the wider is the scope of the science of "wealth."

The abundance of free goods, though *prima facie* advantageous to a community, does not always coexist with the highest degree of prosperity. In tropical and semitropical countries the conditions of living are on the whole easier than in temperate countries. Some sorts of food are free or nearly free, and protection does not need to be provided against the cold of winter. But the climate saps energy, and checks the development of physical vigor and of intellectual capacity. Hence the peoples of temperate regions, from the very obstacles they have to overcome, gain resources within themselves which lead eventually to greater prosperity. So it is with individuals.

He who has always had abundant means at his command often lacks endurance and spirit, and in the end is surpassed in happiness as well as in riches by him who had to face harder conditions at the start.

§ 3. In the preceding paragraph wealth has been spoken of as the result of effort. But there are cases where a commodity is wealth, — is an economic good, — even though it be obtained without effort. A free gift of nature may be wealth, if it is limited in quantity.

On some parts of the seashore the waves dislodge from near-lying rocks quantities of kelp, which is useful as a fertilizer. Like multitudes of other articles, its use is indirect; it does not satisfy wants directly, but is an aid in the operations for satisfying them. Obviously, it may none the less be wealth. If kelp were steadily borne to the shore in such quantities that every one could get all he wished, it would be a free good in the strict economic sense. But if it is deposited in limited quantities on favored spots, and if many farmers are desirous of using it, it will command a price as it lies on the beach, before even the hand of man has touched it. And the same supply which at one time was so abundant as to command no price, may be brought by the growth of population within the circle of things bought and sold, and so become one of the goods with which economic science deals. Meteoric stones, usually disintegrated by heat before touching the earth's surface, in some instances reach the ground. Being scarce, and in our days esteemed for scientific research or even for the satisfaction of mere curiosity, they command a price, and, though the free gift of nature, are not free goods in the economic sense.

The same narrowing of the circle of free goods, and the same widening of that of economic goods or wealth, appear if there be not a natural, but an artificial, scarcity of goods. A supply of water or timber, unlimited in quantity for the needs of a given community, may come by force or by long-settled law under the control of some individual or individuals. By limiting the amount which others shall have, the owners may make such things a source of income for themselves and cause them to enter the list of economic goods. Monopoly *per se* raises some of the questions with which economic science has to deal.

This simplest sort of scarcity may seem to be exceptional; and as to the things which we usually think of as goods or commodities, it is so. The instances just adduced are exceptional. In the vast majority of cases commodities become economic after some labor has been applied to fashioning them. Though scarcity (that is, relative scarcity) still underlies the notion of wealth or economic goods, it is scarcity in the sense that the materials supplied by nature need to be adapted to man's use by his labor. Labor, or effort of some sort, is usually the cause or condition of economic phenomena.

There is one large class of things, however, for which this statement does not hold: limited natural agents, of which land is the most conspicuous. These are not commonly called goods or wares; but they are economic goods in the strict sense, being limited in quantity and of high service in satisfying wants. Agricultural land, power and deep-water sites, forests, mineral lands, — all are often economic goods by virtue of mere natural limitation of quantity. They present, as will appear in due course, some of the most intricate social and economic problems.

§ 4. What is labor, may seem a simple matter. Most people would say that they are more than sufficiently familiar with it. Yet some questions arise concerning it that go to the heart of economics, and the last word on them cannot be said until the very close of the exposition of the whole subject.

Some activities are agreeable, some are irksome. Some are undertaken for the pleasure of doing, some for a reward. Not infrequently the two satisfactions are gained simultaneously from the selfsame activity; it is both a source of pleasure in itself, and it brings a reward.

So far as the nature of the muscular or nervous effort is concerned, no distinction can be drawn between the agreeable and the irksome activities, or between those which are undertaken for pleasure and those which are undertaken for pay. Such severe physical labor, combined with hardship and exposure, as mountain climbing, is done for pleasure by tourists and for pay by guides. The pursuit of athletic sports is the most familiar of recreations and is also a familiar profession. A multitude of occupations ordinarily pursued for gain — woodworking, gardening, painting, acting — are also pursued by many persons for the satisfaction which the doing affords.

None the less it is true that the greatest part of the activity which men carry on in getting a living does not give pleasure. The chief reason seems to be that activity, in order to be effective toward getting a living, must be steady, unvaried, and long-continued; and it must be, in an important sense, not free. The characteristic of most activities that are sources of pleasure in themselves is the element of freshness or novelty, and the absence of compulsion. The guide who climbs mountains year after year, and knows the tracks by heart, soon finds the task a weary one; and this the more, because, in order to earn his living, he must follow his tracks regularly, regardless of his health or spirits at the moment. It is the zest of novelty and the sense of freedom and choice that cause pleasure in the summer's arduous vacation. Inactivity and idleness soon become irksome; but, with few exceptions, steady application to the same task also soon becomes irksome.

In savage and barbarian communities, the men usually confine themselves to the chase and to war. The monotonous work of cultivating fields and of preparing food is left to the women. Though hunting and fishing often entail the most strenuous exertion and the severest hardship, they do not commonly endure long, and they are almost surely varied by changes and respites. The variety and the sudden changes give play for emulation and for satisfying the love of distinction, — that for slaughter also, — instincts which have a powerful effect in many fields of economic activity. An alternation of periods of complete idleness and of feverish activity is characteristic of those early stages of society in which men give themselves to the unchecked satisfaction of their instinctive propensities.

The sort of labor that occupies the mass of mankind in civilized societies, and that which brings the largest product, is mainly of the continuous, monotonous, and irksome kind. This is more especially the case where the division of labor has been much elaborated. The wide extension of the division of labor, as we shall presently see, has been a main cause in modern times of the greater abundance of material goods, and of the extraordinary advance in material prosperity. But it has probably also been a cause of greater weariness and unattractiveness for most labor. Even in the simpler and older form of the division of labor, where one man was carpenter, another smith, another cobbler, there was of necessity a steady repetition of operations and no little monotony of work. But in the remarkable splitting up of occupations which has resulted from the elaboration of machinery in modern times, it is rare that a workman does all the work of his trade, or even knows how to do it. He is no longer a cobbler making a whole shoe, but a factory hand attending hour after hour and week after week to the same minute piece of machine work. Moreover, in a dense population and with strictly enforced ownership of property and of land, he is under compulsion to do continuous work of some such sort, in order to keep body and soul together. He lacks variety, and he lacks freedom. He may find pleasure in exerting himself strenuously at sports; but the labor of getting his living yields in itself little satisfaction.

§ 5. Some sorts of labor, though pursued systematically and continuously, seem never to become wearisome. This is the case with much intellectual labor, especially that of persons who are engaged in the pursuit of knowledge and in the satisfaction of man's insatiable curiosity about the things that surround him. Persons of artistic temperament — painters, musicians, poets — have often so strong an instinctive bent toward one kind of activity that nothing can hold them from it and nothing ever pall the pleasure of the exertion. And any occupation which satisfies the instinct of emulation has unceasing charm. He who can achieve things which few can achieve, and which many would like to achieve, rarely tires of his work. The actor, even though his occupation involves the monotonous and long-continued repetition of the most trifling details, never fails to get a thrill of pleasure from the breathless silence or stirring applause of his audience. Were he compelled to go through his part as often and as rigorously under the cold supervision of an indifferent supervisor, and under that only, how flat and stale it would become! For a similar reason, work of leadership and command almost always is continuously pleasurable. It satisfies the love of distinction and the desire for domination; and it has a real or apparent element of freedom. Hence the work of the employer commonly affords more satisfaction than that of the employee, and often is continued, from mere love of the doing as well as from habit, long after the reward or profit from the exertion has ceased to be valued.

These exceptions should not blind us to the fact that by far the greater part of the world's work is not in itself felt to be pleasurable. Some reformers have hoped to reach a social system under which all work should be in itself a source of satisfaction. It is probable that such persons are made optimistic by the nature of their own doings. They are writers, schemers, reformers; they are usually of strongly altruistic character, and the performance of any duty or set task brings to them the approval of an exacting conscience; and they believe that all mankind can be brought to labor in their own spirit. The world would be a much happier place if their state of mind could be made universal. But the great mass of men are of a humdrum sort, not born with any marked bent or any loftiness of character. Moreover, most of the world's work for the satisfaction of our primary wants must be of a humdrum sort, and often of a rough and coarse sort. There must be ditching and delving, sowing and reaping, hammering and sawing, and all the severe physical exertion which, however lightened by tools and machinery, yet can never be other than labor in the ordinary sense of the term.

Reference has just been made to a greater monotony of

labor in modern times, under the influence of growing use of machinery and growing specialization of labor. But the extent of the change in this regard may be easily exaggerated. Ruskin has dwelt on the charm of the medieval craftsman's task, who felt the joy of work that had beauty and character. Yet this joy was probably shared by few in medieval times, or in any other. Then, as now, most work involved the repetition of the same operations, and was felt to be tedious and exacting. It is not easy for us to picture the conditions of life in earlier societies, organized in a very different way from our own; but it is more than probable that the mass of mankind found their tasks then on the whole no pleasanter or lighter than now.

§ 6. We may hope that, as the material conditions of mankind improve, especially in the countries of advanced civilization, gains will be achieved as regards the irksomeness of ordinary labor. Some alleviation will come from a mere change in the state of opinion in the community. The sense of distinction affects the satisfaction from exertion. A task admired is an attractive task, and one despised is unattractive. The common attitude of the more favored classes has long been to contemn manual labor and those who perform it. Such was the natural attitude in communities based on slavery, or on its successor, feudalism; and such remains too often the attitude of that leisure class which in modern times adopts many of the traditions of feudalism. The growing democratization of society may be expected to change this, and to raise the dignity and self-respect of labor of all kinds, manual or mental. Greater ease of movement between different classes and greater equalization of their conditions will add to the esteem in which all kinds of manual labor are held, and may remove some at least of the causes that now contribute to make it unwelcome.

The chief mode, nevertheless, in which labor is likely to be made less irksome is not by a change in its character or its intrinsic attractiveness, but by a diminution in its severity. It will probably be lightened by the increasing perfection of tools and the increasing use of machinery; though on the other hand, it may be that from this cause its monotony will become no less, perhaps greater. More important is the prospect that the hours of labor are likely to be shortened, and the hours for recreation and variety correspondingly lengthened. The weariness of labor is by no means in proportion to the number of hours spent on it. For a healthy and well-nourished person, the first hours of work are not a source of fatigue. Some writers have indeed maintained that during these earlier hours — barring perhaps a brief initial period of stiffness — there is a sense of pleasure rather than of pain. This may be the case in intellectual activity, and in some handicraft occupations; and the experience is a familiar one in holiday jaunts. But little direct consciousness of pleasure comes at any stage from the stated work of the great majority of men. The difference between the earlier parts of their day and the later is not so much that the former are pleasant and the latter unpleasant, as that fatigue does not begin until some hours have passed, and then becomes increasingly severe with each of the later hours. When indeed the hours of labor are unduly prolonged, fatigue becomes so great and so deep-seated that the period of rest and sleep does not suffice to remove it. The next day begins again with fatigue, and worse succeeds worse. Such was the effect of the factory system in its early stages in England; such is still the situation in backward countries like Russia. Under these wretched conditions, the work of the day has covered eleven, twelve, even fourteen, hours. In the United States, in our own day, some of the steel-making industries, whose operations go on night and day, have had two shifts, in each of which the men worked twelve hours. To cut off one, two, three hours, from such a day's labor is to cut off a much larger proportion of the weariness of labor.

The movement for shorter hours has been one of the most beneficent aspects of the betterment of material conditions in civilized countries during the last two or three generations. The day's labor was first cut down to eleven and ten, partly from the pressure of workmen's organizations and partly from legislation restricting the hours of women and children employed in factories. It is still in process of being reduced. The ideal of the trade unions is now to lower it to eight hours; a limit which has already been reached in the more prosperous and highly paid trades, and is likely to be attained by a larger and larger proportion of manual workers. We shall have occasion to consider at a later stage the significance of this shortening of the period of work, the nature and causes of the gains so secured, and the fallacies which have attached themselves to the short-hour movement.[1] But in itself that movement should have the sympathy of every friend of humanity.

Notwithstanding all the alleviations of the irksomeness of labor, — through moderate tasks, free time for recreation, a rational respect for labor of all kinds, — the larger part of the world's work will always be felt to be irksome. A fortunate minority may work at tasks which are in themselves pleasurable and are not performed chiefly for the return which they bring. But most work is now undertaken for reward, would not be done without reward, and is strenuous and well directed in proportion to the reward. It is doubtless true that the mass of mankind, though they find their labor irksome or repellent, are yet happier than they would be under complete idleness, or with only that fitful kind of exertion which attracts the savage. But labor is commonly felt to be a hardship, and the pay which it secures is the dominant motive for undertaking it. The fundamental problems that arise in economics are concerned with the relation between unwelcome exertion and the remuneration which induces that exertion.

[1] See Book VI, Chapter 56.

CHAPTER 2

Of Labor in Production

§ 1. The relation of labor to production may seem simple. Yet it has been the occasion of great difference of opinion among acute thinkers, and it presents some nice questions.

We commonly speak of a tailor as making clothes, a carpenter as making a table, a cobbler as making boots. The briefest reflection shows that this is a careless use of language. The labor of the tailor but gives the finishing touch to the work previously done by a long series of persons, — the shepherd who tended the flocks, the wool shearer, those who transported the wool by land and sea, the carder and spinner and weaver, not to mention those who made the tools and machinery of these workers. Similarly the carpenter is the last of a succession of persons who worked toward a common end, — those who felled the trees, fashioned the timber, transferred it from the woods, and so on. Many laborers, arranged in long series, combine in making even the simplest commodities.

But it is clearly all these laborers, taken together, who produce the commodities; and can it not be said these alone are the producers of wealth? Wealth has been described as consisting of those goods which are not free. The term refers primarily to things that are tangible and material. Many laborers produce no wealth in this sense. Such are domestic servants, policemen, actors, singers, teachers. Does not their work stand in a different relation to production from that of laborers who make material things and carry on production in the common meaning of the word?

This was the opinion of many of the earlier writers on economics, especially the English writers from Adam Smith to John Stuart Mill. Their view was that only such laborers as turned out material things were productive; all others were unproductive. A liberal interpretation was indeed given to their definition of the productive laborers. Not only those who directly handled materials and fashioned them were included, — the day laborer, the carpenter, and the smith; but those also by whom the operations were guided and promoted, — the employer who directed the manual laborers, the foreman and the engineer, the teacher who trained the engineer. Even the teacher of the humblest workman may conceivably be regarded as contributing to the operations of material production, in so far as the diffusion of even the rudiments of education raises intelligence and adds to efficiency. But with the widest latitude in interpretation, a great range of persons, doing all sorts of work and by it earning a living, remained outside the class of the so-called productive laborers. Domestic servants, lawyers and judges and policemen, all the army and navy, not to mention persons who provided mere amusement, were classed as unproductive. As Adam Smith remarked, "in the same class [of unproductive laborers] must be ranked, some both of the gravest and most important and some of the most frivolous professions: churchmen, lawyers, physicians, men of letters of all kinds; players, buffoons, musicians, opera singers, opera dancers."

This distinction between productive and unproductive laborers was early attacked and long debated. It was pointed out that it seemed to affix some sort of stigma — an accusation of uselessness, of being in need of support from others — on whole classes of persons whose work was admitted to be honorable and often seemed to be indispensable. But this was after all not material; whether or no an "unproductive" occupation was to be regarded as honorable, the essential question was and is whether there are differences between this kind of work and the other which are important for the welfare of the community. It was much more to the point that the distinction led to difficulties and inconsistencies. The musician was regarded as an unproductive laborer; was the artisan who made his instrument — his violin — nevertheless productive? The labor of the violin-maker issued in material wealth, or, as Adam Smith said, in "a vendible commodity." Yet its only object was to make an instrument to be used by the musician; and was not the consistent view that of regarding the two sets of persons as combining for a common result, just as the sheep shearer, the weaver, and the tailor combine in making clothing? And if thus working together for the same end, was one to be set apart as productive, the other as unproductive? All members of the navy and army were classed as unproductive; yet those who built the ships, made the guns and the powder, were supposed to be productive. If one set were unproductive, why not the other?

§ 2. The solution of these difficulties is indicated by a conception which the British economists, though they followed it in other directions, were curiously slow to use with reference to their discussion of productive labor. It points to satisfactions, or *utilities*, as the aim and end of production. We shall see, as we progress, how in various directions economic science gains, and is often brought to unity and consistency, by the analysis of production as ending in utilities.

If it is a careless use of language to speak of a carpenter as "making" a table, it may also be said to be a careless use of language, or, at best, a short-cut expression for a complicated act, to speak of any artisan or set of artisans as "making" anything. The amount of matter in the world is not subject to man's control. He cannot add to it one atom or subtract one atom. All that he can do is to change forms and combination. And just this he does in production. He fashions and refashions material things. He puts them into forms in which they serve his wants. Such is obviously the nature of the carpenter's work, the tailor's, the cook's. It is not less true of those whom we describe as "producing materials." The plants from which man secures the greatest part of his food and most of the materials he uses, get their constituent parts from the soil and the air. What man does is to arrange conditions favorable for their growth. The minerals which he uses are a fixed store in the earth's crust. When we say that coal is produced, we mean that it is brought to the surface and made available for our use.

The modes in which man brings about utilities or satisfactions are many. Not only are plants grown, and coal, iron, copper brought up from the mines; not only are these raw materials shaped and adapted for their different uses, — they are also transported to the places, often very distant, where they reach the hands of those whose wants they finally satisfy. They are bought by traders from one set of persons, and sold again to another; and among the traders there is a division of labor, some buying at wholesale and selling again to the retailers, who dispose of the commodities to their customers. The phrase "place utility" has been used to describe the contributions of those engaged in transportation and trade; and it serves to bring into relief the fact that such persons, though they do not shape or fashion commodities, yet contribute to their utilization.

Now, since the essence of production is that it leads to satisfactions or utilities, it follows that any labor or effort that yields utilities is productive. The musician whose performance brings us pleasure does precisely the same sort of thing as the florist whose blossoms last a few hours. The domestic servant contributes to our ease just as does the artisan who supplies the furniture for our dwellings. No doubt there are gradations in the importance of the wants supplied by different workers. The essentials of life are most important; the conveniences and luxuries come after them; and these gradations, as we shall see, have economic consequences. But they are not significant for our present purpose; they give no ground for distinguishing between those producers who embody utilities in material objects, and those who do not. If we were called on to dispense with the services of some of the producers, we might put aside, as easily spared, first, the buffoons and the opera dancers who figure as unproductive in Adam Smith's list. But we might also put aside at once the scene painters at the opera, the printers of trashy books, the makers of cloying sweets and noxious drinks. And if, on the other hand, we were called on to say what producers we should retain to the last, we should select not only those who supply the material things essential for existence, — food, clothing, shelter, — but also the physician who preserves our health and the teacher who maintains the education on which rests civilization. The distinction between things essential and things dispensable is by no means the same as that between material and immaterial sources of utilities.

We conclude, then, that all those whose labors satisfy wants — all those who bring about satisfactions or utilities — are to be reckoned as taking part in production, and are to be called productive laborers. Certain it is, whatever phraseology we care to apply, that no conclusions of importance for economics flow from the distinction between those who shape material wealth and those who bring about utilities of other kinds. And the test of the value of a distinction or classification is always that significant propositions can be laid down as to the things put into a given class which do not hold for those outside the class.

This conclusion also enables us to dispose of an allied question: Is there nonmaterial wealth? Those who denied the old proposition, — who maintained that labor which did not embody a utility in material objects was nevertheless productive — often maintained that there was such a thing as "nonmaterial" wealth. The phrase certainly is not in accord with common usage. We think ordinarily of wealth as something that can be kept and accumulated, and intend by it tangible things; and in this sense it is a contradiction in terms to speak of immaterial wealth. But if we use the more technical and therefore more precise phrase, "economic goods," we include all those things and services which satisfy human wants and are not to be had free. Services of those whom Adam Smith and his followers called unproductive laborers come under this head.

They are desired and prized, often highly prized; and they are yielded by human effort. The rewards earned by these efforts are an important topic in economic science, and the utilities provided are an important part of the sum of utilities which constitute, in the last analysis, the community's income. If we mean by wealth anything about which economic problems arise, we must make the term coextensive with the term "economic goods"; and then we may speak of nonmaterial wealth.

§ 3. From this interpretation of the terms, it would seem to follow that all labor belongs to the productive class. If not only the butcher and the baker are in this class, but the barber and the fiddler, do any remain who are to be regarded as unproductive?

Obviously, there are some persons who are outside the pale of productive activity. The paupers, thieves, swindlers, ne'er-do-wells, are parasites. Thieves and swindlers often exert themselves severely, though not often continuously. But their activity is purely predatory. They contribute nothing; they simply try to get things away from others. Whether or no we should apply the term "labor" to their exertions, it is certainly not to be called productive labor.

A different question arises as to some labor carried on without violation of the law and without conscious delinquency, yet certainly of doubtful aspect. A quack medicine, containing ingredients which the maker knows to be noxious, or at best harmless, may be puffed by mendacious advertising into widespread use. Can it be said that the labor devoted to preparing it and persistently circulating lies about it is productive of satisfactions, and therefore to be reckoned as productive labor?

To take another case, of still a different sort, what shall we say of the labor given in well-nigh all communities to the production and sale of intoxicating liquors? Among physiologists the settled conclusion is that, though the use of these stimulants in the lighter forms may lead to no serious harm, that of distilled spirits is overwhelmingly bad. It is certain that an immense amount of misery and vice comes from the widespread use of strong liquors; that the diminution in their consumption during the last generation or two has brought betterment for mankind; and that the world would be a much happier place if drunkenness could be stamped out. What has the economist to say of labor given to the production of things harmful?

These cases call for discrimination. They may be cases of fraud and deceit. They may be cases of wants misdirected, but none the less wants really felt and really satisfied.

Fraud and deceit mean that a person does not secure that which he expected and was led to expect. In an ordinary sale, the seller is not presumed by the law to give a guarantee as to the quality of the thing sold: *caveat emptor.* But where a guarantee is given, or a precise description equivalent to a guarantee, the buyer has a remedy in the courts.

The distinction made by the law is substantially that which the economist would make. The quack medicine may be a draft of flavored water or disguised alcohol. But so long as the purchaser wants this sort of thing, and buys because he has a notion it will do him good, the purveyor adds to the sum of satisfactions. The case is different where the purchaser wants one thing, and is deceived into taking something else; since then his felt wants are not satisfied. Intermediate is the case where the purchaser does not know precisely what he wants, and is wheedled into taking something which the other man wants to sell. Here it is often difficult to draw the line. Is the buyer foolish, or is he swindled? Does the seller lie outright, or is he merely expansive in praise of his wares? What the law can do is to aid in making the situation clear; and this is particularly needful where the consequences of misunderstanding are serious. Hence the pure-food and pure-drug legislation, and the legislation requiring that the composition of nostrums be precisely stated on their labels.

Where the want is really felt and really satisfied, the labor that brings satisfaction must be adjudged by the economist productive; and this, even though the ultimate consequences be harmful.

The keeper of a dramshop is a productive laborer, even though he purveys something which often causes misery. To enter on inquiries about the final effect on human welfare would raise many questions of a different sort from those within the strict range of economics; inquiries which, if consistently followed in all cases, would range into almost every field of knowledge. There are physiologists who believe that meat, though men like it, is unnecessary for nourishment and is frequently a cause of disease. Others maintain that such stimulants as tea and coffee are of ill effect; that health and happiness are promoted by abstinence from them. To judge between these various advocates and reformers is no part of the essential task of the economist. So long as a person who buys a thing or pays for a service really *desires* it, the labor which yields him the satisfaction is productive. The economist is concerned to inquire what labor is productive in this sense and what is not, and what are the various aspects and consequences of men's activities in trying to satisfy their wants.

A case which may call for nice distinction between labor that is productive, even though morally questionable, and labor that is predatory, is that of the professional gambler. For example, those who maintain the luxurious establishment at Monte Carlo may be regarded, on the one hand, as simply purveying to that love of games of chance which is so universal as almost to be classed as instinct. So far as they do so — so far as the act of gaming is pleasurable to their customers — they supply a satisfaction, even though it may be desirable for permanent welfare that this craving be kept in check. On the other hand, so far as both parties — croupier and gamester — are merely trying to get each other's money, and care not for the play *per se*, the activities of both are predatory. Just what motive underlies the gamester's wagers may be a matter for nice psychological analysis. No doubt the two distinguishable motives — love of play and cupidity for the other man's money — are often combined. There are certainly instances enough where the pleasure of the play counts for nothing, and where cupidity alone is at work; and then the keeper of the gambling establishment is simply predatory.

Returning now to such articles as were considered a moment ago — drugs and alcoholic spirits, whose effects may be noxious — we may note the obvious distinction between saying that a given kind of labor is productive and saying that it ought to be exercised. Though a want may be satisfied by the labor, it does not follow that happiness, or the best kind of happiness, is promoted thereby. The law may prohibit gambling, or the manufacture and sale of liquor, because it is thought best that men should not have the gratifications at all. Whether or no a prohibition of this kind should be enacted raises questions, to repeat, of very wide range, to whose solution the economist can doubtless contribute, but on which he says by no means the final word. The labor which yields a service may be, in the eye of the economist, strictly productive; but it may be a kind of productive labor which had better not be exercised.

§ 4. The meaning which we affix to the word "productive" is further illustrated by one of those professions which Adam Smith regarded as indeed grave and important, but none the less unproductive, — the law. With the lawyer may be grouped the judge, the policeman, the jailer, — all those concerned with the administration of the law. In a sense, their services are not necessary. They do not conduce directly to the production of material goods or to the rendering of services or utilities to consumers. They are inevitable adjuncts to the processes of production, rather than immediately contributing factors. If all men were honest, truthful, fair-minded, and willing to abide at once by the decision of an impartial arbitrator, the work of the legal profession and of all its hangers-on could be dispensed with, or at least reduced to insignificant dimensions. If virtue were universal, policemen and jailers would disappear, and lawyers would have little or nothing to do. Yet the experience of all peoples shows that — men being what they are — the work of the legal profession becomes indispensable in any complex society. As property is accumulated and diversified, as exchanges between men multiply, as the precise relations between different persons come to be carefully defined by law, the business of interpreting the complex system is put into the hands of a separate profession. The settlement of differences is intrusted to judges; the orderly conduct of affairs is aided by the advice of lawyers; the observance of the law is enforced by the police. No doubt an ill-devised legal system entails more labor of this sort than would suffice under a better system; and the unprejudiced observer must question whether the law of our modern communities works as efficiently as it might. But a clumsy instrument, though it involves more labor than one well adjusted, is none the less useful.

Similar considerations apply to the army and navy. The immediate object of the soldier's work is destruction. He must be supported by the rest of the community; he does not contribute directly to its well-being. Yet military protection has been, through almost all history, an indispensable condition for the sustained conduct of peaceful industry. Like the policeman, the soldier is needed because of the bad passions of man. And even where defense is not necessary, and armaments are maintained from national vanity or senseless rivalry, the soldier nevertheless must be reckoned productive in the sense that he does what people wish to have done and what they pay him for. The army and navy may be only dangerous playthings. But men are not less foolish when they pay for tawdry ornament or vulgar amusement. It is not for the economist to sit in judgment on their tastes.

There is indeed a situation in which a military force is, from the economist's point of view, clearly unproductive. This is where it is used solely and simply for aggression. A pirate is obviously not a productive laborer. Unfortunately many of the heroes of history have been no better than pirates. The armies of the first Napoleon swarmed over Europe, levying tribute wherever they penetrated. No doubt deep-lying historical forces served to bring on the wars of the Napoleonic period. Some conflict was inevitable between the old feudal order of society and that new order which arose with the French Revolution. But the domineering spirit of Napoleon turned the conflict in its later stages to mere aggression on the one side, exhausting defense against aggression on the other. That defense was necessary; yet all the effort applied both to offense and defense was in the last analysis a fruitless application of labor.

Lest this mode of considering the military be judged shallow by some of our fellow economists,—it is likely to be so regarded by many Germans, in whose contemporary civilization preparation for war plays so large a part,—let it be added that the bare economic side of the matter is not the only one to be considered. Complex political and social questions present themselves, quite beyond the scope of a book on economics. No range of topics brings out more clearly the need of considering problems that are partly economic from other points of view as well. Even as a problem in economics alone, the industrial progress of mankind has often proceeded in strange ways. Civilization has gone forward on the powder cart, as in our Civil War. Aggression itself sometimes leads to happier ends. The English first took possession of India in a spirit of sheer rapacity. Yet their rule, resting as it still does on force, has much promoted the material welfare of the native races. And in the conflicts between civilized peoples also, whatever their origin, a better order and a higher prosperity have often emerged from wars that were seemingly causeless. Reflections of this sort will occur to every thoughtful reader, and lead him to qualify and interpret what has here been said of the relating of armaments and wars to the principle which underlies the conception of productive labor.

§ 5. There remain to be considered questions as to the relations of certain kinds of activity to the productiveness of labor. Are any of the business doings which go on in modern society to be judged unproductive?

When unscrupulous persons solicit funds from the gullible, ostensibly for "investment" or "speculation," and in due time run off with the money, their labor, systematic and strenuous though it may be, is obviously predatory. Not only they, but the clerks and assistants whom they employ (whether these be accomplices or innocent), are unproductive. Now it is maintained that, outside the range of operations so clearly predatory as to be made criminal by law, there are not a few others, within the pale of the law, whose economic effect is substantially the same. This is alleged, to take a familiar example, of speculative transactions in general. In our highly organized modern communities, an immense amount of buying and selling is done for a turn in the market. A man buys wheat or cotton which he does not want and which never gets into his possession; he promptly sells his nominal title at an advance in price, pocketing what is called a profit. Is any contribution made to the sum of utilities by such transactions? It may be assumed that the pleasure of the game, which may be an element in gambling with cards or dice, here plays but a negligible part; the motive is simply to get gain somehow. The most conspicuous operations of the sort are on the stock exchange, where sales and purchases take place on an enormous scale with no traceable effect in adding to production or to social income. The business involves an elaborate apparatus, — brokers, clerks, officers, a periodical press of its own. As the clerks of a bare swindler are unproductive, so must be those of the broker, if he is himself in the parasitic class.

But this sort of allegation has been pushed further. A large part of what is ordinarily called "business" has been placed under the same ban. Not only those who are usually called speculators, but those who "operate" in real estate — buy and sell land for a margin of profit — and the bankers who "handle" stocks and bonds are described as mere parasites. Nay, all business men, of every kind, have been condemned by socialist writers as essentially unproductive, — that is, so far as they are not directly doing work of management and superintendence. By them "business" has been adjudged, simply a way of securing a gain through the ignorance or weakness of others, and therefore to be condemned as useless to society.

The questions here raised cannot be answered until after a consideration of some very complex matters. But the mode in which they should be dealt with and the nature of the answers to be sought can be indicated now, even though with some anticipation of later conclusions. Thus, as regards one of the set of operations supposed to be unproductive, — speculative dealings, — it must be admitted that the charge is in part founded. Though some speculative dealings in commodities and securities serve a useful purpose, others are in large part mere wagers, akin in their economic effect to vulgar gambling.[1] Judged by the test which we have set up, — whether the labor adds to the sum of utilities, — all those who engage in mere wagering speculation are unproductive laborers: not only the principals, but the brokers who execute their orders, the clerks who record them, the mechanics who put together and operate the "ticker" in the broker's quarters. All belong in the class whose work serves no useful end.

The same test is to be applied to the activity of business men; but here the balance of gain is much clearer. Though the greater part of speculative dealings is probably of no utility, the greater part of business men's doings has great utility. The indictment of the socialists, which charges that they are predominantly unproductive, far overshoots the mark. The function of the manager or leader of industry is of high service in production. He adds conspicuously to the abundance of commodities and the satisfaction of wants. But it is none the less true that in any large center of industry there will be found plenty of persons engaged in "business" whose doings are essentially parasitic. They pick up a living, perhaps a very comfortable one, by shreds and patches of dealings, by shrewdness in buying and selling, by waiting for land or securities to rise in value. Often they are sober, solid citizens, personally estimable; so indeed are, as a rule, the stockbrokers who provide the facilities for the gambling speculators. These respectable persons would resent with indignation the suggestion that

[1] Compare Book II, Chapter 11.

they belong in the predatory and parasitic class. But one of the most remarkable phenomena presented to the student of economics is the ignorance of all sorts of persons as to their place and function in the industrial world. The broker or merchant, no less than the mechanic or clerk, sees the little corner in which he is at work, and knows nothing of its relations to the community as a whole. The respectability of an employment, and even the spirit in which it is pursued, give no certain clew to its effect on the general welfare.

It is the aim of the legal system under which we live — the system of private property — to inhibit predatory doings. Hence not only physical violence, but fraud and deceit, are forbidden and punished. This aim of the law is in the main attained. He who earns his living in a lawful manner commonly contributes to the sum total of satisfactions. He does what another person is willing to pay him for; or, in the more technical language of economics, he brings forth utilities, and so is a productive laborer. The view, sanctioned more or less explicitly by some socialist writers, according to which the work of manual laborers alone is productive, and all the income-earning and money-making of the well-to-do classes are unproductive, carries the indictment against the existing system too far. But the fact that criticism against the working of private property is exaggerated should not blind us to the fact that there exist opportunities for securing an income or even amassing a fortune, not beyond the pale of the law, yet of a kind which the economist must regard as predatory, and so unproductive.

Some opportunities of this kind are due to imperfections in the law as it stands. With changes in economic conditions, proceedings that once seemed helpful to the promotion of the general welfare, and perhaps at one stage were helpful, cease to be so, or remain so only in part. Thus joint stock companies, or corporations, have proved a device of great efficacy in furthering improvements in the arts and in securing more abundant and varied production. On the other hand, the statutes under which corporations may be organized, especially in our American states, have often made possible precisely that evil of which the socialist critics complain: mere thimblerigging and plundering. The reform of the laws of incorporation in such a manner as to keep the good and reject the evil is now one of the pressing problems in the United States.

To discriminate clearly between the operations that are in the end helpful toward satisfying wants, and those that are not, is sometimes impossible even after the nicest weighing of the results by the best judges. The law, for instance, withholds its sanction from mere wagering contracts. Yet transactions which are wagers cannot be distinguished in outward form from others which are useful to society. There is a vague consciousness in the public mind that some persons are engaged in "legitimate" business, while others doing the same sort of thing, "illegitimately" occupied, are "plungers." But to draw a precise line between those that may be approved and those that may not, is no less difficult for the business man, however intelligent and wide-minded, than for the judge or the economist. So it is with the law of fraud and deceit. As long as men are free to choose for themselves and act according to their own judgments, those who are shrewd and watchful will make better bargains than those who are dull and unobservant. When does one man overreach another, when does he simply leave him to judge for himself as to his own interests? The probabilities are that for the sake of securing the large general benefits that flow from private property and competitive dealings we shall always have to permit some doings that are on the line between the productive and the predatory. If the law brings it about that labor is applied in the main to the satisfaction of wants; if it restrains most of the unproductive doings; if the system as a whole works well, and these predatory operations are only its loose ends, — it will be better to accept them as inevitable and to set off against them the general benefits. Absolute perfection in human arrangements is not to be looked for.

CHAPTER 3

The Division of Labor and the Development of Modern Industry

§ 1. The division of labor is one of the great central facts in modern society. Some of the most difficult questions of economic theory, the most common popular fallacies, the most serious problems of legislation, have their roots in the division of labor.

The division of labor may be analyzed under two heads. On the one hand there is the simpler form, under which a workman carries through the whole of one of the stages in production. The tailor, the cobbler, the carpenter, ply their several trades. On the other hand there is the more complex form, under which there is a splitting up of several operations all belonging to one stage of production. In more primitive stages of industry the shoemaker might be a tanner, and the whole process of converting the rawhide into a shoe thus be in one hand. Nowadays, the shoe itself is not put together by the cobbler; it is the work of a large number of different workmen in a factory, of whom some do nothing but cut the leather, others stitch it, others put on the soles, still others the heels, and so on, with an elaborated parceling of different operations.

Obviously, a hard-and-fast line cannot be drawn between these two aspects of the division of labor. No craftsman carries through from beginning to end any one operation in production. The tailor buys his materials of the cloth maker; the cloth maker buys his wool of the farmer or grazier. The cloth maker and the grazier in turn buy tools of the mechanic, who buys materials from the ironworker and woodworker. On the other hand, the tailor does not necessarily carry his own work through even the whole of the stage with which he is concerned. It may be divided between the cutter and the stitcher; and similarly the cloth maker's may be parceled out between the weaver, the fuller, the dyer. The difference between the simpler and the more complex division of labor is essentially one of degree. Nevertheless, this difference of degree is important. The two sorts of arrangement bring about somewhat different advantages and give rise to different social conditions.

§ 2. Let us consider first the simpler division of labor. This dates far back into antiquity. The familiar crafts are of very old standing. The extent to which their names have been adopted as surnames shows how, among modern peoples, occupations were separated in that comparatively simple state of society, in the Middle Ages, when patronymics were in process of formation. The Carpenters, Masons, Smiths, Weavers, Drapers, Tailors, Dyers, Saddlers, Shoemakers, Millers, Bakers, Coopers, and such other common surnames indicate what sort of division of labor was maintained for hundreds of years with comparatively little change.

The chief advantage in production from this form of the division of labor is the gain in dexterity which comes from the constant practise of the same occupation. So familiar are we with the effect of practise that we assume as a matter of course the skill which comes from it. Reading, writing, the donning of our clothes and the lacing of our boots, are effected with ease, almost without effort, from the ingrained effects of custom and iteration. Piano playing and typewriting are marvelous to the inhabituated, easy to the point of indifference for the practised hand. The acquired dexterity of the craftsman and mechanic make their productive capacity infinitely greater than they would be if each had to carry on a dozen occupations and were half proficient in any one.

Other gains also have been enumerated as accruing from the simpler division of labor. There is a saving in time when the same task is followed without interruption. The carpenter, even though no more dexterous than the farmer, can yet accomplish more in the hour or the day than the farmer who tries to do jobs of tinkering in his spare moments. Something also is due to the adaptation of tasks to the abilities of the workers. There are differences between the inborn abilities of individuals, even as regards tasks for which training and practise are the most important causes of dexterity. Among mechanics a certain proportion only have the sure eye and the deft hand which are required for the most exacting tasks. It is obviously advantageous that they should confine themselves chiefly to these, leaving the less exacting to persons of ordinary capacity. Even for comparatively simple occupations there are differences in the qualifications of individual workmen. The work of a motorman on an electric car seems of the most monotonous sort, easily accomplished by any adult. Yet it requires a certain steadiness and alertness of attention not possessed by all laborers. How far differences of this sort are the result solely of inborn qualities, how far brought about or accentuated by education and environment, need not here be considered. So long as they exist, there is a gain if each individual is called on to do only that for which he has the greatest aptitude.

The last-mentioned factor in the division of labor — the adaptation of tasks to varying aptitudes — is of most importance as between those who work with their heads and those who work with their hands. Though there is mental training as well as manual training, and though instruction and practise tell in the lawyer's trade as well as in the mechanic's, inborn abilities are important in greater degree for the former. This is more particularly the case in all work which calls for initiative, superintendence, direction. There is a difference of far-reaching effect between those who have the qualities for leadership, whether in the arts or in intellectual life, and those who must belong to the rank and file. There is often a very great gain when those who are born leaders can devote themselves solely to the work which they alone can do, or which they can do best, leaving to others, with no such capacities, the routine mechanical or clerical work.

The great mass of men, however, have no special aptitudes. For them, continued practice, begun or aided by systematic training, is the chief cause, even though not the only cause, of skill in any particular sort of work. In the main, the division of labor is a cause rather than a result of specialized capacity. Most dexterous men are so because they have long practised a given art; they do not practise it because they are born with dexterity.

§ 3. Let us turn now to what we have styled the more complex form of the division of labor. This is the salient characteristic of the development of industry during the last century and a half; a development which has gone on with accelerating pace in very recent times. The change in industry and the nature of the new order of things can be described most concisely by saying that the tool has been replaced by the machine.

Though the gain in efficiency from the division of labor arises chiefly from the dexterity acquired by repetition, none of the trades familiar under the simpler division of labor was reduced to the continuous repetition of identical movements. The carpenter, the mason, the smith, the tailor, — each was master of his trade as a whole, and, while gaining proficiency from unceasing practise, yet turned from one part of the occupation to another. The instruments which these artisans used were tools, of varied kinds, adapted to the different parts of their occupations. A "tool," as that word is still commonly used, means a hand tool, put in motion by human force and requiring adaptation, judgment, flexibility.

The gradual elaboration of the division of labor slowly enlarged the number of occupations, diminished the range of each one, and tended to reduce each more and more to an identical routine. Thus the making of cloth was divided between the spinner, the weaver, the fuller, the dyer. The division between the spinner and the weaver, itself one of the oldest, became eventually of much moment, for it gave occasion for one of the epoch-making applications of machinery and power. When the steady repetition of the same movement becomes an important part of an industrial art, it is possible to apply other force than that of man's muscles. No machine, even in the highly elaborated forms of modern times, can rival in dexterity and flexibility the human hand. But whenever the same thing is to be done over and over, the blind forces of nature, working through a machine, can do it as well as the human hand, and indeed better than most human hands. The division of labor in its simpler form gradually was developed to the point where the application of power was possible. The gain from the application of power proved so great that there was a reaction on the division of labor: an inducement to split up the steps in production still further, to reduce more and more of them to the repetition of identical movements, and so to make possible in still greater degree the use of natural forces.

The great change toward the use of machines and power set in during the second half of the eighteenth century. The textile trades felt its influence first. In 1764, Hargreaves invented the spinning jenny; in 1769, Arkwright brought out his rival spinning machine; in 1779 Crompton invented an apparatus which combined the devices of Hargreaves and Arkwright, and brought the spinning machine to a still further stage of perfection. All three were directed to the mechanical repetition of the twisting of the fiber; and water power was soon applied to setting them in motion. Not long afterwards, weaving was also subjected to the same principles. The power loom was gradually elaborated, and in the beginning of the nineteenth century began to supplant steadily the hand loom. By the close of that century, the old-fashioned weaver's trade had become, in advanced countries like England and the United States, a thing of the past. The textile material to which these inventions were first applied was cotton; for this has an even and homogeneous fiber which makes it most readily available for machinery operated continuously at uniform speed. Wool, linen, and silk, being of less even fiber, were subjected to the machine process later than cotton, through a long series of subsidiary inventions. It has not been until our own day that silk, the most delicate and irregular of these fibers, has come to be manipulated on a large scale by power machinery.

Water power was used for the textile manufactures in their earlier stages; but it was soon supplemented and largely replaced by the steam engine. The steam engine was brought by Watt to the stage of effective working in 1781. It was first used on a large scale for the pumping of water out of mines, — an obvious case for the application of power, since it calls for the unchanging performance of the simplest of movements. It was soon applied further, not only to the textile industries and to a wide range of other manufactures, but to transportation. Steam was used in navigation by Fulton on the Hudson River in 1807. An even more important application of steam to transportation came when the locomotive was perfected by Stephenson in 1830. This created the modern railroad, and, as we shall presently see, marked the beginning of a still further development of the division of labor.

The series of great inventions of which these were the most important, brought about what is known as the Industrial Revolution, — a change in the arts, and a consequent change in economic and social conditions, greater than has appeared during a like short time in any stage of human history. Its fundamental economic characteristic has been the elaboration of the division of labor, through the splitting up of the stages of production into separate operations, each one of which is repeated continuously and so may be carried on by the machine. The carpenter's sawing, planing, joining, molding, — each of these is now done separately by machinery, usually in establishments that tend steadily to become larger and larger and to subdivide still more the various operations of the trade. The cobbler of former days put together a shoe by himself; in a modern factory the shoe goes through some eighty different processes. So it is with ironworking, with all the elaborated processes of the textile industries, with printing and bookmaking, not least with the very making of machines and tools. The machines now used are vastly more complex and more efficient than was dreamed of in the early stages of the application of power, and have extended the principle of the automatic repetition of identical movements to tasks long thought too intricate to be amenable to such methods. The work of the hand is not indeed superseded; the skillful workman and the adaptable tool retain a large place in industry; but the range of their work tends to become more and more restricted. Within each branch of industry, as one stage after another is subjected to the machine process, the other stages have a narrower and simpler range, in which inventive spirit constantly finds new opportunities for the application of power. Thus the character and the working of the division of labor have been profoundly and all but universally modified.

The essential gain from this modern development of the division of labor has come from the virtually unlimited store of natural power. Once the identity of movement has been secured, there is no work so heavy, no operation so delicate, but that the machine can repeat it day in, day out. Human labor applied first to putting together the machine, then to guiding the natural forces that move it, accomplishes vastly more than the same amount of labor applied to the making and using of the simpler tools of former days. Coal and falling water are the great sources of power; and though nature does not supply them without limit, the application of machinery has not yet been fettered for human needs by any limitation, nor is it likely to be fettered in the future, as far as we can look forward into it. The labor required for any one operation in production has been immensely lessened by the industrial changes of the last century, and appears likely to be lessened no less rapidly and largely in the century before us.

The period in which we live has been aptly called the age of machinery. Its characteristic phenomena are mainly the results of the use of machinery; and they will engage our attention in many parts of our subject. They are seen in the growth of capital, and the increasing power and importance of the business man who has control of capital; in the spread of production on a large scale, and the tendency to monopoly in many branches of industry; in a new position of the workmen, a wider gap between employers and employees, and a consequent development both of labor organizations and of employers' associations; in grave social problems from the employment of women and children in factories; not least, in a loss of individuality in the working population, and a strengthening of the lines of demarcation between social classes. Of all these consequences of the complex division of labor more will be said as we proceed.

§ 4. The division of labor obviously means that the persons who carry on the several operations of a given branch of industry combine to bring about the final result. It means, no less clearly, that those engaged in different industries combine to satisfy the varied wants of the community. Each contributes his special product to be used by all; each uses the products contributed by the rest. The division of labor may thus be described also as the combination or coöperation of labor.

That combination may conceivably be carried out deliberately, with conscious control and coördination, with immediate sharing of the joint output, and without exchange. In the ancient civilizations of Greece and of Rome we get glimpses of establishments of the rich and privileged in which the several trades are plied by slaves for the benefit of the whole household. In the earlier Middle Ages, also, we find seigniorial possessions, where the serfs have specialized occupations, and contribute in kind to the lord's needs. Even in modern times, we have examples of communistic societies, in which there is a division of labor among the individual members, yet no exchange; each member contributing his part to the common income and each receiving from that income a share deemed equitable. Such a society does not approach so nearly to self-sufficiency as the ancient household or the medieval estate;

it must buy and sell on a considerable scale with the outside world, whereas those earlier organizations bought very few things (salt and iron, for example). Yet within its own limits the division of labor leads to no exchange between members.

Commonly, however, the division of labor has brought with it as a natural corollary the *exchange* of the several commodities produced by different workers. The cases noted in the preceding paragraph are comparatively rare in economic history; at all events, they give no clew to the phenomena of the modern industrial world. There the division of labor almost always means exchange, and the relation between the workers is very different from that in a community where there is conscious and deliberate combination of effort. It is strictly true that the workers in a modern society combine in bringing about a joint output; but the consciousness of coöperation is lost. The individual is not thinking of the joint output. Only if he happens to be versed in the books and theories of economic writers, and bears them in mind in his active hours, is he aware that he is carrying on one small operation toward a joint output and shares in the manifold contribution which others make to that joint output. The things on which he works are not part of a common store, but are private property, bought and sold, cared for and guarded, by each individual for himself. He thinks only of the particular product which he sells, and of the terms on which he can buy other products. He is intent on the results of the exchange thus made, and tries to secure for himself the best terms of exchange. Private property and exchange are well-nigh universally the consequences of the division of labor, and the phenomena of exchange are the dominant phenomena of the modern world.

§ 5. For some centuries preceding the industrial revolution of the eighteenth century, the typical form of exchange was that between the small city or town and the agricultural region immediately surrounding it. This was the period of the simpler form of the division of labor, of the familiar handicraft; the period of the tool, preceding the modern period of the machine. The city of early modern times was the center of an industrial community which was in the main self-contained. Within the city the burghers carried on the arts and crafts. To it the surrounding rural population brought food and materials, and in it they made their purchases. The city craftsmen were united in the gilds which were so conspicuous a feature of the economic organization of that period. Each craft was open only to the members of a gild, who trained apprentices and employed journeymen, and transmitted from generation to generation the knowledge of its trade. The organization of the gilds, and the regulation and restriction of their membership, were inevitable and doubtless beneficial at the outset, assuring protection and mutual aid, and the maintenance of skill in the arts. In later times, their regulations were made the means of monopoly; they had long outlived their usefulness even before the great inventions of the industrial revolution put an end to the economic organization of which they were a part. But these are aspects of the gild system not closely related to our present topic. So far as it bears on the division of labor, it was part of what the Germans call *Stadtwirthschaft*, — the city organization of industry. A map of England and of the greater part of western Europe from say 1350 to 1800 is dotted with a large number of cities of modest size, each the center of a more or less isolated economic area. There was, indeed, some exchange of special commodities between different countries and between the different economic areas within a country; but the main exchanges were between the city and the surrounding agricultural district, and the characteristic stage of the mechanical arts was that of the division of labor between the familiar crafts organized in the medieval gilds.

The steps through which this organization of industry has been replaced by that characteristic of modern times were at first slow and gradual. But in the eighteenth century, the industrial revolution brought a sudden burst of great changes. Without pausing to consider the events of the sixteenth and seventeenth centuries, which prepared the way for these changes, we may contrast the final result with the conditions of the early simpler division of labor, and so understand better the conditions of our own day.

The economic area has been immensely widened. It has come to include the whole of a country, in some respects the whole of the world. There is division of labor not only between the different crafts within a city, but quite as much between different cities and countries. On the other hand, the crafts themselves have been split up into more minute subdivisions, and different parts of each are followed in widely separated localities. These tendencies have been immensely promoted by the modern improvements in transportation, — improvements which have themselves been the results of the introduction of machinery. The use of power, especially through the steam engine, was the dominant factor in the industrial revolution; and in no direction has it had larger effect than from its application to traction and to navigation.

An epoch-making invention was that of the locomotive. Roads had been much improved in England during the latter part of the eighteenth century, when Telford and Macadam devised their methods of constructing roadways. During the same period canals had also been dug, and used to no small extent both in France and in England; and the people of the United States, always driven by their special industrial conditions to search eagerly for improvements in communication, pushed the use of roadways and canals in the first quarter of the nineteenth century. But in 1830 came the locomotive. In this case, as in that of the steam engine, and indeed of almost all great advances in the arts, the final attainment of the successful device was due to a long series of experiments by many contrivers. Stevenson in 1830 perfected rather than invented the locomotive. So the modern railway was created; and thereby began a second industrial revolution, or at least a second phase of the industrial revolution. Side by side with the railway have acted the great improvements in water transportation. The application of steam to navigation, through the paddle wheel, was a comparatively simple matter, and was accomplished early in the nineteenth century. But the paddle-wheel steamer was too clumsy, too liable to damage in storm, for communication across great bodies of water; and it was not until Ericsson's invention of the screw, in the middle of the nineteenth century, that ocean navigation underwent a great change. This change in any case was not so far-reaching as that wrought by the railway; for water transportation by sailing vessels had always been comparatively cheap; whereas land transportation had been slow and dear, and its dearness had imposed great obstacles to the division of labor within large land areas.

§ 6. As Adam Smith remarked in 1776, in the earlier stages of the modern era, the division of labor is limited by the extent of the market. The village cobbler will turn out no more shoes than it is possible to dispose of within the economic area he can reach. To divide the work of shoemaking between the cutter, the stitcher, the heeler, the laster, is not feasible unless as many shoes can be marketed as the combined labor of all will produce. A modern shoe factory, with its elaborate machinery and highly developed division of labor, turns out thousands of pairs of shoes daily. These shoes can find their purchasers only in a large population reached from the central source of supply.

Many other illustrations could be given of the way in which the divison of labor has been pushed farther and farther with the extension of the market consequent on cheapened transportation. Furniture is made nowadays in large factories, often placed near the sources of timber supply and distant from the persons who are to use the articles. The cabinetmaker of olden days has been replaced by workmen who tend and direct a series of machines, each of which performs unceasingly its part in the operations of sawing, planing, grooving, turning, polishing. Plows are no longer made by the village blacksmith, but put together in the great factory and then distributed broadcast over the earth. Unless it were possible so to distribute them, plows could not be made in quantities at the factory, and there could be no elaborated division of labor in making them. One of the most striking results of the widening of the market is seen in the transformation of the butcher's trade. Until within the last thirty years, the butcher carried on his work as he had done it for thousands of years before. His cattle came from near-by farmers, and the meat was supplied to near-by customers. Through the larger part of the United States, he has now been supplanted by the great packing establishment, where cattle are slaughtered by the thousand. In these establishments dozens of different stages in dissecting the carcass are allotted to as many different sets of workmen. The application of power has not here been carried as far as in some other industries; yet at every stage where it is possible, the machine is set to work; and where it is not, the workman is assigned to the unceasing repetition of a single operation.[1] Every part of the animal is used, and every part is manipulated on a large scale under a further minute division

[1] "It would be difficult to find another industry where division of labor has been so ingeniously and microscopically worked out. The animal has been surveyed and laid off like a map; and the men have been classified in over thirty specialties and twenty rates of pay, from 16 cents to 50 cents an hour. The 50-cent man is restricted to using the knife on the most delicate parts of the hide (floorman) or to using the ax in splitting the backbone (splitter); and, wherever a less skilled man can be slipped in at 18 cents, 18½ cents, 20 cents, 21 cents, 22½ cents, 24 cents, 25 cents, and so on, a place is made for him, and an occupation mapped out. In working on the hide alone there are nine positions, at eight different rates of pay. A 20-cent man pulls off the tail, a 22½-cent man pounds off another part where good leather is not found, and the knife of the 40-cent man cuts a different texture and has a different 'feel' from that of the 50-cent man. Skill has become specialized to fit the anatomy. . . .

"The division of labor grew with the industry, following the introduction of the refrigerator car and the marketing of dressed beef, in the decade of the seventies. Before the market was widened by these revolutionizing inventions, the killing gangs were small, since only the local demands were supplied. But when the number of cattle to be killed each day increased to a thousand or more, an increasing gang or crew of men was put together; and the best men were kept at the most exacting work."— Professor J. R. Commons, in the *Quarterly Journal of Economics*, Vol. XIX, pp. 3, 6. It will be noticed that here there seems to be scope for that advantage from the division of labor which is secured from the adaptation of the tasks to the varying abilities of the several workers. Cp. p. 32, above.

of labor. The output in all its varied forms — the meat of all qualities, the fat, the hide, the bones, the horns, the very hair — all is then marketed to millions of people, distant hundreds of miles, sometimes thousands of miles, from the packing establishment. All such elaborate organization and division rests on the possibility of transporting the products a great distance, and so supplying an enormous population from one central point.

§ 7. The great improvements in transportation during the nineteenth century have given immensely wider scope to a phase of the division of labor which we have not yet considered. This is the geographical division of labor.

In medieval and early modern times, those articles only could be transported for any considerable distance which had great value in small bulk. Such were drugs, spices, fine cloths, rare silks and cottons, choice weapons and armor. These were used chiefly by the small circle of the rich; trade in them did not affect the mass of the population. Where water transportation could be used, there was indeed some possibility of trade and exchange in the bulkier commodities. For this reason, England, with her insular position and much-indented seacoast, was able at a comparatively early stage to export such commodities as wool, copper, and tin, and to develop in some degree the geographical division of labor. With the improvement and enlargement of vessels, the greater security of the seas, and the use of the mariner's compass, trade by water gradually grew to greater and greater dimensions. A still further extension came in the latter part of the eighteenth century, when parts of the interior of the civilized countries were tapped by canals. But the most far-reaching development of the geographical division of labor came with the railway; for the railway can reach all parts of the land. The industry of almost every part of the world has been transformed by this mighty solvent.

The United States at the present time presents what is probably the most extreme case of geographical division of labor highly developed under the influence of cheap transportation. The southern part of New England is a manufacturing hive. The food and raw materials there used come from all parts of the world. The wheat and other breadstuffs come from the Mississippi and Missouri valleys; the meat and animal products from the same regions, and some from regions farther west; the cotton from the Southern states; the wool from the trans-Missouri region, Australia, Argentina, China, Siberia. All sorts of manufactured articles are sent out from New England in exchange, — cotton and woolen fabrics, boots and shoes, metal wares, tools and machinery. The anthracite district of eastern Pennsylvania, again, is given wholly to the mining of hard coal; all its manifold supplies come from without. Pittsburgh is the center of a district in western Pennsylvania given wholly to the mining of bituminous coal and to manufactures which use that fuel, such as iron and steel and glass. Here too, the food, clothing, articles of comfort and luxury, are obtained from all parts of the United States and of the world. No part of the country is self-sufficing; each is constantly sending its products to distant regions, and in return receiving the product of distant regions.

An example no less striking of the geographical division of labor is to be found in the present condition of Great Britain. That country now imports the greater part of its food, — four fifths of its breadstuffs, and more than half of its meat and other food supplies. Its wheat comes chiefly from the United States, Canada, Russia, Argentina; its meat very largely from the United States and Australasia. All the cotton and almost all the wool which serve to clothe its people are brought from other countries. These various commodities, as well as the others which come from tropical regions, are obtained in exchange for a great range of manufactures exported. The people of Great Britain, by devoting their labor chiefly to manufactures and exchanging them for the imported foodstuffs and raw materials, get vastly larger returns than they could by producing everything at home. New England and old

England are in substantially the same industrial position. It is probable that neither could support its present population on its own soil; it is certain that neither could satisfy in this way the imperative needs for food, clothing, shelter, warmth, except on very much harder terms and with very much scantier results. Each is dependent on trade with other regions; the main difference being that in the one case virtually the whole of the trade crosses the political border, and in the other a large part of it is within the same nation.

In consequence of this highly developed division of labor, the position of cities is essentially different from what it was in medieval times. They are no longer dependent for food and materials on the agricultural regions surrounding them, nor do these regions depend on the adjacent cities for their supplies of manufactured commodities. As regards the country surrounding them, the cities are centers for the distribution of goods rather than for production. Many cities have special articles of manufacture, and in this sense are producing centers; but their specialties are disposed of over all the world through the distributing centers. The very large cities, with a wide range of miscellaneous manufactures, and with a great distributing trade, overlap in their economic areas.

§ 8. The gains from the geographical division of labor are of two sorts, analogous to the two sorts of gain from the division of labor between individuals. In part they arise from the adaptation of different regions to the production of specific articles, and in part from the proficiency which is the result of exclusive application to one task.

The division of labor between tropical and temperate countries obviously brings the gain arising from specific adaptation. Tropical fruits, spices, coffee, sugar, are exchanged for the wheat and corn of temperate climes. The southern part of the United States, again, has a climate peculiarly adapted for growing cotton; while in the great central plains there is a corn belt and a wheat belt, — great stretches of country with climate and soil peculiarly adapted to one or the other of the staple cereals. The abundant deposits of excellent coal in the western part of Pennsylvania cause that district to devote itself to coal mining and to the industries for which cheap fuel is essential. Extraordinary deposits of iron ore have been found on the shores of Lake Superior, and thousands of workmen there mine the ore, procuring from other parts of the country all the varied articles which they consume. Italy has a climate adapted to the culture of the grape and of citrous fruits, and she exports them to the countries of more rigorous climate. Italy has no coal; she imports it, chiefly from the great beds of Great Britain. The enumeration might be indefinitely extended. It is obvious that there is a gain when the wheat and corn are produced in the regions favoring them, the iron and coal where they are most abundant, the cotton where the soil is best. This geographical division of labor is not indeed all-embracing; there are obstacles to its sweeping application from such causes as the force of custom and cost of transportation. Yet there is a strong and steady tendency toward the pursuit of a branch of production in that place for which the natural advantages are greatest.

Different in origin and basis, though the same in effect, is that division of labor between different regions which rests on the mere fact of specialization and acquired skill. Exchange between individuals, though based in part on differences in native aptitudes, rests in the main on acquired dexterity. So it is in considerable degree between different regions. When once an industry is conducted on a large scale, with elaborate machinery and with a great output, it will tend to be concentrated. But there may be no strong reason for its concentration at one place rather than another. There is no cause in the natural conditions why Bridgeport and New Haven in Connecticut should be specialized centers for the manufacture of metal wares, Brockton in Massachusetts for shoes, Cohoes in New York for knit goods, Nottingham and Bradford in England for laces and woolen stuffs, Lyons for silks, Chemnitz in Saxony for hosiery.

For certain sorts of industries there is simply a gain when a number of establishments carrying on operations of the same sort are clustered together. Subsidiary industries spring up, supplying them with materials or accessories. When workmen skilled in particular operations are required, their selection and adaptation is easier. The mere attractiveness of a city (for most persons) makes it easier to secure and retain a steady force of laborers. Sometimes the first cause of the location of an industry in a particular place has been the energy, ingenuity, resource, of some individual. His capacity as leader builds up an establishment; others then follow his lead. Sometimes the natural adaptation of a spot causes an industry to spring up there, and later to persist from the mere effect of acquired advantage. Thus some of the manufacturing cities of New England, such as Lowell and Lawrence, grew up on sites having water power, before steam power was as fully developed as in later times, and when the transportation of coal was more costly. It is doubtful whether the water power would now cause these centers of population to be built up; but being there, they tend to remain. All through the broad, flat country of the Mississippi Valley there have sprung up cities and towns, of which one is the seat of the manufacture of vehicles, a second of furniture, a third of engines and machines, with no obvious causes why one place rather than another should possess the particular industry. In whatever place the industry is, the advantages of concentration are secured. A wide market from cheap transportation makes possible the conduct of the industry on a large scale and so the use of much capital, of elaborate machinery, of specialization, and minute division of labor.

A considerable part of the division of labor between nations, and a large volume of trade between them, seem to rest on this second cause. Especially as regards manufactured articles, some countries have advantages in production which rest not on natural resources, but on acquired efficiency. England's manufacture of certain kinds of woolen goods, the silk manufacture in France, perhaps the linen manufacture of the north of Ireland, present cases of this kind. This is the real basis of the argument for protection to young industries. So far as the division of labor between countries and their trade are the results of natural differences, they are best left to work out their results without restriction. But so far as they rest on acquired skill, there is at least a possibility that they may be superseded to advantage by similar division of labor and similar trade within the country.[1]

[1] See what is said on this subject in Book IV, Chapter 37, § 2.

CHAPTER 4

Large-scale Production

§ 1. The tendency to large-scale production has shown itself in all civilized countries since the industrial revolution. It has profoundly modified social as well as economic conditions, and bids fair to modify them still further in the future.

The characteristic feature of the tendency is that the size of the individual establishment becomes larger, and that the total number of establishments becomes smaller. In a period of very rapid growth, it may happen not only that each unit becomes larger, but that the total number increases. More commonly, however, the total number decreases, or remains stationary; while yet the individual establishment becomes greater in size, and the productiveness of the industry as a whole is much enlarged. The following figures from the Census publications of the United States, indicating the growth of some great manufacturing industries during the period from 1850 to 1905, will serve as illustration.

Agricultural Implements

Year	No. Establishments	Wage-Earners	Capital (in Millions)	Product (in Millions)
1850	1,333	7,220	$ 3.6	$ 6.8
1860	2,116	17,093	13.9	20.8
1870	2,076	25,249	34.8	52.1
1880	1,943	39,580	62.1	68.6
1890	910	38,827	145.3	81.3
1900	715	46,582	157.7	101.2
1905	648	47,394	196.7	112.0

Iron and Steel

Year	No. Establishments	Wage-Earners	Capital (in Millions)	Product (in Millions)
1850	468	24,874	$ 21.9	$ 20.4
1860	542	35,189	44.6	52.8
1870	808	75,037	121.8	207.2
1880	792	133,023	209.9	296.6
1890	719	171,181	414.0	478.7
1900	669	222,607	590.5	804.0
1905	605	242,740	948.7	905.9

Cotton Goods

Year	No. Establishments	Wage-Earners	Capital (in Millions)	Product (in Millions)
1850	1,094	92,286	$ 74.5	$ 61.9
1860	1,091	122,028	98.6	115.7
1870	956	135,369	140.7	177.5
1880	1,005	187,587	219.5	210.9
1890	905	218,876	354.0	267.9
1900	1,055	302,861	467.2	339.2
1905	1,154	315,814	613.1	450.5

The figures in all three cases tell the same story. The total capital, the total product, the total number of persons employed, increase at a very rapid rate. Not so the total number of establishments. In the case of cotton goods, it remains curiously constant; for iron and steel, increases slightly; for agricultural implements, decreases sharply. There has been throughout the half century a great and combined advance in the average capital, the average product, the average number of employees.[1]

[1] The figures are taken chiefly from Special Reports of the Census of 1905 (Part IV, Table 1, for Agricultural Implements; Part IV, p. 4, for Iron; Special Report on Combined Textiles, Table 1). For iron, the figures for 1850 and 1860, added from the Census Reports for those years, are of uncertain value. The number of establishments making cotton goods in 1880 is swelled by the inclusion under that head of some outlying establishments. Though subject to correction for these reasons and for others, the statistics are sufficiently trustworthy.

In the interpretation of the figures, however, it must be borne in mind that they do not tell the whole story. In at least two of the industries — iron and

These three cases have been selected as illustrations, because they represent different stages in the march of large-scale production. In the cotton manufacture the change during the half century was least. By 1850 that industry was already established on the factory basis, and since then no essentially new forms of organization have developed. The iron manufacture (that is, the making of crude iron and steel) shows relatively a greater change. Most marked of all is the transformation in the third case. In 1850 agricultural implements were still made in the main on a small scale, and by handicraft methods. Since then large-scale production has transformed the industry in even greater degree than the figures indicate; for the stated number of establishments is swelled, and the averages per establishment are kept down, by the survival of a large number of petty shops.

A similar general tendency shows itself in all the advanced countries: large-scale production gains ground. Yet it must not be supposed that the growth is such as to have crowded out the smaller enterprises, or even to indicate that in the course of time they must disappear entirely. Figures enabling comparisons to be made for successive periods and for all the industries of a given country, are not easily found. The following are available, for Germany, and are significant. They show what percentage of the total persons employed in

steel, and agricultural implements — the average per establishment is kept low, and the growth of large-scale operations obscured, by the fact that a considerable number of small establishments survive, side by side with a few very large ones. These few very large ones are really representative of conditions in the industry; but the census figures do not convey this fact. Further, in all three industries, and especially the iron manufacture and that of agricultural implements, combination and large-scale operation have been going on in forms of which the census figures do not take account. The census regards an establishment in any one place as independent and separate, even though it be owned and managed by persons or corporations having establishments of the same sort in other places. As a matter of fact, during the last decade or two, establishments in different places have come largely under the control of the same corporations or individuals; hence the drift toward concentration is more marked than the figures indicate. And, finally, prices of the several articles declined during the half century covered; hence the increase in the average output per establishment was even greater in terms of quantity (in tons of iron or yards of cloth) than in terms of value.

Germany were engaged, at certain dates, in manufacturing establishments of different size.

	1882	1895	1907
Per cent of persons doing work alone	25.2%	16.4%	10.1%
Per cent of persons in establishments employing 2 @ 5 persons	29.9	23.5	19.4
Per cent of persons in establishments employing 6 @ 10 persons	6.0	7.2	6.6
Per cent of persons in establishments employing 11 @ 50 persons	12.6	16.6	18.4
Per cent of persons in establishments employing 51 @ 200 persons	11.9	17.0	20.1
Per cent of persons in establishments employing 201 @ 1000 persons	10.9	13.9	17.3
Per cent of persons in establishments employing over 1000 persons	3.5	5.4	8.1

It will be seen that the one-person establishment, and those employing five persons or less, have lost ground greatly. Those in the next tier (6 to 10 employees) hold their own; all the others gain, and the very greatest rate of gain is in the class of very large establishments.[1]

§ 2. The causes of the growth of large-scale production are to be found mainly in the revolutionary changes in the arts during the last century and a half. Underlying them all is the increasing division of labor and the increasing use of machinery. A necessary condition has been the widening of the market under the influence of the opened transportation.

A tool or machine of any kind is advantageous only if it is used for a number of operations. The greater the number of operations, the more is it worth while to have an elaborate tool, and to give much labor to its making. Machinery moved by

[1] I take these figures from Professor Bücher's paper in the *Zeitschrift für die gesammte Staatswissenschaft*, 1910, Heft 3, p. 430. Professor Bücher points out that for Germany, as for the United States, census figures do not tell the whole story of the growth of large-scale operations, since several establishments forming part of one larger enterprise are frequently reckoned by the census as separate and independent.

power is a highly elaborate tool. The larger the scale on which an enterprise is conducted, the better is the opportunity for using machinery to advantage. The gain from its use arises from several sources. Power itself becomes cheaper per unit as it is applied on a large scale. Both for first installment and for running expenses, a large steam engine costs less, for each horse power, than a small one; which means economy if the establishment is large enough to utilize all the power supplied. Again, subsidiary operations can be carried on to advantage by machinery. The use of steam shovels in handling coal, ores, earth, and of similar instruments for loading and unloading vessels, depends on the work being massed in large quantities at one spot. An ocean steamship of 10,000 tons carries freight more cheaply than one of 5000, and one of 20,000 tons more cheaply still. Wherever the traffic is heavy, as between Europe and the United States, the huge steamship is economical. Where the traffic is less heavy and less regular, as in the trade with South America and outlying regions, the ship of moderate size holds its own. The greatest of the American corporations making agricultural implements, one that illustrates conspicuously the tendency to large-scale production, — the International Harvester Company, — has a machine whose sole work is to shape poles for wagons and harvesters. The machine cost $2500; it saves a cent per pole; it is worth while only because poles by the hundred thousand are made each year.

Other causes, more or less closely connected with the growing use of machinery, have strengthened the tendency to large-scale production. Just as all the several expenses for the plant and power become less per unit as the output enlarges, so the general expenses for administration and counting-room work tend to become less. Clerks are kept more continuously occupied, and more elaborate division of labor among them is feasible. Superintendent and foreman can take charge of the full number of men which each can direct to advantage. One watchman, one engineer, one timekeeper, can usually serve a large establishment as effectively as a small one. All the miscellaneous expenses of general management are less in proportion to a large output.

The mercantile management of a large enterprise — the buying of materials and the selling of the product — also offers opportunity for economy and efficiency. Supplies can usually be bought to greater advantage. This is commonly spoken of as if due simply to greater bargaining power on the part of the large buyer, and to greater pressure of competition among those who wish to sell to him. But in the main it is due to the fact that mercantile operations themselves, and especially wholesale operations, are carried on more economically when on a large scale. Expenses for clerk work, rentals of office premises, and the like, which constitute the main outlays of the wholesale dealer, are no greater for large transactions than for small. Hence brokers and wholesale dealers can sell at lower prices to those who buy habitually in large amounts.

Again, the disposal of the output is often at less expense for a large establishment than for a small one, and often at still less expense for a very large establishment than for a moderately large one. Advertising and notoriety much affect the marketing of sundry commodities. When once appeal is made not to a limited local market but to a large and extensive constituency, the disposal of the great quantities of goods turned out by a modern factory becomes by no means the least difficult of its manager's tasks. All the apparatus for drumming up custom — traveling salesmen, trade catalogues, and the like — is the more effective, and the less costly per unit of product, in proportion as it operates on a large scale. Advertising is most effective when spread over the land with every sort of device; when it is systematized and put in charge of a separate manager. All such elaboration of marketing is both a result and a further cause of a great volume of business.

The utilization of "by-products"[1] is another of the advantages of large-scale production. At the great packing houses which

[1] Better, "joint products"; see Book II, Chapter 16, § 1.

do so much of the butcher's work of the United States, every particle of the slaughtered animal is used, and many things which would go to waste in the small shop become a source of profit. A very large woolen factory finds it advantageous to utilize the fatty matter which is attached to the wool as it comes from the sheep's back. This grease, which must in any case be scoured out of the wool, goes to waste in a smaller establishment; whereas the large mill, by putting in a plant for the special purpose of treating the grease, finds it a source of gain. Great ironworks find it possible to utilize the gas expelled from coal in the coking process; either selling the gas, purified, in a near-by city, or using it at once for fuel in their own furnaces. A large sawmill can put in a plant for burning its own sawdust, dispensing with other fuel for power.

Other advantages of large-scale production arise from the possibilities of experimenting with new devices and new methods. Some ventures will fail, some succeed. In a very great enterprise, the successes may be expected in the long run to outweigh the failures; the enterprise insures itself, so to speak, against the inevitable risks of experimenting. Where operations are conducted on a small scale, the failure of one experiment may ruin the entire undertaking. Again, the best technical skill, the best-trained engineers and chemists, are more easily and more economically employed by the great establishment. As with expensive but efficient machinery, their use is advantageous only for a very large output, and is most economical for the largest output.

§ 3. The limitations on large-scale production arise mainly from the infirmities of human nature. The extension of the scale of operations means an ever increasing reliance upon hired labor and an ever-lessening reliance on spontaneous self-interest. If all men worked with as much energy and spirit for an employer as they do for themselves, the spread of large-scale production would be almost without bounds. A striking illustration of the influence of this limiting factor is shown in the differing tendencies of agriculture and of manufactures.

The operations of agriculture are necessarily spread over a considerable area; and they are not easily subjected to a fixed routine. Both circumstances make supervision difficult. Manufactures, on the other hand, bring the concentration of hundreds or thousands of workmen under a single roof or in a small area. Moreover, in manufactures, machinery means the repetition of identical operations. Hence a routine can be fixed, and workmen assigned to fixed tasks, and their faithfulness controlled, with comparative ease. But in agriculture much must be left to the zeal and intelligence of the individual worker.

The consequence is that agriculture has nowhere shown the same tendency to enlargement of the scale of production which is so unmistakable in manufactures. It is true that some countries are usually spoken of as countries of large farming; England is the type of such a country. It is true, also, that in some parts of the United States (in the North Central region, for example) there has been in recent years a slight tendency to increase in the size of farms. But a farm which is called large is an industrial unit of comparatively small size. One which employs twenty men the year round is considered large; yet a factory employing this number is a small affair. The tasks of twenty men engaged in farming would be spread over several hundred acres, and must present troublesome questions in assigning and supervising the work. Farms of this size are comparatively rare. By far the greater part of agricultural work is done on farms where a single man, having under him perhaps one other or a few others, conducts the operations on his own account. In the early stages of the development of some parts of the United States, so-called "bonanza" farming has appeared for a time. Where great level tracts of fertile land have been suddenly opened to cultivation, as in the interior valleys of California or in the Red River Valley of the Dakotas, wheat culture has sometimes been carried on for a while over thousands of acres, with dozens of men and vehicles and with expensive machinery. But this has proved only a temporary phase. As the fertility of virgin soil begins to be exhausted, and a more varied and careful use of it is called for,[1] these great tracts are split up into smaller units. The head of a large factory can devise means for supervising his men and for securing the execution of his orders. But the owner of a farm can use hired labor to advantage only when his own example and his own oversight supply the needed stimulus.

Some industries, though spread over a large area and presenting difficulties for the supervision of hired labor, are so much more effective when on a large scale that these disadvantages are not decisive. The railway is an example. Many of its employees are necessarily scattered over great tracts of country. The supervision of the innumerable agents calls for an intricate and expensive apparatus of rules and regulations, bookkeeping and auditing. But the work is done so much more cheaply on a large scale that this difficulty and the expense entailed by it are more than offset.

Sometimes, on the other hand, industries which offer possibilities of economy from large operations are for other reasons limited to small ones. Though retail dealings can be conducted to advantage on a large scale, — with economies in purchases and in administration, with better utilization of premises, with more continuous activity by the force of salesmen, — the smaller shops still hold their own. The opportunities for large-scale retailing are availed of in the cities by the so-called department stores; establishments whose growth has been immensely promoted of late years by the improvements in urban transportation. But even in a large city, and especially in its outlying quarters, small or moderate retail shops continue. The reason is that often the purchaser must have his source of supply near at hand. The ubiquitous corner drug store of our American cities persists against large competitors.

A glance at such a volume as the *Statistical Abstract of the United States*, with its summary of the number of establishments and volume of transactions in various kinds of business, shows instructively which among them, for reasons of this sort,

[1] Compare Book V, Chapter 42, § 5.

resist the tendency to concentration. The strictly manufacturing establishments show the characteristic features of the modern movement. Though the volume of transactions becomes immensely greater, the number of establishments becomes less. So it is with the manufacture of agricultural implements, of boots and shoes, of carpets, chemicals, firearms, glass, cotton, woolen and silk fabrics, sewing machines. Those industries which, like the retail shop, purvey more directly to the consumer, or for other reasons must be near the persons with whom they have dealings, increase their numbers *pari passu* with the increase in population and with the volume of their own transactions. Such are blacksmithing, carpentering, plumbing, bread baking, printing, painting, and paper hanging. Here there is no marked tendency toward an enlargement of the size of the individual establishment, still less any victory of great-scale production.

The limitations of men's faculties explain why large-scale operations do not make their way, even in manufactures, with unfailing certainty. What has been said in the preceding paragraphs may seem to imply that the transition to greater size takes place quasi-automatically. This is by no means the case. It depends on the energy, ambition, insight, of individual men. Every new machine, every change to larger scale, involves risks, calls for planning and judgment, is dependent on some individual's initiative. If an indefinite number of individuals were capable of this sort of work, the march of progress would be faster and large-scale operations would make their way more surely and speedily. As it is, these changes wait on the impulse given by the comparatively few individuals who have the capacity for industrial leadership. Occasionally some such individual reorganizes his business upon a larger scale and with more highly developed plant and machinery. Then others follow his lead, and a whole industry is rapidly transformed. This has happened during the last two decades in the iron manufacture, especially in the United States and in Germany. Carnegie in the former, Krupp in the latter, led the way in a remarkable development. Usually, however, the advance takes place by gradual and tentative steps, like those in the growth of the size of ocean steamships. The industrial revolution, so far as regards its pace, has been in reality not a revolution but a slow and gradual change, dependent on the energy and ingenuity of individuals, and limited by the scarcity of men possessing such qualities.

§ 4. A new phase of large-scale production has come to be of great and almost ominous importance during the present generation. Perhaps it should be called large-scale management rather than large-scale production; since it involves not so much an increase in the size of the individual establishments as the combination under single management of several establishments. It takes two forms, which may be described as horizontal and vertical.

Horizontal combination is the union under single management of a number of enterprises of the same sort. They are usually few, and each is usually on a large scale. As the size of the representative establishment in any industry enlarges, and the number of individual establishments shrinks, the stage is finally reached where but a few survive — a dozen, perhaps. These then combine; not in the sense that one huge establishment supersedes the dozen, but that the dozen, while retaining their technical independence, are owned and managed as one. Though large-scale operation may have reached its limit so far as the mechanical apparatus of production goes, some gain may still be secured from united large-scale administration. A typical example is the American Sugar Refining Company. A modern refinery is a huge concern, costing a couple of millions of dollars, and putting out 10,000, even 15,000, barrels of sugar a day. Yet there are limits to its size. Beyond a certain point, enlargement no longer adds economy in operation. When an output beyond this capacity is called for, a second refinery of the same kind is erected, and so on until the total supply is provided. All these refineries, however, may be managed from one common center, with at least possibilities of economy. Their supplies may be bought in common, and distributed among them in such a manner as to insure continuity in operation and the minimum outlay for transportation. This last factor, economy in transportation, is of great consequence where the chief material (raw sugar, in this instance) comes from great distances, and, being rapidly worked up, must be continually and systematically replaced. Machinery may be made identical, or "standardized," in the different works, and its repair and replacement thus facilitated. These and other possible economies may be offset, to be sure, in whole or in part, by the inherent difficulties of large-scale management, — notably the increasing difficulty of supervision. Experience, and especially the test of competition, can alone settle with certainty whether the advantages offset the disadvantages.

Horizontal combination is typical of the so-called "trust." The motive for such union under single management is twofold. Partly it is to secure economy in management; but largely it is to put an end to competition and bring about a more or less effective monopoly. So far as economy is secured, the movement, which has attained such extraordinary dimensions in the last ten years, may be to the public advantage. But if monopoly develops, it has grave possibilities of public disadvantage. How far monopoly in fact is likely to result, and how far cheapening of production is in fact brought about, is still uncertain; time and experience alone can show. But it is clear that in some respects at least, and for some industries, such combination brings an extension of large-scale production and concentrated management.

Different in its essential features is vertical combination, or, as it is sometimes called, the integration of industry. The usual outcome of the division of labor has been that the several steps in production which succeed each other in time have been conducted in independent establishments. But in some important trades there has appeared of late a tendency to unite such successive stages under single management. Thus the iron industry, in the traditional organization, was split up into a number of separate branches. One producer — that is, a capitalist hiring and directing a group of workmen — carried on ore mining, and disposed of his ore to other producers engaged in smelting it into pig iron. Still another producer similarly cut the wood and converted it into charcoal, — this in earlier days when wood supplied the fuel for iron making; or, after coke supplanted charcoal, mined the coal and made it into coke. The pig-iron maker, who had bought the ore and the fuel, sold his product to the puddler or steel maker, who in turn sold his bar iron or steel to the machinist, the builder, the wire maker. Vertical combination, or the integration of industry, appears when all these successive steps are united under single management, — when all the phases of iron and steel making are combined in one great enterprise.

The United States Steel Corporation carries out this sort of combination in a typical manner, and on an enormous scale. Itself a union of previous combinations which had adopted the same method on a scale already great, this corporation owns vast mines of iron ore, of coal, and of limestone. The mines are situated chiefly on the shores of Lake Superior, the coal mines chiefly in Pennsylvania. Most of the ore is carried to the coal, and smelted in the great iron-making district of which Pittsburgh is the center; but in part the coal is carried north and west, meeting the ore halfway, to be smelted at various places on the Great Lakes. To transport these materials, the corporation has its own railways in the Lake Superior region, and in the region from Pittsburgh to Lake Erie; and it owns a great fleet of steamers and barges on the Lakes. The pig iron, made in its own furnaces, is converted into steel of various shapes in its own steel mills. The further operations of converting the steel into rails, structural and bridge shapes, plates and sheets, tubing, and wire, are carried on in still other establishments. In no other industry, and nowhere else in the world, has the experiment of vertical combination been conducted on so great a scale.

The iron and steel manufacture offers an unusually tempting field for vertical combination, chiefly, it would seem, because of the concentration of the supplies of raw material, — coal and iron ore. Those who, at any stage of rising demand, possess the mines of coal and iron, have the whip hand in the situation; hence the manufacturers of the more finished forms of iron and steel have sought to gain control of the mines, by purchase or amalgamation. This tendency has shown itself in some degree in Great Britain, and has proceeded in Germany almost as far as in the United States. The combination of a series of superimposed establishments has now become the normal form of organization in the iron manufacture.

Some tendencies of the same sort are found in other industries. The International Paper Company owns great tracts of spruce forest, cuts the timber and logs, floats them to its own pulp mills, and there manufactures the paper which is used in such enormous quantity by our newspapers. The Harvester Company, already referred to, owns forests and cuts timber; it owns its iron and coal mines, and makes its iron and steel. The Sugar Refining Company owns its forests and makes its barrels. Other industries have shown a similar development in another direction, — in the marketing of goods. The usual arrangement is for a separation between manufacturing and marketing. The shoe manufacturer commonly sells his output to the wholesale dealer or "selling agent," who in turn often sells to an intermediate dealer, the jobber, and sometimes directly to the retailer. But some shoe manufacturers have undertaken not only the making but the marketing of their wares. They have established their own retail shops, scattered in many cities over the country, and through them deal directly with the consumer. Again, the American Tobacco Company, by establishing its own retail shops in great numbers, has likewise combined the distribution of goods with their production.

Vertical combination and horizontal combination may go hand in hand. The American Tobacco Company has attempted to combine all the establishments manufacturing tobacco for smoking and chewing; and the extension of its operations into the retail disposal of its products has been the outgrowth of the endeavor to form and strengthen this all-embracing horizontal combination. The Steel Corporation owns many iron furnaces, many steel mills, many tube works, many sheet-steel and tin-plate works, and thus exemplifies also the union of the two kinds of combination. The Steel Corporation has carried horizontal combination in some branches to the point of nearly complete monopoly; thus it owns virtually all the sheet-steel and tin-plate mills and tube works in the United States. But it produces little more than half the pig iron, and has by no means a monopoly of the steel rails or structural steel. In Germany, the *Stahlwerksverband* (Steel Works Association) has formed a compact pool in the iron and steel manufacture, though one that does not go the full length of completely unified ownership. In Great Britain, on the other hand, while many large works have extended their operations downward to the control of mines and upward to the making of finished products, there is very little of horizontal combination; the several great enterprises go their own way independently. In the case of the boot and shoe manufacturers, just spoken of, who own their own tanneries or sell at retail their own shoes, the combination is vertical only; there is no attempt at horizontal combination.

The movement toward vertical combination is less strong than that toward horizontal combination. The iron trade, which presents so striking a case of the former, is exceptional. The desire to secure control of a limited, or at least concentrated, raw material, which has promoted the integration of the iron trade, has not affected others, in which the sources of raw material are more scattered. In the manufacture of cotton, wool, silk, or flax, there is no indication of any movement for control of the supply of raw material or for vertical combination in any other way. On the contrary, the tendency seems to be rather toward a minuter division. The textile industries in Great Britain and on the Continent have always been split up into separate industries to a greater degree than in the United States. In Europe, spinning, weaving, bleaching, dyeing, printing, are usually carried on as distinct industries. The tradition in the United States has been for the combination of several of these steps — especially spinning and weaving — in one organization; yet even in this country the movement of late years seems to be in the other direction. In the shoe manufacture, while there has been the marketing arrangement just noted, and in some cases a combination of leather tanning with manufacturing, the trend does not seem to be toward greater combination. Some establishments do nothing but make soles, others do nothing but make box toes, and so on.

The movement toward combination, whether horizontal or vertical, is in part a result of the intensified competition which comes with the greater investment of fixed capital and the greater size of the separate enterprises. But very largely it results from the discovery of the possibilities of organization. What are the limits to the size of the enterprise which can be managed as a unit? The single factory, perhaps large, was supposed until comparatively recent times to represent that limit. But as the scale of industry has been enlarged, the operations have been systematized and subjected to more perfect control. The task of management itself has been subdivided. Separate persons are intrusted with the purchase of supplies, the sale of product, the maintenance of plant, the hiring and superintendence of labor, accounting and auditing. The genius of men with great inborn capacity for business has led to even greater perfection of organization. The telegraph, the telephone, improved postal service, have promoted large-scale management as they have large-scale production. These striking changes have been the results of skill, judgment, and administrative capacity in the guiding individuals, and also the cause of an increasing demand for the persons possessing such qualities.

None the less, the larger the scale of operations, the more do its disadvantages appear. There is need for an expensive system of control, — for supervision, accounting, auditing, the effective prompting of energy and economy. The test of competition settles in the long run whether the great combination is the more efficient agent in production. If it can produce more cheaply, it can sell more cheaply, and displace its rivals.[1]

§ 5. Notwithstanding the wastes of competition, and the possible economies of large-scale production, competing establishments hold their own over the greater part of the field of industry. There is no present prospect that competition will be generally supplanted by combination and monopoly.

That competition operates wastefully seems in some cases obvious. The milk of a city, for example, is usually supplied by a number of dealers, each with his own set of customers scattered irregularly over a large area. If all who lived in a given quarter were supplied by one dealer, a clear economy in delivery would be secured. If the whole supply for an entire urban district were under single large-scale management, there would be a possibility of cheapening the product still further, and (what in this case is specially important) of improving its quality. Retail dealers, especially in such things as groceries and foodstuffs, overlap in similar wasteful fashion. Commonly, too, the areas supplied by competing manufacturers overlap. Advertising, again, seems to be in large part designed to induce a customer to turn simply from one dealer to another. If there were no competition, — if one great establishment supplanted ten rivals, — the same wants would make themselves felt, the same purchases would be made, the expense of advertising eliminated, the goods sold cheaper.

Though some tendency is seen toward getting rid of the causes of waste, the tendency is not very marked. With the growth of great cities, large firms and companies have come in great degree to control urban milk supply, yet with little indication that complete and systematic combination is emerging. The great manufacturing "trusts" endeavor to avoid cross freights, by making shipments from that one among their establishments

[1] To this statement of the automatic action of competition there are some qualifications, considered in Book VII, Chapter 63, § 3.

which is nearest the point of delivery. But, as a rule, manufacturers continue to compete and to ship in a seemingly haphazard way. The same is true of retail trade, where all sorts of establishments, great and small, vie for the customer and duplicate facilities in the traditional and apparently wasteful fashion.

The waste is probably less than it seems. Competition keeps every one keyed to a high pitch, nerves the shrewd and alert, weeds out the inefficient. Advertising is part of the mechanism of competition as well as of combination. Not least, competition leaves the purchaser some freedom; he is not subjected to the alternative of turning to one single purveyor or else doing without. Even the most benevolent and considerate monopolist becomes often exasperating; how much more so the ordinary trader when no longer spurred by competition! A choice as to what you would have, and when and how you would have it, satisfies a deep-rooted human instinct. In the advocacy of socialistic organization, the advantages of unified supply are much dwelt on. But the consumer in the socialist state would have to accept whatever the all-controlling public managers put before him. The satisfaction which comes from freedom of choice explains in large part the persistence of competition.

The movement toward combination has been so conspicuous of late years that the extent of the field which it covers has been exaggerated. Agriculture shows it least; transportation, especially by land, shows it most. In mining, there is the striking case of the iron trade; and there is also, in the United States, the striking case of anthracite coal, where the strictly limited area of supply and the close connection with transportation have brought about effective combination. Nevertheless, most mining is still carried on by independent producers. In manufactures, most industries have not reached the stage of combination. Over the greater part of the industrial field, though production tends to be on a larger scale, with great use of machinery and minuter division of labor, competition still prevails.

CHAPTER 5

Capital

§ 1. The increasing complexity of the division of labor and the growing use of machinery have added to the number of separate stages in production and to the length of time over which the whole process is spread. Hence the greater need of a supply of tools and materials, the importance of capital, the problems which relate to owners of capital and to the income from capital.

Production is spread over time in any society advanced beyond the most primitive savagery; and this not merely for the several subdivided steps in production, but for production as a whole. That agriculture takes time, from the sowing of the seed to the reaping of the crop, is obvious. But the sowing is not the beginning, nor is the reaping the end. The seed must have been itself sown and husbanded, and the tools for cultivation must have been prepared in advance. After the harvest, the grain which is reaped may indeed be available for satisfying human needs almost at once; it is so in a small, self-contained community, such as we still see in a village of Hindustan. But in the countries of advanced civilization grain is carried by rail or water to a mill, probably distant; there ground into flour; then carried another distance to dealers; and finally, after a considerable interval, put into the hands of the consumer. Each of these steps not only takes time in itself, but implies the existence of apparatus which has been made in the past and has taken time to make, — the railway or steamship, the flour mill, the warehouses and shops of the middlemen. Almost all the operations of production require first the procuring of materials from nature's resources, then their fashioning with the aid of tools and machinery. Let the reader but consider the mode in which the familiar articles of daily use have come into his hands, — the clothing and the footgear, the furniture and household utensils, the books and ornaments, the house in which he dwells, — and he will see how long has been the series of operations, how intricate the division of labor for each one, and how extended the period from the beginning of production to the final attainment of the consumable or enjoyable article.

This fundamental fact, resting on the complex division of labor, is yet disguised by that very division. The tanner who puts his leather on the market, the farmer who sells his flax, the ironmaster who sells his steel or iron, each thinks of himself as marketing a completed product. By the sale he gets money, and so the command of the enjoyable things he wishes to buy or of the things needed for continuing production. He never stops to reflect what must further be done to the thing which he sells; how it must pass through the hands of a long chain of producers and dealers before it reaches in consumable form those whose wants are finally satisfied.

In modern times, the most significant aspect of this element of time in production is found in the increasing use of machinery and plant of all sorts. Machinery, though it may be simply a more intricate kind of tool, adds so much to the preparatory work that it has greatly accentuated the problems that arise from the spreading of production over time. A factory requires a year or years to build; the machinery in it requires still more time to make. Many years are needed for constructing a railway; a generation for such a work as the Suez Canal or the Panama Canal. The factory, and the machinery in it, exist for the purpose of eventually turning out things to be used and enjoyed. The railway and canal facilitate the geographical division of labor, and serve to promote, through a series of steps which only begin when these means of transportation have been completed, the eventual abundance of things to be used and enjoyed. One simple fact illustrates how marked the tendency toward greater use of plant has been in the period since the industrial revolution began. The world's annual production of iron has multiplied tenfold the last half century, and sixtyfold in the last century.[1] Iron is used solely (the exceptions are insignificant) as an instrument of production; it is the foundation of the material apparatus of civilization; it means plant, tools, machinery. The enormous quantities of it which have been turned out in modern times, and especially during the last generation, signify an extraordinary increase in the construction of elaborate and expensive apparatus, and a corresponding extension of time in the operations of production.

§ 2. If we were to take a cross section of the community's possessions at any given time, we should find them to be of the most diverse sort. There would be, in the first place, such things as iron ore and steel bars, timber and wool and cotton, factories and railways and ships, stocks of all sorts in warehouses, commodities ready for sale in the retailers' shops. And in the second place, there would be houses, furniture, clothing and food, in the hands of those using them for the satisfaction of wants. To the first set of things we apply the term capital, or producer's capital; the second set of things we call wealth, simply, or consumer's capital. The first set we may speak of as unfinished goods, the second set as finished and enjoyable goods. For some purposes of economic analysis they are similar, for other purposes dissimilar. The difference between them is at bottom only a difference of degree; yet is so great as to justify a distinction.[2] For the present, we shall find it convenient to apply the term "capital" specifically to the first set, — to producer's capital. The second set will be referred to as enjoyable or consumable or finished commodities; and only when speaking of them in

[1] The world's annual output of pig-iron was: —

In 1800	825,000 tons
In 1850	4,750,000 tons
In 1870	11,900,000 tons
In 1905	53,700,000 tons

[2] The difference in degree is one as to the time when satisfaction or utility accrues. That time is commonly nearer in the case of consumer's wealth or consumer's capital, and more distant in the case of producer's capital. See what is said below on these subjects, Book V, Chapter 40.

those aspects and relations which offer analogies to the first, shall we refer to them as consumer's capital.

Capital, then, — that is, producer's capital, — is not in enjoyable form; it is not now a source of satisfaction. It exists for the purpose of increasing consumer's wealth. Its relation to enjoyable goods is twofold. On the one hand, it may be said gradually to "ripen" into such goods. On the other hand, it is a means of increasing their supply.

It is easy to see that raw materials, as they are commonly called, ripen into finished commodities. Wool is converted by successive steps into clothing, stone and timber into a house, grain into bread. But a process the same in essentials takes place as to tools and machinery. Suppose a printing machine to last for one year only, being worn out and worthless at the close of the year. The books printed with its aid are the product not only of the labor applied to making the paper and other materials, of that applied by the compositors and other workmen in the printing office, but also of that applied in the construction of the printing machine itself. If we suppose that one hundred books are printed in the course of the year, the machine may be said to have ripened into so many enjoyable goods, and each of these may be said to have embodied in it one hundredth of the labor which was given to constructing the machine. The machine as such has disappeared, just as the paper and ink as such have disappeared; in place of all three we have the printed books. If the machine lasts for ten or twenty years, the labor of constructing it contributes to making a much greater quantity of books, and a smaller fraction of the labor of construction is embodied in each book. So of all machinery and all plant. It wears out sooner or later, and may be said sooner or later to ripen into goods that satisfy our wants.

The most important single cause of the abundance of consumable goods, and so of the improvement in the material welfare of mankind, is found in those forms of capital which are commonly spoken of as fixed, — in tools, machinery, plant. Certainly this has been the most important cause of the remarkable advance in material welfare which the civilized countries have made during the last century. Erect a great cotton or woolen mill, a shoe factory, a large sugar refinery or flour mill, — take much time and apply much labor for getting ready an elaborate apparatus, — and eventually you will secure your product in greater abundance and with less labor embodied in each unit. The making of machinery itself has illustrated this tendency as strikingly as any other branch of production. The manufacture of iron and steel, conducted on a great scale, with elaborate and expensive plant, serves to turn out in cheapness and abundance the metal indispensable for the apparatus of production at large. Locomotives, textile machinery, agricultural implements, not to mention the simpler tools of the mechanic, are themselves made with machinery.

In order that all this application of plant may work smoothly and effectively, the supply of materials must also have been on a large scale; and this again involves prolonged preparation. A great iron furnace, kept in blast night and day, year in and year out, takes into its maw huge quantities of iron ore, coal, and limestone, which, no less than the furnace itself, must be made ready in advance. So the textile mill requires its wool or cotton or silk, the shoe factory its leather, the refinery its raw sugar. Through all the complicated operations the trend is the same; elaborate preparation, production spread over time, much capital, eventual plenty, and cheapness of the consumable goods.

§ 3. In order that there shall be capital and time-using production, there must have been at some previous period a *surplus*. The more of capital is to be employed, the more must there be a surplus to draw on.

In the very earliest stages of the formation of capital, that surplus showed itself directly in the fact of spare time. The first rude implements of stone and bronze must have been fashioned during hours when labor did not need to be given for the satisfaction of imperative wants, — when there was a chance of doing something else. What motives may have influenced man during this stage, and by what chance the first tools were hit on, we cannot guess. Very possibly a mere instinct of contrivance was the moving cause. A reasoned understanding of the gain from having tools and supplies must have set in at an early stage. The choice under the simplest conditions is between the present and the future, — between idleness or amusement for the moment and provision for future needs.

The greater the surplus, the greater the time and labor which can be given for future needs. When the arts are at so low a stage that little is produced beyond the bare necessaries of existence, provision for the future can be made only on a scanty scale. On the other hand, the very scantiness of capital is an obstacle to the efficiency of labor and so to the existence of any considerable surplus. During long ages mankind was thus in a position of double difficulty. Without capital the productiveness of labor was meager, and yet with meager productiveness of labor there was little possibility of creating more capital.

It is not to be understood that the slenderness of the surplus stock was the only obstacle to the creation of capital. Ignorance of natural laws and of the possibilities of tool making, carelessness for the future, were no less important. But without the surplus the very foundation for building up any effective apparatus of production was lacking. Here, as often, the first step was the hardest. Once man had became possessed of some capital, the productiveness of his labor became greater, and thereby the creation of still more capital became easier.

§ 4. In the preceding section we have spoken of capital as being made or created. But capital is also said to be *saved* and accumulated. Both expressions are accurate. If we think of one person or set of persons as being alone concerned with the steps by which capital comes into existence, we can see that this person both provides for the future by saving, and uses his surplus in shaping tools or getting together materials. But in a society having an elaborated division of labor, these two things are rarely done by one person; that is, they are rarely done together by one person for any given item of capital. When all incomes and expenditures take the form of money, savings are made, not by putting aside things in kind for one's own use, but by putting aside money for future needs. On the other hand, tools and other apparatus of production are made for the market by persons who are not consciously providing for the future. They are bought by other persons who wish to "invest," — that is, to get capital. The process by which these separate steps are made to bring about their joint result in the modern organization of industry deserves careful consideration.

Saving may take the form of simple hoarding. The miser who puts away a store of coin, saves and provides for his own or others' needs. But no addition to the apparatus of production results from such saving. Where property is insecure, from the rapacity of a despot or from the feebleness of a government unable to protect against foreign invaders, hoarding is sometimes done on a large scale. In British India, during many centuries preceding the British occupation, both these causes of insecurity existed. Hence those who had means put them largely into the form of specie and jewels, — articles having much value in little bulk and capable of being hid or carried away. The European aggressors of the seventeenth or eighteenth century found great stores of such wealth in Hindustan, not because that country had rich mines, but because the people had attained a considerable civilization and prosperity, and had hoarded long. Notwithstanding the peace and security which British rule has long maintained, the habit of putting accumulated means into this form has continued in India to our own time. In France, for a long period preceding the French Revolution, the peasantry — those among them, comparatively few, who had anything at all in the way of a surplus — put away coins, one at a time, hidden in the chimney or garret, until they had accumulated enough to buy a scrap of land. Fear of spoliation and ignorance of other ways of doing anything with the money caused their saving to take the form of hoarding. No addition to capital was thereby promoted. Nor was there any addition to capital even when the accumulated coins were brought out for the purchase of land. The noble of whom the purchase was made probably frittered away the proceeds, and the only immediate result of the peasant's accumulation was the transfer of land from one hand to another. Such practises continued in France after the Revolution and until the latter part of the nineteenth century, when the war between France and Germany, which shook so many of the established traditions of France, served largely to bring to an end the habit of putting aside hoards of specie.

The great bulk of saving, however, takes in modern times the form of *investment*. Contrast the process of hoarding with what happens when money is put away in a savings bank, — an operation which we may select as typical of the methods of investment in a modern community. The person who leaves his cash with the savings bank commonly thinks only that it is safe, and that he is paid something as interest on it. But the cash is not kept in the coffers of the institution. A small fraction only is retained, to meet possible calls of depositors who wish to make withdrawals. Almost all of it is lent out to persons who use it for making a profit. Now profit arises, in the ordinary course of things, from the operations of production; and the person who borrows money uses it for the purchase of things needed in production. He may be a manufacturer, who erects a building, buys machinery and supplies, hires workmen. He may be a merchant, who buys commodities from the manufacturer, and carries them one stage further in the successive stages which bring them at last to the consumer. Every person who directs production — such as the manufacturer or merchant — uses a large part of his means in buying materials or tools or stores from producers of a previous stage, so recouping them for the outlays they have already made. The money means which are put at the disposal of the business class as a whole are a most important part of the mechanism for adding to the concrete apparatus of production.

§ 5. The fundamental fact in this elaborate mechanism of saving and investment is that advances are made to laborers. One set of persons put aside money means; through various channels, other persons are given command of these money means, and use them to set laborers to work. Here, again, the division of labor between those who carry on the successive stages of production conceals the essential nature of their operations. A manufacturer spends only a part of his means upon hiring laborers directly; the rest he uses in buying plant and materials and in the other expenses of production. But those materials were themselves fashioned by laborers to whom another set of advances had to be made by a previous capitalist. The wholesale or retail merchant hires comparatively few laborers, — only a set of clerks and a porter or two. But he recoups by his purchases of goods the advances of a long series of preceding employers, himself giving only the finishing touches in the whole process. Looking at the operations of capitalists and employers as a whole, and reflecting on the outcome of the division of labor among them and their workmen, we find that all capital is made by labor, and all the operations of the capitalist class are resolvable into a succession of advances to laborers.

These advances, just spoken of as money turned over to laborers, consist ultimately in a provision of commodities for their use. The money is but the medium whereby laborers get command of the commodities which they buy. These commodities — things to eat, to wear, to give shelter — are in the last analysis what the employing class hands over to those whom it employs. Some of the advances were made in the past, and are represented now by plant and materials, still in use, of which the full equivalent has not yet been reproduced in finished form. Some are made from day to day, in the course of current operations. The whole of existing capital may thus be described as a great accumulated surplus which has been used and is being used for maintaining labor, while provision is made for the future. The process of setting laborers to work in the initial stages of production is going on all the time; similarly that of bringing articles to the final stage of consumable form.

The wide separation, in modern societies, of the two acts needful for the creation of capital — saving and the application of labor — is mainly the result of inequality. Persons of the well-to-do class have a considerable surplus over current needs, and save with comparative ease. They own most of the apparatus of production. But most persons in our modern societies are not of the well-to-do class, and have little in the way of a surplus. They have small accumulations, and they are mainly hired by others in carrying on the operations of time-consuming production, and in making and maintaining capital. No doubt, some savings are made by the working classes; and through the agency of savings banks and similar institutions, these savings have increased rapidly. But, while absolutely considerable, they are no large proportion of the total of accumulated means. The greater part of the capital owned and maintained in modern communities arises from the savings of the comparatively small numbers of the more fortunate classes.

A chain of middlemen commonly connects the individual who saves with the laborer to whom advances are made. The employer himself, though he almost always uses some means of his own, commonly is a borrower. He borrows, however, not from the savers directly, but from their various agents and representatives. The savings bank, for example, collects surplus sums from individual savers, yet often deals with the employer of labor only through brokers and other middlemen. It buys stocks and bonds from brokers and banking firms. The banking firms have issued them after long negotiations with the persons undertaking the operations to which the whole series of transactions is in the end directed. Bankers are the typical intermediaries; their essential function is to direct the stream of surplus money income into one direction or another, and to put into the control of one or another group of employers the means for setting laborers to work. Life insurance companies, which collect and equalize funds put aside by many individuals in order to provide for future needs, are among the great modern agencies of saving. Like the savings banks, they commonly make their investments not by direct loans to employers, but through bankers and other intermediaries who take the first risks of production and guarantee the investors a secure return. During the last half century there has been an immense increase in the amount of savings and investments by persons who themselves are neither desirous nor competent to direct actively the operations of production. Hence there has been a great development of the class of middlemen who intervene between them and the active managers; there have been great possibilities of profit for those middlemen, great possibilities of abuse in positions of trust, but also great effectiveness in collecting and investing the savings that underlie the enormous growth in the total capital of modern communities.

§ 6. Not only the creation of capital involves labor and saving; its maintenance does so also.

All forms of material wealth wear out in course of time. Some sorts of capital are indeed very durable, such as irrigation dams and ditches, or granite docks. Some last a considerable time, as buildings and machinery. Others are used up very quickly, as the coal which is consumed under the boiler. All need to be replaced as time goes on; some slowly, in proportion as they last long; some quickly, in proportion as they are rapidly used up. In order that the existing apparatus of production may be maintained, a certain amount of labor must steadily be given to its renewal and replacement. This labor must be supported, and its support means repeated demand upon surplus and savings.

The manner in which this takes place may be illustrated by the depreciation account which appears on the books of every manufacturing enterprise. The manufacturer knows that his machinery wears out, and that, if his capital is to remain unimpaired, he must set aside something annually to replace it. Not only does his machinery wear out, but, in a period of rapid improvement and invention like our own, it fast becomes antiquated, and he must be prepared for the possibility of having to discard it even before it has ceased to be workable. If we assume that its life is ten years, he must set aside annually something like one tenth of its value; to put it more exactly, he must put aside such sums as, invested and compounded, will make up the value at the close of the decade. If he is to secure a permanent profit, he must reckon these amounts as part of his expenses. Yet, in the first instance, the amounts are free sums, or so much surplus, not expected to be used for current expenses.[1] They are presumably used for purchasing new apparatus to replace that worn out; but they are not necessarily so used.

Commonly, capital is maintained intact; not in the sense that the same machinery or materials are maintained indefinitely, but in the sense that, as they wear out, other machinery and materials are regularly produced to take their place. The surpluses which are put aside to balance depreciation are again invested in the same enterprise and the same instruments, or in some other. The habit of saving is strongly intrenched among the well-to-do. Spendthrifts are rare, and such extravagances as occur are more than balanced by the fresh accumulations of new savers and investors. Consequently the making of new capital — of machinery, materials, and all sort of apparatus — goes on constantly. Those persons who in the established division of labor are engaged in the machine-making trades, have the well-founded expectation that their apparatus will be bought to replace that which has worn out. Thus the manufacturer finds new machines already prepared, or at least finds all the materials ready to be put together by other machinery made *ad hoc*. Under the division of labor, provision is constantly made for anticipated needs, and among those needs that of replacing of capital steadily makes itself felt.

The repair of capital, as well as its complete replacement

[1] In practise, the actual setting aside of money, and its investment over a term of years, as a separate fund toward depreciation, is probably rare. Usually, a sum is each year debited on the books against earnings, for depreciation. On the other hand, one or another item of plant is renewed or repaired each year — the whole does not become useless at one fell swoop — and the sums spent for replacement are charged against the depreciation account. In any given year, more or less may be actually so spent than is regularly set aside for depreciation. If less is spent, and the depreciation fund accumulates, it is often used, in a profitable enterprise, for putting in additional machinery or improvements, — it is invested *in* the plant rather than *for* the plant.

when worn out, calls for the recurrent exercise of saving. Some kinds of apparatus must be touched up a little from day to day in order to be in good working order. Such is the case with the roadbed of a railway, which needs almost hourly attention, and would become quite unusable if neglected for a few weeks. The locomotive of a railway, again, is subjected to constant heavy strain, and needs to be sent to the machine shop at frequent intervals; until finally, after perhaps a generation of alternate using and patching, it goes to the scrap heap, and has to be replaced with a new one. The continued maintenance of capital by operations of this sort means the steady application of labor hired (in the last resort) by persons who mean to keep their capital intact.

§ 7. Even at this early stage, some corollaries from the propositions as to capital and saving may be stated. Saving on a large scale is commonly undertaken not merely to provide for future wants, but in the expectation of a separate reward in the form of interest on capital. The theory of interest, which has many complications, will be considered in its due place; it suffices here to say that, under a régime of private property, the receipt of some such return on savings is a condition of the creation and maintenance of the whole stock of capital. Some economists have indeed implied that it is only the first making of capital that calls for the deliberate use of a surplus, and that capital, once made, reproduces itself automatically without any effort on the owner's part, and without any need of stimulus or resource in the way of interest.[1] This view arises from assuming that what is habitually done is done without choice or effort. The habitual replacement of capital takes place not by any automatic process, but because the owners recurrently choose to save and to invest surplus sums as they are acquired. Were there no motive for doing so — were there no such thing as interest on capital — habits would change; and not only the creation of new capital, but the maintenance of that already existing, would be endangered.

[1] *E.g.* J. B. Clark, *The Distribution of Wealth*, Ch. IX.

Such, at all events, would be the result in communities, of the kind familiar to us, in which there is accumulation and ownership of capital by private individuals. What would be the method of accumulating capital under the very different conditions of a socialist community, where all capital was owned by the state, opens another set of questions, which must be reserved for later consideration.[1]

§ 8. In the older books on economics it was often laid down that the distinction between capital and noncapital was merely a matter of the owner's intention. According as he chose between investing and spending, — between providing for the future and enjoying in the present, — there was capital or there was enjoyable wealth. The impression was left that some magic change was wrought in the nature of commodities by the mere volition of their owner. Obviously this could not be literally true. Most articles are by their nature such that they can be used only in one way, — either for present enjoyment or as producer's capital. Iron and steel, for example, to which reference was made in an earlier paragraph, are almost of necessity capital. They are used for making tools, machines, buildings, and can rarely be used for any other purpose. All factories and all materials are in the same case. Almost universally any concrete form of wealth is by its nature fit to be used once for all either as capital or as a source of immediate enjoyment.

Could the owner, nevertheless, exercise his choice by selling his capital (say a factory), and using the proceeds at will for investment or for enjoyment? A little reflection shows that such a disposal cannot change the nature of the factory. Sale means simply transfer to another hand; the factory remains, and its purchaser can use it only as an instrument of production. The individual can change by sale the nature of his own possessions, but he cannot thereby change the nature of the apparatus of production.

Nevertheless, the owner's intention is in the long run im-

[1] See Book VII, Chapter 63, § 5.

portant, nay decisive, in determining whether wealth shall or shall not take the form of producer's capital. As the various kinds of wealth wear out and need to be renewed or replaced, a choice is recurrently presented to the owners as to the way in which they shall use their surplus possessions, — whether they shall continue investment and maintain capital, or cease investment and cause labor to be directed to making consumable goods. For any given period they may have committed themselves irrevocably to investment, and cannot change the form which their property has taken. But as time passes, and the process of using and renewing the various kinds of wealth goes on, they have again the option which they had in the initial stages. They may save and invest, or they may spend and enjoy. However considerable the length of time over which the capital of a community, when once constructed, endures in the shape which has been given it, and however slow the process by which the disposition of the capitalists takes effect, it is still true that in the long run the owners' intention determines whether there shall or shall not be capital.

§ 9. Saving and investment have been spoken of so far as leading to the making of capital. But they do not necessarily do so; and some consideration of the cases where they do not is essential to an understanding of the relations of the individual saver to the general welfare.

All that the individual investor is concerned with is the safety of his principal and the return on it in the way of interest. If a spendthrift wishes to borrow, and gives a sufficient guarantee of repayment, by mortgage or other pledge, a loan is made to him as freely as to a business man who proposes to put up a factory. But the loan to the spendthrift has nothing to do with the making of capital. It leads to the same results as if the original owner of the surplus sums had devoted them to present use. It causes labor to be directed to producing truffles and champagne, not factories and machinery.

Spendthrift loans, incurred by individuals, are common in backward countries, but with industrial progress tend to become relatively unimportant. The Hindu peasant still borrows from the village usurer, as his kind have done for centuries; he will pledge his crops, his land, his very self, to give a feast on the marriage of his daughter. During the transition from the Middle Ages to the modern period, kings and feudal dignitaries borrowed heavily (often from the Jews), in part for crusades and dynastic wars, in part to satisfy the developing taste for lavish expenditure of money income. But in modern times operations of this sort have become of little importance as compared with the total of borrowing and of spending. Pawnbroking has become a petty business. Most borrowing by private persons takes place in the course of investment.

Yet another kind of spendthrift borrowing remains of great economic importance — by governments for war purposes. Where highways or railways or irrigation works are constructed from loans, we have the ordinary phenomena of saving, investing, capital making. But where the sums advanced by investors are used for war expenditures, we have saving and investing, but no resulting capital. We have vast waste by contending armies, and great loans that are — so far as their strictly economic consequences are concerned — essentially of the spendthrift sort.

Every modern state has a great debt, and these debts represent in the main war loans. The national debt of France now amounts to some 3000 millions of dollars; that of England to millions. Both are the legacies (almost exclusively) of wars. The United States borrowed 2500 millions during the Civil War, and our war debt still outstanding (1909) amounts to 1000 millions of dollars. The consols and rentes and government bonds by which these debts are evidenced represent to the individual investor the acme of solidity and security. Yet they are the most intangible of the forms of wealth. They stand simply for claims on the community at large, — an obligation by the public to pay stated sums to the creditors. In no sense do they stand for capital to the community.

This great phenomenon has a bearing on the social significance of interest as a return on capital. Interest means a leisure class. Rightly or wrongly, some persons are supported in idleness by the rest of the community. Against the burden may be set the fact that the community possesses useful instruments which could not have been got except through some one's saving. This is, in essentials, the justification of interest. But in the case of national debts the community has obtained no useful instruments. The justification of the claim to interest by the public creditors themselves is of course in no way affected by this consideration. Their rights must be held as inviolable as those of other lenders. But the social justification of interest would be much less strong if all saving and all investment were for the conduct of war, and if nothing of permanent economic effect remained but endless generations of pensioners.

§ 10. Some further distinctions as to capital call for brief consideration.

An individual thinks that to be capital which yields him an income; but there is an obvious distinction between that which is capital for the community and that which is, in the usual sense, "capital" to the individual.

Stocks, bonds, and securities yield an income to the owner, and are regarded by him as part of his capital. In themselves these are simply evidences of ownership or of indebtedness. A stock certificate states that the holder has certain fractions of ownership in a given concrete thing or set of things. A bond is a mere promise to pay. Bonds are commonly issued as the result of operations of saving and investing which have to do with the making of capital. But, as the case of government securities shows, they may be the result of operations which are quite wasteful. Though capital to the individual, they may or may not signify the creation or the existence of real capital.

Consumer's wealth is not commonly regarded by an individual as part of his capital. A factory; a stock of materials or goods used in business operations; money on hand or in bank, not in the nature of spare cash for current expenses, but a fund or reserve for business purposes, — such things he thinks of as capital. Household furniture, clothing, horses and carriages, he does not so reckon, since these yield him no income. Possibly a dwelling, though occupied by the owner and yielding no direct income, would still be regarded by him as part of his capital; for he might reflect that, if he did not own it, he would have to hire one at a rental, and hence might conclude that his own is equivalent to income-yielding property. Dwellings not occupied by the owner, but let to tenants, would unquestionably be regarded as capital.

Everyday usage is hazy, and "capital," like other common words, is used in different senses. For the purposes of economic study, we shall disregard the individual's point of view, and shall consider the subject of capital, as we shall other subjects, from the point of view which is important for the community. Whether, so considered, there is an important difference between producer's and consumer's wealth, will be discussed at a later stage.[1] It suffices here to say that in speaking of capital, we shall have in mind real things, and not rights to things; and we shall have in mind producer's capital, — those things which are part of the community's apparatus of production.

Some writers have distinguished between "capital" and "capital goods." By the latter term they mean the concrete apparatus of production, — just that to which, in the preceding paragraph, the single word "capital" was affixed. But by the word "capital" alone these writers mean the value of the concrete apparatus; and they sometimes speak as if there were a sort of distillation or essence of capital, distinct from the tangible capital goods in which it is embodied.

It is often convenient to measure and record capital in terms of value and price, — as so much money. In that way alone can the various constituent elements be reduced to a common denominator. An individual usually states his capital as being so much in money value. His capital obviously consists, not of the stated sum of money, but of factories, machines, buildings, merchandise, stocks and bonds, if you please, — the various

[1] See below, Book V, Chapter 40, § 3.

things which make up an individual's "capital." He simply measures it in terms of the price for which the whole would sell. Similarly, we can reckon the community's capital in terms of the price for which the whole would sell. If the total prices, at current rates, of the various factories, instruments, materials, goods in stock, are added together, the sum will give an idea of how much capital the community possesses. It would give a very imperfect idea. Statistics of this sort, occasionally collected by public officials for census purposes, are in many ways misleading. Yet if we wish to measure total capital or total wealth at all, we can proceed only in this unsatisfactory way. Though some forms of capital can be measured in other terms, — machinery, for example, in terms of horse-power, or textile mills in terms of spindles and looms, — the only measurable element common to all forms is that they have value and price, and the only way of reaching a quantitative statement as to the whole is in terms of value and price.

But it is not to be supposed that there is any such thing as capital distinct from the capital goods. The only actual and existent thing is the concrete apparatus of production. Its value or price is merely a relation to other things, a mode of measuring it. Hence in the following pages, we shall commonly denote by "capital" the concrete things, or "capital goods." Sometimes, it is true, convenience in conforming to everyday terminology will require a departure from this usage. We shall have occasion to speak, for example, of the capital of a bank, which is always reckoned in terms of money; and in other discussions the word may refer to the values and prices of things rather than to the things themselves. What sense is meant, will ordinarily be clear from the context.[1]

[1] For some references on Capital, see below, at the close of Book V.

CHAPTER 6

The Corporate Organization of Industry

§ 1. The growth of large-scale operations has caused a great development of combined action by producers and investors; that is, by those who guide production and those who own the apparatus of production. Association by the manual laborers themselves, for the conduct of production, is a different thing. It might conceivably be an important and even dominant form of industrial organization; but in fact it is not.[1] The form which is more important than any other in the modern world is the association in the business corporation of capitalist owners and managers.

The simplest form of association by such persons is the partnership of two or more persons. The distinguishing mark of the partnership in the eye of the law was originally the joint and several liability of the partners for all debts; and this still remains in most cases. Each of the partners is liable individually and without limit for all debts of the firm. A creditor, if his claim is not met according to stipulation, may levy on any one of them, and may secure the full amount of his debt from that one. The mode in which the partners then settle the distribution of the obligation among themselves is a matter with which the creditor need not concern himself.

The distinguishing mark of the corporation is limited liability. The several associated persons contribute to the undertaking, in the form of a subscription to shares or capital stock, a given sum. Their liability for debts is then limited in proportion to the original subscription. Usually it is limited to the precise amount subscribed. When they have once paid in that sum in full, — the par value of their shares, — they can be

[1] See what is said in Book VI, Chapter 58, of coöperation by workingmen.

called on to pay no more. Occasionally there is a different liability. For example, in our national bank corporations, the liability is double; the shareholder may be called on to pay not only his original subscription, but (in case of need for meeting debts) as much more. Some limitation there always is. The shareholder in a corporation is never liable, as is a partner, to the full extent of his means.

The legal distinction between a partnership and a corporation does not run parallel with that which is significant for the purposes of economic study. For the economist, the important distinction is between an association of a very few persons, well known to each other and actively engaged in the undertaking, and an association of a considerable number of persons, strangers to each other and generally investors not closely concerned with the management. Size, though not necessarily significant, yet distinguishes roughly the two kinds of economic organization. It is true that some corporations are small, some partnerships large. But usually the conduct of operations on a considerable scale, and with a considerable number of participants, is in the corporate form; while partnerships usually confine themselves to more moderate undertakings.

During the last half century, legislation in English-speaking countries has greatly modified the sharp distinction which the law drew in earlier times between the partnership and the corporation. The strict rules of the older common law made the partnership a cumbrous form of organization. It had to be wound up on the death of any partner, and it was in other ways hampered in continuity of operation. Accordingly statutes have permitted partnerships to have some of the characteristics of corporations, — continuing existence, inactive members, some limitation of liability. On the other hand, corporations have been allowed to enter on all sorts of industrial fields which formerly were shut to them. Originally, industrial corporations were authorized only where some special public interest was supposed to be involved; as in the case of the great companies for foreign trade in the seventeenth and eighteenth century, of banking corporations, and, in later days, canals, turnpikes, railways, and the like. But the convenience of this form of associated action, compared with the cumbrousness of the partnership, caused a gradual extension of its field, until at present any and every sort of industrial enterprise may be conducted in corporate form.

The consequence is that many business corporations are of small size, owned and managed by a few individuals whose relations to each other are substantially those of partners. The choice between a corporation of this sort and a partnership of the older type is often determined by the peculiarities of the law in the place of action, by its tax methods, by its legal procedure. The fundamental distinction of limitation of liability has ceased to be of vital importance. It is true that a partnership with unlimited liability may be expected to enjoy better credit, since those who lend to it have more to fall back on. But credit in modern times depends very much on the personality and business repute of the borrowers; or, if there be question as to their business standing, it depends on the direct pledge of property. The other conveniences of corporate organization outweigh any disadvantage on the score of credit. Hence "Smith & Jones, Incorporated," or "Smith & Jones, Limited," or the "Smith & Jones Company," supersede plain "Smith & Jones"; but this change in the legal form of organization is of little economic consequence.

Very different, to repeat, is the economic significance of what we may call the true corporation. Here there are many shareholders, directors selected from among them, and managers chosen by the directors, — in other words, a clear separation between owners and managers. This is the sort of organization chiefly found when production takes place on a very large scale.

In our own time, and in the United States, many people associate with the term "corporation" something still different; not only divided ownership and large-scale operations, but special public importance. They think of corporations as having a monopoly power, and therefore peculiarly subject to public regulation. "Public service corporations" are spoken of as if they were *the* corporations. Whether there is a clear line of distinction between the so-called "public" corporations and the others, and whether large-scale operations in themselves bring monopoly and public responsibility, will be considered in another place.[1] For the present we are concerned simply with those aspects of corporate development which have to do with the growth of large-scale production in modern times, and with the modern mechanism of saving and investment. Not only corporations of the "public service" kind, but others which are commonly regarded as having no special duties or relations of a public sort, present these aspects. Hence, in the following sections, we shall speak of "corporations" in the sense indicated above, — those which operate on a large scale, which have many shareholders, and in which investors and managers are clearly separated.

§ 2. The advantages of the corporation for the development of industry have been great.

In the first place, large-scale operations have been facilitated. Many modern enterprises require so great a capital that no individual could supply it. In some of the older books on economics, it was said that such enterprises could be undertaken only by the state; and hence mere size was regarded as a criterion for public management of industry. This reason for resorting to public management can now have no force. Though no individual or small group of individuals be able to furnish the funds needed, the corporate combination of numerous individuals can supply the means for any undertaking, however large.

Limitation of liability has been a chief factor in promoting large-scale operations under corporate organization. Every enterprise involves risk, especially in its first stages. Where the enterprise is large, the amount risked and the consequent liability are correspondingly large. If each individual who took shares were liable for debts, as a partner is, without a limit, investment would be checked. Occasionally it has hap-

[1] See Book VII, Chapter 6.

pened that a great business, conducted in essentials under corporate form, but without the legal safeguard of limited liability, has met reverses and failed. Each shareholder has in such a case been subject to levy for all his property. Thus when the Glasgow Bank failed in 1878, hundreds of small shareholders in Scotland were ruined because each was liable for the debts without limit. Probably few of them were clearly aware of this possibility when they became owners of their shares. The general practise of strict incorporation and consequent limitation of liability had put them off their guard. If experience like theirs were frequent, it would not be possible to gather the capital for large enterprises by contributions from many scattered individuals.

Again, new enterprises, both large and small, and especially those which are large, have been promoted by the limitation of liability. The progress of invention in modern times, the diversification of industry, the increase of productive power, — all this has taken place by successive ventures, each of which meant at the outset uncertainty and risk. It is comparatively easy to induce a person to take a few shares, or even a good number of shares, in a novel undertaking presenting possibilities of profit; but if participation involves also the possible loss of his entire fortune, he will be slow to join. Such a great risk will be taken only if the possibilities of profit be very great indeed; that is, if the prices of the commodity or service in question promise to be high enough to yield an exceptional profit. Limitation of liability and consequent readiness to invest in venturesome operations mean not only that more such operations will be carried on, but that the community will get the output on better terms.

Perhaps most important of all the ways in which corporate organization has promoted the development of industry has been the ease of investment, and the consequent stimulus to saving and the making of capital. In the eighteenth century almost the only possibility of investing in securities was through the purchase of public obligations; and these, though they meant investment by the individual, usually brought no increase in the community's capital. Merchants and persons in active business could indeed manage the investment of their surplus means in factories, warehouses, ships, and the like. But the investor pure and simple could not turn to these. If he did not buy government securities, he had little choice but to buy and improve real property. Real property is not divisible into convenient shares, and involves a good deal of management and not a little risk. The modern security market, on the other hand, offers an almost limitless field for the investment of savings, great and small. Railways, factories, steamships, mines,—all are conducted under corporate form, and corporate obligations representing them can be bought at a moment's notice by any one. Savings have been made liquid, so to speak, and can flow with ease and in any desired volume wherever there is a prospect of their advantageous use. The ease of investment in corporate enterprises has stimulated savings, and, by a reciprocal influence, the unceasing accumulation of savings has made possible an immense increase of real capital under corporate management.

§ 3. The consequences of ease of transfer for corporate shares deserve special attention. It is by no means essential to corporate organization; for conceivably those who have embarked as shareholders in a company might bind themselves to stick to it for good or ill. But transferability is so ancient and so nearly universal that it is commonly thought of as a natural and necessary part of corporate organization.

Transferability, like limitation of liability, is advantageous for the community in that it makes possible a greater division of risks. A person who has invested by taking shares in a given corporation is not thereby committed to the bitter end. If he does not think well of its prospects, or comes across some opportunity which he finds more promising, he can sell his shares to another person who has a better opinion than his own of the original venture. As will be explained more fully in the later discussion of speculation and exchanges, ease of sale in any set of business dealings facilitates venturesome operations, and permits them to be carried on at a smaller margin of profit.[1] It is so with sales of securities and speculative operations on the stock exchanges. The essential advantage of such transactions for the public is that they operate as a sort of insurance against risk, and so stimulate investment, especially in new enterprises.

Transferability of shares probably has another advantage. It tends to bring ownership and control into the hands of the shrewd and competent. Those who judge best of the prospects of an enterprise and who exercise influence intelligently toward its skillful management, buy out those who are less capable. Good judgment is perhaps the most important quality for success in business operations, and tells immensely both for an individual's money-making and for the efficient utilization of the community's labor and capital.[2] Whether the reward which such judgment secures, often so large and so quickly won, is in proportion to the services rendered, may be an open question. But judgment does tell immensely, and transferability of corporate shares aids in making it tell.

Transferability, however, has had some consequences that are not so clearly beneficial. The sense of association for common ends has virtually disappeared among the shareholders of the modern corporation. Though it persists more or less in the closely owned family corporation (the quasi-partnership), it is gone where the holders are many and widely separated. Each looks out for himself; deserts the venture in case of expected loss as a rat deserts a sinking ship, or, if he expects a gain, quickly gathers in from his associates a larger number of shares for his own profit. To sell out when the affairs of a corporation are going badly, to buy in when they are going well, is the height of business acumen. This is quite inconsistent with the original notion of a joint venture for common profit or common loss; but it is not for a moment thought of as violating any principle of morals or of fair play. No doubt it brings the advantages

[1] See Book II, Chapter 11.

[2] Compare Book V, Chapter 49, § 4.

just mentioned: the constant buying and selling minimize risk for the individual, and make for control by the shrewd and able. But it is among the phases of individualism that bring a shock to a nice moral sense.

The extraordinary growth of corporate enterprises, and the transferability of their shares, have brought into existence the modern stock exchanges, with all their conspicuous and sometimes overshadowing influences. The homogeneity of shares and other securities makes them available for purchase and sale by all sorts of persons, and thus peculiarly adapted for speculative dealings.[1] By far the greater part of the transactions on the exchanges have nothing to do directly with the process of actual investment; usually that has been completed before the securities are listed. It is only in the way of anticipation, through the indirect influence of the prospect of easy transfer, that stock exchange dealings promote the increase of factories, railways, concrete capital. Though the gain in this way is real, it is accompanied by a vast deal of unproductive effort in the way of stock gambling; nor is it easy to say whether the social gain on the whole outweighs the social loss. Most persons who discuss these matters have but hazy notions as to what constitutes the social loss or gain. They assume the corporate organization of industry as a settled fact, without discriminating wherein it is really to the general advantage. They assume transferability of shares to be a settled fact, without stopping to think whether the gain from quickened investment outweighs the material and moral loss from gambling. Still less do they consider whether the advantage from more efficient management at the hands of the shrewd outweighs the social disadvantage arising from greater inequalities in wealth.

Transferability often brings still other unwelcome consequences. Control passes not only to the shrewd, but to the unscrupulous also. The directors and other "insiders" who are best informed about the prospects of a corporation play the game with loaded dice when they buy from the ordinary share-

[1] Compare again what is said below in Book II, Chapter 11.

holders or sell to them. This sort of action is not indeed sanctioned, as buying and selling among ordinary shareholders is, either by law or by general opinion. In the eye of the law, a director is in a fiduciary position. He is not allowed to profit from dealings with those whose interests he has in charge, and is under obligation to disgorge any gains from such unfaithful doings. In the corporation of moderate size, whose shares are closely held, violation of fiduciary duty is frowned on by public opinion also. But in the great corporations the rigging of the market and speculative profit from inside information are not condemned with seriousness in business circles; and this largely for the reason that so many play the same game, or try to play it. The whole fry of buyers and sellers of stock are trying to overreach each other. Those who fail lack only the shrewdness or good fortune, not the will, to get the booty. In stock exchange gambling, as in dicing and card playing and speculation in grain or cotton, it is the presence of a great mass of greedy and gullible persons that creates the opportunities for the comparatively few who are strong and shrewd as well as unscrupulous.

It is but just to add that corporate management has often shown a high regard for the duties of directors and officers, especially in the case of those companies of moderate size in which, as has just been said, public opinion is still strong in condemning bad faith. And almost invariably, even in corporations of the most miscellaneous ownership, the rights of the shareholder who is duly registered on the books are scrupulously respected. He gets the benefit of every accruing profit, of every windfall, however ignorant or incompetent he be in the details of management. This sort of regard for the shareholder indeed is a *sine quâ non* of corporate investment. It is like the good faith of brokers in adhering scrupulously to bargains signified only by a nod of the head or a stroke of the pen on a sale-sheet. Without the certain maintenance of the mechanism for carrying on the agreed operations, the whole fabric of corporate investment would collapse. It is in the process of buying and selling, of becoming a shareholder, that there is play for manipulation. And here again it is sometimes difficult to draw a clear line between the exercise of good judgment and the abuse of official position.

§ 4. Another consequence of the growth of corporations has been the increasing power of financial middlemen. The investor has ceased not only to manage capital, but to use care and judgment of his own as to the use of his savings in creating it. The investment banks are the most important real directors of the course of investment. Such are the historic private banking houses of England and the United States — the Barings, the Rothschilds, the Morgans — and the newly-developed large banking institutions of all modern countries, most conspicuous perhaps in Germany. From them "the public" buys its securities, chiefly the stocks and bonds of corporations. This purchase, much affected by the advice and repute of the financing bank, constitutes for the individual the act of investment. What corporations shall be organized, what industries carried on, what railways, mines, factories equipped, is decided by the financial middlemen, in consultation with the more immediately active managers of industry.

Hence the great power of those bankers who secure the confidence and support of numbers of investors. It is common to speak of the "control" of a given enterprise — a railway, a factory or combination of factories, a mine or complex of mines — as being in the hands of an individual or a few individuals; and the public is staggered by calculations of the hundreds and thousands of millions' worth of capital which are dominated by a Morgan or a Rothschild. Control of this sort does not signify necessarily or usually a concentrated ownership of those millions. It does signify concentrated power, based on the confidence which a multitude of investors have in the judgment and leadership of commanding personalities.

The concentration of control in few hands shows itself most strikingly in the United States. Though we have been singularly reluctant to concentrate political control, we have been unhesitating in the acceptance of concentrated industrial control. It is odd that in England, where unification of responsibility has been carried to the maximum in public affairs (at least, in the central government), directors still direct in industry, and the powers of presiding managers are still strictly limited. In the United States, where the tradition of checks and balances continues to shape political organization, directors in industrial corporations are often no more than figureheads, while presidents are benevolent despots. This development of one-man rule has no doubt promoted boldness, efficiency, progress; but it has also concentrated power in a degree to justify uneasiness.

§ 5. Still another consequence of the development and refinement of corporate organization is an advance not only in the ease of making investments, but in the stability of the mere investor's position. The ingenuity of the financial middlemen in vying for the custom and support of the great army of savers, has provided more and more secure ways of investment. All sorts of securities are offered; not only those with risks and with a possibility of large returns, but those with low return and absolute safety. Government securities still possess a special prestige as to safety and hence yield but the lowest rate of interest. Corporate securities are also offered which are hardly less safe, and enable the purchaser to dismiss all worry as to the maintenance of principal and income. The position of the property owner, if he is content with a low rate of return, is highly secure. It used to be said, and is still occasionally repeated, that the maintenance of a fortune calls for as much ability as the making of it; that riches have wings; that it is but three generations from shirt sleeves to shirt sleeves. This is far from being the case in modern times. Chiefly as a result of corporate organization, a sort of abstract or distilled property has grown up, exempt from the vicissitudes of industry. The rich and the well-to-do, if they are content with low rates of return, can make their position almost impregnable, and, through inheritance, can maintain it indefinitely. A leisure class, based not on feudal privilege, but on savings, investment, and productive enterprise, has become a stable part of modern society.

CHAPTER 7

Some Causes Affecting Productiveness

§ 1. The preceding chapters have dealt with such causes affecting the productiveness of industry as the division of labor, the advance of large-scale production, the use and the growth of capital. Some other factors bearing on the efficiency of labor in production will be considered in the present chapter.

Among these other factors is the quality of the laborers. The increase of production depends not only on the marshalling and organization of the laborers and on their equipment with capital, but also on the strength and skill of the individual workmen. These two factors — strength and skill — may be taken up separately.

There is what may be called the steam engine theory of the efficiency of labor. It maintains, or perhaps implies rather than maintains, that the vigor of the laborer is in proportion to what he consumes. The more is turned over to him, the stronger will he be, and the more will he produce; just as the power got from a steam engine depends on the fuel burned in the fire box. Feed your laborer better, and he will be able to do so much more. The proposition is an optimistic and comforting one. It would indicate that higher wages will always pay the employer.

There is a measure of truth in this view. It holds good particularly of the simplest unskilled labor, such as calls for continuous and heavy muscular exertion. Sometimes men are so underfed that their physical strength suffers. Employers of large gangs of laborers find that it pays to feed them abundantly. Military operations which involve heavy labor, and especially those involving long marches, are more likely to succeed if the rank and file get good rations. Millions of people in backward and semi-civilized countries, such as China and India, are underfed. It is probable that their efficiency could be increased by more food and better housing. No small proportion of laborers in civilized countries are in the same situation. Mr. Rowntree, in his investigations on the city of York in England, made an estimate of the money wages which would secure, at current prices in England, the food, shelter, clothing needed for physical efficiency. The sum was about 20 shillings a week for a family of five; and the earnings of one sixth of the wage-earning class in York fall short of that sum.[1] The case is probably no less disheartening for many laborers in all parts of Europe; and, notwithstanding the higher general range of wages in the United States, there may be some workmen — perhaps but few relatively, yet in absolute numbers not insignificant — whose state is equally miserable in this country also.

It may seem that where laborers are underfed, an increase of wages up to the point of nourishment adequate for full physical efficiency will not be difficult to bring about, since the added product will make the added wages worth while. But the case is not so simple as it appears. Though the laborers in general may gain in effectiveness from more ample subsistence, and though the community may become thereby a healthier and happier social body, the individual who makes the advances to the laborers will not necessarily gain. If, indeed, the laborers were slaves, there would be some chance of direct profit from feeding them better. They would remain the property of the master, and he would reap where he had sown. Even as regards slaves, to be sure, it is not always profitable to go to the expense of full feeding. It may be cheaper to work them hard on poor fare, to wear them out in a few years, and to buy new ones for the same wretched round, — a practise said to have been deliberately followed on some Southern plantations in the slavery days. However this may be, it is obvious that the case of free men is essentially different. The gain in effectiveness from better fare inures to the laborer himself. Any employer who

[1] B. S. Rowntree, *Poverty: a Study of Town Life*, Chapter IV.

would make the needed advances could have no assurance of recouping himself. The effects of full subsistence on effectiveness do not appear either with quickness or with certainty. The process is not quick, because time is needed to bring weakened and demoralized laborers into good condition. It is not certain, because some among them are so enfeebled by sustained hardship, or congenitally so weak in constitution, that they will never become able-bodied. Even though a body of underfed laborers, if in hand systematically, could be brought to a pitch of full vigor, the risks and uncertainties, as well as the probability that the regenerated men would betake themselves to employment elsewhere, make it hopeless for a profit-seeking employer to carry out any operation of the kind. It is only under exceptional circumstances, where large gangs of selected men are at work in out-of-the-way places and are therefore under a quasi-compulsion to stick to their job — say in building the Panama Canal or at construction camps in remote regions, — that it is to the immediate interest of the employer to supply the means for ample support.

The class of underfed laborers, comparatively small though it be in modern communities, presents a distressing problem. They are ill paid because they are inefficient; they are inefficient, for one reason, because they are ill paid. Yet they are easily demoralized; too often they remain still inefficient if better paid from charitable funds. Neither physically nor morally do they respond readily to possibilities of improvement. Often the adults are hopeless; the children alone can be taken in hand with prospects of success. Hence even when there is a *prima facie* case for increasing the productiveness of labor by adding to the reward of labor, the precise method of accomplishing the result is hard to devise. Only public or quasi-public action can grapple with the problem; and this must include suppression or elimination of the unfit, as well as uplifting of the potentially capable.

All this reasoning and speculation, however, is concerned only with the minimum necessary for health and strength:

the minimum for health and strength, be it noted, not for keeping body and soul together. Men can live and do work for less than is necessary to enable them to do full work. The minimum for efficiency is above the starvation level. But when they once get what is necessary for complete physical vigor, anything in addition is mere surplus; surplus, that is, in that it no further increases efficiency. If obtained, it must be as the consequence of skill and productiveness; it becomes a result of high efficiency, and ceases to be a cause of efficiency. Nor is the minimum for full vigor a very high one. An abundant vegetable diet, rude shelter, and simple clothing are all that a man needs to do the hardest work which the human frame can stand. The frugal Italian or the rice-fed Chinaman, if only he gets enough of his simple fare, can do as much as the meat-eating Irish-American.

In some of the higher walks of life, the minimum for efficiency is doubtless to be measured more liberally. Something more is called for than that which is indispensable for muscular efficiency. The work of a lawyer, physician, teacher, business-man, calls for alertness of mind and bodily health more than for physical vigor. The requisite response of intelligence will often be lacking if the surroundings dull the mind or enfeeble the spirit. Hence as regards intellectual work we may count among the necessaries for efficiency, varied food, ample lodging, restful relaxation. It is hard to say just how far such sources of enjoyment, procured by a larger income, are really necessary for the best exertion of the mental faculties. Those who are accustomed to comfortable living and to pleasant distractions easily convince themselves that these are necessary to keep them fresh for their work. It is a sort of excuse, too, or justification, of the existing inequalities in income to believe that they are inevitable, in the sense that the work which earns the higher income could not be accomplished without the freer life which that higher income secures. Yet plain living and high thinking are not incompatible. The luxuries and comforts to which most persons of the well-to-do classes are habituated could be in large measure foregone without loss of vigor or freshness. Some comfort, some leisure, some distraction, are doubtless necessary for the best intellectual work. But a modest income and a scale of expenditure much below that of most members of the well-to-do class would suffice.

§ 2. Different from strength are skill and intelligence. These tell strongly on the efficiency of the individual workman and on the productivity of industry at large.

Many of the improvements in the arts depend for their application on a good degree of intelligence. The Hottentot cannot use tools even of a comparatively simple kind because his brain power is not sufficiently developed. Negroes are employed in great numbers in the gold mines and diamond mines of South Africa, but for simple pick and shovel work only. For handling and guiding machines skilled and intelligent white mechanics must be employed. Many of the operations of agriculture require nothing beyond delving and ditching. But the fruitful agriculture of advanced peoples calls for care, discrimination, intelligence, and could not be practised by Indian ryots or Russian peasants. Many routine operations of modern industry can be carried on by any persons capable of giving steady attention. But that very faculty, like the ability and willingness to do prolonged continuous labor, is not a matter of course. It is not possessed by savages; it is a slowly acquired quality of civilized man. No doubt there is a growing range of machine work in which very slender intellectual or moral qualities are needed. In many factory operations of modern times, the human worker is hardly more than another steady and dependable automaton. Along with labor of this sort, however, there must always go some proportion of labor more flexible, more observing, more highly trained. This is the quality of mechanics' work, as distinguished from that of "laborers'" in the narrower sense. Here accuracy, watchfulness, skill, intelligence, are called for; and here these qualities are indispensable for efficiency.

The effect of education on the productiveness of labor is not simple. In some respects, a wide diffusion of education is conducive to greater efficiency of the population at large; in other respects, the extension of education raises economic questions not so easy to answer.

The simplest kind of pick and shovel work seems to be done as effectively by the illiterate workman as by the educated. This is also the case, as has just been remarked, with much modern factory labor. And even in many handicrafts, education is not indispensable for a high degree of skill. The work of the craftsmen of the Middle Ages in Europe, and that of the same class of workers in modern Japan and indeed in some parts of contemporary Europe, show that illiteracy is no obstacle to the deftest use of tools.

Nevertheless, it remains true that a wide diffusion of education is a most effective means toward productiveness. It is effective particularly toward propagating new kinds of efficiency. When an art has once been learned by slow steps, — for thus, historically, mankind has acquired most of the arts, — its mere transmission from generation to generation, its maintenance and even perfection, take place by the simplest imitation, unaided by book learning. But the rapid spread and utilization of improvements are immensely promoted by the ease of intellectual communication. Mere ability to read and write opens at once a whole new world. He who possesses it can learn from the experience of all mankind, no longer from that of his parents and masters only. The extension of such a great improvement as the system of interchangeable parts has depended largely on widespread elementary education. A complex tool or machine — a plow, a reaper, a bicycle — is made nowadays on standardized patterns, each part being a precise duplicate of every other part made from the same pattern. When there is a break, the needed part can be replaced at once. The system makes possible the wide use of intricate apparatus in localities distant from repair shops. But its adoption is possible, in turn, only if those who are to use the apparatus have some general intelligence and if they can read instructions. In the United States the unexampled use of labor-saving agricultural implements, all made with interchangeable parts, has rested not only on the intelligence of the people, but on the universal diffusion of elementary education. The great industrial advance of Germany during the last generation is due in large measure to the same factors.

Technical education obviously has a direct economic effect. The training of civil engineers, mechanical engineers, electrical engineers, conserves from generation to generation the elaborate acquired arts. It promotes, too, the advance of the arts. In the past, great inventions and improvements have probably come as often from the workshop as from the laboratory. Under the conditions of the modern world, and especially with the more methodical application of natural science to the arts, the laboratory is likely to play a larger and larger part, both directly, through the inventions that come full-fledged from the laboratory, and indirectly, through the work of those who have had its training.

All training for the arts and professions tends to become more systematic in the modern world. The engineer gets his fundamental training, not in the workshop or in the field, but in the technological school; the physician or the lawyer gets his, not from the active practitioner, but from the professional school. The same movement is seen in the extension of industrial training to the familiar mechanic arts. Apprenticeship to a craftsman was for centuries the mode in which these arts were maintained and transmitted. But the conditions of modern industry have made apprenticeship ineffective and virtually obsolete. The "master" of former times has well-nigh disappeared; he is replaced by the large employer, out of touch with his individual workmen, whether young or old. Those preliminary stages of industrial training which were in former times provided by apprenticeship should now be undertaken by systematic trade schools, and should be a part of the general system of public education. The time is not distant when the normal entrance to a trade will be through such schools, precisely as the normal entrance to the so-called liberal professions is through their professional schools.

We must distinguish sharply between the effect of such education on individuals and on the community. As between individuals, the wide diffusion of educational opportunities has simply an equalizing effect. For the community, it tends to raise general efficiency; but it is not likely to raise general efficiency in the same degree as it raises the earnings of some individuals. It tends to break down any privileged position which may exist among those who now possess technical or professional skill. It may tend to lower their earnings. On the other hand it tends to raise the earnings of those who are enabled more easily to acquire such skill. The trade unions are usually opposed to the establishment of trade schools, from a fear that it will lower the rate of wages in the more highly-paid trades. This fear, though much exaggerated, is not entirely without foundation. People who descant on the advantages of education, and especially of industrial education, often contrast the high wages of a skilled workman or trained engineer with the low wages of an unskilled laborer, and assume the difference to measure the relative productiveness of the two. They forget that if all men could easily procure the training for the better paid occupation, numbers in that occupation would be greater, and pay in it would be less. Wide and free diffusion of all sorts of vocational training would almost certainly increase the productive power of the community as a whole; but it would also tend to lessen the differences in earnings which now exist, and to lower the earnings of some individuals and some classes now favored.[1]

General education in all its grades, from that of the elementary school to that of the university, though not directed to a clearly defined industrial end, doubtless has its considerable economic effects. Largely it is an end in itself, or at least a means to other ends than industrial efficiency. The mere attainment of knowledge and understanding is a satisfaction

[1] On this subject more is said below, in Book V, Chapter 47.

in itself, to some persons a great joy. Among man's traits none is more remarkable than his insatiable curiosity concerning all things in the heavens and the earth. The satisfaction of that curiosity is one of the constant ends of human endeavor. And knowledge opens the way, it need not be said, to the higher and nobler enjoyment of life. But general education has its more immediate economic effects also. Though reading and writing do not make the ditch digger stronger, and geometry and literature do not add directly to the skill of the mechanic, all education makes for intelligence, discrimination, the utilization of opportunities, the spread of improvements. It makes also for sobriety, honesty, and steady endeavor. The more it is directed to uplifting the character and training the faculties, and the less it follows dull routine, the more does it achieve these ends. Where it fails to achieve them, the remedy, even in the interest of bare industrial efficiency, is still not to curtail it, but to improve it.

§ 3. Not least effective among the forces that bear on productiveness is leadership. It is exercised by business managers, by engineers and technical experts, and by men of science. Economic efficiency is profoundly affected by the success of a community in securing good leaders.

When intricate tools and machinery are put together by skilled mechanics, and when all this apparatus is guided to its productive outcome by still other skilled mechanics, one is tempted to say that here are the real producers. But a little consideration leads to the inclusion with them of the designers,—the inventors and engineers. It requires still further reflection to include also the directors and employers. These last, the business class, seem to some persons, notably to the socialists, to be mere exploiters. The real work seems to be done by the others; the business men sit by and merely levy toll. There is no greater misapprehension. The effectiveness of industry depends on the business man's leadership almost as much as that of an army depends on generalship. Under a complicated division of labor, the various factors of production must be brought together and properly combined. The different kinds of labor and capital must be applied to the best natural resources. The long gap between producer and consumer must be bridged. The skilled mechanic and even the engineer would commonly be helpless without the guidance of the business leader. Especially is this the case where industry is rapidly shifting. Courage, energy, judgment, and command of capital are indispensable for economic progress. Much more will be said, as we proceed, on the significance of industrial leadership.

Another kind of leadership is that of the man of science. The progress of material civilization depends on the understanding of nature's laws. The astronomer, the physicist, the chemist, the biologist lay the foundation for the development of the arts. Their efforts are usually stimulated in greater degree than with most men by motives of the higher sort,—by the single-minded search for truth, or by love of fame rather than hope of material reward. The influence of scientific investigation on the arts, though often indirect and unexpected, is none the less far-reaching. Faraday had no concern for the industrial possibilities when he discovered the induced current; yet how profoundly economic progress has been affected by the dynamo![1]

Leaders are rare. Most men are commonplace. Among the means for promoting progress none are more important than the discovery and stimulation of those who have high abilities.

Freedom of opportunity and diffusion of education are the means for discovering those possessing unusual gifts. Among the classes of men who now lack education and are depressed by illiterate surroundings, there may be many persons of talent and an occasional genius. To the general advantage of a wide diffusion of education is to be added the fact that it helps to arouse and develop all the gifted. It is probable, to be sure, that high inborn capacity is most common among those to whom education

[1] My colleague, Professor C. L. Jackson, has called my attention to Perkin's discovery of purple dye, which led to the aniline dye industry, and to the investigations of Graebe and Liebermann on alizarin, which led to the manufacture of that coloring stuff from coal tar; further instances of industrial changes consequent on the discoveries of pure science.

and opportunity are already open. We touch here on the debatable problem of the origin and significance of social classes. There is evidence tending to show that the well-to-do are in their more favored position because they possess, on the whole, higher intellectual ability. But the proposition, even if established, is subject to much qualification; and certainly it must be admitted that there is among the less prosperous some fund of capacity which fails to be utilized. Though gifted persons are probably less common, in proportion to numbers, among the so-called lower classes, there may be many of them. The full development in these of all their qualities for better efficiency, above all for leadership, is one of the most important objects of widely diffused education.

Freedom and democracy operate to develop to the full the scanty number of leaders. The abolition of class privileges in modern times thus has been not only of political and social consequence, but has had direct economic effects also. The industrial preëminence of England during the eighteenth and nineteenth centuries was due largely to her free institutions. The lowborn person's opportunities to rise, even though restricted, were better than on the Continent, and England profited accordingly. In the United States such opportunities have been more free than ever before in any part of the world, and to this factor, above all others, is due the wonderful material prosperity of the country.

Those possessed of the qualities for leadership must not only be given a free field; they must also be stimulated to the full exercise of their gifts. Inequality of some sort appears to be indispensable as a stimulus.

Obviously we have here a question different from those considered in the preceding pages. There is an essential difference between providing a gifted person with the wherewithal to enable him to do his best and offering him a reward which will stimulate him to do his best. A reward in some way proportioned to the rarity and effectiveness of unusual faculties seems necessary to induce their exertion to the highest pitch. Such, at all events, has been the experience of mankind with the gift of industrial leadership. No stimulus to economic activity has yet been found comparable in efficacy to that of the prospect of large earnings. Inequality of incomes and possessions, so far as based on differences in industrial efficiency, is a most potent instrument toward general efficiency in production.

This, to be sure, is the individualist view. It assumes that most men are influenced in their bargaining and income-earning by preponderantly selfish motives. The extreme collectivist view is that men can be readily induced to the full application of their faculties by other than selfish motives. Neither view can be maintained without qualification. Some sorts of leadership are undertaken with little consideration of reward. Those having the very highest intellectual gifts in letters, in the fine arts, in pure science, exercise them in pursuance of a well-nigh irresistible impulse. On the other hand, industrial leadership and industrial efficiency seem to depend on industrial reward. Whether there are possibilities of stimulating them without inequality, or at all events without great inequality, is a question reaching into the most difficult problems of economics, and its full consideration must be postponed to a later stage.[1] Suffice it to say that material reward, in the shape of high income and the chance of a fortune, has hitherto proved wonderfully potent and apparently indispensable in eliciting and spurring economic leadership.

§ 4. In sum, the effectiveness of industry depends not only on material equipment, but also on what we may call immaterial equipment; not only on accumulated surplus in the way of capital, but on accumulated moral and intellectual qualities. Maintenance and transmittal are not less important for this immaterial capital than for the community's material capital.

Education transmits from generation to generation the acquired attainments of the race, from the rudiments of reading and writing to the most elaborate technical training. Not only

[1] See Book VII, Chapter 65.

these intellectual attainments, but moral qualities likewise, must be handed down to the successive generations. Habits of industry, truthfulness, honesty, sobriety, of consideration for others, of care for the common good, — all these are of slow growth, and rest on repeated example and precept.

In some degree there is transmission also by inheritance. The biologists still differ on the question whether acquired traits are inherited. The more general opinion seems to be that they are not, and that only inborn qualities are passed on from parent to descendant. If this be the rule universal in nature, man also must conform to it; and then some at least of the qualities that mark the civilized man can be maintained only by set training. Others perhaps have been incorporated in his nature by a process of selection, — through the weeding out, in the long course of history, of those having a less civilizable disposition. Human nature changes and improves, and the quality of men is now finer than it was thousands of years ago, perhaps than it was centuries ago. Repeatedly there are projects for hastening the process through design, — by breeding men, as animals are bred, from strains deliberately selected. Without entering here on the far-reaching questions which such proposals raise, it may be said that, for a future as far as we can look into it, the slow and haphazard process of unconscious selection will alone affect the transmission and possible improvement of inborn qualities. As regards the general average of ability and character, heredity leaves man, from one generation to another, on the whole *in statu quo*.

But persistent and repeated training not only keeps mankind *in statu quo:* it offers more immediate possibilities of advance. No less than inherited quality, it contributes to make the difference between the civilized man and the savage. Man's great moral, intellectual, educational capital must be conserved, like his material capital, by unremitting effort; and like that it can be increased by effort. In both ways, the effort is largely altruistic. It results from the cares and sacrifices of parents, and from the conscious endeavor of the community to improve the quality of all its members through the diffusion of education. But it results also in no small degree from the self-regarding motives, — from the desire of each individual to better his own condition and that of his family. Certain it is that man now starts from a vantage ground which makes possible still further advance. Some of his qualities for civilization he has inherited; some of those same qualities he acquires and transmits by constant effort. The outcome of all is the great immaterial capital of the community; a possession not less important for the general welfare, and perhaps not less extensible, than his capital of tools and materials.

References on Book I

On productive and unproductive labor, see the often-cited passages in Adam Smith, *Wealth of Nations*, Book II, Chapter III; and those in J. S. Mill, *Principles of Political Economy*, Book I, Chapter III. W. Roscher, *Political Economy*, Book I, Chapter III, gives an excellent historical and critical account. Among modern discussions, none is more deserving of attention than the paper by Professor T. Veblen, on "industrial" and "pecuniary" employments, in *Proceedings of the American Economic Association*, 1901, No. 1. A recent discussion, with not a little of clouded thought, is in the *Verhandlungen des Vereins für Sozialpolitik*, 1909; especially a paper by Professor E. Philippovich and the discussion thereon.

On the division of labor, Charles Babbage, *On the Economy of Machinery and Manufactures* (1837), is still to be consulted. On modern developments, the *Thirteenth Annual Report of the Commissioner of Labor (U. S.) on Hand and Machine Labor* (1899) contains a multitude of illustrations. A keen analysis of the division of labor in its historical forms is in K. Bücher, *Die Entstehung der Volkswirthschaft* (7th ed., 1910); translated into English from the 3d German edition under the title *Industrial Evolution* (1901). On the industrial revolution of the eighteenth century, see the well-ordered narrative in Mantoux, *La révolution industrielle au xviiie siècle* (1906), and the less systematic but more philosophical account in A. Toynbee, *Lectures on the Industrial Revolution* (10th ed., 1894).

On capital, see the references given below, at the close of Book V. Much as has been written of late on corporate doings and corporate organization, I know of no helpful references on the topics considered in Chapter 6.

BOOK II

VALUE AND EXCHANGE

CHAPTER 8

INTRODUCTORY: EXCHANGE, VALUE, PRICE

§ 1. The division of labor brings in its train the exchange of goods between those who undertake the separated acts of production. Exchange in turn brings the phenomena of value, money, and prices. With these phenomena we shall be concerned in the present Book and in the Book following.

As has already been noted, the division of labor does not bring exchange as a necessary consequence.[1] There may be the self-sufficing patriarchal family, with division of labor but without exchange; or its counterpart, the communistic society, self-sufficing at least in some degree. Even in the modern family, there is division of labor, after a sort, between man and wife. But commonly we consider the family as a unit, and think of the housewife, when she works for husband and family, as working for that of which she is but a part. Similarly, the patriarchal family and the communistic society are considered by their members as economic units. Exchange arises from a separation of interests. As between individuals, it has grown with the growth of private property. Throughout by far the greater part of modern industry, division of labor prevails, and with it private property and labor for one's self and family. Hence exchange and its concomitants, value and price.

Production for one's self holds its own longest in agriculture. Yet even in this industry, division of labor and exchange are rapidly extending in the highly developed countries of our time. In the United States the self-sufficing farmer of earlier days has well-nigh disappeared; and even the stolid peasant of Europe is being transformed by the modern methods of easy communication and easy exchange. Though the farmer still produces part of

[1] See Book I, Chapter 3, § 4.

his own food, especially vegetables and fruit, there is a steady tendency toward widening the range of agricultural products which are bought and sold. Grain is sold by the individual farmer, flour is bought; cattle are sold, meat is bought; milk and cream are sold, butter is bought. In other occupations than agriculture the division of labor has worked out its consequences to the last stage. No labor is given to the direct satisfaction of each worker's wants by himself; all is turned to the indirect process of specialization and exchange. Hence sale, price, value, and the whole mechanism of exchange, become the characteristic economic phenomena.

§ 2. Almost as early as the division of labor, a medium for exchanging the various products came into use. Barter — the direct exchange of products — may be carried on under a very simple division of labor; yet even then it is inconvenient, and as soon as the first stages of savagery have been passed, some use of a medium of exchange appears.

Any commodity in general use will serve passably as a medium of exchange. He who has an article to sell, and cannot find at once the precise kind and quantity of the things he wishes to buy, will accept a staple commodity, with which sooner or later he will be able to procure the things he wants. Hence in various stages of civilization, the most diverse commodities have been used to obviate the inconveniences of barter. In Homeric times the value of things was often stated in terms of oxen; for such occasional exchanges as are made among primitive pastoral peoples are naturally effected in terms of their staple commodity, cattle.[1] For a considerable time in the early history of the colony of Virginia, tobacco was almost the sole article of export, and the chief commodity habitually produced for a market; it became the recognized medium of exchange in the colony. Furs,

[1] Mr. Wicksteed remarks (*The Common Sense of Political Economy*, p. 137) that "there is more evidence in the Homeric poems of the valuation of female slaves, of tripods, or of gold or brass armor, in terms of so many cattle, than there is of any direct transfer of cattle in payment of those goods." It is probably true, also, of the other commodities mentioned in the text that they were used more freely for measuring relative values than for effecting exchanges.

salt, tea, cocoa, have served the purpose with other people. But by far the most widespread among the things so used have been the precious metals, gold and silver. We need not pause at this stage to consider what qualities fit them peculiarly for serving as a medium of exchange, — their luster and consequent attractiveness for ornament, their freedom from rust and deterioration, their homogeneity, their divisibility. Nor need we consider how the device of coining has increased their fitness for carrying on purchases and sales; nor in what ways paper representatives or substitutes for them have come to be so widely used in our own time. These are topics that belong to the subject of money, to which much attention must be given later.

It suffices here to note how completely division of labor and exchange work out their results through the use of money. Every producer gets his return in amounts of money. The exceptions in any of the countries of advanced civilization are so few and are so rapidly disappearing that they serve only to make clear how virtually universal is the rule. Exchange takes place by first selling goods or services for money, and by then buying with the money such other goods and services as are wanted. The fundamental fact of exchange is thus obscured by the very mechanism that so perfectly facilitates it. Just as the coöperation and combination which are essential features of the division of labor are carried on without a consciousness of any combined action, so the process of exchange goes on without the consciousness that it is the aim and end of all buying and selling.

§ 3. The value of a commodity means in economics its power of commanding other commodities in exchange. It means the rate at which the commodity exchanges for others. If a bushel of wheat can be exchanged for a large quantity of other things, — for many pounds of iron, many yards of cloth, many ounces of salt, — its value is high; the possessor of it can procure many of these things. If a bushel of wheat can be exchanged for but few pounds of iron, few yards of cloth, few ounces of salt, its value is low; the possessor of it can procure few of these things. It is immaterial that the exchange does not take place directly, but by the process of first disposing of the wheat for the medium of exchange, — money, — and then procuring with the money the iron, cloth, salt, or other desired commodities. The result of the double operation is the same as if the exchange had taken place by direct barter. Only it is reached by a more convenient method.

The value of a commodity, thus conceived, is its value in exchange. This is very different from its usefulness, or utility, or importance. In everyday discourse, we use the word "value" sometimes to indicate exchange value, sometimes to indicate utility or importance. We speak of the value of iron as greater than that of gold, and the value of wheat as greater than that of diamonds. We mean thereby that iron and wheat are more important, satisfy more urgent wants than gold and diamonds. Yet we also speak of gold and diamonds as more valuable commodities than iron and wheat; then we use the terms "value" and "valuable" in the sense of value in exchange, and mean that exchange and sale take place on such terms that with comparatively little gold and diamonds the owner can secure much iron and wheat. For the purposes of economics this latter sense, exchange value, is the most important.

A third sense, however, may be noted in passing. People sometimes speak of the "value" of a thing as greater or less than that which appears in an actual transaction of exchange. They speak of a house as being "worth" more than they paid for it, or of a commodity or a stock exchange security as selling for less than its "intrinsic value." They mean that the current price is different from the price that is likely to be paid in the long run, or different from the price which they think proper and just. In the sense which we have adopted, value means simply the actual rate in exchange, and there can be no value other than that registered by sales and exchanges. That the word is also used with this third signification, of proper or intrinsic worth, only shows how vague and uncertain is everyday phraseology. Economists have often pointed out how much troubled they are, both in exposition and in their own thinking, by having to employ familiar terms, like capital and value, which in everyday use have various and shifting meanings. For the purposes of economics, one meaning or definition must be selected, and held to with care. In the following pages "value" will be used strictly in the sense which economists have adopted for it, — a relation in exchange.

By the price of a commodity is signified the amount of money which it will command; in other words, its value in terms of the accepted medium of exchange. The notion of price is familiar, whereas that of value is one to which the beginner in economics must become accustomed. In modern times price means, in almost all advanced countries, the amount which is got, in exchange, of the particular money medium which these countries have adopted, — gold. Paper and metallic substitutes for gold are often used, equal in exchange value to the gold, and performing the functions of a medium of exchange precisely as it does. The peculiarities of paper, silver, and copper as money will receive attention in due time. For the present we shall assume that gold is the medium of exchange, and that price is measured in coins of gold, say dollars. Coins, it needs hardly to be added, are simply pieces of gold manufactured with care and containing each a given weight of metal of uniform quality.

§ 4. From the definition of value, it follows that there can be no general rise in values, and no general fall in values. Value is a term expressing the relation of exchange between commodities. If at a given time a commodity procures in exchange less of others than at an earlier time, it has fallen in value; but *pro tanto* those other commodities have risen in value. All cannot rise and fall together. A change in the value of any one of them, or any set of them, means a converse change in the value of the rest. On the other hand, a change in general prices is not only possible, but is one of the familiar and recurring phenomena of economics. Wheat, iron, diamonds, things in general, may all exchange for more dollars now than they did ten years ago; and ten years hence they may exchange for less dollars than they command now.

Evidently a general rise or fall in prices signifies a change in the value of money, that is, of gold. When all prices rise, and things exchange each for a greater number of dollars, the dollar can buy less than it did. Its power of commanding other things is less, and its value has fallen. When every single thing exchanges for a smaller number of dollars; that is, when prices have fallen, the dollar buys more, and its value has risen. The value of money is inverse to the level of prices. When prices are high, the value of money is low. When prices are low, the value of money is high.

The mere fact of a rise or fall in the price of a single commodity, therefore, does not indicate whether or no its value has changed. It may be that this single commodity alone has fallen in price, others remaining as before. In that case the fall in price registers also a fall in value. Or it may be that other commodities likewise have fallen in price to the same extent. In that case there has been a rise in the value of money, and a fall in the value of all commodities as compared with gold; but no change has occurred in the values of commodities *inter se.*

The value of gold, that is, the general level of prices, changes but slowly. Though prices of individual commodities change quickly, all do not change quickly in the same direction. A rise in the price of any one is likely to be accompanied by a declining price of another, or by stationary prices of the others. So gradual are changes in the general range of prices, so uncertain the comparison and offsetting of the complex individual changes, — a rise here, a fall there, no change at all in a third, — that it is often difficult to ascertain for a short period whether a general change has really taken place. If, indeed, an upward or downward movement continues for years, it usually becomes unmistakable. We can ascertain then whether the value of money has risen or fallen, and can measure with some accuracy the extent of the change. But unless the lapse of time exceed two or three years, it is often not easy to determine what has been the general trend; so stable are prices for short periods.

But though general prices and the value of money change thus slowly, the prices of individual articles change quickly and considerably. The price of wool or cotton or iron may rise by ten per cent in the course of a month; and changes are common in the prices of individual articles — of wheat, cotton, copper, coal — by ten, twenty, thirty, per cent in the course of a single year. Where the price of one thing changes, other prices remaining the same, the new price evidently registers a change in value. The ordinary fluctuations in the prices of things hence signify corresponding changes in their values.

For the purposes of an orderly and systematic exposition of economic principles, we shall assume for the present stability in general prices; hence that a change in the price of an article signifies a change in its value. If an individual article rises in price under these conditions, it commands more of other things in exchange, and rises in value; and conversely if it falls in price. We shall thus use the familiar examples of price and money in our illustrations and figures, and shall put aside, for consideration at a later stage, the problems of fluctuations in the general level of prices.

CHAPTER 9

Value and Utility

§ 1. An object can have no value unless it has utility. No one will give anything for an article unless it yield him satisfaction. Doubtless people are sometimes foolish, and buy things, as children do, to please a moment's fancy; but at least they think at the moment that there is a wish to be gratified. Doubtless, too, people often buy things which, though yielding pleasure for the moment, or postponing pain, are in the end harmful. But here, as has already been explained, we must accept the consumer as the final judge. The fact that he is willing to give up something in order to procure an article proves once for all that for him it has utility, — it fills a want.

On the other hand, no less evidently, the value of an object is not in proportion to its utility. Free goods, such as fresh air, pure water, the beauty of nature, may have high utility, though wholly without value. Only slight value may attach to other things having high utility. In our advanced civilized communities the simplest and most wholesome articles of food have low value; they are cheap. Yet they satisfy the most elemental and pressing of wants, and have great utility. So it is of other necessaries of life, as clothing, shelter, or warmth; great utility often goes with low value. On the other hand, some things whose exchange value is high have utilities which we do not ordinarily reckon great. Jewels, tasteless ornaments, a stupid book printed four hundred years ago, — such things sometimes command a high price, though the satisfactions they yield are not of a high order or apparently highly prized.

§ 2. The supply of a commodity, as we all know, closely affects its value. When an article becomes abundant, its price falls; when it is scarce, its price rises. The causes of these fluctuations are two, very different in nature and social significance.

One obvious cause, and that which many persons are likely to think of first, is the difference in means between rich and poor. Those who are able to pay highest, secure the first installments of any commodity that comes to market. If there be comparatively few installments, each will command a high price. As more and more are offered, the price must be lowered in order to bring them within the means of the less rich. Finally, if the supply be greatly increased, the price must be lowered very much in order to make possible purchases by the poor.

But the same result would appear if there were no differerences between rich and poor, — if all persons had the same incomes. Then, also, an increasing supply would bring a decreasing price. The causes which under these altered conditions would yet lead to the same inverse variation are of the second sort; and they are the fundamental causes.

Consider any familiar article of daily use, — the knives, forks, spoons, on your table, the clothing you wear, the house you live in. One set of knives and forks is essential to cleanly eating. A second set is highly convenient, a third somewhat less so; there is a decline in utility, until at last the stage is reached where an additional set is a mere encumbrance. So with clothing. One suit is necessary. A second and a third add to comfort. More and more can be used, yet with a steady tendency to lessening satisfaction with the successive installments. One room in a house, or a one-room house, is indispensable for existence. The added comfort and decency from a second room are very great; and further additions to houseroom continue to yield satisfactions. But though the rate of diminution in utility may be for some time comparatively slow, the tendency still is present, and before long the stage is reached, when more houseroom serves to satisfy only the love of display, not to yield substantial comfort. All things, it may be observed, which minister to the love of display, have the possibility of maintaining this sort of utility in a curious degree.

The mere fact that a thing is rare — that it is of a sort not possessed by others, and so distinguishes its owner — gives utility to things otherwise useless; a notable example is an old postage stamp.[1] Additions to the supply of many classes of articles may for a long time give additional satisfaction, if the individual things be varied and adapted to gratify the love of distinction; as with the garments and houses of the rich. But the tendency to diminishing utility none the less persists. The more of these things you have, the less you prize any one. The addition of a new coat to an abundant supply, of a new room to a house already large, brings less satisfaction than the preceding coats or rooms brought.

To this general tendency we give the name of the principle, or law, of diminishing utility. Successive doses of the same commodity or service yield diminishing utilities. If the doses be continued indefinitely, the point of satiety will be reached. Then further doses yield no satisfaction whatever; the utility of each additional dose becomes *nil.* This principle, as has just been intimated, and as will presently be explained further, applies in strictness only to doses of the same commodity (or service). Vary the thing supplied, — even though different only in small degree, — then the result will not be quite the same. The diminution in utility may be prevented or checked; and the point of satiety may be indefinitely postponed. From the fact that there is a limit to the possibilities of satisfaction from increasing the supply of any one article, it is not to be inferred that limits in utility exist for all articles taken together.

But none the less it remains true that all enjoyments tend to pall if repeated. If any one of us were called on to retrench, — to dispense with some enjoyments now possessed, — he would find himself cutting off first those things least prized, and then in succession various others in the inverse order of their utility; a process which would make it clear not only that some things

[1] No doubt the instinct of acquisition (the "collecting" instinct) plays its part as regards such articles, in combination with the instinct for distinction through display.

have more utility than others, but that some doses of the same thing have more utility than other doses of that thing.

It is this fact of different and diminishing utility that explains the growing variety in the articles produced and the growing complexity of production and consumption. As the productive power of mankind increases, and especially as the commodities in common use become more abundant, labor is constantly turned in new directions. It is given not so much to making more of the same things as to making different things. Abundance without variety means that the approach to satiety is rapid. Bread, in most civilized countries, is cheap, being produced with comparatively little labor. With increase in the effectiveness of industry, more and more bread could be produced with the same labor. But some of this labor turns to other kinds of food as bread becomes cheaper, — to meat, eggs, butter, vegetables, fruit, sugar. A varied diet, such as is possible in modern times, marks a great advance not only over the monotony of savages' food, but over the very restricted diet with which civilized peoples had to content themselves until the last century or two. The essentials of clothing, also, are plentiful and cheap, and a comparatively small part of the labor of a modern country is given to the covering needed simply for health and decency. A vast deal of labor is given to making more convenient and attractive clothing. With the growing productiveness of labor, any one of the familiar articles of everyday use tends to be put on the market in such quantities that people care less and less for additional increments, and the prices of these articles are ever tending to fall. Variety in production must take place if consumption is to respond.

There are articles to which the principle of diminishing utility does not apply as unfailingly as the preceding statement suggests. Though stimulants on the whole show unquestionably the tendency to lessening response, the conscious effect from the first few doses does not always show it. The second or third glass of liquor may be as much enjoyed as the first. Or, to speak of higher things, the second or third reading of noble verse, or hearing of beautiful music, often gives greater pleasure than the first. Again, there are many cases where a preliminary stage of doubtful satisfaction is succeeded, with habituation, by unquestionably greater satisfaction; as with tobacco and oysters. Many a novel article needs to be insinuated into people's liking. As this is brought about (perhaps by skillful advertising), the article reaches a stage where a larger supply of it is sold, not at a lower price per unit, but at a higher. In such cases, however, the tastes of the purchasers may be said to have changed in the interval. At any given stage of taste and popularity, the principle of diminishing utility will apply. It is not worth while to enter on refinements as to whether, in the cases just mentioned, there are real or only apparent exceptions to the principle. The qualifications that may be needed are of no great importance. The tendency shows itself so widely and with so few exceptions that there is no significant inaccuracy in speaking of it as universal.

§ 3. From the law of diminishing utility we are led to the conceptions of total utility and of marginal utility.

Utility can be measured, for the purposes of economic study, in one way only: by the amount which a person will give to procure an article or a service. Enjoyment or satisfaction is subjective. The objective test of it is willingness to pay. What a person will pay for an article rather than go without it, is the only test by which we can ascertain with any approach to precision how much satisfaction it brings him. Hence price, actual or potential, is the economic measure of utility. Not infrequently in discussion of this set of subjects, it is said or implied that the utility of an article *is* the price it commands or might command. This language is inaccurate. Price simply indicates utility.

Consider now how price may measure the utility, to an individual, of several units of a given commodity, — say five oranges. Suppose them to be offered in succession, each being appraised by itself without thought of there being more to come. The first we may believe to be so fragrant and refreshing that the individual would pay 50 cents rather than go without it. The second, yielding less satisfaction, would command only 25 cents; the third would command still less, say 15 cents; the fourth, 10; and the fifth only 5. The total utility of the five would be indicated by the sum of the amounts which the several units would have commanded separately, namely: —

For the first orange	50 cents
For the second orange	25 cents
For the third orange	15 cents
For the fourth orange	10 cents
For the fifth orange	5 cents
For the total supply	105 cents

Suppose now, on the other hand, that the five oranges exist as a stock, possessed together by the individual. All are alike. Take away any one, and the loss of utility or satisfaction will be the same as if any other had been taken away. Each has the same degree of importance for his welfare. As installments or successive doses, they have differing utility. But possessed as a stock, they have each the same economic importance. Any one would be parted with on the same terms as another. And those terms — the price — would be settled by the utility (satisfaction) yielded by the *last* of them if they were enjoyed in succession. The price at which the fifth would be bought (or sold) is the price at which any one of a stock of five would be bought (or sold). That price measures the *marginal* utility, or *final* utility, of the supply. Economic importance; marginal utility; final utility; the satisfaction got from any one unit of a stock, — all these expressions come to the same thing.

It may seem paradoxical to say that all the constituents of a stock have the same economic importance, and that none the less some have greater utility than others. But there is no real paradox. It must be remembered that utility means satisfactions or enjoyments. To possess a stock is not to enjoy it (except so far as, by association of ideas, mere ownership gives pleasure; as in case of a miser's hoard). The stock is necessarily enjoyed, not as a whole, but by installments: and as it comes to be so enjoyed, the successive installments yield lessening satisfaction. Economic importance is something different; it is the satisfaction dependent, not on the whole stock, but on any one of the constituents of the stock. Considered in this way, all the constituents are alike; even though, considered as sources of enjoyment when actually used, they are of varying utility.

§ 4. Let us return now to the relation between the supply of an article and its price. Increase in supply means lower price. It also means lessening utility from the added units. The price of a commodity depends, as the case is commonly stated, on the least of the utilities yielded by the supply, or on final utility. Price, or value, depends on the utility of the last increment. Properly qualified, and properly understood, the principle is sound; and not only so, but of primary importance.

First as to the qualifications. The proposition is true, in strictness, only if we suppose many competing buyers and sellers. And in fact most things are brought to market by competing sellers, and are purchased by competing buyers. Assume now that a given supply, say 1000 oranges, is offered by the sellers. Among the buyers are some whose means are large, others who value oranges highly. Both sets would be willing to pay a high price for a few oranges rather than go without. But there are more oranges than these purchasers are eager for. To induce the rest to buy, or to induce the eager purchasers to buy more, the price must be lowered. As the sellers are many and competing, the price of the whole supply will be uniform. Any one seller, trying to obtain a higher price from the eager buyers, would be undersold by others. There would be one price at which the whole lot would go, and that would be the price which tempted the last buyer; or, to be more accurate, the last purchase by any of the buyers. This last purchase, and the price which must be offered to induce it, would settle the terms for all the transactions.

Next, as to the just understanding of the proposition. Observe that the last buyer and the last purchase have been spoken of, not the last or marginal utility. In the usual statements of this fundamental principle of value, it is said simply that selling price, or exchange value, depends on marginal utility. The assumption is here tacitly made that all the buyers are in the same position and that all have the same means. From this it would follow that a less sum of money paid out denoted a less utility, and that he who bought the last unit of the whole supply was not only the last purchaser, but the purchaser to whom that unit gave the least satisfaction. The fact is, however, that purchasers have very different means, and, as just pointed out, this circumstance is of vast importance in explaining the fall in price which actually takes place when supply is increased. The dependence of selling price on the last purchaser (or the last purchase) is not affected by the inequality of incomes. But the significance of the final purchase for the utility or satisfaction-yielding power of the last installment of the supply is much affected.

The simple and familiar fact that a rich man, when paying out a given sum of money, often gets less satisfaction than a poor man when he pays out the same sum, is expressed in more technical terms by saying that the marginal utility of money is less to the rich than to the poor. A dollar signifies little to the man of means. If he parts with it, his loss in welfare is vastly less than that of the poor man who parts with the same amount. A high price therefore does not necessarily indicate great utility to those paying it. It may signify only that the marginal utility of money is small.

The phrase "marginal utility of money" must, however, be used with caution. Money has utility in a different way from other things. It is valued not because it serves in itself to satisfy wants, but as a medium of exchange, having purchasing power over other things. Gold jewelry is subject to the law of diminishing utility precisely as other things are. But gold coin — money — is subject to it only in the sense that an individual buys first the things he prizes most, and then other things in the order of their less utility. Strictly speaking, the statement that money has varying utility and that there is a marginal utility of money is only a way of saying that the things bought with money have varying utility, and that some among them are at the margin of utility.[1]

§ 5. The conceptions of total utility and marginal utility lead to that of consumer's surplus.

Consumer's surplus is the phrase applied by Professor Marshall (who has done more than any other writer to make clear this whole subject) to the difference between the sum which measures total utility and that which measures total exchange value. The total exchange value of a set of goods is obviously the price per unit (determined by marginal utility) multiplied by the number of units. But the total utility of the units as they come to be enjoyed is a different quantity. Thus, our orange-eater would have been willing to pay for the first orange 50 cents, but had to pay only 5 cents. He had a "surplus" of 45 cents' worth of satisfaction. Using the same figures as before for the supposed supply of five oranges, we get the following comparison between the prices that would have been paid and the prices that were paid in fact; the difference indicating consumer's surplus.

	Potential Price, Measuring Total Utility	Actual Price	Consumer's Surplus
For the first orange....	50	5	45
For the second orange .	25	5	20
For the third orange...	15	5	10
For the fourth orange..	10	5	5
For the fifth orange....	5	5	
For the whole supply ..	105	25	80

The case is stated here in the simplest terms, and on the assumption that the price of this small supply of oranges would be determined as the price of the usual large supply of commodities as they come to market in the actual world, — by marginal utility, or at a price which carries off the last increment. With-

[1] See what is said further on this topic, and on the peculiarities of the value of money, in Book III, Chapter 18.

out stopping now to inquire how far this assumption in fact holds good where a very few commodities are put on sale,[1] let us consider the nature of consumer's surplus, as here typified.

How substantial is this surplus? and how far is this mode of measuring it satisfactory? To ask these questions is only to ask, in different words, how substantial total utility is, and how far we can measure total utility.

One limitation of the first importance has already been indicated when considering marginal utility and its connection with demand. If all persons had the same income, then willingness to pay a given amount for an article might be fairly assumed to mean that the article had the same utility for each of them. But some have greater incomes than others; the marginal utility of money is less to the rich; and the payment by them of a larger sum does not signify a higher utility. A rich man will pay for hothouse fruits or vegetables a sum quite out of the question for a person of modest means. The latter may secure, at a season of greater plenty, precisely the same things for a price much lower. The rich man probably gets no greater enjoyment from his expensive purchase; or, if so (counting as part of his pleasure the gratification of the love of distinction), by no means in proportion to the higher price he pays. If some of the familiar comforts of civilized life become scarce, — fresh milk or good bread, — they would command a high price, even if all persons had the same incomes. But the price would go still higher if there were a circle of persons able and ready to bid heavily for them without making serious gaps in their incomes. The special increase of price resulting from this latter circumstance is indicative, not of specially high utility, but of large means for purchasing utilities.

Still another qualification is suggested by the fact of inequality. Many articles which command a high price satisfy the passion for display. Such are the precious stones, rare paintings, and statues. No doubt many things of this sort — the great works of art — are intrinsically beautiful, and yield

[1] See the next chapter in this book, Chapter 10, § 9.

enduring and unalloyed pleasures; and it is their intrinsic beauty, tested by time, that is at the basis of their high value. Being not only beautiful, but also rare, they satisfy in addition the deep-rooted instinct of emulation and desire for distinction. They have what has been called a prestige value. They command a higher price simply because they are already high in price. Suppose now that such things become common and therefore cheap; that diamonds, for example, become very plentiful, and that their price falls to some such level as that of glass beads. The intrinsic qualities of diamonds would remain; their luster and brilliancy, their hardness. The satisfaction which the previous limited supply had given might be thought, therefore, to remain undiminished. Yet in fact it would be vastly diminished; for diamonds would no longer be evidences of wealth and social station. Consumer's surplus, as measured by the previous high price, would evaporate.

Consumer's surplus is thus unsubstantial for a considerable range of articles now much esteemed and paid for at high prices. Not only the favorite objects of rich collectors, such as rare paintings and books, belong in this class, but many others which are not commonly thought of as belonging there. Handsome houses, fashionable clothes, even choice food, get no small part of their power of yielding utilities from their satisfying the sense of distinction. As to all these, total utility and consumer's surplus are highly elusive.

Another qualification concerns articles at the other end of the scale, — things of simple necessity. Measured in terms of the prices that would be given for the early doses, consumer's surplus is very high for bread, clothing, houseroom, — for the minimum of food, raiment, and shelter. Rather than dispense with these, anything would be given; life itself depends on them. Total utility and consumer's rent may be calculated to be infinite. Certain it is that, were they to become very scarce, their price would go to a very high range; and this, irrespective of whether there were or were not inequalities of incomes among the purchasers. But a question may be raised as to the nature of the utilities derived from these necessaries. The satisfaction they give is of a negative sort. The chronicler of Lewis and Clark's expedition across the American continent narrates that at one stage the explorers subsisted on dried salmon in the form of a tasteless powder, so unappetizing that only the absolutely necessary amount was eaten. Some such situation is in the mind of an ingenious and stimulating thinker, Professor Patten, who has distinguished between a "pain economy" and a "pleasure economy." The first phrase describes that economic stage in which the efforts of man suffice only to yield the indispensable minimum; to prevent hunger, thirst, freezing; to ward off pain, not to yield satisfaction. The second describes that better stage when the first elemental wants have been attended to, and positive enjoyment begins; when food is appetizing as well as sufficient, when clothing and houseroom are attractive. Now, in reckoning total utility and consumer's surplus, we do well to begin only when this second stage has been reached. Let those utilities which are of the indispensable sort be set aside. Only where the stage has been reached of possible comfort, of some choice in the direction of expenditure, can there be anything in the nature of a real surplus of satisfaction for the consumer.

But this is true not only of absolute necessaries, but in a good degree of conventional necessaries. Equipages and horses are conventional necessaries for many members of the Continental aristocracy. They would be immensely missed if the individual had to give them up. Yet the real enjoyment from them is doubtful. So it is with the starched linen and close-fitting clothes of the well-to-do, which are insignia of the wearer's exemption from manual labor. The satisfaction from them is chiefly negative; their loss would be more keenly felt than their presence is enjoyed. Positive satisfaction is indicated in very uncertain degree by the price which under the stress of convention the individual would pay rather than do without such things.

Not the least of the difficulties in the way of measuring utilities by potential prices is the practical one that we have no means of knowing what are the prices that would be paid for the several installments of a commodity. In our illustrative case it has been assumed that the first orange would be so greatly enjoyed as to command a price of 50 cents. But in hardly any actual case do we know what price would have been fetched by the first installment, or by a series of earlier installments. All we know is that they would command much more than that settled by marginal utility for the actual supply. We have some information (though not very much even here) regarding the variations of prices in the neighborhood of the range familiar to us. We observe how oranges, cigars, bread, meat, sugar, go up and down as the quantities become somewhat greater or less than those usually put on the market. But we have no precise knowledge of what would happen if the quantity of any one of these varied very greatly from the usual amount. Statistics of prices, however perfected, throw no light on the highest range that would be paid if supply became very small.

These accumulated difficulties make it impossible to measure in any precise way total utility or consumer's surplus. The figures which have been given for illustration are useful in making the conceptions clear, but are misleading in that they imply accuracy of measurement. We cannot set down the complete price schedule; and even if we could, the differences in incomes, the illusiveness of prestige, the doubtful satisfaction of a pain economy, combine to render a calculation of real enjoyment impracticable. We cannot measure with any approach to accuracy the satisfactions got from wealth.

None the less, total utility and consumer's surplus are not fanciful. That they are real, is shown by their accord with familiar phrases. We often say that we get a thing for less than it is worth to us, meaning that what we give for it offers less satisfaction than the thing we buy. This is merely stated with more care and precision when we say that a consumer's surplus is secured. Though that surplus may not be clear either at the lower end of the scale of consumption, where bare necessaries alone are bought, or at the upper end, where mere vanity is satisfied, it is unmistakable with what may be called the true enjoyments of life. A varied diet, abundant houseroom, clothing and fittings that permanently please the taste, the gratification which all men get from the mimic arts, distraction coming after monotonous work, the pleasures of the intellect, — these are things not less enjoyed when abundant and cheap. They often have a utility much greater than is indicated by the price paid for them. Though their utility be not susceptible of measurement, total utility is certainly large, and consumer's surplus is correspondingly large.

§ 6. The discussion of utility, total utility, and consumer's surplus leads to another question, How state and measure the income of a community?

An individual usually thinks of his income, and measures it, in terms of money. Similarly, the income of a community is usually stated in terms of money. So long as the prices of commodities and services remain the same, this mode of estimating income is for most purposes sufficient. The condition stated — of stable prices — is obviously important. If all money incomes double, and all prices also double, the community is no better off than before. It simply conducts its exchanges with a different scale for the medium of exchange.

Hence we proceed naturally to the next step. Money income is significant simply as a way of measuring the quantity of the things which the money buys. We may think, therefore, of real income in contrast to money income, — of the necessities, conveniences, and luxuries of life. We must reckon, also, as part of real income, the services of those who used to be called "unproductive," — actors, musicians, servants, and so on. The more we can get of such "real" income, of all kinds, the more prosperous we are as individuals and as a community.

But we may go a step beyond. We have seen [1] that the

[1] See Book I, Chapter 2, § 2.

act of production consists in the creation of utilities. Now, just as all production in the last analysis consists in the creation of utilities, so all income consists in the utilities or satisfactions created. Economic goods are not ends in themselves, but means to the end of satisfying wants. In a preceding chapter, we have distinguished between capital and wealth which is not capital, or (in other phraseology) between consumer's wealth and producer's capital. But consumer's wealth, which we may treat in one sense as "real" income, is an instrument no less than producer's capital. It, too, is a means, not an end. Our food, clothing, furniture, may be said to yield psychic income. They shed utilities, so to speak, as long as they last. In the final analysis, the income of an individual or of a community consists of the sum of utilities steadily accruing from its store of economic goods. It consists, that is, of the total utility of all its goods.

Nevertheless, for almost all purposes of economic study, it is best to content ourselves with a statement, and an attempt at measurement, in terms not of utility but of money income or of real income. The reason for this rejection of a principle which is in itself sound lies in the conclusion just reached regarding total utility and consumer's surplus: they cannot be measured.

The other ways of stating and measuring income lead to results of some certainty. We can measure money income. Though our statistics for the total money income of (say) the people of the United States are far from complete, the task of ascertaining that income is not hopeless. Indeed, it has been accomplished for some countries with sufficient accuracy.[1] We can also measure the general range of prices. We know, therefore, whether a given sum of money incomes at one time means more than a given sum at another time. If we know that money incomes have increased, and that the range of prices is unchanged, we are sure that real income, in terms of consumable commodities, has increased.

[1] See, for a recent example, R. E. May's estimate of the money income of the German people in the *Jahrbuch für Gesetzgebung*, 1909, Heft 4.

Further, we can do something toward measuring "real" income directly. We can ascertain what has been the consumption, per head of population, at different times, of such articles as flour, sugar, tea, coffee, cotton, wool, and the like. The results give indications of value regarding the increase of income in terms of commodities. We know that the average consumption of such things has much increased in recent times, and that material welfare has so far advanced.

But how far total utility or "psychic income" has increased, we have no accurate notion. We may feel sure that it has increased in some degree; but whether in the same degree as consumer's wealth, or in less, or even in greater, degree,[1] we do not know. We cannot measure how great total utility was before the increased supply of economic goods, or how great after. The supply of the things which minister to enjoyment can be measured, but not enjoyment itself. Virtually all problems of legislation and applied economics can be settled, and habitually are settled, according to the results in terms of the former sort of income. Hence we do best, for almost all economic reasoning, not to go beyond the tangible and measurable facts of consumer's wealth. Even though consumer's goods be but a sort of capital, and even though total utility be, in the last analysis, the true income, the only kind of income about which we can reach results of quantitative accuracy is that "real" income which consists of enjoyable things.

§ 7. The principle of diminishing utility, if applied unflinchingly, leads to the conclusion that inequality of incomes brings a less sum of human happiness than equality of incomes, and that the greater the inequality, the less the approach to maximum happiness. If additional increments of any commodity yield less enjoyment than preceding increments, the same is true of increments of income in general. A man who

[1] If we accept the distinction between a pain economy and a pleasure economy, and begin to reckon total utility and consumer's surplus only when a surplus over necessaries appears, we may conclude that for a considerable stage after the first emergence of a surplus, total utility increases in greater degree than consumer's wealth.

already has five oranges gains less from a sixth than he who has but one orange gains from a second. A man who has an income of $10,000 gains less from an additional $100 than does the man who has an income of $1000. This is stated in another way in the proposition that gambling between persons of equal income always brings an economic loss. If two men, each having $1000, bet $100, the gain to the winner from the increase of his possessions to $1100 is less than the loss to the loser from the drop of his possessions to $900. All this follows directly from the hedonistic calculus, — from the principle of diminishing utility.

We have just seen that the hedonistic calculus is not to be applied unflinchingly. It needs to be qualified, for example, in its application to the necessaries of life, — to pain economy and pleasure economy. Additions of income (that is, of goods purchasable) which come after the first needs of bare existence have been met, may mean not only an increase of happiness, but a more than proportionate increase. Hence if one half of a people have a considerable surplus over necessaries, and the rest the bare necessaries only, the sum of enjoyments may be greater than if all had the same income, — if the surplus were spread thin over the entire mass.

And it hardly needs to be said that the hedonistic calculus, even where it does lead clearly to the conclusion that enjoyment is subject to diminishing return, does not tell the whole story of human happiness. One of the unfailing sources of satisfaction, deep-rooted in human nature, is the response to the instincts of emulation and distinction. But distinction implies inequality. Though there may be distinction and inequality in other ways, — in rank or fame, — difference in economic possessions has been an immense stimulus and an immense resource to almost all men. The spice and flavor of life would be gone with flat equality.

None the less, it remains true that there is an opposition between inequality and maximum happiness. The opposition becomes obvious when there is very great inequality. High disparity of incomes means a net loss in happiness; the rich gain less than the poor lose. Though some emulation and distinction be essential to a full and happy life, and though some inequality of income be a natural consequence of distinction, such great inequalities as are familiar in modern society, and indeed in all societies advanced much beyond barbarism, cannot possibly bring the most effective distribution of the material sources of enjoyment. Emulation in ostentation palls; it is the least lasting of all the satisfactions derived from distinction. The consciousness, more or less obscure, of the inconsistency between maximum happiness and great inequality underlies the whole modern social movement; for essentially this movement has for its goal a more equal distribution of income. From this flow the characteristic tendencies of our time, — curbing of monopolies, extension of government industry, labor legislation, progressive taxation; last, but not least, socialism. Inequality may be, and probably is, an indispensable spur to the full application of men's best faculties, and an inevitable outcome of free and vigorous industry. But *prima facie* it does not lead to the best distribution of well-being. It is always on the defensive; and the greater and more lasting it is, the more difficult is its defense.

CHAPTER 10

Market Value. Demand and Supply

§ 1. In the preceding chapter the first principle of value has already been stated. The value of an article depends on its marginal utility. It is the price at which the last installment can be disposed of, — the price that settles, in turn, under the ordinary conditions of competition in the market, the price at which the whole supply will be sold. It remains to illustrate this principle further, and to explain in what manner it operates in the complexities of actual life.

Let us first illustrate the main principle graphically. On Figure 1, prices are measured along the perpendicular axis *Y*; quantities, *i.e.* the several installments offered in the market, are measured on the horizontal axis *OX*. Let it be supposed that the first dose, say of sugar, is represented by the horizontal line *OA*, and that this dose would command the price *OP*. Its value would then be indicated by the area *OPA′A*, — the quantity multiplied by the price. Suppose now a second dose to be offered, indicated by the line *OB*. Under the influence of the principle of diminishing utility, its price would sink to *OP′*, and the whole supply would now be sold at this price (or rather, as will presently be explained, at no higher price than this). The total value of the increased supply would now be indicated by the area *OP′B′B*. Add now another dose, the supply being *OC*; the price sinks again, and the value of the whole supply is *OP″C′C*. And so on, with the supply *OD*, the price will be *OP‴*, and the whole value *OP‴D′D*, and with the supply *OE*, the price will be *OP⁗* and the whole value *OP⁗*E′E.

Strictly speaking, under the conditions here assumed, we should not know that the price for the quantity *OB*, for example, was fixed at the amount indicated by the lines OP' or BB'. We should only know that it was not higher than OP' and not lower than OP'' (CC'). In order to induce the supply OB to be taken off, the price must be at least as low as OP'; otherwise, the buyer would not take it. But if the buyer offered less than

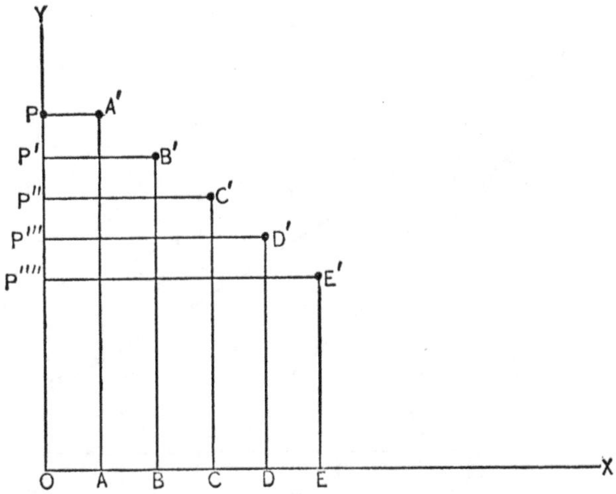

FIG. 1.

OP', the seller would still rather dispose of his supply than have it left on his hands; and until another potential buyer came on the scene, there is no telling what price the seller might not accept. But if another buyer comes, to whom the dose has the utility measured by OP'', and who is willing to pay the price so measured, the seller can compel the second buyer, stationed at B, to pay at least as much as the third competitor, stationed at C, would offer. Price, therefore, would be somewhere between OP' and OP'', or somewhere between BB' and CC'. So in each of the successive stages. The price must be at least low enough to tempt the last buyer, who must be called in to dispose of the whole supply offered. It may go a bit lower than this, until the point is reached at which a new buyer would enter and prevent the more desirous buyer — the more "capable" buyer, as he has sometimes been called — from beating the seller down. If there be a considerable difference between the utilities of the installments to successive buyers, there is a considerable range within which price is indeterminate.

We have already noted, however, that in the ordinary course

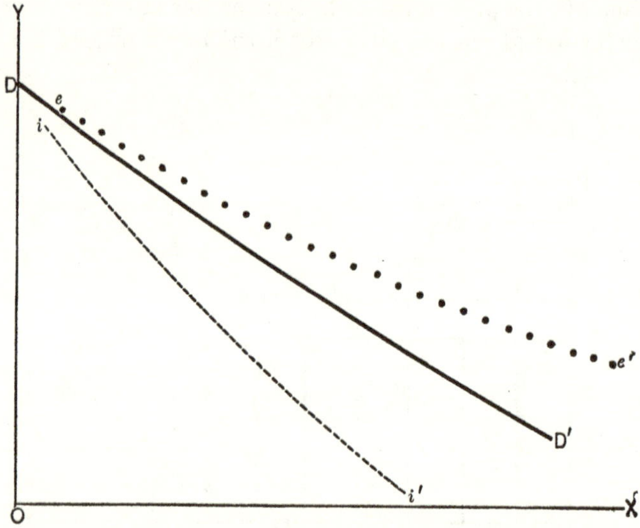

Fig. 2.

of business dealings there are no such abrupt stages in demand as the preceding diagram assumes. There are not a paltry half-dozen purchasers, and a few pieces on sale, for any given article. There are many buyers, to whom great supplies are offered. Among the many buyers, there are always some just ready to step forward; some to whom the utility of the additional dose is only a shade less than was the utility of the previous dose, and who are therefore called into the active purchasing market by the lower price. This situation is described, in the technical language which economists have found convenient, by saying that demand is continuous. Where there are gaps between the utilities to different purchasers, and consequently between the prices they are willing to pay, demand is discontinuous. The successive steps from A' to B', C', D', E' in Figure 1 indicated such discontinuity of demand. The nearer together these points are, the smaller is each step, and the less is the range within which price is indeterminate. For the immense majority of dealings in modern communities, the points are so near together, — the gradation of utility and demand is so close, — that they may be represented as joined into a line or curve. That curve, on a diagram such as is commonly used in graphic illustrations of these principles, always has a smooth downward inclination from left to right, like the unbroken line DD' in Figure 2. It indicates that successive doses of any article have gradually diminishing utility, and must be offered at prices that insensibly become lower and lower as greater quantities are disposed of. It is called the *demand curve.*

The shape which that curve assumes indicates the nature of the demand for the commodity. If it descends slowly, — as does the dotted line ee' in Figure 2, — it indicates that, as greater quantities are offered on the market, new purchasers appear readily and the decline in price is slow. The demand for the commodity is then said to be elastic. On the other hand, a curve descending quickly, like the broken line ii', in Figure 2, indicates that utility or purchasing power diminishes rapidly, that new purchasers do not readily appear, and that the decline in price with increasing supply is abrupt. In such a case the demand for the commodity is said to be inelastic: consumption does not respond promptly to a lowering of price. The cause of inelasticity must be, in some degree, rapid diminution of the utility of added installments; but this cause may be accentuated by inequality in means. If some purchasers are very rich, others well-to-do, many others poor, commodities may meet a highly inelastic demand in the market, but not necessarily suffer a corresponding diminution in their power of yielding enjoyments to mankind.

The demand for necessaries is inelastic. A certain quantity of bread will be bought, whatever the price. No doubt a high price will in some degree check consumption, and a low price will lead to more liberal or careless use. But when the indispensable supply has once been got, the decline in utility from greater quantities is rapid. For articles of this sort, a comparatively small shortage in supply will cause a large increase in price, while a comparatively small redundancy will cause a rapid decline. The sharp inclination of the demand curve *ii′* is the graphic representation of the inelastic demand for necessaries and of the abrupt fluctuations in price under slight changes in supply.

Any article which, though not necessary, is yet clung to with persistence by consumers, has a similarly inelastic demand. Meat, for example, though not a necessary, has an inelastic demand among the well-to-do. On the other hand, the substantial comforts of life — things not indispensable, yet prized by all the world — often have an elastic demand. Such are those articles of food which, though not necessaries, please by their flavor and variety. For almost all except the well-to-do meat is such an article. In the upper part of the supply it has an inelastic demand, in the lower part a very elastic demand. Sugar, fruits, vegetables, tea, coffee, and cocoa have probably an elastic demand throughout the range of supply; so have books, furniture, houseroom, clean and decent clothing.

In general, elasticity of demand is increased by an equal distribution of wealth, while an unequal distribution leads to inelasticity in demand. This effect of inequality illustrates once again the caution which needs to be observed in applying the principle of diminishing utility to the phenomena of value as they appear in modern communities. If all people had the same incomes, diminishing utility would be the one cause acting on the elasticity of demand, and the inclination of the demand curve would be significant of the rate of diminution in the enjoyments yielded by successive increments. In fact, the demand curve is much affected by the circumstance that persons of means can afford to bid high for the first increments, while the great number of those with small means cannot bid until a low price is reached. The lower bids of the latter — signified by a sharply descending demand curve — mean a diminution not so much in enjoyments as in money means. This qualification must be borne in mind when, in the succeeding pages, value is spoken of as depending on marginal utility; that phrase being used, for brevity, to indicate the complex conditions on which depends the price fetched by the last increment of a supply.

§ 2. We proceed to consider now the mode in which the value or price of an article is determined at any particular time, — the problem of market value.

Suppose the supply of a commodity to be fixed; suppose it to be offered on the market by competing sellers; suppose it all to be offered without reserve. Then the value of that commodity will be determined by its marginal utility. If all is not sold at that price by the competing sellers, some part of the stock will not be disposed of. This situation is graphically represented in Figure 3. Given a supply *OS*, the resulting price will be at the point where the perpendicular line *SS′* will cut the demand curve *DD′*. That line ($SS' = OP$) measures the marginal utility of the supply *OS*, and so measures the price at which that supply will be sold.

The total exchange value of the supply is indicated by the area *OPS′S* — the supply multiplied by the price. Total utility is indicated by the irregular area *DOSS′*; consumer's surplus by the (more or less triangular) area *DPS′*. Those purchasers who, rather than go without the article, would have been willing under stress to pay a higher price than *SS′* — as high as *OD* — secure some surplus of satisfaction.

The same proposition, on the mode in which the value of an article at any given time is determined, was stated by the older writers in a somewhat different way. They said that market value was settled by the equation of supply and demand. The everyday way of putting it is to say simply that the value of a thing is determined by supply and demand. This is loose, since it implies that supply and demand are causes that act independently, and are not themselves influenced by price. But demand, in the sort of case here supposed, is certainly affected by price. The lower the price of an article, the more of it will be demanded; the higher the price, the less will be demanded. To say that price depends on demand, therefore, seems to be reasoning in a circle; since, if price is affected by demand,

demand is no less affected by price. Hence the more careful phrase just quoted; the equation of supply and demand. Given a *fixed* supply, there is one price at which the quantity demanded will be just equal to this quantity supplied. To assume that there is one such price, and not more than one, is to assume continuity of demand, as explained in the preceding section, — an assumption that holds good of the vast majority of articles bought

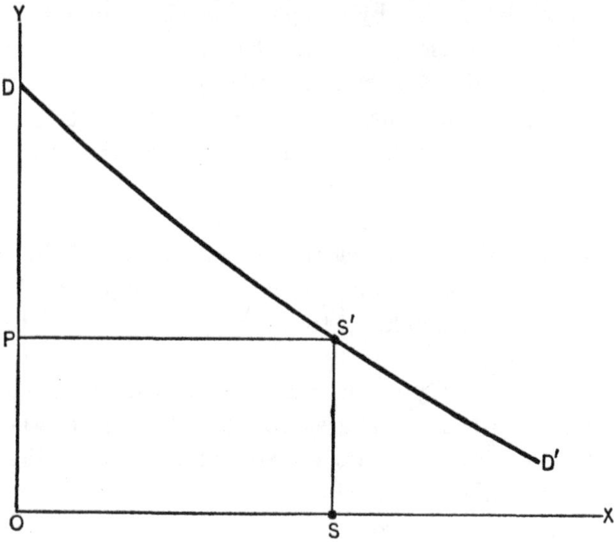

FIG. 3.

and sold in the markets. This one price evidently represents the marginal utility of the supply. Though the phrase "marginal utility" was not used by the older writers, their version of an equation of demand and supply states substantially the same proposition as the more modern one which reasons on the basis of diminishing utility and marginal utility.

§ 3. In both of these statements of the principle of market value, — the older one of an equation and the newer one of the marginal utility of supply, — the underlying assumption is that a fixed quantity is put on the market. But is this assumption tenable? Does it conform to the usual state of facts? We have just said that demand, in the sense of quantity demanded, is not independent of price. Is not the same true of supply? In the ordinary case, it is hardly accurate to say that the quantity offered in the market is fixed, and is independent of price. As price goes higher, more sellers will be tempted to offer their wares, and supply will become larger. As prices go lower, supply will become smaller. Must not the theory of market value be adjusted to variable supply as well as to variable demand?

It is true that in some instances the supposition of a fixed supply is clearly in accord with the facts. When a large crop of strawberries comes on the market, it must be disposed of once for all. There is no keeping back any part of the supply of a perishable commodity. The total quantity on hand must be disposed of for what it will fetch, — for the marginal price. Not very long ago, the list of commodities of this kind was a large one; it included fresh fish, all vegetables and fruits, even meat. But modern improvements for the preservation of most such things, through cold storage and canning, has greatly shortened the list. Most commodities are not put on sale with headlong suddenness. They are offered in installments. They come into the market in a flow or stream, not as an abruptly offered stock. The rate at which they come in, and the amount which will be offered at any given time, depend on the price. A higher price quickens the flow and leads to larger supply; a lower price checks the flow.

It is not difficult to adjust the theory of market value to the case of variable supply. On Figure 4, let SS' represent the conditions of a supply that varies with price, becoming greater as price rises and smaller as price falls. Here, as on the previous figures, quantities are measured horizontally along the axis OX or parallel to it, and prices perpendicularly along the axis OY or parallel to it. At the price SA, we may suppose the quantity OA to be forthcoming on the market. As the price rises, the quantity increases. At the price PP', the quantity offered is OP'; at the price $S'A'$, the quantity offered is OA'. Evidently the line SPS', which is the supply curve, has an upward inclination, the reverse of the inclination of the demand curve *DD′*. A rise in price, which causes the quantity demanded to become less, causes the quantity offered to become greater.

The supply and demand curves, moving in opposite directions, must meet; and in our figure they meet at *P*. The price *PP′* is the equilibrium price, the market price fixed by the play of varying supply and demand. At that point the quantity offered is equal to the quantity demanded: the equation is

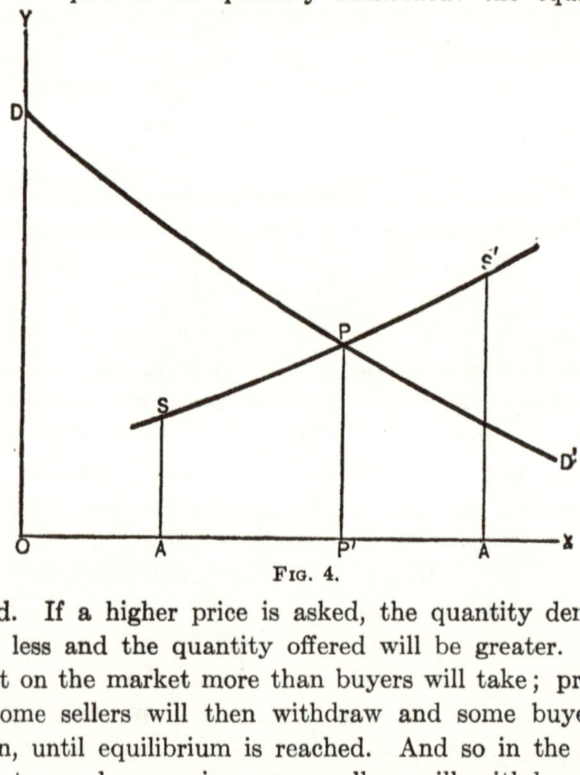

FIG. 4.

satisfied. If a higher price is asked, the quantity demanded will be less and the quantity offered will be greater. Sellers will put on the market more than buyers will take; price will fall; some sellers will then withdraw and some buyers will come in, until equilibrium is reached. And so in the reverse case: at any lower price, some sellers will withdraw, some buyers will be tempted in, and readjustment will again bring the price to the point of equilibrium *PP′*.

§ 4. It has just been said that of these two modes of statement — the one proceeding on the supposition of a fixed supply, the other on that of a variable supply — the second is more in accord with the facts. Yet the first also is so in accord. Both must be had in mind for an understanding of the course of prices in a market.

On any given day, in a well-organized market, the actual settlement of market price undoubtedly takes place through an adjustment of supply as well as through a response from demand. On the cotton exchange or the produce exchange, or in any place where brokers and dealers meet, a process of higgling and bargaining goes on. More or less of the article is offered and demanded, with fluctuations in prices which are usually within narrow limits on any one day and which result in an equilibrium price for that day. But this daily equilibrium price is itself affected by an underlying and more important equilibrium price. While the amount which is offered in the market from day to day — the supply — varies considerably, and varies in response to changes in price, the total amount which can be supplied over a larger period usually is fixed. Take, as a typical case, the price of cotton, which fluctuates on the exchanges from day to day in response to the ever changing play of offer and demand. The total amount of cotton available for the season is not a variable quantity. It is so much and no more, depending on the crop of that season. The price at which the whole will be disposed of depends on its marginal utility or on the equation of supply and demand (whichever mode of statement be preferred) and is the outcome of a total supply which is fixed. The fluctuations in price from day to day oscillate about this seasonal equilibrium price.

Still using the cotton market and cotton prices for examples, we may note that, while the supply for the season is fixed, no one knows in advance with certainty just how great that supply is; still less at what price the supply, even if accurately known, would be disposed of. Hence a period of uncertainty, of rumors and guesses, of selling and buying by brokers and dealers and manufacturers, by any one who chooses to operate on the cotton market, — in short, all the phenomena of speculation. Cotton in the United States (the crop in this country dominates the world market) is picked in the autumn, and the amount harvested is known by December 1. But throughout the summer months there are reports of the condition of the growing plants, which foreshadow, though with uncertainty, the amount of the coming crop. During the picking season more and more certainty is reached. Finally, under modern methods of gathering such information, the amount comes to be accurately known. Then arises the question to what degree the price will be affected by the amount. It is certain that a small crop will command a higher price, a large crop a smaller price. But the conditions of demand or consumption are fluctuating from year to year, no less than the supply from the crops. Just what will be the seasonal equilibrium price for a crop of a given size, no one can say in advance. It is reached by a succession of tentative market prices. From day to day, and from month to month, the market price is settled by the adjustment of variable amounts offered in the market by dealers. For the season, it is settled by the adjustment of a fixed supply to the marginal price at which the whole will be disposed of.

It is not to be supposed that even on a single day is there one price rigidly settled by the equilibrium of demand and supply. Even in the most highly organized markets there may be simultaneous sales at different prices; and, where there are newly discovered conditions affecting the seasonal range, such as a crop report, there may be considerable fluctuations in the course of a day. These oscillations give the opportunity to the astute bargainer. Some buyers, not cool-headed enough to bide their time, will pay more than the equilibrium price. On the other hand, some sellers, unduly anxious lest their supplies be left on their hands, will sell at less. The shrewd and unexcitable person, carefully watching the course of dealings, may buy at one price from the over-eager sellers and sell on the same day at a profit to over-eager buyers. It is sometimes said that all the capital a speculator needs is a pencil and a block of paper, and all the knowledge he needs is a knowledge of human nature. This is by no means the whole story; yet it is true that a certain faculty of judging human nature, and an impassive demeanor, are important in the equipment of the professional dealer, and play no small part in those speculative operations which are discussed in the next chapter.

The more the actual dealings in a market are confined to persons who are shrewd and well-informed, the more probable is it that there will be an exact equilibrium price. And in any market where dealings are habitually conducted on a considerable scale, there will be an equilibrium price which, though not rigid, is maintained between comparatively narrow limits; and that price will represent the judgment then currently held of the probable seasonal price. Here, as in all economic analysis, we have to do not with hard and fast phenomena, but with the wavering doings of human beings. For the sake of bringing out clearly the underlying general probability — a probability which often is so great as to be virtually a certainty — we state our reasoning and conclusions in semi-mathematical form, as in the diagrams and figures that have preceded. But it must be remembered that the conclusions hold good not with mathematical certainty, but simply as statements of tendencies to which the actual market conditions more or less conform.

What is true of cotton, holds of other agricultural commodities, whose supply also is settled by the crops of each season: of wheat, corn, and other grains, of hay, flax and hemp, hops, sugar, tea, coffee. There is always a seasonal price, around which fluctuate the market prices for shorter periods. Virtually this holds of other commodities also. It is true that agricultural commodities show more unmistakably than most others the temporary fixation of supply. The supply of manufactured commodities changes more smoothly and continuously. The amounts offered in the market can often be increased and diminished without waiting for nature's processes of growth. But even here there are important limitations. For any given period of moderate length — a half year or a year — there is something like a fixed supply. Iron, for example, is continuously produced, and the amount of production responds in some degree to the fluctuations in price. But the quantity available for any given period depends on the mines of iron ore and of coal which are open, and still more on the furnaces and works which are ready to smelt and shape the iron. The supply can be increased or decreased only with considerable difficulty. It will not readily decrease, because the existing iron mines and works will be kept going, unless the prospects for profit are very bad indeed; continuous operation is a condition of almost any profit at all. Nor can it be rapidly increased. New mines and works can indeed be added, but this takes time. Again, though the output from the existing concerns does not come on the market at any fixed or regular rate, it is almost sure to be offered for sale within the current season of operations. Thus a seasonal equilibrium of supply and demand establishes itself. Around this seasonal price the current market prices fluctuate, as varying amounts are offered and demanded from day to day and from week to week.

Sometimes dealers, looking far ahead, carry stocks over a considerable period. In this way, the supply on hand, even the seasonal supply, may be sensibly affected, and the seasonal market price may be affected correspondingly. If, for example, the wheat crop in any year is very large, and the price unusually low, some dealers may withdraw considerable amounts from sale, store them, and plan to sell them at a profit in the next year, when a smaller supply and higher prices may be expected. But this is a risky operation. It involves the locking up of large money means. The next season may again bring a large crop. There is the possibility that the wheat held in storage may spoil and become valueless. As a matter of fact, very little wheat (in comparison with the total supply) is carried over from year to year, and the yearly price is determined almost solely by the crop for the time being. It is perhaps otherwise with durable commodities. If iron or copper are unusually cheap, stocks of them may be bought and put aside, with a minimum expense for storage, and with no risk of deterioration, in expectation of higher prices after a year or two. Yet even for these durable articles, such operations seem to be uncommon. Most persons in active business, and especially dealers and middlemen, do not try to look far ahead. They study the conditions of the present and the immediate future, and govern themselves accordingly. The withdrawal of stocks from the seasonal market seems to be no considerable factor in the play of demand and supply.

§ 5. Strictly speaking, the principle of marginal utility applies to consumer's wealth only. Capital yields no utilities directly. Materials, implements, machinery are but means for procuring utilities at a later date. Their utility is a derived one, depending on the utility of the consumable goods they aid in making. Though the principle of marginal utility works out its results for capital goods also, it does so through an intricate process and with some complications.

For example, when the cotton crop is small, the price of cotton rises; marginal utility is greater, we say, for the smaller supply. But the cotton is sold by the planters and farmers first to the dealers and speculators; they sell to the manufacturers; these again, through another set of dealers, sell the cotton cloth to those who wear it. It is the satisfactions got by these ultimate consumers that in the end determine the value of cotton for a given supply. But the manufacturers are the immediate buyers; and it is they who are commonly spoken of, in the language of the market, as the "consumers" of cotton. They are often in a position in which they *must* buy cotton. They have a plant which must be run if it is to earn anything at all, and a force of workmen which, to remain efficient, must be kept together. Each manufacturer wishes to keep his plant working at full capacity, and his workmen fully employed; yet with a small crop, there is less cotton to be worked up. On the other hand, the extent to which consumers will pay at a higher rate for the diminished amount of cotton cloth is an uncertain factor. The manufacturers try to get from the merchants and dealers to whom they sell, a higher price for cloth corresponding to the higher price of cotton. Both these sets of business men will say that it is the high price of cotton which *causes* the high price of cloth. Yet the reverse is at bottom the case; only because the cloth can be sold at a high price does the raw material command a high price. How close the correspondence in price will be, how much the investments and commitments of the manufacturers will affect the situation, how the calculations and transactions of cotton dealers and speculators, and cloth merchants and buyers, will act on prices at any one date and through the season,—these are matters on which the action of the fundamental economic forces is slow and uncertain. There are analogous complications when there is a very abundant cotton crop. Then manufacturers are not prepared to work up an unusual supply of the raw material; merchants and retailers are not certain how far and at what prices they can find a market for additional quantities of cloth. Though cotton cloth is a commodity having an elastic demand, raw cotton, despite the fact that demand for it is derived from that for cloth, may show from season to season fluctuations such as one would expect in a commodity for which the demand is inelastic.

Other kinds of capital goods are to be used for durable tools and plant. Such are iron, copper, timber, brick, stone. In the end, the demand for these also rests on the utility of the enjoyable commodities made with them; they also have a derived utility. But proximately the demand for them is from persons who wish to use them in connection with new investments. When the prospect of profit is good, the prices of these things rise; when the prospects are bad, their prices fall. Hence their prices are closely connected with those alterations of activity and depression, of good times and bad times, which are among the most puzzling of economic phenomena. It is true that their market price is settled by the amount which the last purchaser — the least eager of the buyers — is willing to pay. And in the end, no doubt, what that purchaser is willing to pay depends on what he can get in turn for the consumable goods made with the aid of the capital goods. But the chain of connection is a very long and irregular one, and the market price is universally affected by current expectations as to investment activity. It would be absurd to apply to these articles any strict principle of marginal utility. That principle, like others in economics, works out its results only in the long run, and with all sorts of qualifications and complications.

§ 6. Retail prices might be expected to illustrate most clearly the play of marginal utility; for here enjoyable goods are sold to their consumers, and the utilities from them are nearest realization. Yet in fact retail prices seem less subject to the working of supply and demand than wholesale prices.

Retail prices are governed proximately by custom. People pay the traditional or going price. Even the amounts which they purchase appear to be governed by custom; they buy the quantities which they are in the habit of consuming. And the retail prices which establish themselves as customary seem to be governed by wholesale prices. The retail dealers charge more when there is a considerable and apparently definitive rise in wholesale prices; and competition among themselves causes them to charge less when there is a considerable and lasting fall. No doubt, the accommodation of retail to wholesale prices is slow. When wholesale prices rise, shopkeepers hesitate to ask more, partly because each one fears that his rival may entice a customer away by keeping to the old price for a while. Conversely when wholesale prices fall, no shopkeeper willingly gives his customer the benefit of the change: he waits until some competitor precipitates it. But the two sets of prices in the end move together. Though retail prices are governed proximately by custom, they seem in the end to follow wholesale prices.

But all this is in appearance only. The consumption of every commodity is affected by its price. A rise in price checks purchasers, a fall in price stimulates them. Though it would appear that people continue to buy simply what they are used to buying, this is true only of buyers who are above the margin, — those who have been enjoying a consumer's surplus. There are always some just on the margin, to whom, at the ruling price, the purchase is just worth while and who cease buying when the price goes up. And conversely, when price falls, there are always some additional purchases. How great the changes in consumption are with rising or falling price, depends on the elasticity of demand. But some degree of sensitiveness there always is. So certain is this, that the wholesale dealers reckon on it in advance, and at once accommodate the current prices in the wholesale market. It is they who usually are best informed regarding the general situation. They know when a crop is short, or a new source of supply has been opened, or an invention is cheapening production and increasing the amount offered in the market. It is they, too, who can best observe when the habits of consumers are undergoing change and so are affecting the purchases of a commodity. In case of an increase in demand, any one retailer may indeed notice that his customers are buying more than before; but this may seem to him an isolated phenomenon. He simply orders more from his wholesale agent, and expects to sell more at the old price. But when orders from many retail dealers thus come in to many wholesalers, the market responds and price goes up. The retail dealer then charges more to his customers because he has paid the wholesaler more for his goods; the real influence at work being that the customers, taken as a whole, want the goods more. Here, as in all the phenomena of value and price, the stocks held by dealers, whether retail or wholesale, have an effect in preventing abrupt changes, and sometimes obscure and delay the restoration of the equilibrium of supply and demand. In the end, however, that equilibrium, resting on the demand of the marginal purchaser and so on the principle of marginal utility, settles both wholesale and retail prices.

In the earlier stages of industrial life, and even in many countries which have attained a comparatively advanced stage, retail prices are fixed by a direct process of higgling between sellers and buyers. In the very earliest and most primitive stages, indeed, when exchanges are few and sporadic, higgling plays a very important part. There is then nothing in the nature of a market price or customary price; and the astuteness of the bargainers, the needs and whims of the moment, even the possibility of physical force, affect the terms of exchange. As the division of labor is extended farther, and continuous exchange and sale develop, something like a market price establishes itself. That market price is likely soon to become a customary price, representing roughly an equilibrium of current demand and supply; but, though customary, it is likely also to be subject to bargaining, and to vary more or less from the customary rate.

In the highly developed countries of modern times, bargaining in retail dealings has been almost entirely discarded. The dealer sets a price at which he will sell, and at that price the purchaser may take the article or leave it. The tacit understanding is that the price so fixed shall be the current or market price, and that it shall be the same for all customers at the shop. The practise of fixed prices saves a vast amount of time and friction. The purchaser need not be on the watch to discover what other dealers are asking, and what is the going price; while, if he is not a marginal purchaser, but is enjoying some consumer's surplus, he need not be on his guard lest the dealer take advantage of his potential demand. The ease of everyday purchases and the efficiency of labor in retail operations are immensely promoted. Retailing on a large scale, conducive as it is to economy of labor, would be impossible without the practise of fixed prices. In many parts of the continent of Europe it has not been fully adopted. There the retail dealer still asks, not the price which he will take once for all, but a price which he hopes to get from the individual purchaser, and which he is prepared to lower if the purchaser bargains shrewdly. The result is friction, waste of time, and inefficiency.

§ 7. The current market rate is what people usually have in mind when they speak of a "fair" price. This is what the retail dealer is expected to charge as his fixed sum. If he asks a higher price than is usually asked at the time by other dealers for the same thing, — still more, if he asks a higher price from one purchaser than from another, — he is said to be charging unreasonably, or overreaching, or even cheating; and he is likely to lose his custom. There is often a similar attitude in regard to wholesale prices. Many large dealings in the wholesale market are concluded, in the great civilized communities, on the principle of fixed prices. A manufacturer or merchant in search of a given article orders what he wants from an agent or correspondent of established reputation, with the understanding that a fair price — that is, the ruling market price — will be charged. Here, as in retail dealings, confidence in honesty, and acceptance of prices as they stand, conduce to the easy dispatch of business. Underlying all, however, is bargaining somewhere, — a more or less overt adjustment of price to supply and demand. What is a fair price in the fundamental sense — what is the really just price at which goods shall be sold — are questions much more difficult than is supposed by most persons who use the phrases. Indeed, few who talk of fair and unfair prices are conscious of the problems involved. But they are problems not of exchange, but of distribution, and therefore taken up at a later stage of the inquiry.

§ 8. The discussion throughout the preceding pages has proceeded on the assumption that utility to the buyer is the only aspect of utility that needs consideration. The seller is supposed to put his wares on the market once for all, and to dispose of them, sooner or later, on such terms as their utility to buyers makes possible. But may not utility to sellers also affect price, by affecting supply? May not part of the supply be withdrawn by the sellers, for their own use? Would not the extent of this withdrawal depend on the price, and so introduce a further complication in the theory of market value?

It is entirely conceivable that utility to sellers should thus affect price. In the case of the five oranges, supposed above, it is conceivable that the holder of them might consider the possibility of enjoying one himself, and would be led to do so more and more as the price descended. At fifty cents he would readily part with one of his oranges, but at five cents he might conclude to eat one, and so withdraw part of the supply. And if we suppose, not one seller with a few oranges, but many sellers with many oranges, and suppose that among these sellers there is a considerable possibility of withdrawals for consumption, we have a new problem, more complicated than that of sales based on utility to buyers only. A great deal of intellectual ability has been given by economic writers to the analysis of this problem, and to the careful statement of the terms of exchange that would result under various hypothetical conditions.

But almost all this subtle analysis is in the air. Under a developed division of labor, utility to sellers does not affect value. Men produce with no reference to their own consumption. They produce for the market. The supplies in their hands of the things made by them are so great that the importance to them of any unit is *nil*. They throw their product on the market without reserve. No doubt, if that product were very great indeed, — such as to make the marginal utility to purchasers almost *nil*, — the sellers might stop to consider whether they could not use some fraction of it themselves. Farmers may consume more apples when a very heavy crop causes apples (on the trees) to be nearly valueless. But any supply created by effort and with a view to sale is rarely so far increased that price sinks near zero; and where by mischance price is very greatly lowered, the effect of utilization by the makers (sellers) is so slight as to be negligible. Virtually the whole supply is, in the ordinary case, offered once for all on the market.

The case would be different if supplies got into people's hands without reference from the start to sale and disposal. If they were rained down from heaven, in small amounts, price would be affected by utility to sellers quite as much as by utility to buyers. In early times, before division of labor and exchange had developed far, sporadic exchanges took place, we may imagine, under these apparently simple, though really complex, conditions. But they must have taken place either with very vague consciousness of utility, or under the influence of customs which greatly affected the actual terms of exchange. Ingenious hedonistic calculations probably throw little light on what happens in the stray exchanges of barbarians.

There are, however, in the modern world occasional cases where exchange is affected by utility to sellers. When a fine old picture or a family heirloom is put on the market, its price may depend much on the attachment which the owner feels for it. Articles of this sort, of sporadic and limited supply, are in any case largely indeterminate in value; since buyers are few, and demand is discontinuous. Their price may be made still more indeterminate by the fact that the seller (or sellers) may set store by the few specimens. The same is true, though in very much less degree, of dwellings adapted to individual tastes. The ordinary house, planned like many others of its class, comes on the market on nearly the same terms as other goods of homogeneous supply. But an odd house, built to suit the owner's idiosyncrasies of taste, stands more or less by itself. Its selling price may depend not only on the going price for houses of this range of desirability as estimated in the general market (that is, as estimated by buyers), but also on the attachment which the owner has for this particular one.

CHAPTER 11

Speculation

§ 1. The phenomena of speculation connect themselves with the settlement of market prices. Something more may now be said on the good and ill of speculative dealings.

The term "speculation" is used in various senses. Often it implies the buying and selling of things by a person whose main business in life is different, — "dabbling" in the market by "outsiders." But as often it implies buying and selling by persons who expect to make their living or their fortune by dealing in one commodity or in certain sets of commodities, — persons who are "professional speculators." These are sometimes distinguished again from "legitimate" dealers, — the wheat merchant, the cotton factor, — who buy and sell a commodity year in and year out, and are permanent middlemen for those who have it to sell and those who wish to buy it. Between these various sorts of persons there are insensible gradations. All their operations have their effect in determining market price; and all are more or less in the nature of speculative dealings.

The fundamental effect of speculation is to promote the establishment of the equilibrium of supply and demand. It tends to make daily market prices conform to the seasonal market price, and to make the seasonal market price such that the whole seasonal supply is disposed of. Those who are skillful and painstaking in estimating the seasonal supply, and are shrewd and experienced in foreseeing the effect of a given supply on price, are the persons who are likely to make money in speculation. They buy when others offer at a price lower than the facts of the market warrant; they sell when others bid a price higher than the facts warrant. The more the dealings of the market are confined to buying and selling between such shrewd and experienced dealers, the more likely is it that the seasonal price will be quickly and smoothly reached, and the less will be the fluctuations in price. With the inevitable uncertainties as to the amounts of the forthcoming supplies and the conditions of consumption and demand, there will always be differences of judgment between even the most expert dealers. There will be fluctuations in price, some ups and downs, some unexpected gains and losses, — "speculative" profits or losses. But the general effect of speculation is to lessen fluctuations, and promote the smooth course of exchange and consumption.

This lessening of fluctuations is advantageous alike to the ultimate consumers, and to those manufacturers who in business parlance are often spoken of as the "consumers" of a raw material. For the ultimate consumers, say of wheat, the early and exact adjustment of price brings more even utilization of the available supply. If the crop be short, some lessening of consumption is inevitable; and it is better that the deficit be spread through the season. The sooner and the more exactly the higher price is reached, the more likely is this result. Conversely, a large crop is better sold at a low price throughout the season than at prices ranging from high to low as the season progresses.

The good effect of speculation in this direction has been illustrated from the experiences of older days, when wide fluctuations in the price of food were common. Under modern conditions, with great areas of supply brought into competition by railways and steamships, abrupt changes in the supply of most foodstuffs and raw materials are rare. A poor crop in one country or section is likely to be offset by a good crop elsewhere. The seasonal supplies do indeed change, and prices go up and down under their influence; but the variations are seldom great. But under such conditions as existed under the limited geographical division of labor before the eighteenth century, great fluctuations were common. Then the area from which any district or city got its food and materials was strictly limited. A crop deficiency meant a short supply, and necessitated the adjustment of consumption to that short supply. The dealers or speculators or "forestallers" who secured the supply and at once demanded high prices for it, brought about the inevitable adjustment, and caused a more even utilization of the stock in hand. All this was reasoned out by some of the older writers on economics, and led them to a warm defense of speculators and to a condemnation of laws aimed against speculation. Very likely their defense of speculation was carried too far. The process of buying from the farmers did not necessarily take place under active competition by the dealers or speculators, nor did that of selling to the consumers; and the gains of the speculators were enhanced by the ignorance or heedlessness of both farmers and consumers, and might easily be thought larger than could seem reasonable. We know very little of the details of what took place in these early days, and are prone to project into them ideas or conclusions based on our own experiences. But none the less it is probable that even in those times the influence of speculation was in the main to lessen fluctuations and promote the expedient rate of consumption. It is certain that this is its tendency under the modern conditions of wide markets, full information, active competition.

The development of cold storage in recent times has led to precisely this sort of evened distribution of supply under the influence of dealings that are essentially speculative. Fruit, meat, fish, eggs, no longer come on the market in spasmodic and irregular amounts. Supplies that are heavy at one time are bought by dealers, put in storage, and held for sale at a later period of scantier supply. Prices are more equable, and on the whole the profits of dealers are probably less. There is less risk to them, and the community gets its supplies at a smaller charge for their services as middlemen.

§ 2. The process of lessening fluctuations and distributing risks is much promoted by the practise of dealing in "futures," — a practise with which the term "speculation" is especially associated. Goods are bought and sold not only for immediate delivery, but for future delivery as well. The person — say the dealer — who undertakes to deliver in the future a certain quantity of wheat at a certain price may not have in his possession the goods he sells; indeed, in the common course of such dealings in the modern markets, he usually does not have them. He gauges the probabilities of the future, and undertakes delivery on the terms which those probabilities suggest. Virtually, he guarantees a certain price for the future, and takes his chances as to whether the guarantee will bring him gain or loss. The buyer is then relieved of the risk. The advantage of this security is easily seen. The miller, for example, may wish to close a contract for the sale of flour in the future. By securing the needed wheat at a guaranteed price, he is freed from all the risk of ups and downs, and can give his undivided attention to his proper business of manufacturing flour.[1]

Hence it has happened, since the establishment of exchanges and the development of their varied operations, that millers carry on their business with a much smaller margin of profit than formerly. The difference in price, weight for weight, between wheat and flour, is much less than it was thirty or forty years ago, and the public gains in so far. When, for example, the flour-milling industry was first established at Minneapolis, — where the falls of the Mississippi supplied power for grinding the wheat of a region singularly adapted to its growth, — the possibility of profit for the miller was great. But he then underwent also the chances of loss from fluctuation in the price of wheat. As the exchanges developed, and with them

[1] Even if he is not contracting for the future sale of flour at a given price, but is simply manufacturing continuously for the market, he can escape by this same mechanism from the risk of fluctuations in the price of wheat. When he buys a given quantity of wheat to be ground into flour, he can sell for future delivery the same quantity of wheat. Thereafter, as wheat goes up or down, he loses as much by the one of these transactions as he gains by the other. The fluctuations no longer trouble him. This is the common practise among "conservative" millers. Cotton manufacturers also are getting more and more into the practise of thus "hedging" in their purchases of raw cotton.

the practise of dealing for future delivery, he was able to free himself from these chances. The consequent regularity and solidity of the industry contributed to its systematic development on a great scale, and so to the cheapening of flour. Inventions and improvements, no doubt, contributed greatly; but the elimination of market risks had an important share in reducing the difference between the price of wheat and the price of flour. Both in merchandizing and in manufacturing, the growth of large-scale transactions, though it has increased the gains of those individuals who have the ability to carry on large operations, has lessened the margin between buying price and selling price, and so has operated to lower prices for the consuming public.

The dealer or speculator who has sold for future delivery does not usually run all the risks of the transaction himself. He is likely before long to buy from another dealer, for future delivery, some part of what he has contracted to deliver, perhaps the whole; that other dealer, in turn, shifts part of the business to a third; and so on. The process of gauging the course of the market fluctuations is hardly ever carried through the whole of a season by one person for any one transaction. The dealers constantly buy and sell among themselves, and divide risks and profits and losses. It is extremely rare, consequently, that any one dealer or any one person buys at the lowest price of a season and sells at the highest price, making the utmost possible gain; or that any one buys at the highest and sells at the lowest price, incurring the maximum loss. Every dealer has losses as well as gains. On the whole, if he is shrewd and experienced, he gains more than he loses. He may lose money in one season, but he will make money in another, and in the long run he will earn something in the nature of a professional income. If he is gifted with unusual ability for such operations, he may make gains almost invariably, reap great profits from large transactions, and close his career with a fortune.

§ 3. When commodities are produced on a large scale for distant markets and for scattered purchasers, and middlemen become necessary links in the division of labor, it is inevitable that the middlemen should arrange to be near each other for the convenient disposal of their business. A street corner may serve as a meeting place. Traders in one commodity will settle near each other in a given street; hence in every great city there are dry goods streets, hardware streets, boot and shoe and leather streets, and so on. When, in a populous and thriving country, commodities are produced in large quantities and are necessarily dealt in by many persons, an exchange is set up,—a room or building where the traders meet at fixed hours. Rules are agreed on, governing and interpreting their transactions in such detail that enormous sales are effected by a nod of the head, and are recorded on scraps of paper with a few figures and initials. The actual dealings on exchanges are often done by brokers only, who are middlemen for the middlemen. They act simply as agents, earn their living by a commission (usually an extraordinarily small one) on sales and purchases, and buy or sell for any one who chooses to transact business through them.

The smooth dispatch of business on exchanges is further assisted by the "standardizing" of the articles dealt in; that is, by grading and classifying them according to quality. This process puts an end to all disputes regarding the quality of the things contracted for. Thus grain is examined, as it reaches the Chicago market, by publicly appointed inspectors, and is graded as being No. 1, No. 2, No. 3. Thereafter, when a purchaser has his wheat delivered to him, neither he nor his vendor need inquire further whether it is of the stipulated quality. Delivery of elevator receipts, certifying the grade, satisfies all contracts. Any article that is homogeneous in quality, or is easily classified into distinct grades, can thus be dealt in with the minimum of friction. Grain is the typical commodity of this sort. Cotton is similar to it, through its evenness of quality. Wool, which varies remarkably, is much less susceptible of rapid speculative purchase and sale. Attempts have been made to standardize iron, and in England a system of semi-official grading exists under which large transactions in it are carried on; but in the United States and on the Continent this mode of dealing in iron has never come into considerable use.

§ 4. Against the advantages which professional speculative dealings bring are to be set serious evils. These evils are made possible and are enhanced by the very facilities which enable speculation to work out its good effects.

When once a commodity has been standardized, a new possibility opens; anybody and everybody can deal in it. Ordinarily, he who buys an article must know something about it. He must be able to judge whether what is offered to him is good or bad in quality, worth more or less. But on an exchange where commodities are officially graded, no such questions arise. Only price, present and future, need be considered. Any one can buy if he thinks the present price low, or sell if he thinks it high. Such buying and selling are done, on an enormous scale, by large numbers of persons who do not possess or wish to possess the articles they buy or sell, and whose only concern is to make a profit by taking advantage of fluctuations in prices. They virtually bet on the future price of the commodities, and gamble about it as men gamble on cards or on horse races. In form, their dealings are like any others on the exchange. The brokers receive from these "outsiders" orders to buy and sell, and by the rules of the exchange are held responsible for delivery at the stipulated time. The brokers, in turn, hold their customers to this same responsibility. But, though thus in form like any other dealings, on the better-known exchanges, — the cotton and grain exchanges, for example, — the immense majority of the transactions have in view no *bona fide* business. The machinery which has been devised for the easy and rapid transaction of business is utilized for gambling on a large scale.

Here we have an example of unproductive labor. Of course, dealers, middlemen, brokers, are useful, and their labor is productive, so far as they serve to facilitate exchanges under an elaborate division of labor. Just how much labor can be usefully given to this sort of work, it would be difficult to say. If the only persons engaged in the transactions were merchants and dealers who systematically and continuously gave their time and effort to it, their number would adjust itself automatically to the work required, — much as the number of carpenters or physicians adjusts itself to actual needs. But where there is "illegitimate" speculation on a great scale, the number of brokers and dealers accommodates itself to this new demand for their services. Not only the labor of the speculators, but that of their agents, is unproductive; it adds nothing to the output of society. In no country is there so much of this parasitic activity as in the United States, for here all the conditions favorable to it are found, — a highly developed division of labor, markets and exchanges on a great scale, and a population both venturesome and prosperous. "Business" to many an American means simply speculative gambling.

Unquestionably, the "outside" speculators, or the "public," are, like all amateur gamblers, losers as a class; and most of them are in the long run losers individually. The shrewd and experienced professional dealers know better than they the probable course of prices, sell to them and buy from them to advantage, and on the whole make money from them. Occasionally an able or lucky person makes a hit, and carries off a large share of plunder from a successful operation on the exchange. This then acts on the imagination of others like a great prize won in a lottery. The chances that the speculative public will lose are almost as great as the chances that the purchasers of lottery tickets as a whole will lose: they amount almost to a certainty.

Unmistakable as are the evils of speculative gambling, it is exceedingly difficult to check them by legislation, still more to put an end to them. The common law already makes void transactions which are sales in form merely, and which contemplate a settlement only of the difference between present and future price. But on the exchanges all transactions purport to be, and in strict legal effect are, for the actual delivery of the commodities. An obvious remedial measure is to prohibit buying and selling for future delivery, since it is in connection with such contracts that the gambling operations most often take place. But this would put an end, also, to the benefits which the community gets from contracts for futures; and it is a question whether the loss would not outweigh the gain. The common opinion of American and English economists is against the prohibition of future contracts, which, so far as grain is concerned, has been put into effect in Germany. Yet the evils of speculative gambling are so great that something may be risked for the purpose of lessening them. Lotteries and avowed gambling houses have been prohibited, and the law does its utmost to prevent wholesale betting on horse races; and all it can do to stamp out other forms of gambling is welcome. No doubt, the most effective remedy would be a better moral standard for all industry, and an aroused public opinion against all kinds of gambling. But the worship of wealth, and the well-nigh universal desire to make money on easy terms, even though at the expense of others, together with the close association of this sort of speculation with business dealing rightly deemed legitimate, render it difficult to bring public opinion to bear.

§ 5. What has been said in the preceding sections applies in the main to stock exchange speculation also; but the problems appear here in accentuated form. Here, too, advantages are to be set against evils. The advantages, it is true, are of a different sort from those secured by grain and cotton exchanges. They arise, not from the lessening of fluctuations or the facilitation of large-scale dealings, but from the promotion of investment.[1] They are real and important. But the evils are no less real, and are intensified by the unusual ease of entering on the transactions. Stock exchange securities are ideally homogeneous and standardized. One share of a given corporation's stock is precisely as good as any other share. If it is easy for any one to buy

[1] See Book I, Chapter 6.

grain or cotton, even though he has never looked at the articles, it is still easier for any one to buy stocks and bonds, even though he knows nothing about the corporation that issues them. At the same time, fluctuations in the prices of securities are large and frequent. Opinion regarding their probable course depends (or seems to depend) quite as much on general judgment and general prospects as on expert information. Hence rampant speculation, by outsiders and insiders. Here, as in the case of commodity speculation, the "public" loses in the immense majority of transactions. The professional speculators and dealers get the advantage of the miscellaneous public, both because they are better informed regarding the real prospects of the enterprises whose securities are dealt in, and because they are (by a process of quasi-natural selection) persons shrewd in judging human nature and quick to take advantage of the irresolute. Yet notwithstanding the constant losses, there is an unfailing stream of persons who take fliers on the stock exchanges. There are probably few Americans of the well-to-do classes who have not at one time or another tried their hands at a stock speculation; and there are a great many who habitually gamble in stocks. The immense majority of these dealings are concentrated at the New York Stock Exchange, which is at once the greatest institution in the world for facilitating investment and the greatest of gambling hells.

The evil from the situation arises not only or chiefly from the losses of the unsuccessful speculators. What these lose, others gain, and usually there is not much to choose between winners and losers. The economic loss arises primarily from the waste of much brains and energy on unproductive doings. The waste is more than that of the labor given directly, — the labor of the brokers and their under-strappers, and of the speculators themselves. It is increased by the demoralization of many men in the community who take no great direct share in speculation. Like all gambling, it distracts from the sober, continuous work on which the common welfare rests. Morally, it is no less harmful. In every aspect the evil is one of the greatest in contemporary society.

It must be frankly confessed that no really promising remedies have been suggested. Some excrescences have been aimed at in recent proposals for reform in New York — proposals which look to improvement through the revision and enforcement of the rules made by the exchanges for themselves. Such things as rigging of the market, "wash sales," manipulation of prices with intent to deceive, are to be thus prevented. But even if all of these tricks were cut out, the main evil would remain. In Germany a more drastic remedy has been tried, — the requirement of publicity in stock dealings, through enrollment of names and transactions on a register open to general inspection. It is expected that men will refrain from stock gambling, as they will from many doings of doubtful aspect, if they must be seen in the act. Such a requirement would be met in the United States by the objection that it intrudes on the sacrosanct secrecy of business, an objection commonly brought against public supervision of every sort, yet in itself of little weight. Much more serious is the objection that in Germany the regulation has in fact had little effect: stock speculation has remained much the same in character and amount. Possibly this is because of the difficulty of effective enforcement. At all events, though the evil is there, no clear remedy of a direct sort is in sight. Greater regularity of all industry would lessen fluctuation in values, and so lessen speculation; but this would be at the cost of progress. Better public opinion would lessen "outside" speculation; but the enlightenment of public opinion proceeds very slowly.

CHAPTER 12

VALUE UNDER CONSTANT COST

§ 1. In the preceding chapter, the adjustment of value was considered under the supposition that supply was fixed; fixed, not indeed for the day or the week, nor rigidly over any length of time, but fixed on the whole for the season or the period of production. But even for the agricultural commodities whose production is seasonal, there is variation in supply over a series of seasons. For other commodities there is clearly a considerable and sometimes rapid flexibility in supply. The amount produced and put on the market changes more or less easily. In what way do the variations in supply take place, and in what way do they affect the value of commodities?

We may begin by taking the simplest case, and, for the purpose of bringing into sharp relief a principle, make again an extreme supposition. In the preceding discussion of demand and supply and of market value, an absolutely fixed supply was assumed at the outset. Let now the other extreme be assumed, a supply absolutely flexible. Suppose a commodity produced, under the simplest conditions, by a large number of persons. Suppose that all these persons are competing with each other; that any one of them can easily engage in producing the commodity, and as easily withdraw from producing it. Suppose all to be carrying on operations under the same conditions, no one of them producing more cheaply than another. Such a commodity would be brought to market under conditions of constant cost, and would be sold at a price conforming to that cost. At any moment its value would indeed be determined directly by its quantity, — that is, by marginal utility as analyzed in the last three chapters. But if its value, so determined, were greater than its cost, more persons would be led to engage in its production, supply would increase, and value would fall. If its value at any time were less than its cost, some persons would withdraw from its production, supply would decrease, and value would rise. The greater the ease of entering on the industry and of withdrawing from it, the more rapid and certain would be the adjustment of supply to that amount which would just sell at cost price. If perfect flexibility in supply be assumed, the adjustment of value to cost would be perfect, and the article would always sell for just what it cost to produce it.

Before proceeding further, a word of explanation, and in some ways of warning, is needed, as to the sense in which cost of production is here spoken of. The term is used in very nearly the ordinary commercial sense; it refers to the outlays which an employing capitalist must make in order to get a commodity to market. Chief among those is the outlay for the wages. Charges for material are another item. These charges, it is true, commonly imply that another capitalist has previously paid laborers to make the materials, which then have been sold to the particular employer in question; hence the latter may be said to have indirectly hired these other laborers also. Not only the wages paid to workmen, directly or indirectly, must be included, but a reasonable remuneration for the employer's own time and trouble. This remuneration, like that of the workmen employed, is to be reckoned according to current market standards, — what a workman or an employer of this kind would ordinarily receive for his labor. Again, interest on the capital used is to be included, reckoned also according to the current market rate. If the employer borrows the capital, he must pay the current rate of interest on it. If he owns his capital, he considers that he could get a return on it at that rate by lending it out to some one else; and he regards interest on his own capital precisely as he regards remuneration for his own labor, — something for which a return at the usual rate is to be expected. It will be noticed that rent paid for land is not included in this enumeration, although a business man would include it in his reckoning of cost. The reasons for this omission will be made plain when the subject of rent comes up for consideration.

These various outlays, or equivalents of outlay, are sometimes spoken of as "expenses of production." When that term is used and is distinguished from "cost of production," emphasis is laid on the fact that the employing capitalist is concerned solely with what he pays for labor, for materials, for the use of free or fixed capital. When, on the other hand, the term cost of production is used so as to imply a distinction from expenses of production, reference is made to the sacrifices undergone; to the labor of the hired workman, and not to his wages; to the trouble, anxiety, and work of superintendence of the employer, not to his profits or ordinary gains; to the previous saving by which the capital has been accumulated, not to the interest on that capital. As will be seen at a later stage, some of the most important and difficult problems of economics connect themselves with the distinction between cost of production in the sense of labor and sacrifice, and expenses of production in the sense of outlays.[1] For the present, however, we need not do more than point out the distinction, in order to make clear in what sense we are speaking of cost. We mean by it outlays of a capitalist. If we should think of a workman, or set of workmen, producing independently and without being hired by employers, we should reckon cost of production for them, not in terms of hours or days of work (*i.e.* sacrifice), but in terms of the wages they would ordinarily get for their work.

§ 2. The mode in which value would be adjusted under the conditions of constant cost and absolutely flexible supply is indicated on Figure 5. The cost of the commodity is indicated by *SO*, the distance from the horizontal axis *OX* to the line *SS'*. Whatever the amount of the commodity produced, that cost remains the same for each unit brought to market; whether the quantity be *OA*, *OB*, *OC*, the cost per unit is the same. Hence *SS'*, indicating the conditions of supply, runs parallel to *OX*. Let the line *DD'* indicate the conditions of demand, as in pre-

[1] See Book V, Chapter 48.

vious diagrams. It descends as quantity becomes greater, price falling with the increase in supply and the consequent lessening of marginal utility. The supply of the commodity would then settle at the amount OB or SB'. The demand and supply lines

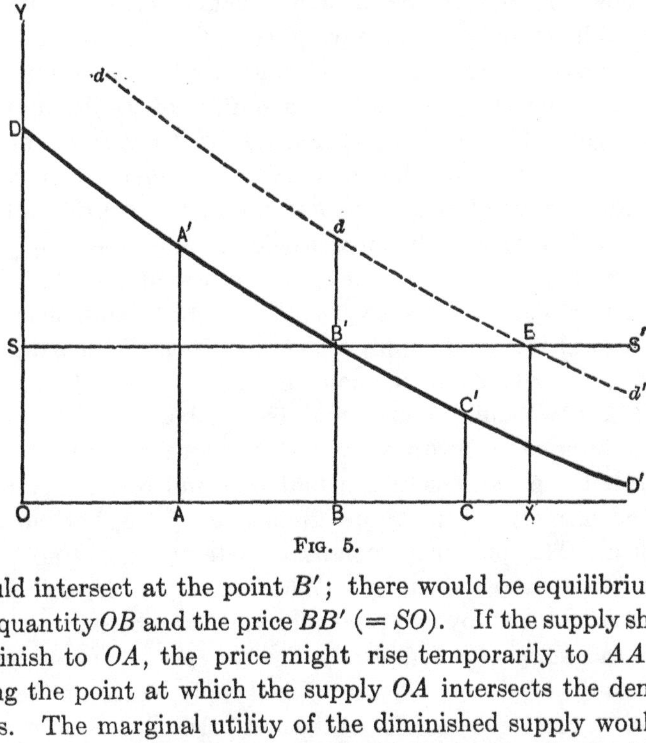

FIG. 5.

would intersect at the point B'; there would be equilibrium at the quantity OB and the price BB' ($= SO$). If the supply should diminish to OA, the price might rise temporarily to AA', A' being the point at which the supply OA intersects the demand lines. The marginal utility of the diminished supply would be raised to AA'; the smaller supply (OA) would sell at a higher price. But that higher price would lead, under the conditions of constant cost, to a prompt increase in supply. Producers would be getting more than sufficed to induce them to bring the commodity to market. They would compete with each other, increase supply, and so bring down price. If the supply should be increased, not only to B, but to C, the total being then OC, they would overreach themselves. For the amount OC, the price would be CC', the point of intersection with the demand line being then C'. This sum (CC') is less than cost; some producers would promptly withdraw; supply would again diminish. For the quantity *OB*, the price is just sufficient to make production worth while to all, and at that amount the supply would settle.

If now for any reason demand should increase, quantity would so increase as still to leave price at the same point. Suppose a change in fashion, or other cause leading to an increased demand. This is represented by a shifting of the demand line to the right. It is now *dd'*, whereas before it was *DD'*; at each several price, more of the commodity is demanded than was demanded before at that price, and the marginal utility of any given supply is greater than it was before. With the supply *OB*, the price, under these new conditions of demand, would be not *BB'*, but *BB'd*, — higher than cost. Supply would again increase, until the total supply was *OX*. Then the demand line would be intersected at the point *E* and price would be *XE* = *BB'*. A new equilibrium would be established, not with a change in price, but with a change in quantity supplied.

Under the conditions of constant cost and free competition, demand or marginal utility determines not price, but quantity supplied. The proximate condition determining value is indeed always marginal utility. Where supply is fixed, price is settled once for all by marginal utility. But where cost is constant and supply is completely flexible, price cannot depart far from the level fixed by cost. The supply on the market will be such as can be disposed of at the cost price.

§ 3. The assumptions made at the beginning of this chapter — constant cost, flexible supply, free competition — are never, in a literal sense, in conformity with the facts of industry. There never is a case when these conditions are exactly fulfilled. None the less, there is a wide range of industry in which an approximation toward their fulfillment is found, and in which the principle of value under constant cost explains the broad facts.

Cost is never exactly equal for all producers. In this chapter, constant cost has been spoken of; but it is not material whether we speak of constant or of equal cost, if changes in the general level take place simultaneously for all the producers. An invention or improvement may lower cost for all; the horizontal supply line on the diagram may be lowered; but the result is merely adjustment to a new level, not the introduction of a new set of conditions. If, however, the lowering of cost takes place not at the same time for all the producers, nor in equal degrees, we have a new principle and a different case, — production at varying cost. This is what in fact happens when inventions bring about a reduction in cost. The change takes place by successive steps. The more shrewd and enterprising of the competitors introduce the improvements first; others follow suit; gradually all adopt it. And by the time all have adopted one improvement, another may be introduced, and the same steps are again gone through. If there be a succession of changes, — and such are likely in the highly progressive modern industries, — equality of cost never exists. There are always some producers who are turning out their goods at lower cost than others.

None the less, there is, over probably the greater part of the industrial field, a tendency to equality of cost. The differences in cost are not permanent; the process is simply one of gradual and irregular adjustment to the new level, instead of prompt and even adjustment.

Some writers have stated the difference between actual conditions and long-run tendencies, by distinguishing between a static and a dynamic state. In a static state competition has worked out its full result, and, unless there are permanent causes of variation, commodities of the class here considered are produced at a uniform cost and always sold at a price corresponding precisely to that cost. In a dynamic state, there is flux and change, variation in cost, oscillation of price. Yet the dynamic state tends to subside into the static. Unless there be incessant reappearance of disturbing forces, the dynamic state will cease.

The real problem is thus not whether price is in strict conformity to a cost of production uniform for all competitors, but whether there is rough approximation to this situation and a tendency toward its full attainment in a static state. And such a tendency, to repeat, exists over a very large part, probably the larger part of the field of industry. A comparison has often been made to the tendency of the ocean to keep its level. Tides, currents, storms, cause disturbances, and it is never true in a literal sense that the level is maintained; none the less, there is a normal level, and the actual height of the water tends to conform to it. Or a comparison might be made to the tendency of the air to maintain a certain pressure. This pressure (measured by the barometer) is said to be 29.9 inches at sea level. In fact, it may be more or less, and rarely does the barometer stand precisely at the normal figure. None the less, it oscillates about that figure, and tends to return to it. At any height above sea level, there will again be oscillations, with a different range, and with a tendency to return to the new normal figure.

§ 4. By way of illustration and explanation, some of the disturbing causes may be briefly considered.

Most universal, perhaps, is lack of flexibility in supply. There never is complete ease of variation, such as to bring about the steady accommodation of supply to the precise quantity which will sell at the cost price. Even under the simplest conditions of handicraft production, there is no such flexibility. As plant and machinery become more important, every considerable change in output involves time and expense. Though there is some flexibility in the output from an existing plant, it does not go far. Any considerable increase in supply involves the making of new plant, and any considerable decrease involves the abandonment of some of the old. Changes of this sort, involving a readjustment of the preliminary investment, not only take place slowly, but are much affected by vague general sentiment. Business men, not much less than others, go with the crowd. When the belief gets abroad that such and such an industry is "a good thing," they flock into it with no very careful calculation. On the other hand, when affairs go ill, it is with reluctance that existing plants shut down.

When the signs of increasing demand show themselves, new plants are at first constructed slowly and hesitatingly; then, at the later stages of a sustained increase, with uncalculating excess. Hence the oscillations of modern industry, often affecting many trades at once, and bringing in their train industrial crises.

The prices of things subject to rapid changes in demand are especially fluctuating, even though they be produced under conditions approximating those of constant cost. Almost all textile goods that are used for outer garments are affected by the caprices of fashion. For textiles worn by women, the changes in the demand are extraordinary. The stuff which is for the moment in fashion cannot be turned out as fast as the women want it; while that which was in fashion but a year ago can hardly be sold at any price. Amid such sharp changes in demand, supply cannot be easily accommodated, and the conformity of price to cost works itself out only as a rough sort of average.

The conformity of price to cost depends, of course, on the free competition of producers. So far as there is combination or monopoly, it does not work itself out. One of the most uncertain problems of modern industry is the extent of monopolistic combination, — combinations so effective that there is no longer even an approximate determination of price by cost. Large scale production tends to limit the number of individual competitors, and facilitates monopoly conditions. But the change in this direction, striking as it has been in the last half century, has not gone so far as to displace competition over more than a limited range of industries.[1] Over the greater part of the economic field competition is still in force, though often irregularly and spasmodically, and the tendency is still for the prices of things to conform to their cost.

An important obstacle to the play of competition sometimes arises from custom and good will, — from brands, labels, trade-marks. Where producers and consumers are separated

[1] Compare Book I, Chapter 4; and Book VII, Chapter 63.

by a long chain of intermediaries, the consumers often look to some external and familiar mark in deciding which among competing products they will select. Hence the immense part played by advertising. It is a familiar saying in business circles that it pays to advertise a good article. Certainly it pays, and sometimes pays enormously, to create and maintain good will. He who has induced many people to get into the way of buying a particular brand, may sell at a price higher than that of his competitors, or sell in greater volume and with more steadiness. No doubt this sort of advantage does not come by accident. It is slowly created by shrewdness, patience, persistence. The profitableness of a trade-mark is due at the outset to the business ability of some individual, and connects itself with questions, to be considered later, concerning the variations of gains among individual business men. In fact, the whole problem of competition and cost is a fundamental one; it ramifies into all parts of economics; and all its aspects can be taken up only step by step as we proceed.

Where production is on a large scale, a very slight difference in price, or change in price, may make a great difference in profit. In railway operations, an extra twentieth of a cent in the charge per ton per mile may mean millions of dollars in revenue. In sugar refining, an extra tenth of a cent per pound on refined sugar means the difference between moderate gains and great gains. What is thus true of a difference in price, is, of course, true of a difference in expenses: he who saves a tenth or twentieth of a cent per unit of output is on the way to fortune. Many of the great combinations which are supposed to make vast monopoly profits, and which in fact make unusual profits, do so by a very small margin. Price exceeds cost by only a fraction, but profits exceed the normal amount by a large total.

Those staple articles which are used regularly from year to year in much the same quantities are sold at comparatively even prices, which are surprisingly close to constant (*i.e.* uniform) costs. So it is with flour, with the ordinary kinds of cotton cloths and of boots and shoes. Here are businesses of cents: a fraction more or less means the difference between profit and loss. An able business manager, quick to introduce all improvements, will be turning out his goods at a cost lower by only a trifle than that of his competitors; or, having succeeded in making a reputation for a particular sort of shoe or a particular brand of cloth, he may get a price a trifle higher than others get. By either slight differential advantage he will make large profits. Other things are commonly sold with a wider "margin of profit" — *i.e.* a wider difference between expense per unit and selling price — because there is more risk, more irregularity, more balancing of possible losses against the expected rates of gain.

All these things need to be taken into account when it is said that price is governed by cost of production, — a proposition which, to repeat, holds good only as a statement of a tendency, of an approximation to what would happen in a "static" state.

CHAPTER 13

Value and Varying Costs. Diminishing Returns

§ 1. Let us suppose now that the several producers who compete with each other in putting a given article on the market have not the same facilities; that for some of them the expenses of production are greater than for others. We need

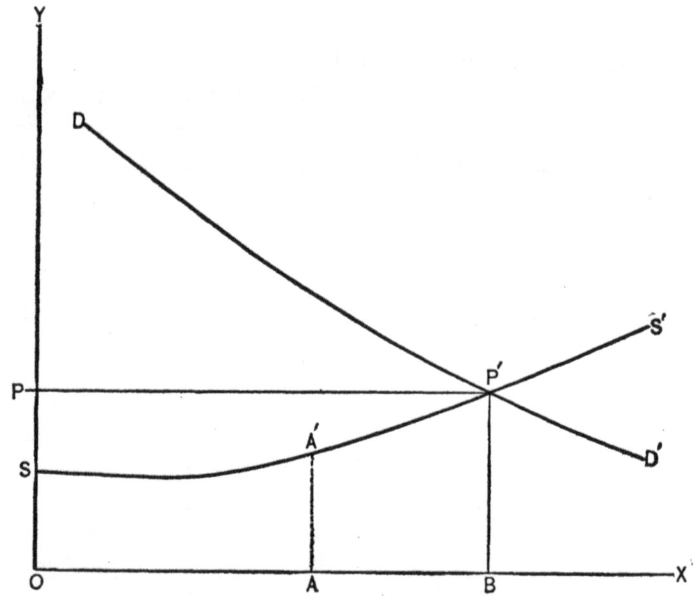

Fig. 6.

not concern ourselves for the present with the question why there are such differences. Let us assume them to exist, and consider what consequences follow.

The situation is illustrated by the diagram. The conditions of demand are again indicated by the descending line DD'. The conditions of supply are indicated by the rising line SS'.

The varying distance from the horizontal axis *OY* to the line *SS′* measures the varying cost of different installments of the supply. Some producers — those most favorably equipped — can put the commodity on the market at the comparatively low cost *OS*. Perhaps a certain moderate quantity can be so produced at constant cost. If the conditions of demand were such that only this moderate quantity were wanted at the constant cost price, — if the demand curve were to intersect the supply curve somewhere near *S*, — the normal price would be *OS*. So far the case would be identical with that studied in the preceding chapter. But now the conditions of demand, as indicated by the line *DD′*, are such that a much greater quantity is wanted at the price *OS* than can be furnished at that price. The supply put on the market increases, but as it increases, additional installments can no longer be produced at the cost *OS*. With the quantity *OA*, for example, the cost of the last installment reaches *AA′*. As more is produced, cost still increases, indicated by the continuing ascent of the supply curve from *A′* to *P′*. At *P′* finally the demand curve is met. At the price *BP′* (=*OP*) the quantity *OB* can be disposed of. Equilibrium is established; the quantity demanded equals the quantity supplied; and price settles at the amount BP′.

The whole supply will be sold at the price *OP* (= *BP*); and the selling value of the whole, *i.e.* the quantity multiplied by the price, will be indicated by the rectangle *OPP′B*. It is true that the more fortunate producers could sell the commodity to advantage at a less price. At the price *OS* or *AA′* they would still find it worth while to bring it to market. But the total quantity which will meet the demand at an equilibrium price cannot be supplied unless producers less fortunate contribute their quota. These will not do so unless they get their higher cost price *BP′*. At that price the whole supply will be disposed of. The more favorably situated producers will get the price necessary to induce their rivals, who have poorer facilities, to contribute to the supply.

We may speak of the producers at *B*, whose cost of production is BP', as the marginal producers. Their cost price is also the measure of the marginal utility of the commodity. Marginal cost and marginal utility thus coincide; and when they coincide, there is equilibrium. If the quantity supplied should increase beyond B, in the direction of Y, marginal utility would be less, and marginal cost would be greater. Supply could not long be maintained beyond the point B, for producers would then be receiving less than cost. So long as the conditions of demand and supply remained as indicated by the lines DD' or SS', price would settle at the amount BP'.

The relation of demand and supply to value is somewhat different here from what it was in the cases discussed in the preceding chapters. Where the supply of a commodity is fixed (the case which underlies the reasoning of Chapter 10), the value of a commodity is settled by the conditions of demand; that is, by the marginal utility of that supply. Where, on the other hand, the cost of a freely produced commodity is fixed (the case discussed in Chapter 12), the value of the commodity is settled by the conditions of supply; that is, by cost. Demand in this case determines, in the long run, only the quantity which shall be put on the market. But in the case now under consideration, the conditions of demand and of supply both have a permanent influence in settling price. As the quantity shifts, not only does marginal utility vary, but marginal cost. A lessening of demand would not only lessen the quantity put on the market, but would also lessen marginal cost. Conversely, an increase of demand would not only cause more to be put on the market, but would also raise normal price, since the additional quantity would be produced at greater cost. Hence demand and supply — marginal utility and cost — mutually determine normal price.

The economist who has best set forth the general theory of value, Professor Marshall, has ingeniously compared the influence of demand and supply to the working of a pair of scissors. If one blade of a pair of scissors is held still, and the other moves, we may say that the second does the cutting.

Yet it could not cut unless the other blade were there. So when supply is fixed, we may say that demand settles value; yet it does so only because supply is there and does not move. When cost is constant, we may say that cost settles value. Yet it does so only because there is a demand for the commodity, and because supply readily adjusts itself to the amount which will be demanded at the cost price. If cost is variable in the manner discussed in the present chapter, both supply and demand — both cost and utility — exercise a mutual influence on normal price. Both blades of the scissors are in motion. All the various manifestations of value (under the conditions of an advanced division of labor and of exchange flowing from that division) can be analyzed as interactions of supply and demand. Neither can be said to settle value independently of the other.

§ 2. The differences in advantage between producers may be due to permanent or to temporary causes. According as they are temporary or permanent, they are of very different significance for the theory of value and for the welfare of society.

Differences of a temporary sort are the most common. They are so common that they may be said in one sense to be universal. As indicated in the last chapter, it probably never happens in communities familiar to us, that all those engaged in a given industry are carrying on their operations in the same way. Some have better plant, better organization, better location, than others; can bring their products to market at less expense; and, selling at the same price, can reap larger gains.

But these differences, if their causes are not permanent, tend constantly to disappear. If one man has better plant or machinery than another, and if there be no permanent reason why the second should not also set up the better outfit, he is likely sooner or later to do so. If he does not do so, he is likely to be driven out of the market. Others will adopt the more effective method of production, will increase the quantity they put on the market, and will be able to undersell him without foregoing a profit. Where the methods of cheapened production are open to all, they are sure sooner or later to be adopted by all.

We say, sooner or later; for the process takes time, especially when changes in the arts are rapid. The civilized world has been for generations in a dynamic state. More or less temporary causes of differences are constantly appearing, disappearing, and reappearing. At any given time, the usual conditions are not those of uniform cost, but of varying cost.

But under these conditions value cannot be said to be determined by marginal cost of production. Value is always determined proximately by the marginal utility of the supply. Given the total supply that comes on the market, — whether put on in large sudden doses, or by gradual increments, — and the price will be such that the whole is sold. For the marginal producer this price may or may not be equal at any given time to cost. With the oscillations of demand, and the various causes of nonadjustment to normal conditions which were considered in the preceding chapter, the season's price may be such as to make the marginal producer prosperous, or such as to make him a bankrupt. If he becomes prosperous, his more enterprising and successful rivals, the infra-marginal producers, become even more so, and are tempted to extend their operations. If he is on the way to bankruptcy, they may yet be able to hold their own. In time, he disappears, and his better-equipped or better-situated rivals supplant him. In time, too, it is cost of production at their hands which acts on supply, and thus acts on price. In other words, disregarding temporary and seasonal fluctuations, the principle of constant cost regulates long-run value where there are non-permanent differences between rival producers. In such a case, it is cost of production at the hands of the more capable and better-equipped producers, not cost of production at the hands of the marginal producer, that settles the long-run price as distinguished from the market price.[1]

[1] Compare what is said in Book V, Chapter 50, §§ 1, 2.

The situation is otherwise where there are permanent causes of difference between producers. Then cost at the hands of the marginal producer does settle the long-run price. The point about which oscillations range, and to which price tends to conform, is cost for the least advantageous producer. Without him, the total supply cannot be enlarged to the point at which there is an equilibrium of normal supply and demand. If there were no limit to the amount which the more advantageous producers could bring to market, — if this fortunate set of producers could increase the output indefinitely at constant cost, — the marginal producer would be driven out, and the conditions would be those of constant cost. There being such a limit, he must be called on for the maintenance of supply, and there must be in the long run a price which will make it worth his while to contribute. Value is then determined in the long run by cost to the marginal producer; but at what point in the varying scale of costs that producer will be, depends on the conditions of demand.

§ 3. Instead of speaking of varying cost, or increasing cost, we may speak of diminishing returns.

Increasing cost and diminishing returns are opposite aspects of the same tendency. Looking again at the diagram, we may see that the marginal producer at *B* has, for the same addition to the supply, greater expenses than the better-situated producers at *A* and *O*. As the quantity put on the market increases along the axis *OY*, cost for every fresh installment becomes greater. With every proportional increase in outlay, there is a less addition to the supply, — a tendency to diminishing return.

It matters not whether we say that the tendency to diminishing return is felt by the infra-marginal producers themselves, or by those whom we have regarded as the marginal producers. It is felt by both. There is an increase of cost as supply increases, and the price must be such as to make the increased cost worth while. Those who are better situated may find, as they try to enlarge their contribution to the supply, that they cannot do so on the same relatively easy terms as for the earlier installments: they encounter diminishing returns. Or this same difficulty may be met by others who add to the supply. Given the tendency, the result remains that normal price settles at the point of cost of production for the last increment. It would be more accurate, therefore, to speak of the marginal product or marginal increment, than of the marginal producer, as fixing the long-run price.

Though we use the term "cost" in this series of chapters in the sense of outlays by a capitalist, and measure increasing cost by the increase in outlays as additional supplies are brought to market, the cause of this rising cost is commonly an increase of cost in the other sense, — cost in terms of labor, exertion, sacrifice, or disability.[1] When additional supplies of a commodity bring permanently greater expense to the producing capitalist, this result is usually due to the fact that more labor is required or a greater volume of capital is called for, *i.e.* more saving by those who furnish the capital. The distinction between expenses of production and cost in the sense of labor and sacrifice, though it will be found of great significance for some problems, is not important here. Where expense increases permanently for successive additions to supply, — where returns diminish in proportion to outlay, — we have also diminishing returns in the sense that the same labor yields a lessening output. That part of the theory of value which we are considering in this chapter has its foundation mainly in some unalterable conditions in the world about us: in the fact that nature enables labor to be applied less advantageously under some conditions than under others, and that the continued application of labor on even the most advantageous sites meets sooner or later a tendency to diminishing return.

§ 4. In what circumstances, and over how great a range of industries, do we find varying cost, or diminishing returns? In general, differences in cost are permanent in the extractive industries, — in agriculture, forestry, mining.

In agriculture, good land yields more to labor than land less

[1] See Chapter 12, § 1.

good. The prairies of Illinois are more fertile than the stony fields of New England, and the black earth of Russia than the sandy soil of Brandenburg. All the climatic factors — such as sunshine, precipitation, the length of the seasons — have their influence, as well as the physical and chemical constitution of the soil. Of these and their effects we shall have occasion to say more at a later stage; it suffices here to emphasize the obvious fact that there are differences.[1]

Not only are there such differences, but there is further an unmistakable tendency to diminishing returns on any plot of land. The amount of produce which can be obtained from the best land is limited; and the amount which can be obtained from that land under the best conditions is limited. By applying more labor and capital, it is usually possible to add to the produce from a given piece of land; but it is not possible to get more produce in proportion to the addition of labor and capital. Hence there are permanent differences, not only between different soils, but between the successive applications of labor and capital on the same soil. So agricultural production presents typically the application of the principle of value which we are now considering.

In forests, likewise, there are obvious differences of the same sort. Some are better than others. Advantage in location and accessibility plays no less a part than advantage in the size and character of the timber; yet either kind of advantage counts. Mines present differences of an analogous kind; they are affected both by accessibility to the market and intrinsic productiveness. Both forests and mines have industrial peculiarities, especially in their development during very modern times; but of both, the general conditions of varying cost and diminishing returns hold good.

In manufacturing industries, which shape and transform the materials brought out by the extractive industries, the principle of diminishing returns is applicable in less degree. But, though the differences in cost between competing producers are commonly

[1] See Book V, Chapter 42.

of the transitional or "dynamic" sort, they sometimes have permanent causes. One manufacturer may have more water power than others, or an unequaled site on a harbor front. In the earlier days of the development of power and machinery, a first-rate water power was of great advantage. Later, steam largely superseded water power; partly because of the great advances in the efficiency and economy of steam engines, partly because they could be set up at any desired place, and so permitted better access to markets or to materials. In recent years the generation and transmission of electric power has again made falling water more important, and may prove the cause of enduring differences in the effectiveness of manufacturing establishments. In the main, however, the poorer establishments do not maintain themselves indefinitely side by side with the better. They are steadily displaced by the better, and these by the still better. The causes of difference are not as permanent, nor do they affect so many branches of production, as in the extractive industries.

CHAPTER 14

VALUE AND INCREASING RETURNS

§ 1. In the preceding chapter the theory of value was applied to the conditions of increasing cost or diminishing returns. We turn now to the reverse conditions, those of diminishing cost or increasing returns.

Suppose that, as additional supplies of a commodity are produced, the cost of each unit becomes not greater, but less. Such a tendency is represented in the Figure 7 where line *SS′*, indicating the conditions of supply, has a downward slope. The line *DD′*, representing the conditions of demand, necessarily has a downward slope, indicating the diminishing utility of successive increments. Equilibrium will be reached at the point

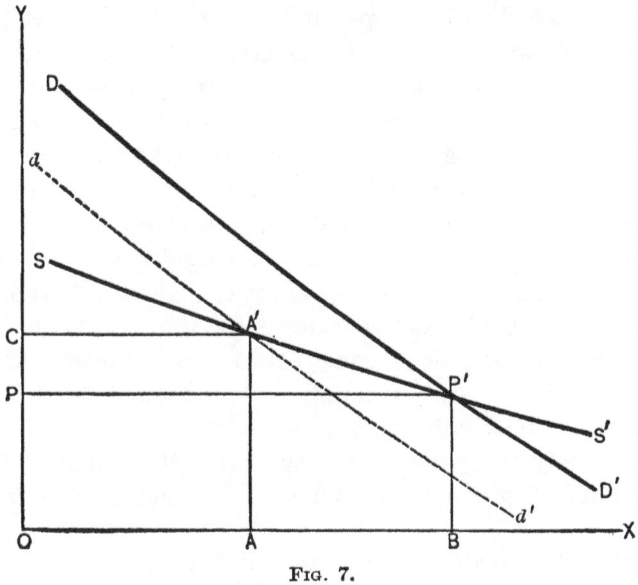

FIG. 7.

where the two curves meet, at *P'*. At that point the quantity brought to market sells at the price *BP'*, which equals its cost of production. The total quantity put on the market will normally be *OB*, and its total selling price will be *OPP'B*.

It is to be observed that this figure represents a situation different in essential respects from that represented in Figure 6 in the preceding chapter. In that case some among the competing producers were supposed to contribute to the supply at less cost than others. They reaped a producer's surplus. In the present case, however, all producers are on the same plane; all have the advantage of lessening cost and increasing returns. No portion of the supply continues to be produced at a cost different from the marginal cost. With the supply *OB*, for example, the cost per unit of the commodity is *BP'* for each and every producer. If for any reason the supply should be reduced, cost for each unit would be greater. Suppose, for example, that demand should decline, the demand curve shifting to the left, to *dd'*, so as to intersect the supply curve at *A'*. The quantity normally supplied would then be *OA*, selling at the price *AA'*. All producers would find their cost per unit higher than when the quantity supplied was *OB*; for *AA'* is greater than *BP'*. But at neither price would there be differences between producers. Total cost and total selling value in either case would be represented by parallelograms; at the price *AA'* by the area *OAA'C*, and at the price *BP'* by the area *OPP'B*. There is no such phenomenon as surplus gain to any producer.

This case differs, again, from that considered in the latter part of Chapter 12. There the effect of a general lowering of the supply schedule was considered, on the supposition that the reduction was due to some extraneous cause not directly connected with increase in supply. Here the reduction is supposed to be directly due to such an increase: the mere fact of greater supply brings a decline in cost per unit of supply. Cost, uniform for all producers, becomes less for each as more is produced.

All these three cases, on the other hand, are alike, in that long-run results are considered. Uniformity of costs, and the automatic decline in cost for all producers with increasing supply, never are found in industry. Where the conditions are favorable for a general decline in cost, some producers, as we have seen, take advantage of them more promptly than others; and so long as this "dynamic" situation continues, we have a lowering of cost for some producers, but not for all. This situation, however, will not endure: those who do not avail themselves of the improvements are underbid and driven from the market, and the "static" state of uniform cost is approached. The case would be different if those who had the better facilities were not subject to competition from others on even terms, and could not themselves increase their output indefinitely at lower cost. With such a limitation to their advantages, we should have precisely the case of varying costs, as discussed in the preceding chapter. Here cost is supposed to be uniform, but not constant, — it becomes less per unit as the number of units increases. The long-run result is an interaction of demand and supply; both blades of the scissors are cutting.

§ 2. What now are the industries in which there is a tendency to increasing return, and what are the causes of this tendency?

The first question is comparatively easy to answer. The tendency appears in manufacturing, in transportation, in mining, — in all the industries in which we have seen the tendency to large-scale production. In agriculture, though it sometimes appears as a passing phase, it is not ordinarily found at all; and the same is true of systematic forestry. The greater the extent to which plant and machinery can be used, the more concentrated the industry and the smaller the area on which a given volume of production can be turned out, the more probable is the tendency to lessening cost and increasing return.

The second question calls for some discrimination. Increasing returns may be due to external economies or to internal economies, — again phrases suggested by Professor Marshall, and pointing to forces different in character and effect. Further, increasing returns may be due to changes in the arts, or may take place even without them. It is not always easy to separate those causes of increasing return which act under static conditions from those which act under conditions of progress in the arts. Yet it will make the subject clearer if at the outset we take up the two cases independently.

First, consider external economies. These are such as arise outside of the establishment which gains thereby in efficiency and in diminution of cost. An example at once simple and typical is the diminution in cost of machinery and adjuncts, as these are made in larger quantities. The more cotton mills there are, and the more machinery they use, the larger the scale on which the machinery itself can be made. As the machinery becomes cheaper the expenses of the cotton manufacturer become less. Again, the construction of large steel ships in the United States is now carried on for a much smaller tonnage than in Great Britain. Consequently various adjuncts needed for ships, — compasses, capstans, winches, donkey-engines, sundry vessel fittings — are called for in much larger quantity in Great Britain, are systematically and uniformly made on a larger scale, and are cheaper for the shipbuilder. These external economies would indeed be at the disposal of the American shipbuilder if he could buy such things in Great Britain without restriction. But the United States imposes on them a heavy customs duty. Within the country, they are made in less quantity than in Great Britain; indeed, often they have to be made separately for each ship. Whether procured from abroad or at home, they are therefore dearer. In consequence, the shipbuilder finds this item of expense greater than it would be if ships were built in large numbers in the United States. Still another example is in the boot and shoe manufacture. When this is carried on extensively, and especially when a number of establishments are in the same locality, subsidiary industries arise which supply cheaply the special tools, materials, and fittings, — the shoestrings, eyes, metal fittings, the paper boxes for packing, not to mention the machinery. The gain in external economies of this sort is one of the reasons for the concentration of an industry in a given place; of shoe manufacturing in Brockton and Lynn, of silk manufacturing in Paterson, of cotton manufacturing in Lowell and Fall River, of metal wares in Bridgeport. In every such place the factories, merely because of their number, command resources and economies which an isolated establishment finds hard to secure.

An important gain of this sort comes from the presence of a large experienced labor force. In almost every establishment the workmen are more or less shifting. The changes are more frequent in industries exposed to seasonal fluctuations, as the boot and shoe manufacture is, or to irregularities in demand, as in the case of establishments making machinery. They are less frequent where steady wants are supplied by staples, as in the soap manufacture, and where long-established businesses are conducted by firms of settled prestige. In many ways they are unfortunate, yet seem to be an inevitable outcome not only of the variations in demand for labor and its supply, but of the monotony of factory labor. Certain it is that workmen come and go, and new men must be found to replace those who leave. They are more likely to be found in manufacturing centers, and in centers where there are industries of the same sort or of similar sorts. No doubt there are drawbacks for the employer in such centers. His laborers are more likely to be organized in unions, and to press for higher wages; and the expense of urban sites needs to be considered.[1] But the fact that manufacturing towns grow shows that they offer net advantages. In an isolated establishment, the loss of a few skilled and trained workmen may cripple the whole. But in an industry which has grown to considerable dimensions, and which is concentrated in certain towns or districts, there is a general diffusion of skill in its various branches. The smooth and continuous conduct of operations is promoted by this external economy.

§ 3. Internal economies are those which arise within the

[1] Compare what is said in Book V, Chapter 43.

establishment itself, and are independent of the general growth of the industry. All the gains from the extension of large-scale production (as distinguished from increasing volume of production) are of this sort, — the gains from larger plant and more effective power, from greater specialization of machinery, better handling of materials, more elaborate division of labor among the workmen, and more refined adaptation of each man's task to his capacity. One of the most interesting questions in regard to these advantages and their limits is the extent of the gain which comes from horizontal combination, — from the union under single management of a number of single establishments each of which has developed within itself the more immediate internal economies. It is not certain how far, in the long run, horizontal combination leads to still further internal economies. Nor is it clear how far vertical combination, or the integration of industry, leads to internal economies. It seems to do so beyond doubt in some of the great industries of modern times, especially in the iron manufacture. But in other directions it has not made such unmistakable progress. In most industries, the enlargement of the industrial unit beyond a certain point, whether in combination horizontally with similar units or vertically with related units, does not seem to lead with certainty to internal economies.

If internal economies were attained indefinitely as the scale of operations increased, the stage would be eventually reached of complete concentration and complete monopoly. If each establishment, or each combination of establishments, found as it grew in size that its efficiency and its economies increased, the successively enlarging enterprises would undersell those rivals who failed to enlarge, and finally nothing would be left but one giant in sole possession of the field. This is the theoretically complete "trust," able to undersell all rivals by virtue of its economies in production. Such a trust has a monopoly, but evidently a tempered monopoly. Prices cannot be raised beyond the point at which producers who operate on a smaller scale can compete. If the rate at which internal economies accrue is slow, — if the cheapening of production from each enlargement of the scale of operations is slight, — this check on the power of the monopoly is substantial.

§ 4. In the first section of this chapter, the supposition was tacitly made that there is only one point of equilibrium under conditions of increasing returns, and the Figure on p. 190 was constructed on this supposition. But a very little con-

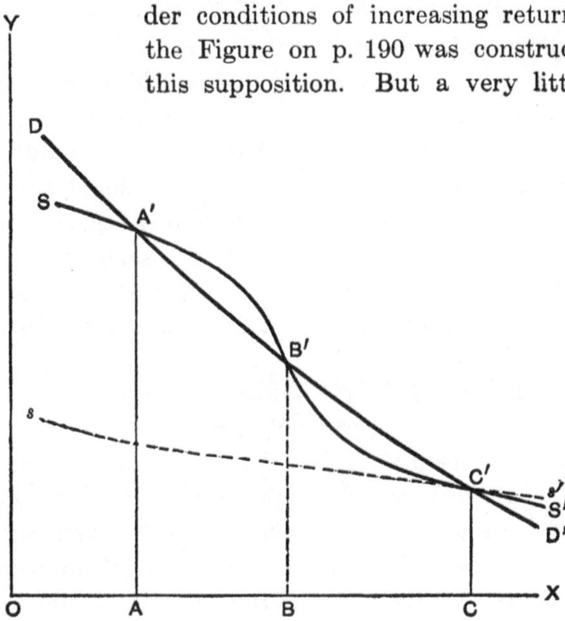

FIG. 8.

sideration shows that there may be two points of equilibrium. The demand and supply curves have the same inclination, and may intersect at more points than one. The above Figure (Fig. 8) illustrates this possibility. SS' intersects DD' at A', again at B', again at C'. (Let the reader disregard for the moment the dotted line ss'.) A' is a point of stable equilibrium; so is C'. B' is not a point of stable equilibrium. It is true that the demand and supply curves intersect at this point. Immediately beyond B', however, the demand curve is above the supply curve; demand price is higher than supply price. An increase of output beyond B would be profitable to producers, since the commodity can be sold, in the quantities between *B* and *C*, at prices higher than cost of production. But *C′* is again a point of true equilibrium; since the supply price beyond *C′* is higher than the demand price, and an increase of supply beyond *C* would be unprofitable. Both *A′* and *C′* are thus, to repeat, points of stable equilibrium. Price might settle at either, and remain at either It is indeed conceivable that a body of venturesome producers would extend supply beyond *A*, confident that cost per unit would decline unfailingly with increase of total output, and that eventually (after *B* was passed) demand price would again be above supply price. But the outcome of expansion of this sort must appear uncertain. If equilibrium were established at *A′*, it would presumably remain; yet if it were established at *C′*, it would also remain. Theoretically there may be an indefinite number of such points of stable equilibrium.

But though there is this possibility of several points of equilibrium, actual conditions probably present very rare instances of the sort. A steep slope like that of the line *SS′* is less representative of what usually happens than a gentle slope like that of the dotted line *ss′*. Such a dotted line is likely to meet *DD′* but once (at *C′*, the third point of intersection for *SS′*). It is not widely different from the horizontal line which represents the conditions of constant cost.

External economies are most likely to affect cost in the manner last described. As a rule, they operate slowly, almost imperceptibly, bringing a steady tendency toward lessening of expenses with increase of output, yet a tendency so gradual that for any given season or series of seasons the conditions may seem to differ little from those of constant cost.

Internal economies, on the other hand, sometimes are rapid in their introduction and operation. This happens especially when great changes take place in the arts, and when a new commodity is brought into use.

Changes in the arts and inventions, though they do not necessarily affect either the total output or that of the individual establishment, yet commonly affect both. The cheapening of goods which results from improvements usually stimulates demand in considerable degree, causes the total output to be larger, and so brings into operation external economics as well as additional internal economics. Improvements have commonly been in the direction of larger plant and more expensive machinery, greater division of labor, production on a larger scale. Not infrequently the arts have advanced so fast as to cause an abrupt diminution of cost, leave the equilibrium of supply and demand unsettled for years, and afford at least the possibility of more than one point of equilibrium. Bessemer's invention immensely reduced the cost of steel making; it also involved expensive plant and machinery; it gave great opportunities for large-scale production and highly elaborated organization; it thus led to very rapidly declining cost. The application of machinery to watch making has led to similar results; and in this case the commodity was one subject to a very elastic demand, hence with a possibility of multiple points of equilibrium.

New commodities, introduced suddenly or rapidly, often bring a strong tendency to decreasing cost with increasing supply. When first offered, they are strange to the buying public, must break the crust of habit, must wait for a readjustment of other devices and wants. Being thus marketable in small quantities only, they are produced on a small scale. As they become familiar and in wide use, the quantity that can be sold greatly increases, production on a large scale becomes possible, both internal and external economics are introduced effectively, and cost of production declines rapidly. The demand schedule for such articles often shows a high degree of elasticity, especially in the lower ranges, as the articles come into common use. The history of the bicycle illustrates this development: its slow introduction in the early stages, its rapidly increasing favor when once accepted and generally used, its rapid decline in cost and price when produced in larger quantities and on a larger scale.

Not infrequently it happens, however, that a new commodity is patented or in some other way falls under single control. This situation brings a new complication, arising from monopoly: the subject of the next chapter.

CHAPTER 15

Monopoly Value

§ 1. A monopolized commodity will be sold, by a person doing business for gain, on such terms as will yield the largest net revenue. We may assume, at the outset at least, that persons possessed of a monopoly act with shrewdness, and adjust their supply with intelligence and success so as to secure this maximum gain.

We say, adjust the supply; for this is the mode in which the monopolist can affect price and profit. The conditions of demand are beyond his control. When once the supply is settled and put on the market, the price at which it will sell depends on the play of demand. In this regard, monopoly value presents no peculiarities. Its special problems arise in so far as the monopolist can make the supply larger and smaller at will. With a given supply, put on the market *en bloc*,[1] the price will be the same whether it is in the hands of a single person or of several competing persons. There is some one price which measures its marginal utility, — some one price at which the whole can be sold, and no more than the whole, — and that price will rule.

This proposition, like so many in economics, needs to be taken broadly, as a statement of a tendency, not of literal detail; with precisely the same allowance for irregularity and imperfect adaptation that must be made for any general statement on values and prices. Most men in active business would at first blush deny it. They would say that a combination or monopoly can secure a higher price than competing persons can, even for the same supply. They know that a higher price can be obtained, in the first instance at least, from the middlemen, the wholesale or retail dealers, to whom

[1] See § 4 in this chapter for the significance of this qualification.

the monopolist usually makes his direct sales. When producers are competing, these dealers are very apt to play off one against another, and to induce the shaving of an offered price by threatening to turn to a competitor. No doubt, if all of the dealers do this successfully, competition among them will tend to lower prices in the end for the retail purchasers. At that final stage, it will appear whether the prices are such as to bring about the equation of supply and demand. But competition among dealers, and especially among retail dealers, operates with friction; and the lower prices which competition among manufacturers causes these to concede to dealers may redound for a considerable time to the dealers' profit, not to that of consumers. Conversely, a monopoly may squeeze the dealers, so to speak; charge them higher prices, which yet they do not find it feasible — for some time, at least — to pass on to consumers. And even when such a rise in prices reaches consumers, the effect on their purchases is not immediate or automatic. If indeed the rise is great, and the demand for the commodity is elastic, a reduction in purchases will be prompt. The monopolist will find almost at once that he cannot sell the same supply at higher prices. But if the rise in price is not great, people will very possibly continue to buy for some time what they have been in the habit of buying. They may be uneasy and irritated by the higher charge, yet for the moment may not adapt themselves to the new situation by curtailing their purchases. The monopolist may then hold the raised price for a while, even if it reaches consumers. Meanwhile, in a growing community, new consumers may be added, or the old consumers may get larger incomes. An increase in demand may overtake the higher price, and make it permanent; and then it will seem as if the mere fact of monopoly had caused prices to rise.

The position of middlemen as buffers, easing and delaying the pressure of the forces at work, appears even more strongly in the case of producer's goods. As has already been said,[1]

[1] See above, Chapter 10, § 5.

the play of demand and utility is much modified in the prices of such things, — iron, copper, timber, wool. The connection between the price ultimately paid for finished goods by consumers and the ruling price among dealers for materials is often a slow and uncertain one. Still slower is that between the materials for tools, like iron and copper, and the consumable articles which in the end the tools serve to make. Here there is a possible influence of monopoly on price which would not appear if the monopolist sold an enjoyable commodity directly to the consumers.

It is to be noted, further, that the first step taken by a monopolist is usually to settle his price, not his supply. The holder of a patent, for example, will offer the patented article at a given price; he will not usually determine in advance the amount which he will put on the market. If he finds that, at the given price, he can sell more than he expected, he will add to the supply. If he finds that he cannot sell so much, he will let the stock which he has on hand go off gradually, and in the future will add to it slowly and cautiously. In other words, he experiments with the supply which he can dispose of at the price fixed; and perhaps, as time goes on, lowers or raises his price, according to the response from purchasers. Probably he is only half conscious that his control over price rests on his control over supply; yet the shrewd business man is very rarely in doubt that this is the fundamental condition for keeping a price above the competitive level.

§ 2. The power of a monopolist over price being exercised, then, fundamentally through his control over supply, let us examine further in what way the control is exercised.

The simplest case is that of a supply which has cost nothing, — something in the nature of treasure-trove. Such a fixed supply, if put on the market *in toto*, will fetch a given price. But the owner may reason that a less supply will fetch a higher price. If the demand be inelastic, half of the supply may fetch more than double the price, and so yield a larger gross sum. It will then be in the interest of the monopolist to destroy half the supply, and put on the market only the remaining half. If the demand is elastic, it will more probably be to his advantage to put the whole on the market. The price per unit, to be sure, will be lower than if only half were sold, but not so much lower as to make the gross yield less. It is usually to the interest of a monopolist to restrict sensibly the supply of a commodity subject to inelastic demand, and to be liberal with the supply of one subject to elastic demand.

Suppose next that the supply is not fortuitous, but is produced by the monopolist under the ordinary conditions, with capital invested, laborers hired, sundry expenses of production incurred. Then the monopolist will aim to obtain not the largest gross amount, but the largest net profit. And that net profit he will try to make larger than the usual profits of capitalists. It may be assumed that in any case the monopolist would be able to secure on his capital, by investment in other directions, interest at the usual rate; and that for his own labor of direction and superintendence he would be able to secure the reward usually accruing to labor of the same skill and assiduity. Those normal gains we reckon among the expenses of production, or at least not as due to monopoly. It is the excess above them that constitutes *monopoly* profit.

It is probable that few monopolists consciously separate their gains in this way. They rarely distinguish between monopoly profits proper and ordinary returns for their capital and labor. They simply rejoice that they pay dividends at ten or twenty per cent, or are able to be munificent in salaries to themselves and their associates. If closely questioned, however, they would soon distinguish the share in these gains which is due to monopoly alone. It is that share, monopoly profits in the strict sense, which now interests us.

If the monopolist produces his commodity under the conditions of constant cost, his calculation of net profit will be simple. Figure 9 will illustrate it. The cost of producing the commodity is there represented by the distance from O to C, and is the same whether a large or small amount of the commodity be produced; it is $OC = AC' = BC''$. The price at which any given quantity will sell depends on the conformation of the demand curve DD'. If a quantity OA is put on the market, it can all be sold at the price AA'. The total cost of this quantity is $OCC'A$. Monopoly profit will then be indicated by the area

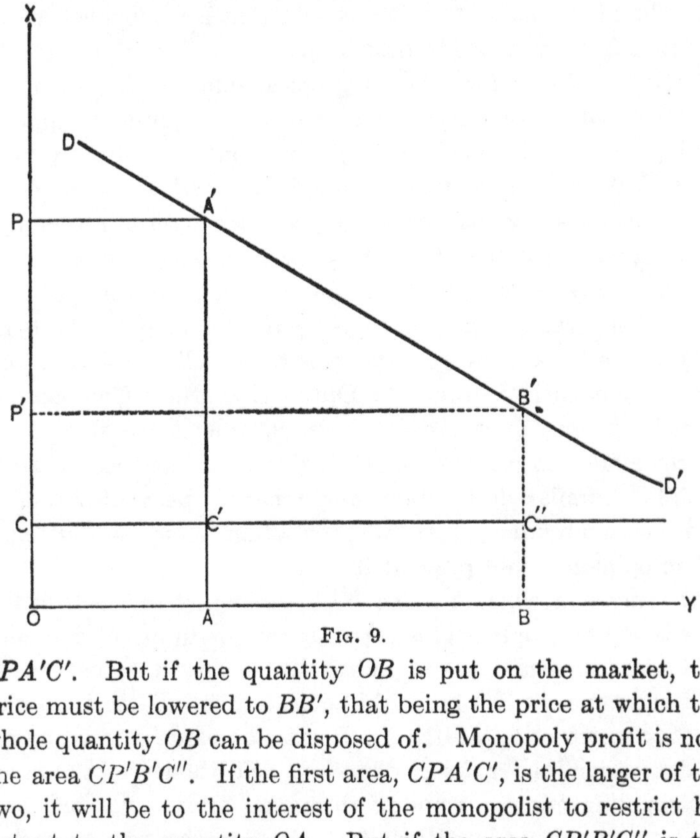

FIG. 9.

$CPA'C'$. But if the quantity OB is put on the market, the price must be lowered to BB', that being the price at which the whole quantity OB can be disposed of. Monopoly profit is now the area $CP'B'C''$. If the first area, $CPA'C'$, is the larger of the two, it will be to the interest of the monopolist to restrict his output to the quantity OA. But if the area $CP'B'C''$ is the larger, it will be to his interest to enlarge his output to the amount OB. As has already been said, the elasticity of demand has an important influence on the calculations of the monopolist. If demand is elastic, — if a lowering of price will greatly stimulate consumption and purchases, — the line DD' will have a gentler slope, and the quantity which can be disposed of at the price OP' will be greater than OB. The parallelograms indicating gross receipts and monopoly profit will be longer, and larger in area. Under such conditions it is probable that monopoly profit will be larger for a comparatively low price than for a high one.

In the preceding section it was said that a monopolist might find it to his advantage to destroy part of a supply, in order to sell the remainder for a larger gross amount. But such destruction can take place very rarely. Fortuitous supplies, coming into a monopolist's hands without cost, hardly ever occur. When a monopolist's supply is produced, and costs something, it is obviously easier and cheaper to refrain from producing a part of it than to destroy a part after it has been produced. Only from miscalculation or causes beyond control (such as superabundance of crops) may a monopolist find destruction to his advantage. It seems to be well established that in the eighteenth century the Dutch East India Company at times burnt part of its crop of cloves in order to be able to sell the remainder at prices so much higher as to increase its gross receipts. Similar destruction would hardly be ventured in a modern community; fear of retribution from an outraged public opinion would prevent it.[1]

The mode in which a monopolist commonly proceeds in the adjustment of supply is illustrated by the conditions of diamond production in recent years. Virtually all new diamonds come from the mines at Kimberley in South Africa. These are under the single ownership of the De Beers Company, formed by an amalgamation, under the guidance of Cecil Rhodes, of a number of competing mines. Some of the mines are not worked, and the total supply is intentionally limited to the amount which can be sold to best advantage. .The demand for diamonds, after a certain point, is highly inelastic. They are bought chiefly for purposes of display. Scarcity and high price are the basis of

[1] When a publisher prints a limited edition of a book, and then distributes the type, he may be said to wipe out part of the supply in order to sell at a higher price the restricted portion which he prints.

their utility; if very abundant, they would be little prized. Hence it is clearly to the advantage of the De Beers Company to curtail production and limit the supply.[1] Were the commodity one like copper, with a very elastic demand, it might pay such a monopolist to work the source of supply to its utmost capacity.

§ 3. Suppose now that the monopolized commodity is produced, not under the conditions of constant cost, but under those of diminishing cost (increasing returns). The calculations of the monopolist then become complex. He must consider on the one hand the extent to which price will fall as a larger supply is put on the market, and on the other hand, how much cost will fall as more is produced. The situation is again easily illustrated by a diagram.

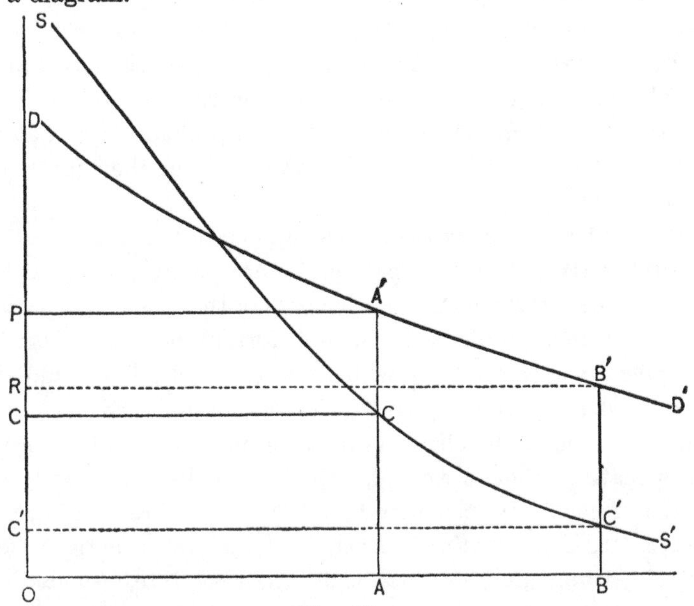

FIG. 10.

[1] The De Beers Company controls 95 per cent of the world's diamond production. See G. F. Williams, *The Diamond Mines of South Africa*, Vol. I, p. 291; Vol. II, p. 161.

I have referred to the diamond monopoly as if it presented a case of constant cost. This is not probable in the case of mines, least of all where the occurrence of the product is as irregular as in diamond mines. But the motives that lead to a curtailment of supply are essentially the same.

On Figure 10 *DD′* has a slight inclination, representing a very elastic demand. *SS′*, the supply curve, has a steep inclination, at least in its upper range, representing a very rapid decline in cost per unit as supply is enlarged. If the monopolist produces and puts on the market the quantity *OA*, he will find the cost per unit to be *AC*, and the total cost to be *COAC*. That supply will be sold at the price *AA′*; the gross receipts will be *OPA′A*, and the monopoly profit will be *CPA′C*. If, on the other hand, the quantity produced is the larger amount *OB*, the cost per unit will be only *BC′*, and the cost of the total supply will be *C′OBC′*. That supply can be sold at the price *BB′*. The gross receipts will be *ORB′B*, and the monopoly profits will be *C′RB′C′*. Evidently the monopoly profit will be much greater with the lower price than with the higher price; this because the conditions assumed are those of very elastic demand and of rapidly decreasing cost. The less elastic the demand, and the less rapid the decrease in cost, the more probable is it that the monopolist will find it to his advantage to limit the supply and keep up the price.

The reader will easily see that a number of maximum monopoly profits and ruling monopoly prices are possible. To express in one single statement all the elements of the case would require mathematical formulation. Such a formulation, however, has an appearance of accuracy which is often misleading; and this is true even of a comparatively simple diagram like that given above. Some of the elements in the situation must be more or less a matter of guess work for the monopolist; especially the degree of elasticity in demand, and the rate of decreasing cost with enlarged production. Even in the case of a perfectly unrestrained monopoly, — and such are very rare, — monopoly price is usually fixed by a sort of rule of thumb. Though probably at a point considerably above the competitive price, it is not settled by any refined calculation of the precise point of maximum profit.

Sharply decreasing cost, or increasing return, is most likely to appear where articles are newly introduced. At first these are bought and used in small amounts. Later, as they become familiar and widely used, they are produced in larger quantities, and the principle of increasing returns applies. Not infrequently new articles are monopolized, being protected by patent or copyright laws. They then give a most apt illustration of the working of the principles here under consideration. Thus, the Welsbach mantles attached to gaslights were long protected by patent in all advanced countries.[1] They enabled a much better light to be had for a less expenditure on gas, and they contaminated the air less. The demand for them was highly elastic. They were produced much more cheaply in large quantities. Hence, though monopolized, they were sold at a price which, per unit of product, was not greatly above cost price; none the less, on the enormous quantity which could be sold, they yielded monopoly profits very great in the aggregate.

A situation essentially similar appears in the case of copyrighted books. Books conform to the principle of decreasing cost. The expense of typesetting and of making the stereotype plates is the same whether one thousand copies be printed or fifty thousand. The other expenses of bookmaking — paper, presswork, binding, and the like — are tolerably uniform per unit, yet some of them show slightly diminishing cost as more books are printed from the same plates. On the whole, the cost per unit is much less for a large edition than for a small one. A common device of publishers is to issue a limited edition, often with numbered copies, and dispose of it at a high rate to collectors and other persons who prize the possession of a rare thing. They calculate that the profit will be greater from a small edition at a high price, than from a large edition at a low price. The same result appears with scientific books, which often appeal to but a small circle of readers and for which the demand is inelastic. The few copies printed are sold at a comparatively high price to those who desire them. Were they salable in large quantities, their cost and probably their price would be lower. On the other hand, new books which many people may be tempted to

[1] This patent expired in the United States in 1906.

read — popular novels, for example — are sold at the outset for a lower price, for they present the conditions both of decreasing cost and of elastic demand.

It is obvious that under conditions of increasing cost (diminishing returns) the situation of a monopolist will again be different. The probability of a sharp limitation of supply is evidently greater if the increase of supply entails greater cost for the additional output. If the demand be highly inelastic, the monopolist will certainly be disposed to restrict his output very much; for the price he can get will rise much with lessened supply, while his expenses will fall. And even with an elastic demand, he will have to reckon, not indeed with rapidly falling price as output increases, but with some increase in cost. Monopoly, however, with diminishing returns is probably rare. It may appear in the case of some uncommon mineral products, obtained from a single source of supply or a few combined sources (the South African diamond mines may present an example). On the whole monopoly conditions, complete or partial, are much more likely to be found with commodities produced under constant or under increasing returns.

§ 4. Monopoly presents another possibility, — different installments of the supply may be sold at varying prices. Under competition, one price prevails throughout the market; no one seller is allowed by the others to get a higher price. In the preceding paragraphs it has been tacitly assumed that the same holds good under monopoly. But it does not necessarily hold.

Look, for example, at Figure 9 (p. 203) representing monopoly under the conditions of constant cost. The monopolist cannot but look with longing eyes at the possible profits represented by the area $CPA'C'$. It is true that the one uniform price yielding him the largest gain may be the price OP' ($= BB'$), at which his monopoly profits are $CP'B'C''$. But may he not get in addition the extra profit potentially to be had on the quantity OA, which would sell, if put on the market by itself, at the price AA'? May he not charge a high price to the richer or more eager buyers, while selling at a lower rate to those not able or willing to pay the high price?

To sell directly and openly at varying prices to different purchasers is, to be sure, not always feasible or politic. There is the possibility of resale by the favored purchaser. Moreover, the instinct of equality or "fair treatment" is to be reckoned with. Its violation arouses a feeling of resentment, which may affect purchasers or lead to hostile legislation. Hence the monopolist, if he discriminates, is likely to disguise his discrimination. But in some degree he will not infrequently secure from the upper strata of buyers that higher price which would otherwise inure to them as consumer's surplus.

Thus the monopolist may put the commodity on the market in installments. He may sell at a high price first to those whose demand is keenest; and then, after a pause, put on the market a further supply at a lower price. Substantially this is often done by publishers with copyrighted books, especially such as are reasonably sure to have a considerable vogue. A first edition is offered at a comparatively high price. After a season or two, a much cheaper "popular" edition is put out, tempting a whole army of buyers for whom the first edition was too expensive. There is, indeed, some pretense of a difference between the two. The popular edition is printed on cheaper paper, has a less elaborate binding, or may be in paper cover. But the difference in cost between the two forms is usually small, and by no means accounts for the difference in selling price. That difference results in the main from the publisher's effort to tap in succession the several strata of buyers.

Something of the same sort happens not infrequently in the case of patented articles. These may be sold at a high price for the first installments put on the market, and at prices much reduced as the great mass of buyers are sought. There is, to be sure, another factor, already referred to. Being patented, the articles must be of a new sort; since the law gives the monopoly, or patent, only on the ground of this novelty. The market is necessarily uncertain. The patentee is likely to proceed cautiously. The moderate quantity put on the market at the outset does not allow the advantages of large-scale production; hence, though price is high, cost also is high. If it were certain from the start that the article would find a wide sale, large plant and elaborate division of labor might be applied from the beginning, great quantities might be produced, a small part sold at once at high prices, the rest stored away until it was time to satisfy the demand at lower prices. But this involves risk. Commonly, the earlier installments are produced and sold tentatively, and the advantages of low cost are not reaped until the possibility of large sales at low prices is proved by successive experiments.

A direct instance of discrimination in price seems to be supplied by the telephone. This is a monopoly in most communities, and indeed, whether under private or public management, ought to be a monopoly. The commodity, or service, is not of a transferable kind; hence one obstacle to discrimination — possible resale — is out of the way. Telephone rates are commonly adjusted on the basis of what the user can pay; they are higher in cities and in thickly settled districts than in rural districts. Some parts of the variations in charges are doubtless due to differences in cost, but in the main they seem to be the outcome of monopoly conditions.

A converse case occurs when a monopoly charges a level rate to all persons, under conditions which would lead competing producers to charge rates varying according to cost. Probably the uniform five-cent fare on American street railways could not be maintained but for monopoly conditions. Custom, convenience in collection, and a disposition to conciliate the public, account here for the one rate of fare which the monopoly charges. The most striking case of this sort, however, is where a public authority carries on an industry as a monopoly. The uniform rate of postage on letters is to be explained largely in this way. The two-cent rate is highly profitable on short distance letters, and especially on letters in the large cities. If competing producers carried on the business, some of them would enter this profitable part of the field and carry letters there for much less than two cents. Private individuals or corporations who might undertake letter service in outlying districts of thin population, especially the rural districts, would have to charge considerably more; or else the government would have to do the work at a heavy financial loss. The existing monopoly enables the government to cover the loss in one region from the profit in another. The postal service is administered at a very moderate uniform rate, either with profit, as in European countries, or at a comparatively small loss, as in the United States. The social and educational advantages of thus conducting the service, as a monopoly with uniform rates, are too obvious to need emphasis.

§ 5. The possibility of charging different prices to different purchasers explains the phenomenon of "dumping," — that is, the disposal of commodities in a foreign country at one price, and to domestic purchasers at another and higher price. In the absence of monopoly, — that is, if producers were competing freely, — all purchasers would get commodities at the same price. The producers might, indeed, gain collectively by selling part of the supply at a low rate, and the rest at a higher. Where market conditions are disadvantageous, and where the total supply cannot be sold on remunerative terms, there is a strong inducement to resort to such tactics. But no one producer will sacrifice himself for the benefit of the rest; he will not slaughter the whole or a part of his stock in order that others may gain. If, however, all were to carry out an agreement to sacrifice each a specified share of his supply, reserving the remainder for higher prices, the object might conceivably be accomplished. Here, to be sure, there is this obstacle: a possibility that the favored purchaser may resell to those from whom it is proposed to exact the higher price. But if the favored purchaser is a foreigner, and if a heavy duty on imports prevents him from sending back the "dumped" commodity to the domestic market, the obstacle is removed. The domestic price can then be kept higher, and the gain from this source may outweigh the loss on the dumped sales to foreigners; especially if the commodity be one for which the demand is inelastic and of which an increased supply on the domestic market would greatly depress the price. If the operation be carried on by a compact monopoly, it is possible that the foreign sales themselves will be at remunerative rates, and that the higher domestic price will yield monopoly profits still further enhanced.

The more complete the monopoly, the more likely will be inequalities in the nature of "dumping." Even in cases of halfway monopoly or temporary monopoly, something of the sort may happen, though the discriminations will be less striking and less continued. Any producer or vendor of a "specialty" — a particular brand, an unusual commodity — is apt to be for a time in a position of semi-monopoly. So far as he controls the given article, he may find it advantageous to get rid of part of his supply in a foreign country, or in any out-of-the-way region, in order not to "spoil" his domestic market. Where control of the market rests only on good will, or on established plant and reputation, the extent to which dumping can be carried is obviously less than in the case of a firm and enduring monopoly. Where, on the other hand, many producers are steadily competing in the sale of a staple commodity, dumping will not arise at all.

§ 6. Complete and unqualified monopoly is rare. Hence too much stress should not be laid on the theory of monopoly price in explaining the phenomena of actual life.

A monopoly exercised by a government for fiscal reasons gives perhaps the best chance of exacting the full monopoly profit. When the Khedive of Egypt, in the days before the English occupation, maintained a monopoly of the salt trade, he probably squeezed out of it remorselessly all that could be exacted from his unfortunate subjects. But generally fiscal monopolies do not exercise their power to the utmost. They are not uncommon in civilized countries, being simply a method of securing public revenue by monopoly management instead of by taxes. Such are the tobacco and salt monopolies in Austria and Italy, the tobacco monopoly in France, the spirit monopolies in Switzerland and Russia. These are rarely exploited up to their maximum yield. A given net revenue, varying according to the financial needs of the several states, is sought, and the adjustment of supply and of prices is pressed no further.

Patented and copyrighted articles, again, seem to fulfill the conditions of perfect monopoly; the law forbids competition once for all. But the holder of such a monopoly must reckon with the competition of more or less available substitutes, and thus is compelled to abate his prices and enlarge his supplies more than he would otherwise do. Copyrighted books, for example, must meet the competition of other copyrighted books of a similar kind, not to mention those on which the copyright has expired. A first-rate textbook yields a good monopoly profit, sometimes a very high one. Yet if the price be put too high, others, little worse, can be used in its place. The gain from a copyrighted or patented article often arises not so much from selling it at a higher price than others of a similar sort, as from selling much more of it at about the same price. This gain is obviously the greater if the conditions of production are those of decreasing cost.

In other cases, also, of real or apparent or halfway monopoly, there are commonly checks. Many so-called monopolies lack a legal basis and even a solid industrial basis. Such is the case with most of the "trusts" which have been formed by horizontal combination. They must be ever on the watch against competitors, and very few, if any, are in a position to exercise unrestrained monopoly power. Others, again, though more securely founded, must be on their guard against regulation or displacement by public authority. Such are the so-called "public service" industries, — the railway, the street railway, the telegraph, the telephone, the gas companies. Both of these sorts of cases, so important in modern industry, will engage our attention as we proceed. Here it suffices to note that the monopoly is in one way or another qualified.

Finally, the dullness or torpor of a monopolist must be reckoned with. The strict reasoning of the theory of monopoly price assumes him to press his advantage shrewdly and to the utmost. He may do nothing of the kind. The spur of competition — the one force which more than any other stimulates enterprise and business intelligence — is lacking. The secure monopolist is likely to be content with a good comfortable profit, and to let well enough alone. It may happen, indeed, that another and shrewder person will see the possibilities, will buy out the inert possessor, and proceed to manage the affair with more vigor and profit. Such has been not infrequently the course of events in the public service monopolies of modern times, especially in those whose possibilities of profit have been connected with changes in the arts and the rapid growth of great cities. But this is not a matter on which prediction can be ventured. The actual working of monopoly, while it conforms more or less to the theoretical analysis, is often highly uncertain and irregular.

§ 7. It remains to say a word about one form of monopoly which frequently comes into public notice, the "corner." This word usually implies not that the sources of production have come permanently under monopoly control, but that the available supply has been got for the time into a single hand. Recurrently, persons of speculative bent try their hands at this operation, buying up the whole supply of an article, and then selling it, if possible, at a large profit.

So far as the ordinary course of market prices is concerned, mere cornering has no effect. If supply remains the same, price to consumers will not be more or less because an article is in single hands. Yet the cornerer may make money. If so, this is because he has foreseen more quickly or more shrewdly than others a shortage in the seasonal supply. By buying the whole of it at moderate prices from producers or dealers less shrewd, he may profit by an advance. But that advance was certain to come sooner or later. The profit is not obtained at the expense of consumers. The question is simply which set of producers or middlemen will accurately gauge the market price of the season and profit accordingly. This is especially true of articles that are in consumable form, or very nearly in consumable form. Such is ice, the supply of which, in regions depending on natural (winter-frozen) ice, is absolutely fixed by the contingencies of the weather; or a vegetable like tomatoes, the crop of which, for canning purposes, has sometimes been bought out by speculators engineering a corner. The price of these things is settled with much precision by the play of demand and supply, *i.e.* by marginal utility, and it matters not to the consumer whether that supply be in a single hand or not.

In the case of producer's goods, such as metals and raw materials, the possible effect on prices from a corner is greater, for the reasons already indicated. Provided the corner is rigorous, — provided all the available supplies and avenues of supply are effectively controlled, — there is at least a possibility that middlemen and producers who are committed to operations in which the raw materials are needed, will be mulcted for a higher price than would rule without the corner.

Quite another situation appears when the persons against whose purses the corner is aimed are not the consumers, but other dealers and speculators, and especially the speculators who have been buying or selling for future delivery. Most speculators are simply betting on future prices. They are doing so, in the majority of cases, with incomplete or ill-interpreted information. A speculative corner is commonly directed against those who have sold for future delivery, — that is, those who have agreed to sell for a given price, at a fixed date in the future, something which they do not own. A shrewd and daring person, or even one not shrewd but only daring, who believes that many persons have oversold for future delivery, may try to buy up the whole supply available at the stipulated date. If he succeeds, he may then dictate the price at which they must buy *from him,* in order to keep their engagements; and the difference between that price and the price he has paid for his purchases makes the profit of the corner. Evidently the persons who are directly affected are not the consumers, but only other dealers and speculators. In so far, it is a case of diamond cut diamond.

Yet the consuming public is by no means without its concern in these speculative corners. Some of its purchases may be of a sort that cannot be postponed, and must be made at the ruling market price. This buying comes from those more eager or necessitous persons, who would ordinarily get the article at the normal market price, and would secure a consumer's surplus. During the crucial period of a corner — say during the month of May, if wheat for May delivery is the bone of contention — wheat will sell at an artificially high price. The cornerer is intent on buying every part of supply that comes to market, to prevent his opponents from getting the means of satisfying their contracts. These opponents, in turn, are under no less pressure to secure the supplies. Until the struggle is over, — until either the corner "bursts" because the cornerer finds he cannot possibly buy the entire supply, or else the "short sellers" acknowledge themselves defeated and "settle" with their opponent, — so long the market price is high, and those who are under the necessity of buying for *bona fide* use must pay accordingly. When the struggle is over, price goes back suddenly to the normal level for the season, or even below that level. Most consumers are no worse off than before, and sometimes are better off, in consequence of the rapid disposal of supplies long withheld from the market.

Successful corners are rare. Usually those who attempt them underestimate the supply and overstrain their credit. When the bidding of the contending speculators raises prices, all sorts of unexpected nooks and crannies prove to have scraps of supply that are hurried on the market to take advantage of the golden opportunity; while the usual consumption is curtailed, and so far leaves more of the usual supply available. In order to hold the corner, enormous sums must be provided, always by borrowing on a vast scale, with hypothecation of what is already controlled; and the insistence of a large creditor may precipitate a collapse. Where the commodity is not, like agricultural products, the subject of seasonal cultivation, but is continuously produced, the difficulties in the way of a corner are even greater. In 1887–1888 a noted attempt was made by a group of French speculators, headed by one Secretan, to corner copper. At once copper poured in from every part of the world, and all sorts of unknown or half-worked mines added to the product. The corner, after keeping up prices for many months, and causing disturbance and expense to those whose purchases had of necessity to be made during its operation, finally failed disastrously; its promoter was led to suicide, and a great French bank which had lent him large funds was compelled to suspend payments.

CHAPTER 16

Joint Cost and Joint Demand

§ 1. Not infrequently commodities are produced at joint cost; the same operations which turn out one in the group turn out another also. Such are mutton and wool; beef, hides, and horn; copper, gold, silver from ores containing these diverse metals; cotton fiber and cotton seed. Commodities produced at joint cost are of interest to us because of the peculiar problems of price which they present.

A perfect example of joint production is that of cotton fiber and cotton seed. To make the fiber marketable, the seed must be separated from it; all the expenses of cultivation and of ginning are necessarily incurred for the two together. But the prices per pound at which fiber and seed sell are very different. For every pound of lint (fiber) there are about two pounds of seed. At the prices of recent years (1903–1908) the fiber has sold at about ten cents a pound; the seed at about one half cent a pound. It may be assumed, with little divergence from the facts, that cotton is produced under conditions of competition, and that there is a large margin at which the cost is practically constant. Fiber and seed between them therefore sell, taking their average prices over a series of years, for what it costs to produce them. But the apportionment of this total price between the two joint products depends on the relative demand for them, or, in the terms which we have learned to use, on their marginal utility. The marginal utility of the cotton fiber from a given crop is much greater than the marginal utility of the seed produced along with it; hence cotton sells at a much higher price per pound.

It follows that an increase of demand for a commodity which is produced jointly with another, may cause a fall in the price of that other. If the demand for cotton increases, its price will rise. This will not directly affect the price of seed, for which the supply and the conditions of demand remain the same. But the higher price of cotton is likely to stimulate production, and more both of fiber and of seed will be brought to market. The conditions of demand remaining unchanged for seed, its price must fall as supply is enlarged. Production will be increased until, in the end, the two between them will again sell for their joint expenses of production. But as the seed now sells at a lower price, the fiber must sell at a somewhat higher price; and the definitive outcome of the greater demand for fiber will thus be a larger output of both constituents. It will cause a higher price for the one and yet entail a lower price for the other. The opposite effect would follow if demand for one of the articles should become not greater, but less.

In most instances of joint cost, the situation is not so simple as this; for usually each article entails some separate items of expense. It is rare that, as with cotton fiber and cotton seed, all the expenses are incurred, to the very last stage, jointly for the two. The common case is more like that of wool and mutton; though produced in the main at joint cost, each brings some special expenses of its own. The wool must be sheared; the sheep must be slaughtered and dressed for mutton. Wool and meat must each sell for at least the special cost connected with them, so a minimum price is set. In what proportion the remaining (joint) cost will be secured from the two will then depend on the play of demand, as in the simpler case of cotton fiber and seed.

The phrase "by-products" is often applied to denote some of the commodities produced at joint cost. When one of them habitually sells at a much lower price than the other, it is spoken of as a by-product; or when a material for which no use has been known, comes to be utilized and to have a market value, it is so described. Both reasons explain why cotton seed is commonly spoken of as a by-product, not, as in strictness it should be, as a joint product. One of the most striking instances of joint cost is in the utilization of the various parts of slaughtered animals. The hide, the bristles, the bones, the horns, the hoofs, the blood, the various organs, all are turned to some sort of use, — usually with items of special cost pertaining to each. As the meat is the most important and familiar product, the others are commonly called by-products.

The advance in the arts of production, especially under the influence of chemical science, has led to the utilization of many materials previously wasted, and so has made the principle of joint cost of wider and wider application. Wool, produced at joint cost with mutton, further illustrates also this aspect of the principle. As wool comes from the sheep's back, it contains much fatty matter, which must be got rid of before the fiber can be used for textile purposes. This matter, formerly waste, has in recent times been extracted, in some degree refined, and has proved useful in treating leather and for other purposes. Similarly, cotton seed, itself a joint product, supplies not only the oil pressed out of it (and that oil of various grades, serviceable for various purposes), but also the oil cake remaining after extraction, which is used as food for cattle. The slag which comes to the surface of the molten matter in a pig-iron furnace, and of which vast quantities formerly accumulated near the furnaces (some parts being perhaps turned to account locally as ballast under railway ties), has lately been used as a material in the manufacture of cement.[1] Coal tar, one of the by-products from the making of gas and coke, has been found by chemistry to contain the materials for cheap and effective dyestuffs, and also for important drugs. The crude oil which comes from the coal-bearing strata, and which has formed so wonderful an addition to man's resources during the last half century, is the basis of a number of products, having partly joint cost and partly special cost, — kerosene (illuminating oil), naphtha, gasoline, lubricating oil, dyes, paraffin and candles, vaseline.

For the utilization of some joint products a large plant is indispensable; as in the case of wool grease or coal oil prod-

[1] In Germany the slag left by the Thomas and other basic processes is the most important source of supply of phosphorus used as fertilizer.

ucts. In so far, the advance of the arts has promoted the growth of large-scale production, and so has intensified the social problems which arise from it. Large-scale production, in turn, may lead to monopoly, or largely facilitate it. Then another complication appears. Either monopoly alone or joint cost alone entails consequences for value which diverge far from the simpler cases. When the two are combined, a variety of interacting forces must be considered, — joint and separate cost, marginal utility and elasticity of demand, monopoly and maximum profit, and the effects upon monopoly of possible competition, of public opinion and public regulation, and of inert management. The Standard Oil Company in the United States illustrates all these complications. It has had a more or less effective monopoly, due to various causes, among which large-scale production and the utilization of joint products have played their part; and these various joint products have been marketed at prices influenced by all the factors mentioned in our discussion of monopoly, except probably that of inert management.

Whenever a very large fixed capital is used not for a single purpose, but for varied purposes, the influence of the principle of joint cost shows itself. Of this the most striking instance appears in the adjustment of railway rates — a case, however, so complex that its consideration is best postponed to a later chapter.[1] Where a large plant is used for producing one homogeneous commodity, — say steel rails or plain cotton cloth, — the peculiar effects of joint cost cannot, of course, appear. True, if such a plant, or combination of plants, has a monopoly or semi-monopoly, there may be varying prices for different portions of the one homogeneous product; there may be "dumping," as in the case of steel rails.[2] But this is a very different phenomenon from that of value under joint cost.

§ 2. A different case from joint cost is joint demand where what is wanted is not a single article, but a combination of

[1] See Book VII, Chapter 60, especially § 3.

[2] See above, Chapter 15, §§ 4, 5.

articles. Thus a demand for dwellings is a demand for the completed accommodation. The purchaser is indifferent to the prices for brick, wood, glass, hardware; all he looks for is the house which combines these various materials.

If we suppose an increase in the demand for houses in a given district, and a rise in their prices, the change will be reflected in a rise in the prices of the several materials. If the materials were used solely for the reconstruction of houses, and if they were put on the market under the same conditions, — all equally limited in supply, or all equally extensible in supply, — there would be no reason for expecting a greater rise in price for one than for the others. But the conditions of supply, as of demand, are likely to be different for the several constituents. Some may be easily obtainable in unlimited quantities at short notice; some may be temporarily or permanently limited. So far as any constituent is solely devoted to the given purpose and is limited in supply, so far is it likely to be peculiarly affected by the changes in demand for the joint product. Those constituents which serve other purposes also, and hence are on the market for miscellaneous sale, will be diverted toward the joint product by the increase in price; enlarging supply here will check in some degree the rise in price. If the supply of any constituent be unlimited and easily extensible at constant cost, its price will not rise at all. Supply will promptly respond to the new demand, and the effect of that demand will appear solely with the other constituents. And if all the constituents except one be easily procured in larger quantities, and if their supplies thus respond quickly to an increased demand, that exceptional constituent will get the full benefit of the increase in price.

The different kinds of labor needed in building operations, as well as the different kinds of materials, illustrate the working of joint demand. A demand for houses and business premises means a demand for all kinds of workmen, — for unskilled laborers, for bricklayers, masons, and carpenters, for plumbers and electricians, and (in the case of high structures in American cities), for ironworkers. Some of these occupations are so widespread that an increased demand for a particular kind of labor in any one place easily draws an increased supply. This is most obviously true of ordinary manual labor, — plain pick and shovel work. More of it can usually be got with little difficulty from other places. With the rougher kinds of carpenter's work the situation is similar. But it is different with the highly skilled trades, and with those to which access is fettered by trade-union restriction. Here it is more difficult to add to the labor supply. Hence increased activity in building may have the effect of very greatly raising the wages of the workmen in these groups, while bringing comparatively little change for the others. Such a result has in recent years appeared frequently in American cities, strikingly so in New York. The rapid growth in urban population, combined with great improvements in building methods, has brought about astonishing activity in adding to and in remodeling dwellings and business premises. Certain kinds of laborers, not easily increased in supply by recruiting from other occupations or from other places, have been in insistent demand,—such as plumbers, tile workers, electrical workers, housesmiths (*i.e.* structural ironworkers). These have felt more than the others the demand for the joint product, and have secured extraordinarily high wages. Artificial restriction of the supply by trade-union regulation has played no small part in securing for them an exceptionally larger share of the possible gain.

Ordinarily, joint demand has not the same sort of permanent effect on value that joint supply has. In the long run, the conditions of supply are the more important in affecting value. Though it is true, as appears most strikingly in the cases of increasing cost and of monopoly value, that there is a constant interaction of supply and demand, the dominant forces for most commodities are those of supply. Where an increased joint demand affects most strongly some one commodity or some one kind of labor, because that happens to be the constituent whose supply is least easily extensible, there is none the less likely to be an increase in its supply. A readjustment of value takes place of the same sort as would have taken place if the demand had been not joint, but solely and separately for this one thing. If more brick is wanted, more will be produced; and an increased demand for houses, though it may for the moment raise the price of brick, will not do so permanently. But the situation is different with joint cost; an increase in the demand for cotton fiber may have a permanent effect in lowering the price of cotton seed. The immediate effect of an increase of demand is usually greater in case of joint demand; but the ultimate effect is usually greater in case of joint supply.

References on Book II

Easily the first and most valuable book to be consulted on the theory of value is A. Marshall, *Principles of Economics* (6th ed., 1910), especially Books III, IV, V. An admirable introductory sketch is in T. N. Carver, *Distribution of Wealth*, Chapter I. On the play of utility, see P. H. Wickstead, *The Common Sense of Political Economy* (1910); Chapter II of Book I and Chapter III of Book II are valuable supplements to Marshall's discussion of consumer's surplus. Compare, also, M. Pantaleoni, *Pure Economics* (English translation, 1898), Part II.

On speculation, consult H. C. Emery, *Speculation in the Stock and Produce Exchanges of the United States* (1896).

The so-called Austrian theory of value, in which stress is laid on utility as dominating value, is set forth most fully in F. Wieser, *Natural Value* (English translation, 1893). A more compact statement is in Böhm-Bawerk, *Positive Theory of Capital* (English translation, 1891), Books III and IV.

BOOK III

MONEY AND THE MECHANISM OF EXCHANGE

CHAPTER 17

The Precious Metals. Coinage

§ 1. We have already considered the part which money plays in the division of labor.[1] It is the medium by which exchanges are effected, and by which the consequences of the division of labor are worked out. It is the medium, too, in which the relative values of commodities are expressed. At any given time, the price of a commodity registers its value. If iron sells for one cent a pound, and copper sells for ten cents a pound, their relative values are as one to ten. If the price of copper rises to twenty cents, iron remaining as before, their relative values become as one to twenty. But if iron sells for two cents, and copper for twenty, their values remain as one to ten; and what has happened is a change in their value relatively to the cents. A rise in both prices has taken place, which means a fall in the purchasing power of money; that is, a fall in its value. Thus money, though an accurate measure at any given time, is by no means necessarily an accurate measure for different times. The most difficult monetary problems are those concerning the variations in its own value, that is, concerning the fluctuations in the general range of prices.

We have seen also that, while any commodity that is in general demand may serve the purposes of a medium of exchange, the most important by far have been gold and silver. Throughout most of the period over which the historical record extends, they have been the main constituents of the circulating medium. During the last century, they have been supplemented to a high degree by paper substitutes or equivalents, and monetary conditions have been by this process profoundly

[1] See Book II, Chapter 8.

affected. But specie[1] is still, and bids fair long to remain, the basis of the medium of exchange for all advanced countries. We can best begin the discussion of monetary questions by treating them as if specie were the sole constituent of the medium of exchange; introducing thereafter the several qualifications which arise from the use of paper money and of the complex credit instruments.

§ 2. Historically, the chief reason why gold and silver became the money metals was that they satisfied the craving for adornment. Things that minister to the deep-rooted love of display are in unfailing demand; and any commodity that is in unfailing demand may perform passably the functions of a medium of exchange Hence the wide variety of things that have so served, — cattle, grain, salt, furs, tobacco, and what not. It is the luster and sheen of gold and silver that caused them to be highly prized in the early stages of civilization, when other ways of producing these effects were not known. The glitter of the bauble is the origin of the monetary use of the precious metals; precisely as glass beads and scarlet cloth are serviceable for barter by explorers who push into those regions (now few) where savagery is still unaffected by the conventional ways of civilized man.

Other qualities contributed greatly to making gold and silver the money metals. They are singularly free from liability to deterioration. Rust does not affect them. They retain their luster with unusual constancy. Most important of all, they have proved to be sufficiently abundant for money use, and yet not so abundant that they have ceased to be prized. Any metal that is fairly scarce might be selected for monetary use. Iron was used in the early days of Rome. Copper was used to a considerable extent in later times; and it is still in use, though only under conditions that deprive it of much significance. In the course of time, both iron and copper have been discovered and produced in such great quantities

[1] I use "specie" to signify gold and silver used for monetary purposes, whether coined or uncoined.

that they have ceased to have any special value from their rarity. Gold and silver remain comparatively scarce. Though common, and very widely distributed (gold perhaps most widely distributed of all), they are rarely found in large amounts, or under conditions which enable great quantities to be secured at small cost. Highly productive mines have been not infrequently discovered, and during our own time new sources are being exploited to a striking extent. Some of these changes have had far-reaching effects on prices and on the modes of use for the two metals. Some of them, too, have caused the question to be raised, at one time and another, whether silver, or gold, or both, might not become so abundant and so cheap as no longer to be fit to serve as money. On the whole, however, their scarcity and high cost have continued. Though now produced in quantities that are enormous as compared with those of former centuries, their annual production is still very small as compared with that of iron, lead, copper, tin, and zinc.[1]

The continued use of gold and silver for money rests very largely on convention, not on the intrinsic factors of beauty and scarcity. Once established as the money metals, they retain their position to a great degree by force of custom. Anything which passes readily from hand to hand has value from its mere acceptability. The strong influence of convention and habit is illustrated by the wampum of the American Indians. These strings of shells, originally sought because fancied for ornament, were in course of time accepted, without thought of their ornamental qualities, as a medium of exchange

[1] The total production, the world over, of the more familiar metals was in 1900: —

	Metric Tons
Pig Iron	41,000,000
Lead	860,000
Copper	486,000
Zinc	471,000
Tin	85,000
Aluminum	7,800
Nickel	7,500
Silver	5,650
Gold	388

for the Indian tribes and the early settlers. Among certain African tribes, tiny axes (called bikei) serve as the medium of exchange. It is clear that they are conventionalized survivals from a time when the purpose was served by real axes, which had the prime quality of general acceptability.[1] Paper money illustrates the same tendency. In the first stages of its use, it had to be really exchangeable on demand for specie; otherwise it would not be taken in payment. But once people were used to it, and accustomed to seeing it received by every one and paid out by every one, it proved able to circulate as money with little reference to its convertibility into specie.[2] Specie has had for many centuries the established position which paper money has secured within very modern times. Just because all the world accepts it as money, it is peculiarly fit to serve as money.

Further, the fact that specie serves so universally as money tends to maintain its value, by giving it a utility for social prestige. Many of the non-monetary purposes for which gold and silver are used have become of minor importance. Brass and sundry imitations often do as well. Between the serviceability of plated ware and solid silver there is no substantial difference. The one great utility which the sterling metal retains is like that of the diamond, — it satisfies the love of distinction. The fact that gold and silver are used as money keeps up their value; the fact that they are valuable gives them utility for display; and this in turn serves to sustain their value for monetary as well as for non-monetary uses.

§ 3. Coins are stamped and certified pieces of metal. Uniformity, and consequent ease in reckoning prices, are made possible by coinage. The fact that the metals can be split up into pieces absolutely uniform is one of the qualities which fit them for monetary use; though, to be sure, it is a quality possessed not only by gold and silver, copper and nickel, but by other metals as well.

[1] See Miss Mary Kingsley's *Travels in West Africa*, p. 320.
[2] See below, Chapter 23, § 1.

Coinage has been almost universally carried on as a public function. In all advanced countries it is now so carried on without exception. Conceivably, private persons might undertake it, the users of money being allowed to judge of the weight and fineness of the pieces as they are allowed to judge of the quality of the spoons and forks which they use. In this way silver is used to the present day as the medium of exchange in China. But the convenience of coins as a medium of exchange would be immensely lessened if every one had to ascertain for himself whether each piece was what it purported to be. Governments therefore reserve to themselves the monopoly of coinage, and punish as a crime the manufacture by private persons of money pieces. Historically, a strong reason for the public monopoly of coinage was the desire of kings and princes to make a profit by coinage operations, often dishonestly, through intentional debasement of the coin.[1] In modern times, however, the monopoly is maintained because through it alone uniformity in the circulating medium can be secured.

Coins are so manufactured that they cannot be clipped or whittled without easy detection of the defect. Hence designs are always put on both sides, and the edges have corrugations (milling) or lettering. If the coins were simply round flat pieces of metal with smooth edges, shavings could be scraped or cut from them without easy detection. Such "sweating" was common in earlier days, before the art of coinage had been perfected. Modern machinery turns out pieces so skillfully manufactured that troubles of this sort have practically ceased.

Coins, again, are never made of pure metal Gold and silver, without alloy, are soft, and coins made of them alone would wear out fast under active use. Hence a small percentage of base metal — usually copper — is added, the mixture giving the needed hardness and toughness. In most countries, gold and silver coins are 900 fine; that is, they contain 900 parts in gold or silver for every 1000 of gross weight. This is the

[1] For a modern instance of the same sort, see Slatin's *Fire and Sword in the Sudan*, pp. 541–543.

fineness of the coins of the United States. Great Britain still coins her gold pieces with a fineness of $916\frac{2}{3}$; that is, the proportion of alloy is not 1 in 10, but 1 in 12.

In the typical case, and that which we shall for the present alone consider, there is free coinage. That is, every holder of bullion may bring it to the mint, and, no matter how much he brings, have it converted into coin. The cost of manufacturing the coin is usually borne in modern communities by the public; but not necessarily. The mint may return to the applicant coins containing a slightly less amount of specie than the bullion which he presented. The difference retained by the mint then constitutes a charge to meet its expenses, in whole or in part. Such a difference or deduction is called a seigniorage (a name derived from the exclusive coinage rights of the king or feudal seigneur). Where a seigniorage is charged, the exchange value of coin may exceed to that extent the value of bullion. The mints of most countries, however, return to the person who presents gold bullion precisely the same weight of fine gold in the shape of coins. Sometimes, indeed, this return is not immediate; there is a delay corresponding to the length of time required for the manufacture of the coin. Thus, in the United States, a period of six weeks usually elapses between the delivery of bullion and the return of coin. Such a delay may cause the value of bullion to be slightly less than the value of coin, even though there be free coinage without seigniorage, since there is a loss of interest during the period of waiting. These causes of divergence between gold bullion and gold coin — whether seigniorage or delay in coinage — have ceased to be of appreciable importance.

Not only can gold bullion be converted into coin at the mint without charge, or for a trifling charge, but gold coin can be readily converted into gold bullion, either by private melting, or by arrangement, common at the mints, for giving bullion in exchange for coin at fixed rates. The situation is very different with silver, copper, and nickel, which are not freely coined, and which present problems of their own. As for gold, it may be said, without substantial variance from the facts, that bullion and coin are interchangeable.

The rate at which coin is given for bullion is the "mint price of gold." In England the mint price of standard gold is £3 17*s.* 10½*d.* per ounce; each ounce is manufactured into sovereigns at this rate. In France the mint price of fine gold is 3447.74 francs per kilogram, in Germany it is 2790 marks per kilogram; the figures again indicating how many francs or marks are manufactured from the kilogram of gold. Because the amount of gold coin given for bullion never varies (so long as the coinage legislation remains unchanged), people often speak of the value of gold as unvarying. Accustomed to think of all exchanges and all values in terms of price, they think of the value of gold as the price (the mint price) of gold bullion. But obviously the value both of gold bullion and of gold coin is really a very different matter. It depends on the general range of prices of commodities, or, rather it *is* the general range of prices; and this is by no means free from variation.

In the United States, the phrase "mint price of gold" is not often used, because our coinage legislation proceeds not by specifying what number of dollars shall be manufactured out of a given weight (say an ounce) of gold, but by specifying how much gold the dollar shall contain. The dollar is required to contain 23.22 grains of fine gold. Dollar-pieces are no longer coined; they proved too small for convenient use; five-dollar pieces are coined with five times this weight of gold, ten-dollar pieces with ten times the weight. The mint price of gold, if that phrase were used with reference to our coinage system, would be $20.67 per ounce.

§ 4. Before closing this introductory chapter, something may be said of the place which money and the mechanism of exchange hold among the factors that bear on the prosperity of a community.

Every person sells his wares or services for money, and commands the wares and services of others in proportion as he has more or less money. It is natural to suppose that what brings prosperity to the individual brings prosperity to all. Yet a moment's reflection makes it clear that here, as so often, the inference is not warranted. If all persons sell their wares for more money, no one gains thereby. The individual gains from having more money only if others have *not* more money, — if he can buy from others at as low prices as before. If all prices and all money incomes are high, no one is bettered thereby. Money is the means by which each person procures the comforts and necessaries of life; or, to speak more accurately, it is the medium by which each person exchanges the particular things he produces or owns for the various commodities which he wishes to buy. The more money there is, the more of this medium is used in every act of exchange. But prosperity depends on the abundance of the things exchanged, not on that of the counters used in effecting the exchanges.

This is so obvious that mere statement suffices for proof. None the less, it happens often that people who are half trained, and see only one aspect of economic phenomena, believe that abundance of gold or silver, or of paper substitutes for them, is the one thing needful to make the world better off. Many educated and intelligent persons, who would scorn to hold this opinion in its crudest form, yet hold some phase of it by implication. Thus, in connection with trade between one country and another, most people assume that such a state of foreign trade as brings money into the country leads to prosperity, while such a state as carries money out leads to adversity. All notions of this sort are the results of half thinking. The flow of specie into a country or out of it, in the course of international trade, is usually a matter of indifference. Where it is a matter of consequence, the mere increase or decrease in the supply of money is only the first step in a series of events that may affect the country's prosperity.[1] Whenever a person speaks of that which "brings money into the country" (or into the city or the village) as being good for it, the probabilities

[1] See the discussion of international trade in Book IV, especially Chapter 32, and Chapter 36, § 1.

are that he has not mastered the elementary principles of economics. One of the simplest of these principles is that money is primarily an instrument for enabling the division of labor to work out its end with smoothness, and that, barring some niceties presently to be considered, its large or small supply is a matter of no consequence.

But though the quantity of money, and the consequent use of more or less of the counters in each operation of exchange, be matters of indifference, the universal use of money in exchanges is by no means a matter of indifference. It has not merely the obvious effect of facilitating the division of labor and so promoting the output from the operations of production: it has ulterior consequences no less important. Without it neither merchants and traders nor manufacturers could carry on large-scale operations. All the phases of large-scale production, with its far-reaching social consequences, are dependent on a developed and smooth-working money régime; it is indissolubly connected with capitalism and capitalistic enterprise. It underlies all lending and borrowing, all investment, the issue of corporate securities, financial operations of every kind. It has psychological effects as well as effects obviously economic. It affords a universal goal for the instinct of accumulation and possession, creating an environment in which every one strives for money, half forgetful of the purposes which the possession of money serves. All things are put in a pecuniary light, all effort is proximately to make money, all efficiency and all product are measured in terms of money. Though not the fundamental cause underlying the problems of the unequal division of wealth and income, it is yet a condition of the emergence of these problems in the characteristic modern forms: social classes distinguished by differences in money means, capital owned by comparatively few. From one point of view the least essential part of the organization of production and distribution, it is from another point of view the one essential part. Without it, the characteristic modern problems could hardly be imagined.

CHAPTER 18

THE QUANTITY OF MONEY AND PRICES

§ 1. What determines the value of money? That is, what determines the general range of prices? The value of money obviously is high when the general range of prices is low; for a given amount of money will then buy much of other things. Its value obviously is low when the general range of prices is high; for a given amount of money will then buy little of other things. What, now, causes its value to be high or low, prices to be low or high?

The first step toward answering this question is to understand the relation between the quantity of money and its value. The fundamental relation is a very simple one. Double the quantity of money, and, other things being equal, prices will be twice as high as before and the value of money one half. Halve the quantity of money, and, other things being equal, prices will be one half what they were before, and the value of money double. That an increase in quantity tends to lower value, is a proposition holding good of all commodities. The special proposition concerning money is that its value tends to vary precisely in proportion to its quantity. This constant relation does not hold good of any other commodity. Double the quantity of wheat, and its value will probably fall to much less than half of what it was before. Double the quantity of sugar, and its value will probably fall by no means to one half. For both wheat and sugar, the outcome will depend on the elasticity of demand. But in the case of money, there is no question as to elasticity of demand, and no such difficulty in prediction. The value of money, under the simplest conditions, is exactly inverse to its quantity.

This is what is called the quantity theory of money. Concerning it a hot controversy has long waged. It has been vehemently denied; and often it has been erroneously stated. Rightly stated it conforms to the facts, but it must be rightly stated and understood. In the preceding paragraph it has been put boldly, with the purpose to bring out clearly the fundamental truth. But the reader will note the phrases "other things being equal" and "under the simplest conditions." Great qualification and elaboration will be required before the bold statement can be made to fit the complicated phenomena of actual life, especially in modern times. The last word cannot be said until a long series of topics have been covered.[1] For the present, let us consider the essential ground on which the proposition rests, and some of the simplest qualifications.

These essential grounds are found in the nature of the demand for money. People often say that the demand for money is without limit. They mean thereby that any individual desires to secure possession or control of as much as he can. But he desires possession or control as a means, not as an end. Money is not eaten or drunk or directly enjoyed. It is a means of getting other commodities; it is sought in order to be spent. We may set aside, as negligible, the case of the miser who gloats over money for its own sake, and also some other possible cases of hoarding. All the money, whether any individual has control of much or little of it, is spent sooner or later. The demand for it — what is offered in exchange for it — consists of the commodities on sale. But the commodities on sale are simply all the commodities that are to be exchanged. The demand for money, in any given community at any given time, is *constant*. It is not subject to change because of the greater or less range of prices. Whether goods sell for less or more, all of them will still be sold, and will still be offered for money. Hence, when there is twice as much money, the same number of commodities will be offered for the money, and prices will be twice as high as before.

[1] See Chapter 31, at the close of this Book.

In other words, there is no such thing as elasticity in the demand for money. The principle of marginal utility is not applicable. When wheat and sugar are offered more abundantly in the market, their value falls according to the decreasing utility of successive increments. The total sum spent on any one commodity — the quantity sold multiplied by the price per unit — may become greater or less as the number of units grows larger. But the total amount of goods offered for money, which constitutes the demand for money, is not affected by its value. That total remains always the whole number of commodities that are exchanged through this medium. The general process is the exchange of the whole number of commodities for the whole number of money pieces; the equation fixes the value of money according to the relative abundance of money and of goods.

§ 2. Let us now begin to introduce the explanations and qualifications of this fundamental principle. In the first place, we should not speak of the whole number of commodities, or even of the whole number exchanged; but only of the number exchanged through the medium of money. Some goods are consumed by those who produce them, and do not enter the circle of exchange at all. Such are agricultural products consumed by those who grow them. These evidently do not constitute at any time demand for money. But with the growing elaboration of the division of labor, the proportion of goods so used tends to become steadily less. In a country like the United States at the present time it is not far from the truth to say that all things that are produced are exchanged.

Nor is it far from the truth to say that all things exchanged at all are sold for money and exchanged through money. So far as barter is practised, there is obviously no demand for money. Goods exchanged by barter constitute demand directly for each other. But barter has disappeared even more completely than production for one's own consumption.

Much more important is a qualification as to the rate or manner in which goods and money meet each other in exchange. The preceding statements seem to imply that all the goods are exchanged for all the money in one transaction. Obviously this does not happen. At any given moment, or on any given day, only a fraction of the goods is being sold, and only a fraction of the money is being used in purchases. Here, as elsewhere in economics, we should have in mind a flow rather than a fund. The total stock of commodities is indeed sold sooner or later, and may be conceived as a fund. But only a portion of it actually comes to the monetary market in any one day or week or other unit of time, the rest following in orderly sequence. There is a flow of goods into actual exchange. Similarly, the total quantity of money does not constitute a fund, but flows into actual use for purchasing goods in a tolerably regular sequence.

The phrase "rapidity of circulation" has been used for money, to indicate this obvious fact. Of the total money actually on hand in a community a portion only is at any given time at work, so to speak. The money idle in our pockets does not directly affect prices; only that which is buying goods at the counter does so. What proportion is at work, depends on the habits of the people. It is affected by their geographical distribution and by the character of their industries. In a thinly settled agricultural section, where access to shops is not easy or frequent, a larger portion of the money is likely to be idle than in a thickly settled manufacturing or commercial section. The temper of the people is a factor. If they are confident of themselves,—perhaps unduly confident, and thoughtless of the morrow,—they are likely to spend money as fast as it comes into their hands, and let little of it remain idle at any time.

These remarks apply to the larger transactions of merchants and dealers as well as to the everyday purchases of consumers. Traders and producers always have on hand more money than they are using in purchases; the proportion depending partly on the nature of their business operations, partly on their temperament. The fact that these classes, in countries like the United States, use not actual cash, but checks against bank deposits, does not alter the situation; it only supplies another illustration of the difference between the fund of money and its flow.

The total of their deposits in banks constitutes the fund; the checks by which purchases are effected from day to day constitute the flow. Though we are anticipating in speaking of deposits and checks, whose use as substitutes for cash will be considered in due time,[1] it may be noted that the same principles are applicable to this more complex monetary medium as to money in its simplest form. In every form, the medium of exchange has its flow, or rate of use, — its rapidity of circulation.

Similarly, goods have their rapidity of circulation. In more familiar language, they have their rate of turnover. This also depends obviously on a great variety of circumstances. It is likely to be rapid in a large city, slower in the country. It is affected, like the flow of money, by the temper of the people. It is likely to be quicker in an energetic and restless country like the United States than in a more slowly moving country like France. It is likely to vary in different parts of the United States. It varies, too, in different branches of trade. The turnover of a grocer's shop is more rapid than that of a hardware dealer's, that of a flour mill than that of a textile factory. Yet the flow of goods as a whole takes place steadily and continuously, and in a given community with a surprisingly regular course.

Thus the proportion of money which is actually buying goods is not accidental; it is determined by the silent force of custom. It may be irregular for an individual, but over thousands and millions of individuals it follows a steady course. The flow of goods to market takes place at a similarly regular rate. Hence we may argue with confidence that if the total quantity of money be increased, the proportion of it used in making purchases at any given time will be correspondingly increased.

Suppose, for example, — to use an illustration of Mill's, — that suddenly every one in the community has twice as much money. The only thing that can be done with it is to spend it. There is nothing to alter the habits of the people; nothing to cause a larger proportion to be kept in the pocket or in reserve.[2]

[1] See below in this Book, Chapter 24, § 3.

[2] See, however, what is said below, in § 5.

The quantity of goods remains the same, nor is there anything to alter the mode in which people and dealers bring their goods to market. The flow of money will be doubled, the flow of goods unchanged, and prices will be twice as high as before.

The same effect which would ensue from a doubling in the quantity of money would ensue also from a doubling of its rapidity of circulation. If twice as much of the total stock is steadily in use for purchasing goods, the effect is the same as if the quantity were doubled without any change in the ways of using it.

The propositions which were laid down in the opening paragraph obviously assumed that the quantity of goods, and the flow of goods into exchange, remain constant. So much was implied by the qualification "other things remaining the same." Needless to say, the quantity of goods does not always remain the same. If it be doubled when the quantity of money is doubled, prices will be unchanged. If goods be doubled, money being the same, and the flow of goods to market unaffected, prices will fall one half. If the flow of goods to market — their rapidity of circulation — be so affected that twice as large a proportion of goods are regularly offered, prices will again fall one half.

Rapidity of circulation is greater for money than for goods. To put it in other words, the proportion which, at any one time, the money actually offered for goods bears to the total supply of money is greater than the proportion which the goods offered for money bear to the total supply of goods awaiting exchange. The reason for this difference is obvious. Money can always be used without delay in purchases; goods can often be sold but slowly. Money need never wait for a buyer; goods must often wait for one. Many commodities have necessarily a slow turnover, as hardware and household furniture. Other things, like dwellings to let, warehouses, and factories, are in the market only by fractions or installments, — only the utilities which they shed, so to speak, are being offered for sale, — and their disposal is sluggish. Money comes into the market quickly. Though there may be hoards, and occasionally an accumulation of unused money in the hands of people who are getting larger incomes than they are used to, money in the main is kept at work briskly, at a rate greater or less for any given time and country according to the ways and customs of the people.

These various corrections and qualifications of the simple fundamental principle the reader will hereafter be supposed to bear in mind. We shall speak of the value of money as determined by its quantity; meaning thereby that, if other things remain the same, an increase of the total stock of money brings a corresponding increase in the flow of money used in making perchases and adds *pro tanto* to the money offered in exchange for commodities.

§ 3. Let us proceed now to inquire how far the monetary supply of specie is different from its total supply.

The precious metals are used in the arts as well as for monetary purposes. But the demand for them in the arts follows no such special law as does the demand for money. Utility or satisfaction-yielding quality determines the demand for gold trinkets and implements in the same irregular way as it determines the demand for wheat or sugar. The quantitative effect of an increase of supply is unpredictable; the elasticity of demand may show any scale of gradation.

If the same proportion of the total supply of gold and silver were always used in the arts, this difference between the monetary and the industrial demands would be of no consequence for the theory of money. But that proportion is not necessarily the same. To a certain degree it is influenced by the very value of the monetary supply.

If, for example, prices and money incomes in general should go up, in consequence of greater abundance of gold, gold bullion would not advance; since, as we have seen, gold bullion is always at the same price in terms of coin. For gold jewelry, spectacles, and the like, the raw material would be as cheap as before; they would advance in price only so far as the expense of manufacturing them from the bullion would be greater. Relatively to money incomes they would be cheaper than before. This greater cheapness would almost certainly cause more to be bought than before, and a greater proportion of the bullion would be diverted into the arts. A scarcity of gold, and consequent fall in prices and incomes, might be expected to have the converse effect. Gold articles would be relatively dearer, and presumably would be bought in smaller quantity than before. The industrial consumption would divert less gold from the mint.

Even without a rise or fall in the value of gold (*i.e.* in general prices), changes in habits and tastes affect its industrial consumption. Gold jewelry may become more fashionable, gilding and gold leaf more in vogue, gold spectacles may be thought more convenient or becoming. A greater proportion of the available stock will then be removed from the monetary supply.

Of these two sets of causes, the first seems to have less effect than the second. Changes in general prices rarely occur on such a scale as to bring about considerable results of the sort stated. The price of jewelry and other gold articles is affected not only by the price of bullion, but by the expenses of manufacture. These expenses fluctuate in correspondence with changes in general prices. If all prices go up, that of bullion will indeed remain the same; but wages and other items of outlay in manufacturing jewelry will go up as other goods and services do. An advance of twenty-five per cent in general prices is a very marked one. Yet such an advance would mean, not that gold articles would remain unchanged in price, but only that their prices would lag somewhat behind the general advance. They would go up perhaps twenty per cent, instead of twenty-five. The effect on their consumption would probably be small.

The second factor that bears on the industrial use of the metals — changes in habits and fashion — seems to be of more importance. The great growth of wealth during the last half century has led to a larger use of gold in the arts; precisely as it has led to a larger use of diamonds. Not until recent years was any methodical attempt made to ascertain the extent and growth of this use. For the decade from 1880 to 1890 the industrial consumption of gold (including export to the East, of which more will be said presently) was estimated to be, in terms of dollars, about $60,000,000 a year. In 1908 the amount was supposed to be double, — about $114,000,000 for that year. Some part of this reported increase was no doubt due to insufficient counting in the earlier period; but none the less, an increase there undoubtedly was. The change was by no means in proportion to that in the total production of gold, which was about $100,000,000 a year in 1880–1890, and no less than $440,000,000 in 1908. In the earlier period, more than half of the gold produced was diverted from the monetary use of Western countries; in the later year, less than one third was so diverted.

The total stock of gold in the world was estimated in 1900 at about $9,000,000,000, of which something more than one half was in use as money, the rest in use for the arts. What is in use for the arts may be regarded as practically lost from the monetary supply. A part of it, no doubt, returns sooner or later to monetary channels; for plate, jewelry, and the like are sometimes melted and perhaps are then coined. But most of it is definitively lost. Whatever part returns has been little influenced by the value of money. Changes in fashion and habits chiefly determine the remelting, just as they chiefly determine how much shall go into the arts in the first instance. In the main, the use of the precious metals in the arts goes its own way, leaving for the monetary supply the annually accruing surplus of production over and above the independent industrial consumption.

This separation of industrial from monetary use is more complete at present than it was in earlier times. In medieval Europe a link might be cut from a gold chain and used in making a payment; and the cavaliers melted their plate freely to supply funds for the Stuarts. In British India, where conditions continue in many ways medieval, the silver ornaments of the natives and their rupees were interchanged constantly and freely until very recent times; notwithstanding the new position of the rupee since 1893,[1] they still remain to a certain degree interchangeable. Even in advanced countries some shift from monetary to industrial use takes place to this day; but, as has been said, there is an increasing tendency to sharp demarcation and to the settlement of the industrial use by independent causes.

The industrial consumption of silver has shown, like that of gold, a marked growth in recent times. In the United States it seems to have more than quadrupled in the period between 1880 and 1906.[2] This change, like the other, is due in large part to increasing wealth and to a fashion for silver plate and trinkets. No doubt it is due also to the lower price of silver. The price of silver has fallen since 1873 about one half. But the case of silver is different in one important respect from that of gold. Silver is no longer a freely coined metal; it does not become money in the same way as gold. Silver bullion, like tin or copper, has its price in terms of gold, and its use in the arts is affected by price through the same mechanism as tin and copper. The use of gold is affected, as we have seen, through the more obscure and unfamiliar influence of ups and downs in general prices and in general money incomes.

§ 4. Still another diversion of gold and silver from monetary use is important for the countries of Western civilization. This is the drain of specie to the East, which has been going on for centuries, and seems likely to continue for a long time in the future.

In the trade between the West and the East, and especially that between Europe and India, as far back as we have any definite knowledge about it, the merchandise sent from the East has exceeded in money value that sent in return from

[1] See below, Chapter 21, § 5.

[2] In the United States, it seems to have been less than five million ounces a year in the early eighties, and over 20 million ounces a year in 1902–1906. See the Report of the Director of the Mint on the *Production of Precious Metals*, 1906, p. 27.

the West. A balance has remained steadily due to Eastern countries, and has caused a steady flow of gold and silver, and especially of silver, to go to them in payment of the balance. The excess thus due has sometimes increased, sometimes declined. It has fluctuated with the variations in demand for the several commodities exchanged between the two regions, with the accidents of seasons and crops, with the appearance of new articles of export on either side. On the whole, the balance to be paid by Western countries has tended to become less in the last ten or twenty years, largely because sundry goods of Western manufacture have been called for in greater amount by the Eastern population (petroleum, for example, and cotton cloths). But a balance to pay there has been for centuries, and still is. Hence specie steadily flows to the East.

This specie is lost to the Western countries as if it had been absorbed once for all in the arts, — almost as if it had been dropped into the sea. It disappears from the monetary and industrial supplies of Europe and America. India — chiefly British India — has been aptly described as a sink, into which flow gold and silver, and especially silver, never to return.

The explanation of this complete diversion and almost disappearance lies in the unusual industrial conditions of India; conditions which are found in other parts of the East also, though nowhere else so strikingly. China is in a somewhat similar situation, and Japan formerly was; but India, and especially that part which is now British India, has played much the most important rôle in this curious monetary experience. The region has long had an enormous population; in 1900 some three hundred millions. This population is mainly agricultural; it is ignorant and stolid. It uses metallic money almost solely, — very little paper money or other substitutes. The rapidity of circulation of its money is low. Moreover, the people are given to the use of both gold and silver for ornament and for hoarding. The bracelets, rings, and jewels serve both to gratify vanity in the present and to store purchasing power for possible want in the future. Hence great amounts of specie can find their way into India, and flow into use, without much effect on general prices; indeed, for long periods, without any measurable effect at all on prices. No such steady inflow could well take place into a Western country without influencing prices. As will be seen when the subject of international trade is reached, a continued large absorption of specie by a highly organized industrial community is not possible. A large inflow will raise prices; this will tempt imports and check exports; then the flow of specie in payment for excess of exports will cease. But in a country like India the response of prices to increasing specie supply is very slow indeed. In the course of generations, it is true, a response will be found. During the last half century, and especially the last quarter century, prices and money incomes in the East have gone up, not to a marked degree, but appreciably;[1] but during the preceding centuries the upward movement, though probably there, had been so slight and slow as not to be clearly discernible. The rending of old bonds of caste and custom, the growing habituation to security of property, the opening of railroads, have much affected the industrial and monetary situation. But it still remains true, and will probably long continue so, that great quantities of the precious metals steadily flow to the East, to stay there; affecting prices and the value of money, it is true, but so gradually that the flow is rarely checked, and is resumed with new force whenever a large new supply is added to the stock of Western nations, or whenever the demand for Eastern commodities causes an upward movement in their export.

§ 5. In one important case an increase in the supply of money may affect its mode of use, and so introduce a new factor. This is where an added supply facilitates a transition from barter to a money régime. This sort of case cannot occur when once exchange by money is fully established, when all goods and services are sold for money. Then an increase

[1] See a paper by F. J. Atkinson, on "Prices in India, 1870–1908," in *Journal Royal Statistical Society*, September, 1909.

in the quantity of money means simply that two gold or silver pieces, or five, or ten, are used where one had been used before. Adam Smith supposed this to have been the only important consequence of the increase in the European supply of specie which came in the sixteenth and seventeenth centuries from the American mines.[1] Gold and silver plate indeed became thereby more plentiful, — "a real conveniency, though surely a very trifling one." For the rest, Adam Smith goes on, "in order to make the same purchases, we must load ourselves with a greater quantity of gold and silver, and carry about a shilling in our pocket when a groat would have done before." But this was not the only change that took place. The greater plenty of specie contributed to its use in transactions previously effected without it, and caused still other transactions (exchanges) to be carried on which before had not been carried on at all.

The period (about from 1550 to 1650) was one of great industrial transformation. The economic régime of the Middle Ages was being rapidly displaced. Under that régime, the division of labor and exchange had been much limited, and a large proportion of the exchanges and payments that did take place were effected in kind, — that is, by barter, not in money. It is conceivable that the break-up of such a situation, and the substitution of a complete monetary régime, should come about without any change in the supply of money. This would mean that the same supply must suffice for a larger number of transactions, and that prices must go down. But in communities so tied by custom as were those of Europe at the time, this process could have taken place, if at all, only with the greatest difficulty. The mere absence of a supply of specie, adequate for carrying on a larger volume of transactions without a great lowering of prices, was an almost insuperable obstacle to the extension of monetary exchanges. The new specie vastly facilitated the transition. It supplied a lubricator, so to speak, for the smooth and rapid working of the more

[1] Compare what is said of this great change in the next chapter.

effective machinery of exchange. It penetrated quickly and easily into all western Europe, and made possible a much wider adoption of money payments; not only without the distress, real or fancied, that lower prices bring, but, through the abundance of the supply, with markedly higher prices. Thereby the division of labor was extended into many new industrial fields, and the ease of exchange was made greater in many fields where such a division already was practised. A real advance in the efficacy of production was secured, and a real gain in welfare.[1]

None the less, Adam Smith's view, though historically incomplete for the particular case, was in principle sound. He wrote at a time when people still had false notions of the advantages from the plentifulness of the precious metals. Being intent on disabusing them of such notions, he was led to overlook the real advantages which a community may secure from the easy procurement of a needed medium of exchange. But when once this medium of exchange has been procured, and when once it is in fully effective use, reasoning like Adam Smith's is not to be gainsaid. If ten times the labor were given to gold mining that is now given, and ten times the gold were thereby got, the world would not be better off; ten gold pieces would simply be used in every transaction where one is used now. The process of transition, to be sure, — the change from lower to higher prices, or *vice versa,* — would bring some important consequences of its own; but these would not affect the final outcome. Barring the transitional effects, it is immaterial whether prices are low or high, whether many tokens or a few are used to facilitate each act of exchange.

[1] Some dim understanding of this fact — a groping toward a substantial truth — probably contributed to the over-importance attached to a plentiful supply of specie by the writers of the seventeenth century, and commonly by those of the eighteenth century also. But the beliefs of these "mercantile" writers were also much affected by the political power of those princes who, at a time when feudal dues were being replaced by money taxes and payments, and when the money dues were yet hard to enforce, had the command of plenty of specie. And mere confusion of thought further explains their attitude. Here, as on so many subjects, things which seem simple when once they have been cleared up, were long puzzling to men of high intelligence.

It has been suggested by some writers that there is still another way in which the play of utility may affect the relation between the quantity of specie and its value; it may affect the monetary use directly. When money becomes more abundant, people, it is said, will use it less constantly. They will keep more of it in their pockets, use less in purchases. The merchant, too, will keep in his till a larger balance when money is plentiful than when it is scarce. But this, in my judgment, is not a probable result. There is no good reason to suppose that money will be used in a different way when there is more of it. If, indeed, the increase in quantity takes place under circumstances that destroy its general acceptability (as in the case of excessive paper money) the use of money and the demand for it will be affected.[1] But a mere increase of specie, or of other sorts of money enjoying general acceptability, will not affect its flow into use or lessen the effectiveness of each unit in the shaping of prices. Any individual, it is true, who gets a larger *share* of the total money on hand may thereby be led to change his ways of using it. A prosperous person ordinarily keeps a larger reserve of cash, in proportion to his income and his purchases, than one of slender means; and the rapidity of circulation of the money that goes through his hands is less. But if all persons in the community have more money than before, so that its distribution among individuals and classes remains the same, the mode of using the circulating medium will not be affected. The same proportion will be applied to purchases in any given period, and prices will go up in proportion to the general increase in quantity.

§ 6. In this chapter, be it remembered, the principles underlying the value of money have been treated on the assumption that specie alone is used. This case is obviously very different from the complicated one which we find in the actual conditions of civilized countries, where not only specie, but paper money and an intricate credit machinery, are used in effecting payments.

[1] See below, Chapter 23, § 1.

But the same principles hold good here, if adjusted. Instead of saying that the general range of prices depends (other things being equal) on the quantity of specie, we must say that it depends on the total quantity of money means, or of the available *total purchasing power* in terms of money. In proportion as this total purchasing power becomes greater or less, prices will rise or fall, — other things, such as the flow of commodities for sale into the market, being still assumed to be the same. A very troublesome problem is the relation between this total of purchasing power on the one hand, and the total quantity on the other hand of gold or other freely coined specie. This problem cannot be solved until the whole range of substitutes for specie and the whole machinery of credit payments have been examined.[1] The conclusions of the present chapter must therefore be taken as provisional. Yet it may be said at once that they do hold good in the long run of the actual course of affairs. For short periods, even for many years, it is often difficult to trace any connection between the quantity of specie and prices. Even in the long run, it is never possible to trace that precise inverse relation to the value of money which has been deduced in the preceding pages. On the other hand, in the long run, a relation between the volume of specie and prices is in fact to be discerned; while the precise quantitative relation between prices and the total purchasing power in terms of money remains unshaken.

[1] See below, Chapter 31, where the theory of prices is restated with the qualifications amplified.

CHAPTER 19

THE COST OF SPECIE IN RELATION TO ITS VALUE

§ 1. The value of money has been considered in the preceding chapter so far as demand and supply directly affect it. But the supply of specie, like that of any other article, is affected by its value. When value is high, the supply is likely to become greater; when it is low, supply is likely to become less. Specie comes from surface deposits and from mines, — chiefly from mines. What are the conditions of supply?

In general, articles yielded by mines show the phenomena of varying costs and of diminishing returns. Some mines are better than others; any one mine tends, as more is extracted, to encounter sooner or later increasing costs. On grounds of general reasoning, we are then led to expect that the value of the precious metals will conform in the long run to their cost of production at the poorest mine, or at the poorest part of the best mines. It will conform, we should expect, to the marginal cost of production.

In fact, however, no close correspondence, nor even a rough correspondence, can be made out between the cost of the precious metals and their value. This, at least, is the situation with regard to gold. For silver the correspondence is perhaps in very recent times closer, yet through most of human history it has been equally uncertain for silver and for gold. The main causes of this lack of conformity with the theoretical scheme are three, — the durability of the precious metals, the aleatory character of mining, and the irregular discoveries of new sources of supply.

Of these three causes, the most important is the first. The durability of the precious metals brings it about that changes in current output affect the total stock very slowly. For most commodities the supplies produced five years ago are quite out of the market. This holds good even of durable articles like iron and copper. The iron mined five years ago may indeed be still in existence, but it has been fashioned into implements and is committed to uses which practically withdraw it from the market. So far as gold and silver are used in the arts, they also are, in the main, withdrawn from the market. But gold and silver used as money remain in the monetary market indefinitely. Even if cost of production is greatly reduced, and the annual output greatly enlarged, as has been the case in recent years, the monetary stock changes but gradually, and value is affected but slowly.[1]

Next, the very conditions of production at the mines have been irregular through almost the whole course of history, and, though perhaps less markedly, remain irregular to this day. The irregularity appears in mining not only for gold and silver, but for all metals. It is difficult to ascertain in advance what will come out of a hole in the ground. For those mineral products which occur in large masses, under conditions enabling systematic tests and samples, the element of uncertainty and risk, though ever present, is at least greatly less. Such is the case with coal and iron ore. Copper mining seems to be much more speculative; gold and silver mining, even more so. With these the elements of uncertainty are great, and the obstacles in the way of an adjustment of value to marginal cost correspondingly great.

The aleatory character of the production of gold and silver has been accentuated by another circumstance. Mining for them has always had a peculiar fascination, and cool-headed calculation has been absent more than in other mining. In gen-

[1] The world's monetary stock of gold was estimated in 1907 at roughly $7,200,000,000. (Helfferrich, *Das Geld*, edition of 1909, p. 203.) The product in that year was $440,000,000; deducting the gold used in the arts (130–150 millions), there remained for the year a net addition to the monetary stock of say $300,000,000, or about 4 per cent. As compared with any period except the present decade (1900–1910), this was an extraordinary addition to the supply, absolutely and proportionally.

eral, it might be expected that there would be successes enough to offset (with some rough approximation) the failures; prizes against the blanks in the lottery. But, as is so commonly the case with avowed lotteries, the blanks are overlooked, the prizes only are seen. A gold mine, in everyday speech, stands for riches. Statesmen, explorers, investors, have been deceived by the glamor of mining for specie. The profitableness of such mining depends, not on getting the specie, but on getting it with sufficiently little labor and expense. A large output may be got at an expense so high as to wipe out all profit. But people have been constantly tempted to gold and silver mining without rational weighing of yield and cost. The late Professor Soetbeer, a very well-informed and sagacious observer, came to the conclusion that as a whole the production of the precious metals was carried on at a loss. Most persons who have engaged in it have overestimated the possible prizes. They have disregarded not only the blanks, but, to a large extent, the inevitable expenses.

In very modern times, gold and silver mining have come to be carried on more systematically, on a larger scale and with less risk. This change is due to the improvements in mining methods which make it possible to extract the metals from low-grade ores. In former times, the main sources of supply were pockets of very rich ore, and very rich alluvial deposits. The occurrence, however, of such lucky finds is irregular, and their continued productivity, even after they have been hit upon, is even more irregular. But there are other deposits, where the ore has a small content of fine metal, but is very large in amount and is easily tested and measured. By establishing a great plant, and treating vast bodies of ore, quantities and profits can be secured with hardly more irregularity than those in mining iron ore. The same is true of alluvial mining when conducted not on chance deposits in the beds of streams, but on whole hillsides washed by powerful hydraulic machinery. Methods of this more businesslike sort have brought the great increase in the output of gold and silver during the generation just passed.

Third, and closely connected with what has just been said, is the influence of new sources of supply. This factor has played an important part in the production and prices of all the metals, especially in modern times; as, for example, in regard to iron and copper. It has always had special importance with the precious metals, because of that amalgamation of old and new supplies which results from their durability. When new and rich mines have been discovered, the output from them has not displaced existing stocks, but has simply been added to them. It is so, also, with the output from the unsuccessful mines. Though poor mines may have been unprofitable to those exploiting them, the gold and silver yielded by them have contributed permanently to the amount in use. Hence the monetary stock at any given time has been a jumble from rich mines and poor mines; ancient supplies from forgotten sources have mingled with new additions from well-known regions; there has been accidental discovery and scientific exploitation; the whole finally constitutes one vast homogeneous mass, exerting its influence on value through its total quantity.

§ 2. These general statements can be illustrated by considering the history of some of the great changes in the supply of the precious metals.

By far the most remarkable change in recorded history took place between the middle of the sixteenth and the middle of the seventeenth century. Then the production and supply of both gold and silver were revolutionized. For the sake of simplicity, gold has been chiefly spoken of in the preceding pages. But until comparatively recent times silver was a more important monetary metal than gold. Gold and silver were used interchangeably at the period of this great revolution, and the supplies and the values of both may be treated for this period as if they were one.

During the Middle Ages and the Renaissance specie had been comparatively scarce. Some supplies had been left over from the days of the Roman Empire; and there was some production, especially of silver, in Germany, Sweden, Bohemia, Spain. The general range of prices was low. So far as can be made out from a comparison of the commodities dealt in then and now, prices in the fifteenth century were only one fourth or one fifth of what they were in the nineteenth. It must be remembered, too, that payment in kind was still largely prevalent; hence the supply of gold and silver which was on hand served to carry on exchanges for only a limited part of the commodities produced and used. The discovery of America led in the sixteenth century to a sudden enormous increase in the supply. The conquest of Mexico in 1519–1521 and that of Peru shortly afterward enabled the rapacious Spaniards to seize large accumulated treasures. Even more important was the production from the rich mines of these countries, — mines partly known already to the natives, partly discovered by the Spaniards. By far the most important were the mines at Potosi, discovered in 1545. Silver was chiefly produced, and it was in the form of silver that the monetary supply of Europe was chiefly increased. In the first decades of the sixteenth century the total production of silver had been on the average 1,500,000 ounces a year. It rose to near 3,000,000 ounces in the period from 1521 to 1544, and in the period beginning with 1545 (the year of the opening of Potosi) it leaped to 10,000,000 ounces a year. About the last figure it remained for two centuries thereafter.[1]

This great mass of new specie was brought to Europe by the Spanish treasure fleets. A share was captured on the way by the English and Dutch buccaneers; but most of it reached Spain, and thence made its way over Europe. Very large amounts never went into circulation in Spain, but were sent by the Spanish monarchs, especially Charles V, Philip II, and Philip IV, to meet the expenses of their armies in Italy, Germany, France, and the Netherlands. Through one channel or the other, the silver and gold reached all Europe. In part, as was noted in the preceding chapter, it simply enabled exchange by money to supersede exchange by barter; it percolated, so to speak, into spaces not previously

[1] Figures for the annual production of the precious metals are given regularly in the reports of the United States Director of the Mint.

occupied. But even with this absorption, the increase in quantity was so great as to swell the amount of money relatively to the commodities exchanged, and so to bring about what is known as the price revolution of the sixteenth century.

The total supply in Europe has been estimated thus: [1] —

	Gold (Ounces)	Silver (Ounces)
In 1493	17,682,500	225,050,000
In 1544	26,202,250	295,458,500
In 1600	38,322,800	771,600,000
In 1660	48,225,000	1,005,330,500

Stated in terms of dollars, this means that the stock of gold and silver, taken together, rose from about $580,000,000 in 1493 to $1,620,000,000 in 1600 and to $2,500,000,000 in 1660. By the middle of the seventeenth century, prices had risen to double or treble what they were at the opening of the sixteenth century. The change worked itself out chiefly during the hundred years from 1550 to 1650, — a century of far-reaching industrial transformation in many directions, and of social and political changes as important, all complicated and affected by the great rise in prices.

The great advance in prices — the fall in the value of money — was due unquestionably to the increase in the quantity of specie. But it would be misleading to speak of it as determined or measured by a corresponding change in cost of production. The miserable laborer — more than half slave — in Peru and Mexico was forced to his work in the mines by the brutal Spaniard; great quantities of specie came from the rich mines; but it would be absurd to speak of any commercial adjustment of value to cost.

[1] I take these figures (converting kilograms into ounces) from Wiebe's *Geschichte der Preisrevolution im 16. und 17. Jahrhundert*, p. 281. They are at best very rough estimates. The figure for 1493 (the starting point) is most uncertain of all. Moreover, the estimates are for the total metallic stock, not for the monetary stock. My own impression is that the increase in monetary supply itself was greater than these figures indicate; but one can have nothing more than an impression, no certain knowledge.

By the middle of the seventeenth century something like a state of equilibrium had been reached. The supplies of specie from the mines, it is true, continued to be as large as they had been since 1545, and even increased somewhat during the eighteenth century. But the total stock on hand had been so swelled that the continuing additions were of much less proportionate effect. A fair degree of stability in value had come from the durability of the accumulated stock. There was, moreover, a steady advance of population and wealth, an improvement in the arts, and so an increase of the quantity of goods presented for sale. Hence during the second half of the seventeenth century and the greater part of the eighteenth, the range of prices was tolerably stable, with rather a downward than an upward trend. During the first half of the nineteenth century, the trend of prices was distinctly, though not rapidly, downward. This downward movement was not due to any decreased supplies of specie; on the contrary, the production of silver increased considerably, and that of gold held its own. But the great expansion which had followed the industrial revolution of the eighteenth century was in full swing, and the quantity of transactions increased more rapidly than the monetary supplies.

§ 3. Another far-reaching change in the production of precious metals set in about 1850. It was gold that now was chiefly affected. Gold deposits of extraordinary richness were discovered almost simultaneously in California and Australia. The production rose from an annual average of something like 500,000 ounces in 1820–1840 to an annual average of over 6,000,000 ounces in 1851–1860; and this rate of production was maintained, with no marked changes, for nearly half a century. Stated in terms of dollars, the annual gold supply rose from, roughly, $10,000,000 in 1820–1840 to about $125,000,000 in 1850–1895. During the twenty-five years from 1850 to 1875, as much gold was produced and added to the world's stock as had been produced during the three and a half centuries from 1492 to 1850. If the dividing line be put at 1840 (for there was already a marked increase from 1840 to 1850), it appears that the gold product between 1840 and 1875 markedly exceeded that between 1492 and 1840. The change in the monetary stock was of course much greater. Of the amount which had been produced between 1492 and 1850, a large proportion had been lost by absorption in the arts, by abrasion, and (so far as European countries were concerned) by exportation to the eastern hemisphere. The total monetary stock of gold in Europe was in 1850 about 38,000,000 ounces, or, in terms of dollars, about $780,000,000. So sharp was the increase in production that, by 1860, the total monetary stock (after allowing for industrial consumption during the decade) was reckoned at 88,000,000 ounces, or about $1,800,000,000. In ten years the monetary supply of gold had doubled.[1]

The effect on prices after 1850, however, was not comparable to that of the earlier period. Price did indeed rise after 1850 in Europe and the United States, and remained at a comparatively high level for about a quarter of a century. But the advance was one of only twenty or thirty per cent. No such revolution in prices took place as that which followed the discovery of America.

The explanation of this slight effect from a cause apparently so powerful is to be found in several directions. There was a steady increase in the demand for money. The civilized world was progressing fast, and the volume of commodities produced and exchanged was enlarging. Next, — and probably this was more important in the decades immediately after 1850, — the new supplies of gold were added to an existing stock composed, not of gold only, but of both gold and silver, and of the two metals coined and used with equal freedom. In that stock silver had been the major constituent in 1850. Finally, the new supplies of gold in part served simply to displace silver. Of this process of substitution more will be said when the topic of bimetallism is reached.[2] It suffices here to note that in France

[1] I take these figures from Soetbeer's *Materials on the Silver Question*, 1887 (English translation, p. 150).

[2] In the next following chapter.

and other bimetallic countries, much gold simply took the place of silver, the silver being lost to civilized countries by steady exportation to the Orient. So far as such substitution went on, the new supplies of gold served to alter the composition of the metallic money of Europe, but not to add to its total volume. There was indeed a net addition to the total volume, and an addition more than in proportion to the greater volume of commodities. Hence a rise in prices took place; but only to that moderate extent which has been indicated.

§ 4. We pass over for the present the period of falling prices in the last quarter of the nineteenth century, since that period can be best considered in connection with bimetallism. In the production of gold, another great change has been taking place during the closing years of the nineteenth century and the opening years of the twentieth. The annual output of gold had remained nearly stationary after the Californian and Australian discoveries of 1850. During the decade 1880–1890, there had been some slight tendency to decline, but no marked change. Thereafter production rose rapidly; it doubled before the close of the nineteenth century; it quadrupled within five years thereafter. In 1880–1890 the annual production had been on the average something like one hundred millions of dollars. In the year 1900 it was over 250,000,000; in 1908, 440,000,000. The change has been almost miraculous. The total production of gold was as great during the eighteen years, 1891–1908, as it was during the forty years, 1850–1890; and during each of these periods it was much greater than it had been during the centuries that elapsed between 1493 and 1850.[1]

This vast addition to the stock of gold has been the foundation of the rise in prices which has taken place in the Western nations, and indeed the world over, during the last decade (1900–1910). What other causes have been at work, and to

[1] The production of gold may be grouped as follows: —

Aggregate during the 257 years, 1493–1850 ....152,000,000 ounces.
Aggregate during the 40 years, 1850–1890 ....232,000,000 ounces.
Aggregate during the 18 years, 1891–1908 ....240,000,000 ounces.

what extent the simple quantity theory must be modified in accounting for the higher prices, need not here be considered. The increase in the gold supply has been the dominant cause. It cannot be foreseen how far that increase will go, or how far it will contribute to yet higher prices. One circumstance which operated as a drag on the upward movement of prices in 1850–1875 is not now present, namely, the displacement of silver. Gold has won its victory. Silver has been displaced once for all, or at least reduced to a subsidiary place. The additions to the gold supply are in the main *net* additions to the monetary stock of Western countries, and additions of extraordinary amount. No doubt, the great and steady growth in the volume of commodities brings an increasing demand to meet the increasing supplies of gold; but whether the demand grows in proportion must be doubted.

The new supplies of gold have been derived, as already remarked, chiefly from low-grade ores; that is, from great deposits of ore having a very low content of gold, but capable of being worked systematically on a great scale. It is profitable to mine ore which yields only $10 (half an ounce) to the ton; that is, ore which contains gold in the proportion 1 : 75,000.[1] The most notable source of this kind is in South Africa, where the mines of the Transvaal have tempted the fortune hunters and led to the subjection of the sturdy Boers. The so-called reef there is of great extent and calculable richness. Of late the Transvaal mines alone have produced annually nearly as much as the world's annual output in the richest period of the Californian and Australian discoveries. Similar deposits are worked, by the same improved methods, in the United States, and indeed in all parts of the world. American mining engineers and managers have been foremost in this march of improvement. As a result, the efficiency of labor in producing specie has been increased to the same degree as, nay, of late to a greater degree than in producing coal or iron or most manufactured commodities.

[1] There are even mines, worked with handsome profit, in which the ore contains only $2.50 gold to the ton, or one part in 300,000.

It is obvious that any uniform increase in the gold supply, even though great, tends to become progressively less in its effect. Each increment enlarges permanently the existing stock; and the succeeding increments, though equally great, are less in proportion to the stock as enlarged. The increase in supply takes place by arithmetical progression; it would have to take place by geometrical progression in order to continue to lift prices at the same rate as at the start. The monetary supply of gold doubled between 1850 and 1860. But after 1860, the stock on hand had been so much enlarged that, though the same annual output was maintained, the rate of enlargement in the total supply was much relaxed. When a stream of water floods a valley, the first inflow raises the level very fast. As the inflow continues, there is a widening of the area over which the water spreads, and the same addition to the supply produces a steadily lessening effect in raising the surface. So it is with an increase in the supply of the money metals.

§ 5. At the beginning of this chapter it was said that we should expect gold to be governed in value by the principles that apply under varying costs and diminishing returns. That is, we should expect value to be determined, in the long run, by cost at the poorest source of supply, or at the marginal mine. In fact, however, over periods as long as it is commonly worth our while to consider, the relation is more nearly the opposite. It is not so true that cost at the marginal mine governs value, as it is that current value determines what sort of mine shall remain in operation and shall become the marginal mine.

This inverted relation is due to the operation of two of the factors noted in the first section: the durability and consequent large accumulated stock of gold, and the irregularity in the discovery of new supplies. The great stock on hand determines or at least underlies the value of the specie. Those mines that are workable at this value continue to yield their supplies. Those that are not workable at this value cease. (We disregard here the aleatory character of gold mining, which causes no little production even at a loss.) The richer mines, which yield a large profit at current values, *a fortiori* continue to yield supplies; very probably the major part of the annual output comes from them. Value does not accommodate itself to cost at their hands, because of the slow influence of the annual yield on the total stock. A decline in the value of gold — that is, a general rise in prices — makes things harder for the poorer mines, and some of them cease operations. But cessation on their part may have but a negligible effect on the total stock. Search for new mines is constantly going on. All new ventures add something to the annual yield, even though many of them are unprofitable and therefore only of temporary effect. Some of the ventures are highly successful, and on occasions — as in California and Australia in 1850, and in the Transvaal since 1890 — contribute huge supplies suddenly. It might be expected that a high value of gold (that is, low prices) would stimulate the search for it, a low value (high prices) dampen the search. Some such tendencies there doubtless are. But they are overshadowed, in their effects on total stock and on value, by the steadiness of the total stock and the irregularities of discovery and exploitation. Historically, therefore, it is very difficult to discover any but the loosest connection between the cost of gold and its value. Over long periods — for generations at a time — the value of the metal determines which among the mines are able to hold their own. It is not these mines that determine the metal's value.

This proposition, at all events, seems now to hold good of gold. Until very recent times it held good of silver also. During the great silver flood which followed the discovery of America, the mines in Germany and other parts of Europe had to accommodate themselves to the new range of prices and the new value of silver. Those which were no longer profitable under these new conditions ceased operations; and the silver production of Europe shrank sensibly during that period. Within the last thirty or forty years, however, silver has been put into a very different position. It has become, in the main, an industrial metal, like tin, copper, nickel; and its value is determined now by causes essentially the same as those acting on these other metals. This great change in the position of silver is the main subject of the following two chapters.

CHAPTER 20

Bimetallism

§ 1. In the preceding pages no attempt was made to consider the relations between gold and silver. The supply of specie was treated as if gold and silver constituted a homogeneous mass. Throughout most of monetary history, however, problems and difficulties have arisen in the endeavor to treat the two metals as homogeneous. These difficulties became accentuated in the nineteenth century, and finally resulted, at the close of that century, in the displacement of silver from the position of a freely coined money metal. This change, one of the most notable in monetary history, was brought about in a surprisingly short space of time. For long centuries silver had been freely coined, and had been the more important monetary metal; it was discarded from this use in the brief course of one generation.

Both before and after the great inflow of specie from the Spanish-American mines, the two metals were used interchangeably. Silver was relatively the more plentiful, and the more commonly used. It was entirely possible to coin each metal independently, and let the two sorts of pieces circulate together, but not on any common basis. Yet it was highly convenient to link them together in some way, so arranging their denominations that they could be used interchangeably. Gradually the double standard system developed: both metals were manufactured into coins of the same or similar names and denominations. The method is illustrated in the system of the United States. The silver dollar contains $371\frac{1}{4}$ grains of pure silver, or $412\frac{1}{2}$ grains of silver $\frac{9}{10}$ fine. The gold dollar contains (or rather, if coined, would contain) 23.22 grains of pure gold, or 25.8 grains of gold $\frac{9}{10}$ fine. Their weights are to each other as 16 to 1 (15.988 is the precise figure, commonly spoken of as 16). This is the coinage ratio; the silver dollar contains sixteen times as much pure metal as the gold dollar. Similarly, in France, the five-franc piece of silver contains 347.22 grains of pure silver, and the corresponding piece of gold would contain 22.4 grains of pure gold. The coinage ratio in this case is 15½ to 1.

Under the pure and simple double standard both metals are freely coined. Any holder of silver bullion can bring it to the mint, and have it manufactured into coin without limit of quantity; and the holder of gold bullion has the same right. Moreover, all coins, whether silver or gold, are made full legal tender for the payment of debts; that is, of debts contracted, as most debts are, simply in terms of so many dollars or francs. These two elements — free coinage and full legal tender — are the essentials of the complete double standard.

§ 2. When the double standard is adopted, the question arises whether the ratio at which the metals are coined by the mint and are thus given purchasing power in the form of money, conforms to their relative value as bullion. If at the mint 16 ounces of silver are coined in the market into as many dollars as 1 ounce of gold; and if, as bullion, 15 or 15½ ounces of silver can be sold at a price equivalent to 1 ounce of gold, — no one will bring silver to the mint. The silver will be more valuable as bullion than as coin; and experience proves that a very small fraction of difference suffices to decide that the metal shall not be presented for coinage. If, on the other hand, silver as bullion can be sold only at the rate of 16½ or 17 ounces of silver for 1 ounce of gold, no one will bring gold to the mint. The holder of an ounce of gold can get for it at the mint only as many coined dollars as he can get for 16 ounces of silver. By exchanging his gold in the market for 16½ or 17 ounces of silver bullion, he can get more coined dollars; and accordingly he will present at the mint silver bullion only. To repeat, a very small variation between the ratio fixed at the mint and that which rules in the open market, will cause one or the other of the two metals to be the sole one presented at the mint for coinage.

The metal which tends, under such conditions, to be presented at the mint is said to be overvalued. The metal which is not presented, and which indeed may be subjected to the opposite process of being melted into bullion from coin, is said to be undervalued. Strictly speaking, the mint regulations do not put a valuation on either metal; they simply state the conditions of coinage. But the regulations, when they are those of the complete double standard, do lay down, in an effective way, a relative value. Where silver is coined at a ratio of 16 to 1 with gold, and silver is worth in the market 15 to 1 of gold, the coinage system says that 16 ounces of silver are required to buy as much as 1 ounce of gold; the market says that 15 ounces suffice. Silver is given a higher value in the market, a lower value by the mint; by the mint it is undervalued. And where silver is worth 17 ounces in the market, it is overvalued at the mint if coined at this same ratio of 16 to 1. The mint then says that 16 ounces of silver are required to buy as much as 1 ounce of gold, but in the market 17 ounces are needed to buy as much.

That metal which is overvalued will tend to become the sole constituent of the metallic circulating medium. It alone will be presented at the mint for coinage. This, to be sure, will tend to withdraw it *pro tanto* from the bullion market; and this process will tend to raise its value as bullion. Conversely the undervalued metal, not being presented at the mint for coinage, will tend to be more plentiful in the market as bullion; and this will tend to lower in turn its value. The offer of free coinage under the double standard thus in some measure exercises a steadying influence on the relative value of gold and silver; a fact which, as will presently appear, has been of no small importance in monetary history. But if there be a permanent force at work which brings about a continuing difference, even though a slight one, between the market valuation and the mint valuation, then the undervalued metal will gradually go out of circulation, the overvalued metal will come more and more into circulation, and eventually the metallic money will consist of the overvalued alone. If there is a considerable and sustained variation between mint and market valuations, this process will work itself out very quickly; the cheaper or overvalued metal will displace the other in a very short time.

No country's history presents a simpler illustration of these principles than that of the United States. When our coinage system was established in 1792, the complete double standard was adopted, at the ratio of 15 to 1. That ratio was chosen after careful inquiry; but it proved to differ from the market ratio, which was about 15½ to 1. At least this ratio was accepted about ten years later for the coinage system of France. Silver accordingly was overvalued at the United States mint, and gold was undervalued. No gold was presented for coinage, and the metallic circulating medium consisted wholly of silver.[1] In 1834, in consequence of various causes, —

[1] Silver dollars of United States mintage were, in fact, little used in this earlier period. The coins were chiefly of foreign mintage, largely Mexican dollars, which passed current at rates specified by law for their receipt in payment of public dues. The foreign coins took the place of the United States coins because they were abraded or light weight. (Note what is said in § 3 about Gresham's Law.)

The changes in the coinage system of the United States are shown in the following table. The coinage ratio, it must be remembered, rests on the relative weight of pure metal in the coins.

United States Coinage

Year	Gold Dollar			Silver Dollar			Ratio
	Standard Gold (gross weight of coin)	Fineness	Pure Gold	Standard Silver (gross weight of coin)	Fineness	Pure Silver	
	grains		grains	grains		grains	
1792	27.00	916.66/1000	24.75	416	892.4/1000	371¼	15 to 1
1834	25.8	899.225/1000	23.2	416	"	371¼	16.002 to 1
1837	25.8	900/1000	23.22	412½	900/1000	371¼	15.988 to 1

The pure content of the silver dollar has remained the same throughout, —

partly a reaction against undue use of paper money, partly an irrational desire to use gold because of the discovery of what were supposed to be large deposits in North Carolina, — the ratio was abruptly changed. It was made 16 to 1. It overvalued gold as much as the old ratio had overvalued silver. Gold alone was now presented at the mint for coinage. Silver gradually drifted out of circulation and out of the country. The change was virtually from a silver standard to a gold standard. After the California gold discoveries in 1850, the change became pronounced. Great quantities of gold were coined at the mint, and silver quite disappeared. Arrangements were indeed made (in 1853) for the use of silver, as subsidiary coin, and in later years its coinage into legal tender dollars was resumed; but these later modes of using silver present new questions, of which more will be said shortly.

§ 3. The tendency of the overvalued metal to drive out the undervalued is often termed Gresham's Law. The name is derived from a Sir Thomas Gresham of the sixteenth century, who gets undeserved fame, as if he had been the discoverer of the tendency. The "law" is simply the commonplace fact, long recognized, that where coins of different bullion value circulate side by side, the poorer, if there be enough of them, will displace the better. The cheaper money metal will be used by preference in presentation at the mint and in making payments; the dearer will be used by preference in the arts or for bullion purposes.

An important illustration of this tendency is in the displacement of full-weight coins by light-weight or abraded coins of the same metal. Until very recent times the machinery for manufacturing coins worked slowly and somewhat imperfectly. It was difficult to turn out a great many coins rapidly; and the coins

371¼ grains of fine silver. The change in ratio was accomplished in 1834 by lessening the amount of pure metal in the gold dollar. In 1837 further minor changes were made, bearing chiefly on the proportions of alloy in the coins. These proportions had previously been irregular. The fineness was now made $\frac{9}{10}$ for both gold and silver, and at the same time a slight addition was made to the pure content of the gold dollar, making a trifling change in the coinage ratio.

minted not only were subject to ordinary abrasion, but, in consequence of uneven mintage, were specially subject to clipping. New and good coins were therefore likely to be picked out for use in the arts or for exportation, while only the poorer pieces remained in circulation. Such seems to have been the common situation of silver coins until far into the nineteenth century. Silver coin, because of its more frequent use, is more subject to abrasion than gold. It is, moreover, more likely to pass current and to remain in circulation, even though abraded; for, since it is used in minor transactions, a trifling deficiency in bullion content, even a considerable deficiency, is likely to be disregarded. People commonly accept the smaller pieces as they are offered in payment, without troubling themselves to inspect them. Hence — to give an example — in the United States during the period from 1792 to 1834, when silver was the money metal in circulation, foreign silver pieces of various mintage were in actual use. These foreign coins had been authorized for use in public payments, because at the beginning no United States mint or coins existed. When the mint was established and coins were issued from it, the new coins could not displace the foreign pieces, being full-weight and preferably used for the arts or exportation. Hence the coinage, which seemed futile, was discontinued, and only the more or less inaccurate foreign coins remained in circulation. Difficulties of a similar sort were long encountered in all European countries, from the Middle Ages through the eighteenth century. The remedies for them are simple: first, the plentiful and accurate manufacture of full-weight coin; second, the withdrawal of all legal sanction (such as receipt in payment of public dues) from other coin; and third, the redemption at the public charge of pieces which become worn by ordinary wear. It was formerly common to enact that pieces which had suffered in weight beyond a certain tolerance should not only lose their validity as legal tender, but should be redeemed at the mint merely as bullion, not at their face value. The holder, thus called on to suffer the loss in value from abrasion, tried to pass them on to another person. Since the payment of ready money is usually welcome to the payee, even coins much abraded remained indefinitely in circulation. It is now the common practise, and the sound one for governments, to redeem at their face value all coins which have not been intentionally clipped or sweated.[1] At the same time, the machinery for providing new and good coins is amply adequate. Hence the particular troubles here described have well-nigh disappeared.

§ 4. The difficulties commonly experienced under the double standard have caused resort to another mode of using both metals together. Gold is made the only freely coined metal and the only one having complete legal tender quality, and silver, though still coined, is not coined freely, but in limited amounts and solely for use as a minor coin. This method was first systematically followed by England when she adopted the single gold standard in 1816. It has since been adopted, so far as subsidiary silver is concerned, by all the civilized countries, and has become a normal accompaniment of the existing gold standard system.

The system of the United States may serve as an example. The high value of gold makes it unavailable in minor payments. The smallest gold piece which can be conveniently used is the quarter eagle ($2.50), corresponding to the British half sovereign, the German ten-mark piece, the French ten-franc piece. Even the quarter eagle and the corresponding coins of foreign countries are of doubtful serviceability; they are easily lost or overlooked, and are subject to comparatively rapid abrasion. A piece of the sovereign or half eagle size ($5) is the smallest gold coin that is thoroughly satisfactory. Yet a multitude of transactions must be settled with money of smaller denominations. Silver coins are convenient in sizes from the ten-cent piece to the dollar piece. For the smallest transactions, even silver has not bulk enough; for these, resort must be had to nickel and copper.

Under the complete double standard it may well happen that, if silver is undervalued, all the silver coin, large and small,

[1] The United States, however, redeems gold coins at their face value only where the depreciation is not more than one-half of one per cent.

will disappear and that an inconvenient scarcity of small change will ensue. This is precisely what happened in the United States under the system which was adopted in 1834 and 1837. Silver then was undervalued, and gold gradually took its place. When finally the California gold poured in abundantly after 1850 and gold coinage at the mint assumed large dimensions, silver completely disappeared from circulation. Hence in 1853 an act was passed which created the subsidiary system in this country. Silver coins were authorized, — half dollars, quarters, and dimes, — containing so light a content of fine silver that no one would be tempted to export them or to melt them for the arts. The silver half dollar, for instance, was made to contain (and still contains) 172.8 grains of fine silver, or 345.6 grains for two half dollars. The silver dollar, whose free coinage at that time was still authorized, contained (and still contains) 371¼ grains. If all silver coins had been freely minted at the rate newly adopted for the half dollars and for the other subsidiary coins (345.6 grains to the dollar), silver would then have been overvalued, and in turn would have displaced gold. But something very different from free coinage was put into operation. No private person was entitled to present silver at the mint for conversion into small coin. The government itself bought the silver bullion in the market, and alone arranged for its coinage. The amount which the government thus bought and coined was limited to the quantity supposed necessary to meet the needs of small-change transactions. Thus the silver coins would not be exported, and yet would not displace gold. To guard against possible abuse, it was further provided that the subsidiary coin should be legal tender only up to a limited sum, now fixed at $10.

Obviously, the government makes a profit by an operation of this sort. The overvalued silver coins are paid out by the government in its ordinary disbursements, or are exchanged by it for full-value gold. In either case there is a profit. This also is often called a "seigniorage," though it differs in important respects from the seigniorage which may be charged on the freely coined and full-value pieces.

Such are the essential principles of subsidiary coinage. Substantially the system had long been followed as to the copper and nickel coins adapted for petty transactions. These have been token coins ever since gold and silver came to be used as the standard metals. In fact, the underlying principle — an artificial value due to limitation of quantity — was followed, or attempted to be followed, in the "billon" coins common in Europe from the Middle Ages until the first part of the nineteenth century. These were pieces in denominations for small transactions, having some percentage of silver, but chiefly alloy, issued by kings and princes primarily for profit, and given a circulation within their territories. The issues were often excessive; the opportunity for profit was abused. In this regard, as in so many others, coinage practise during the nineteenth century was greatly improved, and now is well-nigh perfected. No state now coins subsidiary pieces, whether silver or nickel or copper, with a view primarily to profit. The profit accrues because it is incident to the best method of providing a convenient medium for small transactions.

The regulation of subsidiary coin is carried on with variations of detail in different countries. The quantity coined is sometimes fixed at so much per head of population. Thus in Germany subsidiary silver is minted at the rate of 15 marks (formerly 10 marks) per head of population; in France at the rate of 7 francs (formerly 6 francs) per head. In Great Britain no specific limit is set; the Bank of England arranges for the coinage of such amounts as experience from time to time shows to be needed. In the United States, also, no limit is set.

To prevent any possible depreciation of the subsidiary coin, it is usually redeemable at its face value by the government treasuries when presented in reasonable quantity. Thus in the United States subsidiary silver coins are redeemable when presented in sums of $20, in Germany when presented in sums of 200 marks. The same object is accomplished by receiving them without limit of quantity in payment of public dues, as is done in France.

CHAPTER 21

Bimetallism, *continued.* The Displacement of Silver

§ 1. We turn now to a consideration of the relation between silver and gold during the nineteenth century and to the train of events which ended in the virtual discarding of silver and the general adoption of the single gold standard.

The double standard, as has already been said, prevailed over almost all Europe until very recent times. It was chosen by the United States, in 1792, as the normal system. It was maintained by France when in 1803 she established her present system of decimal coins. In England, it is true, the single gold standard, with silver for subsidiary coins only, was adopted in 1816. England had had, through the eighteenth century, a nominal double standard, with a circulation composed in fact chiefly of gold. In 1816 the gold standard was formally and definitively established. But on the continent of Europe in general the double standard prevailed, with a stock of metallic money made up, as a rule, chiefly of silver. France alone had a circulation in which gold, though by no means the largest constituent, yet was important side by side with silver. That great country emerged from the wars of the Napoleonic period in a prosperous state; and her greatness, continued prosperity, and her large stock of both metals had an important influence on monetary history for over half a century.

It has already been said that the very existence of the double standard tends to bring the relative values of gold and silver toward the ratio chosen. When a supply of the overvalued metal is attracted to the mint, so much less of it is left in the open market. Its value tends to rise, it becomes less overvalued, perhaps ceases to be overvalued at all. When, on the other hand, a supply of the undervalued metal is melted or exported, so much more of it comes on the market. The additional supply tends to lower its value, and the market ratio comes nearer to the mint ratio. A country having a double standard may be said to be in the position of one who offers to buy and sell at its coinage ratio (say 15½ to 1) any quantity of gold and silver that may be offered. This is not literally the case; the country does not directly buy gold and silver bullion. But its free coinage of both is tantamount to purchase, so long as a supply of both metals remains in circulation, and the substitution of one for the other can actually take place. When once either metal has completely displaced the other, this consequence no longer appears.

Some effect of this sort was produced by France during the second quarter of the nineteenth century; and a marked effect was produced in the third quarter.[1] Whenever the price of silver fell in terms of gold, silver tended to be sent to France for coinage, and gold tended to flow out of France. Whenever the price of silver rose in terms of gold, gold tended to be sent to France for coinage, and silver tended to flow out. A high price of silver in terms of gold means, of course, a low market ratio, while a low price of silver means a high ratio.[2] During the greater part of the period from 1820 to 1850, the price of silver was somewhat lower than the equivalent of the French ratio of 15½ to 1. Silver tended to flow into France; gold tended to flow

[1] The first quarter of the nineteenth century was much disturbed; moreover, our information as to the flow of specie into and out of France is exact only after 1822. Hence the narrative in the text is confined to the second and third quarters.

[2] The relation of the ratio to the usually quoted price of silver may be stated thus: —

At the Ratio of	The Price of Fine Silver in United States Money is	The Price of Bar Silver (.925 fine) in British Money is
16 : 1	$1.2919 per ounce	58.93*d.* per ounce
15½ : 1	1.3336 per ounce	60.83 per ounce
15 : 1	1.3780 per ounce	62.86 per ounce

out. The French circulation then consisted chiefly of silver; the proportion of gold was not large, and a very great substitution would have led to the complete disappearance of gold. That stage was nearly reached, but not quite. France was growing in population and wealth, and there was the basis for a large net increase in the stock of specie. Much of the added silver made its way into circulation without displacing gold, and the outflow of the latter metal, though it seems to have come very near to exhausting the stock in circulation, did not entirely do so.

After 1850 the situation abruptly changed. The unexampled supplies of new gold from California and Australia were poured into the world's markets. The price of silver rose; the ratio fell. It became advantageous to send gold, not silver, for coinage into France. A very great influx of gold took place, amounting for the decade 1850–1860 to over three thousand million francs ($600,000,000). A corresponding, though by no means an equal, outflow of silver took place. For in this period, as in that preceding, France increased her metallic stock, with the difference that now the addition was all in the form of gold, whereas before it had been chiefly in the form of silver. The silver which was steadily exported from France tended to keep down the price of silver bullion in the market, and so maintained the market ratio not far from 15½ to 1, though now with a tendency to a figure lower than 15½ rather than higher.

The bimetallic régime in France during the period immediately following 1850 thus served to steady both the general range of prices and the ratio between gold and silver. A great part of the new gold simply displaced silver in France. The superseded metal, again, made its way very largely to the East. The constant movement of specie to the East, which has already been described, happened in this period to be unusually large. There the silver was absorbed without sensibly affecting prices even in those regions. The free opening for coining both metals in France has been justly described as operating like a parachute to arrest the fall in the value of gold. Some fall — that is, some rise in prices — did indeed take place; but it was less sharp than would have been the case without the French coinage influence.

This episode has been cited by the advocates of bimetallism, and justly, as an illustration of the benefits that may come from their system. Some critics have maintained that the result failed of attainment, so far as concerns the relative value of gold and silver, because the market ratio was not perfectly steady. It fluctuated, tending to be a trifle above 15½ to 1 before 1850, a trifle below after 1850. But no one would maintain that an unfailing steadiness at the price exactly equivalent to a ratio of 15½ to 1 was either possible or in any significant degree desirable. It suffices if a reasonable approach to steadiness is secured. Some fluctuations, according to the changing currents in international trade and in the foreign exchanges, are inevitable; so much will become clear when at a later stage the subject of the foreign exchanges is taken up. In essentials, the bimetallists can point to the French experience, certainly during the period after 1850, as counting in favor of their system.

§ 2. Later in the nineteenth century another change set in, not quite so abrupt as that after 1850, but no less unexpected. The production of gold had reached its maximum about 1860, and thereafter barely held its own. The inflowing new supplies were still very great as compared with any period before 1850; but they spread over a larger area, and they were met by an increasing volume of goods. The industries of the civilized world were rapidly expanding, and the demand for money on the whole kept pace with the supply. On the other hand, a change began in the production of silver. Great discoveries were made in the United States, the beginnings of an increase in the productiveness of silver mining as striking as that which had taken place in gold mining. The price of silver in the market fell slightly about 1865. Silver no longer flowed out of France, and some silver flowed in. The market price for a few years was equivalent almost exactly to the ratio of 15½ to 1. Then in 1873 it fell more sharply, became equivalent to a ratio of 16 to 1, and led to a new inversion of the movement; gold began to flow out of France in large quantities, and silver began to flow in.

This inversion proved unwelcome. Gold had come to be regarded, reasonably or unreasonably, as the preferable metal. The practise of England, the leading industrial country, was the main cause of this preference. The German Empire, when reorganizing its currency system in 1871, adopted the gold standard once for all, influenced chiefly by the English example. The coinage of the United States had been, after 1850, practically on a gold basis. France, not wishing to lose her gold, in 1873 stopped the free coinage of silver. In this measure France no longer acted alone. With other countries she had formed in 1865 the Latin Union; the other countries being Belgium, Switzerland, Italy, and Greece.[1] The main object of the Union was the adoption of a uniform decimal coinage system, based on the French franc. Complete bimetallism, with free coinage of both metals at 15½ to 1, was also adopted; and thereafter all these countries had to act in common in their mint and coinage legislation. France was by all odds the most important power in the Union, industrially as well as politically. With the checkered and interesting history of the Union we have not space to deal. It served a useful end by promoting the spread of the rational franc (decimal) system, but it led to much friction and inconvenience between the adherent countries. So far as the coinage of silver was concerned, the states of the Latin Union found it necessary to act together. The decisive steps were taken in 1873–1874; then free coinage ceased, though not all of silver coinage. In 1873 France, acting alone at first, limited the amount of five-franc pieces (that is, of full-tender silver) which would be coined at the mint. Belgium, also acting alone, imposed a similar limitation in 1873. In 1874, the Latin Union, by a special agreement, prescribed the same policy for its mem-

[1] Greece joined the Latin Union in 1868. Spain adopted the franc system, but did not join the Union. Greece and Italy, though members, have counted for less than the other countries, because their currency, during practically all of the time when action regarding silver coinage was under consideration, was on a paper basis. As to the working of paper money, see Chapter 23, below.

bers, the amount of five-franc pieces to be coined being apportioned among them. Limitation was soon followed by complete cessation. In 1878 the coinage of five-franc pieces was stopped; and it has never been resumed. Bimetallism came to an end.

The cessation of silver coinage left the metallic circulation of these countries in a situation not different on the surface from that of bimetallism, yet in essentials very different. Gold and silver coins continued to circulate side by side, and maintained the relative values assigned to them at the mint. The silver five-franc pieces were not subsidiary coins; they were legal tender without limit in payment of debts. Yet in important respects they were like subsidiary coin. They were no longer freely minted; and their intrinsic or bullion value was different from that which they had as coin. The price of silver bullion continued to fall after 1873 and after 1878. If free coinage of silver had been retained in France and the Latin Union, silver would have been presented at their mints in larger quantities. But it was no longer accepted. Gold alone was freely coined. The silver coins were as good as the gold for payments within each country, and indeed throughout the Union, since they were of uniform shape and content. They were (and are) legal tender without limit; and they were received without limit in payments to the government for taxes and other dues. Large quantities of gold, on the other hand, were also in circulation. This gold had to be in use, in addition to the silver. If the monetary supply had been confined to the silver alone, its limited quantity would have caused prices to be low; this again would have caused imports to be small, exports to be large; money would have flowed in; and the only kind of money which now could flow in was gold.[1] The silver five-franc pieces, like the subsidiary coin, were given an artificial value by the limitation of their quantity; and their value conformed to that of freely coined gold.

[1] The reasoning here anticipates what will be said later of the working of international trade. But this part of the theory of international trade is so simple that its bearing will be readily seen. Compare Book IV, Chapter 32.

To this situation in France and the Latin Union, never established by design, but reached through a succession of unforeseen steps, the name "limping standard" has been applied. The silver coin, though intrinsically of less value than the gold, hobbles along, maintained at equality by being coupled with its stronger associate. The same situation has developed in other countries also, partly by deliberate action, partly by steps taken with as little intent as in the Latin Union of bringing about a limping standard.

§ 3. Germany adopted a limping standard deliberately, though only as a transitional measure. As has just been said, her gold standard was adopted in 1871, when a uniform coinage system was created for the newly established empire. The monetary unit was the mark, whose gold content is nearly that of the English shilling; that is, the twenty-mark piece is not far from the English sovereign. The metallic circulation, however, had been before that time chiefly of silver, largely in the form of thaler pieces having a silver content equal to that of about three and one half francs. These thaler pieces were in part withdrawn and replaced with new gold pieces. But in part they were left in circulation. Their complete replacement with gold was a task which it was thought best (and wisely so thought) to carry out gradually. No new coinage of thalers, of course, was permitted. Those left in circulation were declared legal tender at the rate of three marks for the thaler. Notwithstanding their insufficient intrinsic value, they were left on a parity with gold precisely like the silver five-franc pieces of the Latin Union, — by the limitation of their quantity, by their full legal tender power, and by their acceptance in payment of all public dues.

The original intention had been to leave the thalers in circulation only during a comparatively brief period of transition. It was expected that from time to time, as they were received in the public tills, they would be withdrawn, melted into bullion, sold as such, and replaced by gold coins. This process, indeed, went on for a few years. But after 1873 the price of silver fell sharply, and sales of the metal were a losing business. Moreover, the advocates of bimetallism bitterly opposed the sales. The German government, by way of partial concession to the bimetallists, and also from a cautious desire to await the future as to the supplies and availability of the two metals, in 1879 stopped the withdrawal of the thalers and the sale of the bullion. For many years thereafter the thalers remained in circulation. In 1900, however, steps were finally taken toward getting rid of them, though in a way somewhat different from that originally contemplated. The act of that year provided for their retirement by gradual recoinage into subsidiary money. The permissible amount of subsidiary coin, which had been originally ten marks per head, was then raised to fifteen marks; the additional quantity of such coin was to be got by using the old thalers. Most of the thalers were soon recoined, and the rest will disappear as the increase of the population of Germany calls for more subsidiary coin. Virtually, the limping standard has ceased to exist in Germany.

§ 4. In the United States a result exactly similar to that in France has been brought about, without intent, through a succession of compromises and half measures. The history of this episode cannot be fully understood until price movements and paper money have been dealt with. So far as the silver situation is concerned, it will suffice to state briefly the important events.

In 1873 the coinage of silver dollars — that is, of the full tender, freely coined silver — was dropped in the United States. It was in this year, too, that France suspended free coinage; but the coincidence in date was fortuitous. The United States in 1873 had only paper money in circulation; depreciated paper, or so-called fiat money. If there had been specie in circulation (and for some important purposes specie was in use, though not in active circulation), that specie would have been gold. After the coinage changes of 1834 and 1837, and the influx of new gold that began in 1850, gold alone had been the real basis of the monetary system. The existence of a nominal double standard had been forgotten. In 1873 the coinage legislation of the country was overhauled and consolidated, in the expectation, realized in 1879, that paper money would be given up soon and a specie system reëstablished. In this revision of the statutes, the silver dollar was dropped from the list of coins that could be struck. Therewith bimetallism, long obsolete in practice, was formally ended by law. The change naturally attracted little attention. In later years, when a strong agitation for renewed use of silver had sprung up, the dropping of the silver dollar was often called "the crime of 1873." It was supposed to have been stealthily done by persons interested in securing the gold standard. In fact, it was done quietly because nobody at the time thought it of any moment.

After 1873 a period of depression and of falling prices set in. A strong party in the United States wished to check the fall, and welcomed any legislation which would add to the quantity of money in use.[1] For a generation, there was agitation for a return to complete bimetallism, — to the free coinage of both gold and silver. At the old ratio of 16 to 1, and at the market prices of silver after 1873, this would have meant the actual coinage of silver alone. Yet this radical step, though often it seemed impending, was never taken. By way of compromise two great measures were passed, each providing for a large though limited quantity of overvalued silver dollars.

In 1878 the so-called Bland-Allison Act was passed, requiring the monthly purchase by the government of not less than \$2,000,000 worth of silver bullion, nor more than \$4,000,000 worth; this bullion to be coined into dollars of the old content ($412\frac{1}{2}$ grains of standard silver, $371\frac{1}{4}$ grains of pure silver). The minimum only under the act was in fact bought and coined, — \$2,000,000 worth of silver. The number of dollars obviously was more then two million a month. If the price

[1] Not a political party is here meant; neither Democrats nor Republicans were consistent in their policy as regards silver coinage. The silver party was made up of adherents from both political parties.

of silver, in terms of the money which the government used in buying it (this money was gold after 1879) happened to be low, more silver bullion could be bought with the fixed sum of $2,000,000 and a larger number of dollars coined; if the price was high, less bullion could be bought, and less dollars coined. In fact, during the period from 1878 to 1890, when this act was in force, the outcome was the monthly coinage on the average of about two and one half million silver dollars, or thirty million a year. These dollars were precisely like the French five-franc pieces; overvalued, limited in quantity, full legal tender, and in every respect as valid for payments as gold.

In 1890 a second measure was enacted, again a compromise between free silver coinage and rejection of silver. Without entering on the details of this complicated and luckless statute, it may be said, in sum, that during the three years of its life (it was repealed in 1893) silver was purchased by the government which added eventually not less than 218,000,000 silver dollars to the country's money supply. Under the act of 1878, there had been coined, in round numbers, 352,000,000 such dollars. When these operations finally came to an end, a total of 570,000,000 dollars of overvalued silver had been injected into the circulating medium.

It is not so much in the form of coin, as in that of the silver certificate, that the silver has made its way into actual circulation. This kind of paper money, as the name indicates, is merely a certificate or warrant stating that so many silver dollars (one, two, five, as the case may be) are held in the government vaults and will be paid to the bearer on demand. Since the paper representatives are for most people more convenient than the somewhat bulky dollars, their issue has greatly facilitated the actual circulation of the additional money.

Evidently the possibility of adding these hundreds of millions to the monetary supply of the United States, and yet keeping them equal in value to gold, has rested on the fact that this is a huge country; and not only a huge country, but one whose industry advances at a prodigious rate. In addition to the silver, there are other forms of overvalued money. The bank notes and government notes in circulation, which will be described in the ensuing chapters, may also be said to be overvalued. An indefinite increase in the quantity of all this overvalued or "fiduciary" money would mean the eventual expulsion of gold. Indeed, at one time, between 1890 and 1893, the rate of increase, under the act of 1890, was so great that gold seemed about to be expelled; and this probability was one cause of the remarkable crisis of 1893, and of the repeal of the act. In recent years, the population, resources, and industrial output of the United States have advanced by leaps and bounds. The quantity of commodities offered in exchange for money has risen enormously. Hence gold has not only remained in the country, side by side with the silver, but the quantity in monetary use has much increased. The consequence has been that the overvalued silver has had its stronger companion side by side, and has been held up to an equal value; it has been as good as gold.

§ 5. One other important event remains to be noted, the last in the chain of those which deposed silver from its former monetary place. In 1893, the same year in which the United States ceased its purchases of silver for coinage into dollars, British India put an end to the free coinage of silver. The flow of specie to the East, already referred to,[1] had always been chiefly in the form of silver. British India, by far the most important country of the East, had coined that silver freely into rupees (whose bullion content is about two fifths that of the United States dollar). The continued fall in the price of silver caused serious embarrassments, of which more will be said elsewhere.[2] After long and patient waiting, the British government in India finally took the drastic step of closing its mints to silver. Thus in one year, 1893, the last two great markets for silver — the United States and British

[1] Chapter 18, § 4.

[2] Chapter 23, § 5; Chapter 32, § 6.

India — were closed. This was just twenty years after the France mint began the great change.

The bottom seemed to drop out of silver in 1893. Its production had been steadily increasing for a quarter of a century. Before 1870 the annual supply from the mines had been about thirty million ounces. After 1870, it rose thus: —

		Million Ounces
Average annual product in the 5-year period	1871–1875	63
” ” ” ” ” ” ”	1876–1880	79
” ” ” ” ” ” ”	1881–1885	92
” ” ” ” ” ” ”	1886–1890	109
” ” ” ” ” ” ”	1891–1895	158
” ” ” ” ” ” ”	1896–1900	165
” ” ” ” ” ” ”	1901–1905	168

So great a fresh supply pressing on the market, with most mints closed to free coinage, caused a steady decline in price. In terms of United States money, the ounce of silver fell from $1.29 in 1873 to about $.90 in 1892. The American purchases under the acts of 1878 and 1890 did not serve to prevent that decline, though doubtless they made it less abrupt. With the two closures of 1893 (in the United States and British India), the price fell sharply to $.67. In 1894 it was on the average about $.64.

Since 1893 silver has maintained, on the whole, the levels reached in that year both as to production and price. The production has not sensibly diminished or sensibly increased; the price has been in the neighborhood of $.60 an ounce. At that price the market ratio is about 34 to 1. It follows that the silver dollar contains less than half its nominal content; that is, as metal it is worth less than fifty cents in gold. The French five-franc pieces are overvalued to a similar degree. Silver has become in all the leading countries a commodity like any other, fluctuating in price according to market conditions. It is bought in large quantities by governments for manufacture into subsidiary coin, and the demand for this purpose has proved to increase steadily. It is used in the arts in growing quantities; and the East still absorbs considerable amounts, partly for monetary use, partly for ornament, partly for hoarding. That its production continues undiminished, notwithstanding the great fall in price, indicates that its marginal cost is not greater than the price that has ruled during the last fifteen years (1893–1908).

It will now be obvious why, as was stated in the preceding chapter, the value of silver is related to its expenses of production in a different way from what it was in former centuries, and in a different way from gold. Silver no longer has a free opening in monetary use. The annual supply can no longer be added, as can that of gold, to a vast monetary stock. What part shall be added to the circulating medium in the form of subsidiary coin depends on the purchases which governments choose to make. The annual supply is sold, like that of other metals, at whatever price it will fetch. The price corresponds in a rough way to its marginal cost, and is in a rough way determined by its marginal cost. The existing silver coins of the countries of the limping standard are kept at an artificial value; but this artificial value has no influence on the value of the newly accruing output from the mines.

§ 6. Two entirely different questions of principle arose during the course of the deposition of silver. One concerned the relative values of gold and silver, and the effects on those relative values of bimetallism and of monometallism. The other concerned the general range of prices and the effects on prices of bimetallism and monometallism. The bimetallists contended that their system conduced to a more stable ratio between silver and gold. They also contended that it conduced to a greater stability in prices. On the first question they were probably in the right; on the second question the verdict of recent history has been on the whole against them.

We have seen, in the case of France, that the very existence of complete bimetallism — free coinage of both metals — tends to keep the value of the two metals in correspondence with the ratio. Suppose now that the industrial area over which free coinage prevailed had been very much larger than France. Suppose that not only France and the Latin Union, but England, Germany, the United States, had coined silver and gold freely at the French ratio of 15½ to 1. From this vast area the expulsion of gold would have been difficult, nay, well-nigh impossible. The countries mentioned include all those in which gold is freely coined on a great scale, or at least all those in which gold was so coined during the period of the great fall in silver. Whither could the gold have been driven? The ordinary avenue of departure — exportation — could hardly have been followed, since there were no important countries to which large quantities of gold could have been exported. A rapid rise in general prices would perhaps have stimulated a markedly increased industrial consumption; but this would have been a slow process, coming to its term long before all the gold had been absorbed in the arts. A rapid rise in general prices, again, might conceivably have checked the production of gold; but this, too, would have been a slow and uncertain process, having its term like the other, — at the point where the poorer mines had been brought to a stop. The monetary stock of gold would have remained in monetary use without great change, and would perforce have remained in circulation side by side with silver. This result would have been the more probable because, if the leading countries had adopted bimetallism at a common ratio, the lesser countries would have been likely to join them. International bimetallism, applied unflinchingly by the leading countries, would have brought about the proximate object, — the concurrent circulation of the two metals as money, and a market value corresponding to the mint ratio.

This conclusion is subject to possible qualification. It rests on the assumption that people in general, and the business community in particular, would accede to the regulations contemplated (and in part prescribed) by governments. Thus, silver would be made a legal tender in payment of debts, and therefore as good as gold for a vitally important monetary use. Conceivably, however, general opinion — general prejudice, if one is disposed so to call it — would boycott the use of silver. As will be seen in connection with the history of paper money,[1] the power of government in forcing the use of a particular kind of money has its limits. To make money legal tender is by no means necessarily to make it pass in general circulation. But in the special case here supposed for silver, it is not probable that a government would have overpassed the limits within which it would affect the use of money. Silver was in most parts of the world, in the period from 1873 to 1893, a familiar and not unwelcome form of money. True, in Great Britain it was not familiar, and much prejudice in that country, and in the United States and Germany also, would have had to be overcome; yet the obstacles against the acceptance of the new situation would hardly have been insuperable.

The direct obstacles in the way of international bimetallism were political. There never was a chance for the conclusion of a compact. Great Britain at no time was willing to accede, except as to British India, which would not have brought any new strength to the bimetallic league. Without Great Britain, Germany would not come in; without at least one of those countries, the United States would not. Whatever the abstract possibilities of united bimetallism, the project never had a working prospect of realization.

§ 7. Very different is the second question that arose, regarding the stability, not of the ratio between the metals, but of the general range of prices. And this, obviously, is by far the more important question. It does not matter much to the community (though it may very greatly concern the mine owners) whether silver exchanges for gold at the rate of 15 to 1 or 30 to 1. But it matters very much whether prices go up or go down or remain stable. That they should remain as stable as possible is the desirable situation. How far would international bimetallism have promoted this result?

The answer to this question depends on the extent to which the total supply of specie — gold and silver — would have been affected. In the year 1890 the answer seemed doubtful.

[1] See below in this book, Chapter 23, § 1.

The production of gold then seemed virtually stationary. That of silver, on the other hand, was rapidly mounting, in face even of a steady fall in the price of silver. The opponents of bimetallism maintained that silver, once restored to free coinage, would be produced in immensely greater quantity. Under modern mining methods, vast known deposits of low-grade silver-bearing ore can be treated; the question is not one of discovery or speculation, but simply of calculable profit. Raise the price of silver to $1.33 an ounce (the price in United States gold corresponding to a ratio of 15½ to 1), and floods of silver may be expected to come out. Some cool-headed observers predicted that the addition to the monetary stock would be so huge as to double prices in ten years. The bimetallists on the other hand said that the increase in output would not at all be so great, and that, with a stationary or declining output of gold, and with a great area over which the total stock could spread, the change in prices would be slow, and so far as it did take place rather beneficial than otherwise.

Whatever doubt there may have been regarding the probabilities of the case — and there was much, about 1890 — was set at rest by the new conditions governing the supply of gold which set in after that date. The wonderful increase in the annual product of that metal has already been described. The danger of a scant supply of gold — so scant as to keep prices moving downward — disappeared. If silver had been freely coinable as well as gold, the total supply of the two metals would have increased without fail at a portentous rate. Even at the low prices of silver which have prevailed since 1893, the production of that metal has not diminished; it has remained stationary. At doubled prices, it would surely have increased rapidly, and so have added much more to the supply of specie. Bimetallism would have led not to stable prices, but to prices even less stable, and advancing even more rapidly, than under the single gold standard. The extraordinary increase in the production of gold has put an end, probably forever, certainly for an indefinite period, to all proposals for rehabilitating silver.

CHAPTER 22

CHANGES IN PRICES

§ 1. Two topics will be taken up in the present chapter: first, how to ascertain and measure whether changes in prices have taken place; second, what are the consequences for good or ill of such changes. Of the causes of the changes nothing more will be said for the present.

The measurement of changes in the value of money would be easy if all prices went up and down together. But this they never do. Some prices go up, while others go down. Occasionally in times of very great and rapid movement, all prices change in the same direction. Even then, they do not all change to the same extent; some rise or fall in less degree than others; hence, though the fact of a change in a given direction may be clear, the extent of the change becomes difficult to measure.

To get a summary expression of the general trend of prices, resort is had to the method of index numbers. An example will best explain how an index number is constructed. Suppose that on January 1, 1900, the price of iron was $15 a ton, of wheat $1 a bushel, of cotton 10 cents a pound, of wool 40 cents a pound. These are called the base prices. Later prices are expressed in relation to them, usually by stating them in terms of a percentage. Suppose that a year later, on January 1, 1901, the prices of these four commodities have come to be $20 for iron, $1.25 for wheat, 10 cents for cotton, 36 cents for wool. Then the actual prices, and the percentage relation between them, would stand thus:—

	1900		1901	
	Base Price	100	Price	Percentage to Base
Iron	$15.00	100	$20.00	133
Wheat	1.00	100	1.25	125
Cotton	.10	100	.10	100
Wool	.40	100	.36	90
Total		400		448
Average (arithmetical mean)		100		112

The index number was 400 for 1900, and rose to 448 for 1901. Reduced to the arithmetic mean, the index number for 1900 was 100; that for 1901 became 112. Sometimes index numbers are given in the first form by simple summation; such, for example, is the mode in which the well-known index number of the *London Economist* is made up. More often the numbers are averaged. The base average, of course, is always 100; the average for any other year is then a percentage of the base average. In the example just given, the index number shows a rise in prices of twelve per cent; or, rather, as the very word "index" implies, *indicates* a rise to that extent.

If, now, instead of four commodities, fifty or a hundred were treated in this way, we should feel some confidence in the indication obtained as to a general change in prices. If the summarized result as to a large number of articles is an advance of ten or twenty per cent in the index number, it is tolerably certain that most commodities have gone up in price. No doubt it is possible that the result has been due to the fact that half the commodities went up a great deal, and that the other half went down, though but moderately. But an examination of actual changes, even a cursory one, almost always shows, where a marked change has occurred in an index number, that the large majority of prices have moved in the one way indicated. The index number serves, therefore, to point to a fact, — that on the whole prices have gone up.

§ 2. Other modes of reaching index numbers are proposed, the arithmetical mean being criticized as crude and inadequate. Some of the suggested improvements may be briefly noted, and the usefulness of the simpler method tested by comparison with the results from those more complex.

The geometrical mean has been advocated; and sometimes also the harmonic mean. Of the geometric mean it is said, with undoubted truth, that its use will mitigate a misleading effect on the index number from extraordinary fluctuations in the price of a single article. With the use of logarithms the geometric mean is easy to ascertain; and it has quite as good a right to be entitled a "true" average as the arithmetic.

Another proposal is for the use of the median. Let the index numbers be made up, not by averaging, but by ascertaining mid-way points. Arrange the several price quotations for any year (reduced to a uniform basis as for the other methods) in numerical order, and then ascertain that figure which stands in the middle of the series, — that figure on either side of which there are an equal number of quotations. For various sorts of observations the median is thought by statisticians to be at least as significant as any average; and though comparatively unfamiliar, it is easy to use. Even more than the geometric mean, it prevents an extremely high or low price of some one article, or of a very few articles, from having an undue influence on the index number.[1]

Entirely different is the improvement of the simpler method

[1] Thus if a series of price quotations, reduced to a basis of 100, were

86	102
90	106
94	110
97	120
100	

the median would be 100. If the last figure were not 120, but 150, the median would still be 100.

There being in this series an odd number of figures, the median is *the* middle one. If there were an even number, the median would lie between the two middle figures, and would be in so far indefinite. But where there are many figures, as is always the case with price quotations, the median is sufficiently precise.

For an illustration of divergence between the median and the arithmetic mean, see Chapter 23, p. 318.

itself — the arithmetic mean — by taking account of the relative importance of the different articles; or, as it is technically put, by *weighting* the articles. A change in the price of wheat, for example, is of much more importance than a change in the price of wool. If wheat were to double in price, the purchasing power of a given income would be seriously affected; if wool were to double in price, much less. The varying importance of different commodities may be regarded in the construction of an index number by assigning weight to the commodities in the proportion of their consumption. If the community as a whole spends four times as much of its income on wheat as on wool, wheat may be counted as if it were four articles and wool as if it were one. If twice as much is spent on cotton as on wool, cotton may be counted as if it were two articles; while iron, on similar assumptions, may be counted as three. The prices just used for illustration would then be made up into an index number as follows: —

	1900			1901		
	Weight	Base Price	Weighted Base	Price	Percentage of Change in Price	Weighted Change in Price
Wheat	4	$1.00	400	$1.25	125	500
Cotton	2	.10	200	.10	100	200
Wool	1	.40	100	.36	90	90
Iron	3	15.00	300	20.00	133⅓	400
Total	10		1000			1190
Average			100			119

This weighted average indicates a rise in prices from 100 to 119, whereas the simple average indicated one from 100 to 112 only. And the weighted average is plainly the more significant; since the higher prices of widely used articles like wheat and iron are more important than the lower price of the less used wool.

Though the weighted index number is clearly preferable, the application of this more refined method presents difficulties. It is not easy to ascertain the consumption or relative weight of the several articles, especially where a very large number (100 or more perhaps) are included in the list. Moreover, the consumption of the different articles varies. Changes in habits take place; one article may be much less used in 1910 than in 1900; how readjust its weighting and the whole weighted index number? These difficulties, and others that might be instanced, though not insuperable, add to the complications of weighting.

In regard to all these suggestions, whether for improvement in the arithmetic mean or for the use of a different mean, it must be borne in mind that no index number corresponds to a real thing. It is not like the mean of certain observations in natural science — such, for example, as those for measuring the distance between the earth and the sun — of which any one may err, but whose average will point to a single specific fact. An index number points to no single fact. It gives, to repeat, only an indication of the general trend of prices. People often speak and think loosely on this topic, as if an index number told the whole story once for all. There is no one change in prices. There is a medley of many changes, different in direction and degree. All that we can hope to secure by averaging and summarizing is some concise statement of the general drift.

Now experience in the application of the various methods to the same sets of figures shows that the simple arithmetic mean, when applied to a sufficiently large number of price quotations, gives substantially the same results as more refined methods. If many articles are in the list, some of much importance, some of little, it is unlikely that all the important articles will fluctuate in one direction and all the unimportant in another. If they did so (as in the example just given), weighting would be indispensable. But the fluctuations in fact are likely to be distributed among the several classes in much the same way. An unusual change in the price of a particular article, whether it be consumed in large amounts or in small, will not affect greatly an average made up from many price quotations. And in practise it has been found that the simple unweighted average brings results not very different from those obtained after weighting. Similarly, it has been found that the method of the median does not yield, for such fluctuations in prices as take place under a specie standard,[1] results substantially different from those of either the simpler or the weighted arithmetical mean.

This similarity of outcome is illustrated by the following chart, showing the course of four index numbers reached in different ways, all based on the same quotations of prices.[2] One represents the simple arithmetic mean of 250 price quotations; the second, another arithmetic mean of the same prices consoli-

[1] Compare what is said below, Chapter 23, p. 318.

[2] The four series are: —

(1) The Department of Labor's arithmetic means, for prices of 250 articles.

(2) Professor W. C. Mitchell's rearrangement of the same price figures: "The Bureau's list of commodities contains anomalies such as the inclusion of a single series [of quotations] for wheat and ten for cotton sheetings; two for hogs and three for glassware, etc. The result is most unscientific weighting in what purports to be an unweighted index number. To remedy this obvious defect, I have combined the series for nearly identical articles, thereby reducing the number of series to 145." — *Journal of Political Economy*, May, 1910, p. 372; cp. the same writer's *Gold, Prices, and Wages under the Greenback Standard*, p. 19.

(3) The median for the same (145) series of quotations, as calculated by Professor Mitchell.

(4) A weighted index number for 50 staple articles, selected from among the 250 (145); the weighting being on the plan of the Gibson index, but revised by Professor Mitchell.

The figures of the four series are: —

	I Arithmetic Mean of 250 Quotations	II Arithmetic Mean of 145 Quotations	III Median of 145 Quotations	IV Weighted Index Numbers from 50 Quotations
1890	112.9	114.1	112	114.0
1891	111.7	112.7	111	113.9
1892	106.1	106.1	107	105.1
1893	105.6	105.0	104	105.2
1894	96.1	95.6	96	93.9
1895	93.6	92.8	94	93.9
1896	90.4	88.8	90	86.6
1897	89.7	88.7	91	89.2
1898	93.4	93.5	94	95.0
1899	101.7	102.5	100	103.4
1900	110.5	111.3	109	111.6
1901	108.5	109.6	107	109.2
1902	112.9	113.7	110	116.2
1903	113.6	113.8	111	115.3
1904	113.0	113.9	112	116.3
1905	115.9	115.8	114	117.9
1906	122.5	122.3	119	123.4

dated into 145 quotations; the third, the median of these same 145 quotations; the fourth, a weighted index number of 50 among these commodities. The prices are at wholesale, in

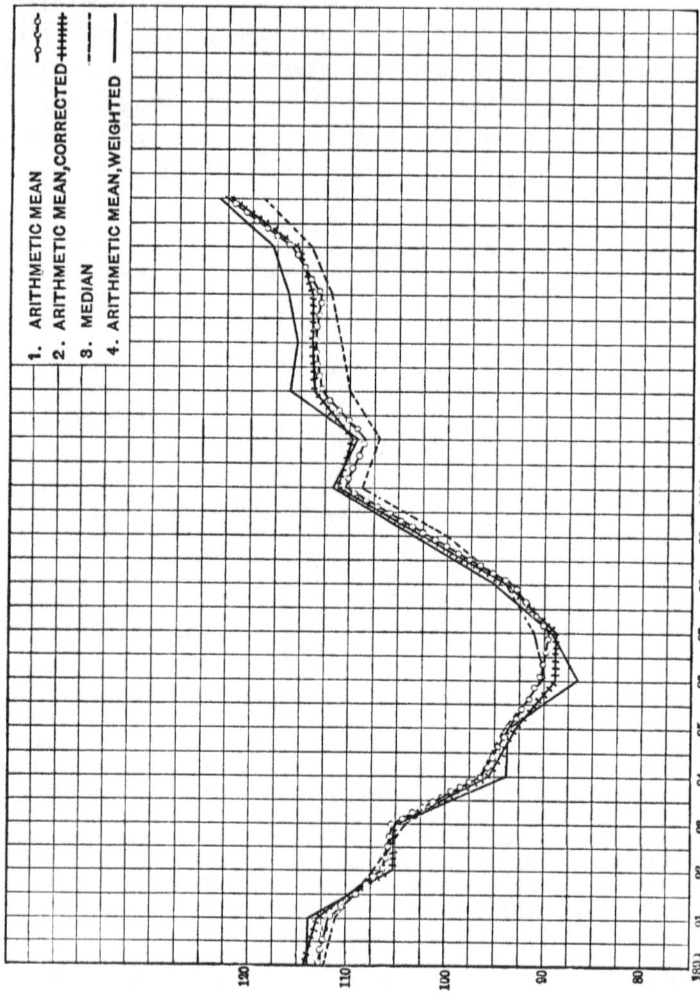

the United States, for the period 1890–1906; the "base," indicated by 100, is in each case the average (arithmetic mean) for the decade 1890–1899.

§ 3. A rise in prices is of advantage to debtors; a fall in prices is of advantage to creditors. When prices go up in the interval between the contracting and the paying of a debt, the debtor, on returning to his creditor the amount of money borrowed, returns less in the way of commodities. Conversely, when prices go down in the interval, the debtor, on returning the same money, returns more in the way of commodities.

Most changes in prices are slow; from year to year there is little variation. Most debts, on the other hand, are for short periods of time. Hence fluctuations in general prices do not ordinarily cause injustice or serious embarrassment. Even over a period of several years the dealings between debtor and creditor are usually carried on with sufficient equity. An index number change of five per cent in a single year is unusual. Commonly our observations must extend over two or three years if we are to make sure that any general rise or fall is really in progress. A change of five per cent or ten per cent, as registered in an index number, would probably be little noticed by most debtors and creditors. Each would be concerned only with the particular articles bought or sold by him; and these articles might remain unchanged in price, or move in a different direction from the index numbers, or in different degree. It is only abrupt and marked changes in prices that disturb the usual approximate equity of debt payments. Under a specie standard, such changes do not take place; this much is brought about by the durability of specie and the consequent slowness of changes in the total stock. Violent changes, over short periods of time, take place, if at all, from resort to irredeemable paper money. There is a sound basis for the attitude which most people take, of regarding specie as stable in value and measuring incomes, possessions, debts and credits, once for all in terms of money.

The case is different with debts having a long time to run. As to these, even under a specie régime, there is a considerable possibility of injustice and hardship. In the course of twenty years, possibly in the course of ten, marked changes in general prices may occur, and with them marked injustice to debtors or to creditors, as the case may be. Though obligations running over such a long period are not often contracted by individuals, they are not uncommon on the part of corporations and of governments. European governments, to be sure, when they borrow, usually do not undertake to repay the principal sum at any given date; they promise only the regular payment of a stipulated rate of interest. They reserve the option of repaying the principal (either at times expressly stated or at their discretion), but they need not repay unless it suits them. In such case they have a protection against loss from price changes, though their creditors have none. The United States government has often borrowed on long time, and exposed itself to possible loss; a practise, however, which has been kept in recent years within such moderate limits as not to forebode substantial difficulties. Many of our great corporations, however, and especially the railway corporations, have borrowed quite without regard to possible price changes, and indeed also with disregard of possible changes in the rate of interest. Bonds have been issued payable after the lapse of twenty, forty, even one hundred, years, without provision for redemption in the interval. Who can say what will be the range of prices after the lapse of decades or of a century?

Such long-time obligations find a market because most investors (like other people) think of the value of money as unchanging, and because they are glad to have an income, supposed to be fixed, guaranteed for a long time. Corporations, on the other hand, when they wish to raise great sums of money, adopt the devices which will entice the investor. Yet in such engagements both debtors and creditors take great and unpredictable risks. Under monetary systems as they now are, and are likely long to remain, these risks can be avoided only by restricting all loans to periods of a moderate number of years.

§ 4. A different question as to justice between debtor and creditor arises from the fact that money wages and other money incomes do not necessarily move in the same way as the prices of commodities. In the preceding sections, it has been tacitly assumed that these two movements — of prices and of money incomes—proceed *pari passu*. But they do not always do so. One may lag behind the other; or the movements may be in opposite directions.

Suppose, for example, — to take the sort of case which, fortunately, is most probable, — that industry is progressing, the arts are advancing, the prosperity of the community growing. This means that real incomes are becoming larger; that the commodities and utilities at the command of the community as a whole, and on the average for each person, are more abundant. The concrete way in which that abundance must show itself, where all transactions and all exchanges are carried on through money, is in cheapness of goods relatively to incomes. Goods may become cheaper, money incomes remaining the same; or money incomes may become greater, prices remaining the same; or some intermediate relation may appear. In any case, prices and incomes will not move together. Relatively to prices, money incomes will rise.

Thus, during the period of falling prices after 1873, money income on the whole did not fall. The evidence to prove this relates chiefly to the familiar crafts and to unskilled or little skilled labor; since comparison of wages at different times is here easiest. Money wages on the whole did not fall after 1873; they rather tended to rise. So it was as to those rates of wages which are euphemistically called salaries,—the pay of teachers, corporation employees, public officials. The same upward tendency, or, at the least, stationary tendency, showed itself in the more irregular money incomes of professional and business men. With rising or stationary wages and incomes, and with falling prices, real incomes, in term of commodities and of utilities, must have gone up substantially. Obviously, this was the natural outcome of industrial progress and cheapened production. That same outcome of progress and cheapness, however, must be expected to appear in a period of rising prices; only in this case in a different way. If prices advance, money incomes must advance at least as much, if real income is to remain the same. If the same fundamental forces are at work to promote progress and relative cheapness, wages and all money incomes must advance even more than prices. If the increasing gold supply of the last ten years proves in fact to bring about continuously rising prices, we must expect that this change will be accompanied by an even greater rise in money incomes.[1]

What, under such circumstances, are the relations between debtors and creditors? With prices falling and incomes stationary, debtors, paying their debts with the same amount of money, repay to creditors more in the way of commodities. This may be called repayment according to a labor standard. It is true that the debtor pays back more commodities than he got; but those commodities represent the same money income and (presumably) the same amount of labor as before. It may be fairly argued that the debtor suffers no injustice, if at the time of repayment he has the same money income as when he contracted the debt. The creditor simply shares in the greater cheapness of commodities due to improved production. Suppose, on the other hand, that there are stationary prices and rising incomes. The debtor, paying back the same money, pays back also the same commodities. It may again be fairly argued that the creditor suffers no injustice. He gets back precisely what he lent, in terms both of money and of goods. He can be said to suffer hardship only in that he fails to share the full advantage of progress. He does not experience, as others do, rising receipts with stationary expenses. The results in the two cases are different; yet in each it may be plausibly argued that the outcome is just, or at least not unjust.

It is fortunate that this intricate question of justice does not present itself in such a way as to involve the likelihood of any serious departure from the familiar and accepted principles of equity in debt payments. Just as movements in general prices

[1] Long-run effects are here had in mind, and especially those long-run effects which are to be expected from steady gains in the efficiency of industry. The proximate effect of increasing gold supply is, as pointed out in the next section, to cause prices to rise faster than the wages of hired laborers (though not faster than all money incomes). It is only in the long run that this effect is counteracted by that of continued improvement in the arts.

proceed slowly, and therefore do not entail serious injustice as regards most debts, so the relative changes of prices, money, and money incomes proceed slowly. Thus the inverse movement of wages and prices between 1873 and 1896, referred to a moment ago, could be noticed only after careful observation of five-year and ten-year periods. Again, if it proves true — as there is reason to expect it will in the long run — that rising prices during the next generation will be accompanied by money incomes rising still more, this change also will come slowly and gradually, as the ultimate result of the irregular march of improvements in production.

If it be asked, none the less, which of these two situations — stationary incomes with falling prices, or rising incomes with stationary prices — brings the more equitable adjustment of the relations between debtor and creditor, the answer cannot be given with ready assurance. The problem involves a consideration of the whole problem of the right distribution of wealth, and more particularly the question whether equal return for equal labor is the right basis for dealings between man and man.[1] In this case, as in most others, we must be content if the outcome is satisfactory on the whole; if clear injustice is avoided, even though that which is ideally just be not attained. The monetary use of the precious metals brings advantages which outweigh its disadvantages. Specie in the main has brought, and still brings, stability of prices. It is an invaluable safeguard against crude experimenting and arbitrary change. The system of private property and free exchange works better under a specie standard than it seems likely to work under any other medium of exchange yet discovered. Though the standard inures sometimes to the advantage of debtors, sometimes to that of creditors, and though sometimes it brings complex conditions under which very difficult questions of equity arise, — none the less, we must be satisfied if it brings on the whole a satisfactory working arrangement. No part of the existing organization of society rests more frankly on a utilitarian basis than the use of specie as the medium of exchange.

[1] See Book VII, Chapter 64, § 3.

§ 5. The proposal for a multiple standard as a means of remedying the effects of falling and rising prices on debtors and creditors is to be judged by this same utilitarian standard. Briefly, the proposal is as follows. Let there be kept accurate records of the prices of a great number of commodities, and let the index numbers show at stated periods how the general level has changed. Let debtors then repay creditors in such way that the same quantity of commodities be returned the creditors. Thus, if the general index number rises from 100 to 110, let the debtor who has borrowed $100 pay back $110; for only by the repayment of this larger sum does the creditor get as much in the way of commodities as he gave. Conversely, if the index number falls from 100 to 90, let the debtor pay back $90 for every $100 that he borrowed.

To any such scheme there are various objections. The uncertainty as to the best way of computing index numbers, the varying results reached by different methods of equal validity, the difficulty of recording with certainty the actual changes in prices, the inevitable margin of error, — here is one set of objections. Another arises from the possibility, just discussed, that money incomes may change in a different direction from commodity prices; though this is commonly evaded, in discussions of the multiple standard, by the tacit assumption that a *quid pro quo* in terms of commodities is necessarily just. The conclusive objection, however, is that under the multiple standard certainty and calculability would cease to exist in all transactions involving postponed payments. No man would know, when contracting a debt, what he would be called on to repay when it became due. He would have to watch each monthly or quarterly report of the index-number bureau, and guess in the meanwhile how his affairs would have to be adjusted. It is true that, as things now are, changes in the prices of the particular things which each person buys and sells cause uncertainty. But every one in business necessarily watches these changes and adapts his doings from day to day to the shifting conditions; indeed, so to watch them, is a main part of business. To add to this inevitable cause of uncertainty another from unpredictable changes in index numbers would make all industrial operations irregular and halting. If the scheme were put into effect, people would rebel against it at the first trial. Or, if it were arbitrarily maintained, the speculative element in all transactions would become more marked, risks would be greater, the margin of gain for middlemen would become wider, the action of competition less smooth and less effective. The business classes in the end would recoup themselves from the rest of the community for the trouble and risk imposed. The plan has been rightly called one for a "fancy" monetary standard. Whether from the point of view of difficulty in administration or of the outcome under the best conceivable administration, it must be rejected on any sober consideration.

§ 6. It might seem that, barring the effects on debtors and creditors, rising or falling prices are not of consequence. It is certainly of no consequence whether a community reaches finally a stage of high prices or of low prices. The only difference in the end is whether many counters or few shall be used in exchanges. But the process of reaching the end may bring results of its own. It is maintained by many that the transition to higher prices brings good results, the transition to lower prices bad results.

Periods of rising prices are, in fact, commonly periods of prosperity. In part, to be sure, that prosperity is rather apparent than real. People so habitually reckon their incomes and resources in terms of money that they think themselves better off when money incomes go up. They disregard, in some degree at least, the fact that their expenses go up also. But it is not merely a matter of deceptive appearances. The business class feels a stimulus from rising prices; and so long as the management of industry is in the hands of the business class, that which stimulates its members to activity commonly acts as a real stimulus to productive industry. In part, no doubt, the effect on business men, as on others, is psychological. They think they are gaining when prices rise, whether in fact they do or do not gain as regards the purchasing power of their incomes; and this appearance of gain spurs them to activity. But they secure also real and substantial advantages.

These advantages do not arise chiefly from the fact that business men are debtors. They are both debtors and creditors. It is true that in relation to the investors, they are debtors. But the men of large affairs — the wholesale merchants, the manufacturers, the bankers — are creditors quite as much as debtors, in relation to the rest of the community; and it is the large-scale men who give the tone and temper to the business class.

The chief explanation of the optimism and activity which business men as a class show in times of rising prices arises from the relation which they as a class hold to the laborers as a class. At bottom their main operation is to hire laborers; and they hire laborers to advantage at such times, because the prices of commodities go up faster than money wages.

That wages go up more slowly than prices is one of the best-attested facts in economic history. It holds good of almost all sorts of hired persons, — not only manual laborers, but clerks, overseers, teachers, salaried officials. It is due mainly to the force of custom, which is especially strong as to wages; and it is strengthened often by the lack of bargaining power among laborers. It is connected with many peculiarities in the dealings between employers and employees, and especially with the position of the employer as feeling the brunt of any industrial change. Of the fact there can be no question; when prices rise, the wages of hired workers do not rise as fast.

But, as has been already said, and will be more fully explained at a later stage,[1] the operations of capitalists as a class, and of business men as the managers of investment, are resolvable into a succession of advances to laborers. Their total expenses consist in the last analysis in a series of wages payments. To the extent that prices of commodities advance faster than expenses for the labor they buy, the payers of wages gain.

[1] Of all these matters, more is said in the chapters on Business Profits and Wages, in Book VI, Chapters 49, 50, 51. Cp. also Book I, Chapter 5, § 5.

It is familiar experience that those business men gain most in periods of rising prices whose operations involve in largest degree the payment of wages. The mere trader or merchant usually gains least; the prices of the things he buys go up almost as fast as the prices of the things he sells. The manufacturer who buys few materials, and whose expenses are chiefly in the direct purchase of labor, profits most of all. Such, for example, is the situation of a highly integrated enterprise like the United States Steel Corporation, which hires laborers directly [1] to dig iron ore, mine coal, convert the coal into coke, transport these materials, smelt and shape the iron and steel. When the prices of the iron and steel go up, it gains hugely, since its main outlay, for wages payments, is nearly stable. Those iron and steel makers, however, who have to buy iron ore, or coal and coke, gain comparatively little; the prices of their materials go up *pari passu* with those of their products. The business man who is nearest the ground, so to speak, — nearest the laborer, — profits most from the relative stability of wages.

Conversely, the business class as a whole commonly loses in periods of falling prices. Then, the same forces tending to keep wages stable, a fall in prices brings loss. Probably wages feel the effect of falling prices less slowly than they do those of rising prices. The employer's superior bargaining power enables him more readily to stave off the loss, just as it aids him in reaping the gain. But some loss there is, for the same fundamental reason, — on him falls the first effect of any change.

Whatever the business class thus gains in periods of rising prices, may appear to be obtained at the cost of others; and conversely as to their loss from falling prices. What the employers gain (in the first case), the laborers *prima facie* lose. And it is true that the activity and prosperity of flush times are a doubtful boon to the laborers.[2] But in one respect they

[1] That is, through its subsidiary corporations. Between the subsidiary corporation there is nominal purchase of materials.

[2] It may happen that money wages do not overtake at all the advance in prices. Such seems to have been the result of the great price revolution of the

seem really to gain; employment is more constant, for the pace of industry is more even as well as more quick. Periods of falling prices are more likely to be periods of slackened enterprise and irregular employment. The energy and consecutiveness of operation depend largely on the temper of the business class. They are the leaders, and on their hopes and fears depends the course of modern industry. The gains which are reaped by them, in times of rising prices, may be needlessly high, and out of proportion to their services to society; but in return something is got in the way of unhesitating and sustained activity.

The effects of falling and rising prices on business profits are modified in that complex case, referred to in the preceding section, where prices and money incomes do not move together. If there be, in consequence of general improvements in the arts, falling prices but stationary money incomes, it would seem that no depressing influence will be felt in business circles. What concerns the business man is not price per unit of product, but total receipts from his output compared with total outlays for that output. He may pay out as much per unit of labor, and receive less per unit of product, and yet may make profits because there is more of product per unit of labor, — this being the result of greater efficiency of labor. On the other hand, if there be rising wages and rising prices, though prices rising in the end less high, — the sort of movement which is likely to appear when there is growing efficiency of labor and at the same time rapid increase in the money supply, — the business class will feel an exhilarating influence no less than in the simple case of rising wages and rising prices. Though prices be stationary, yet the total receipts from the output will be greater, since more is turned out per unit of labor; and though wages rise, they are likely to rise less fast than gross receipts. In the first case, the depressing effect of falling prices is mitigated or overcome by improvements in production. In the second case,

sixteenth century. When this had run its course, prices (of food, at least) had risen more than money wages, and commodity wages had definitively fallen.

the stimulating effect of rising prices is accentuated by improvements. The first case seems to have appeared in the period of falling prices and stationary wages from 1873 to 1896; the second case during the period of rising wages and rising prices during the period that followed 1896.

§ 7. Another influence of changing prices may be on the rate of interest.[1] If prices rise, the creditor loses; but it may be that he will secure a higher rate of interest at such times, and that this will offset the loss from payment of the principal in depreciated money. And conversely, if prices fall, the debtor may get his loan at a lower rate of interest, thus securing an offset against the loss to him from lowered prices. It is conceivable that this sort of compensation will take place steadily, even automatically, and that thereby all disturbing effects on the relations between debtor and creditor will be obviated.

There can be little question that periods of rising prices are, in fact, usually periods of higher interest rates, and that during periods of falling prices interest rates are lower. The explanation of this fact has been the occasion of much critical discussion, and cannot be said to be entirely clear.

It would seem to be tolerably certain that there is no *conscious* adjustment of the rate of interest to changes in prices; and this for the simple reason that such changes can rarely be foretold. Sometimes, to be sure, persons who are versed in economic theory and economic history believe that conditions exist which will lead to a rise in prices. Such was the case after the Californian and Australian gold discoveries of 1850; such has been the case in recent years (1900–1910). But the rise in prices after 1850 was much less than had been expected by very competent persons;[2] and it may be that the similar expectations held by some good judges in our own day will

[1] The topic taken up in this section will be better understood after reading the chapters on Banking and Crises in the present Book, and those on Interest and Business Profits in Book VI. It may perhaps be postponed until these have been read.

[2] Chevalier, a distinguished economist, and by no means a closet economist, immensely overestimated the probable effects of these gold discoveries.

prove mistaken. Certainly the fall in prices which took place after 1873 was unexpected. And whether or no a few persons can foresee price changes, the great mass of lenders and borrowers do not even think about them. Except in times of extraordinary fluctuations (such as are due to paper money), they regard money as fixed in value. They reckon their gains and losses as well as their interest payments in terms of money only. They do not trouble themselves with adjustments of the "real" rate of interest to coming changes in prices.

It is possible, none the less, that there may be some adjustment by an unconscious process. If all who are debtors are seen to be gaining in times of rising prices, and if it becomes current opinion that buying on credit and borrowing are profitable operations, there may be a press of demand for loans, and so a rise in the rate of interest. The converse phenomenon of slackened demand for loans and low rates of interest may show itself, for reasons of the same sort, in times of falling prices, when those who have borrowed are seen to be often in straits.

There are other causes, however, which go far to explain the oscillations in demand for loans and in the rate of interest. Among these, and in my judgment a weighty one, is the fact of higher business profits due to the comparatively slow advance of money wages. Borrowers are mainly "producers"; that is, they are mainly business men engaged in guiding the operations of production. In times when their prospects for gain are good, — and such is the case when wages lag behind rising prices, — all want more "capital"; that is, more money means that will give them command of more capital goods and more labor. Though interest depends in the long run on other factors than business profits, it is derived proximately from business profits, and follows these in its ups and downs. The gains which the members of the business class make in times of rising prices, and the losses they incur with falling prices, go far to account for the corresponding oscillations of interest.

Still another cause is to be found in the working of the machinery of credit. In the preceding paragraphs, activity in business operations has been spoken of as a result of rising prices. But it is also a cause of rising prices. Even though there be no influence of a distinctly monetary sort (such as an increase in the specie supply), prices may go up from the general expansion of credit, — a phenomenon of which more will be said in its proper place.[1] It suffices here to point out that, as between active times with high rates of interest and dull times with low rates of interest, there is an interaction of cause and effect; or, more accurately perhaps, there are sundry effects all due to one commanding cause. Both rising interest and rising prices are in large degree due to a common cause, — the general fever of activity; and both falling interest and falling prices are promoted by a common cause of the same sort, — industrial lethargy.

Certain it is that there is no exact or automatic relation between fluctuations in prices and fluctuations in the rate of interest. Some writers have supposed there is; that when prices fall, interest so falls that the debtor's gain in the interest rate offsets his loss from lower prices. Conversely, when prices rise, interest is supposed to rise just enough to offset the creditor's loss. But such adjustment as statistical inquiry reveals seems to be but partial; the creditor or debtor, so far as they get alleviation from shifting interest rates, get only a partial alleviation. And this partial alleviation is not the result of any conscious adjustment, still less of any automatic correction of inequities in debt payments. The roughly parallel movements of prices and rates of interest are not explicable in the main from anything in the way of calculation by debtors and creditors. If this process tends to promote equity in the dealings between these classes under the existing monetary régime, it is partly the result of other causes acting on the interest rate, but mainly because, after all, fluctuations in prices are slow and their effect in disturbing the outcome of most credit transactions not considerable.

[1] Chapter 29, especially § 3.

CHAPTER 23

Government Paper Money

§ 1. In this chapter we shall consider paper money issued by governments, and particularly inconvertible or irredeemable paper money. All paper money contains on its face a promise to pay; but in the case of government paper that promise is more often broken than kept. The most perplexing and at the same time most instructive problems relating to paper money arise when it is not what on its face it purports to be, — when it is not convertible into specie.

Inconvertible paper has been called *fiat* money, because its use as money and its value depend on the mere command of the political authority. The extent to which the edict of the sovereign or legislature can cause a scrap of paper to serve as money, and to maintain its value as money, may be both overstated and understated. Historically, all money has had its origin, directly or indirectly, not in any compulsion or even in any deliberate selection, but in the customary acceptance of some commodity of general serviceability. When, however, such a commodity has once come to be habitually used as money, public authority can very much affect its value and the mode in which it circulates. Paper pieces, similarly, can be made to serve as money by mere government fiat only when a people has already become habituated to the use of a paper medium of exchange. Modern communities began using money of this sort on a considerable scale in the latter part of the seventeenth century, when public and semi-public banks issued promises to pay, which readily passed into circulation because really convertible into specie. By the eighteenth century, paper substitutes for metallic money had become so familiar that the way was easy for the issue by public authorities of inconvertible paper. Partly by taking advantage of the established habit, partly by mere force of law, governments found it possible to make promises to pay that were only nominal circulate as freely as gold and silver.

Let it be assumed that those conditions exist without which there can be no circulation of inconvertible paper, — some habituation to paper promises to pay, and a strong government. Let it be assumed further that the government exerts its strength to bolster up the paper which it issues. This is done commonly by making the paper a legal tender for debts (*i.e.* for those expressed simply in current money) and by making it receivable at its face value for taxes and other public dues. Suppose that by these means the paper is made to circulate freely, passing from hand to hand as readily as specie. What then determines its value?

Evidently, the reasoning already set forth as to metallic money will hold good of paper money also: its value, too, will be determined by its quantity. If it is issued in the same quantity as the specie previously in circulation, and if it completely displaces that specie (as ordinarily it will), the range of prices will be precisely what it was before, and the value of the paper will be as great as that of the specie had been. If it be issued in twice the quantity of the specie, prices will be doubled, and the value of money will be one half. These statements are subject to the same qualifications that would have to be applied to specie itself. They assume that rapidity of circulation remains the same, and that the quantity of commodities and their mode of coming to market remain the same, — qualifications which have been already discussed. They assume, too, that the use of credit substitutes for money, and especially the bank methods of credit, are unchanged, — important qualifications which remain to be considered. Yet all these corrections in no sense touch the essential truth; the value of freely circulating paper money depends on its quantity. Though it be quite inconvertible, though there be no prospect of its redemption in specie, it will retain its value and perform all the functions of money. It will obviously have a *prima facie* advantage over specie, in that it will cost the country less. Gold and silver can be produced only with much labor. Paper money costs but a trifle. A cheap and apparently serviceable medium of change is substituted for a dear one.

All this, to repeat, rests on the supposition that the paper money circulates freely. It does not necessarily circulate freely. Conceivably, people will distrust the government, or dislike to use paper, or for whatever reason refuse to accept it readily in current transactions. Then it will either not get into circulation at all, or it will have a value determined in a different way. Of this sort of possibility a striking illustration appeared in the state of California during and after our Civil War, from 1862 to 1879. The government of the United States issued paper money in such a quantity as to cause prices to rise and the money to depreciate. In California, as in other states, the paper was legal tender, and was receivable for public dues; nor was there any distrust or hostility towards the federal government. But there was a strong feeling — call it prejudice or reasonable preference — in favor of gold and against paper; a feeling due to the fact that California was then in the first stage of her great gold discoveries, and that gold was a plentiful medium for all transactions. Every debtor had the legal right to pay off his debts in depreciated paper. But if he did so, he was a marked man (the creditor was likely to post him publicly in the newspapers), and he was virtually boycotted. Throughout this period paper was not used in California. The people of the state conducted their transactions in gold, while all the rest of the United States used the inconvertible paper.[1]

The same factor — widespread unwillingness to use the paper — affects its circulation and value with highly dramatic effect, when a government grossly abuses the possibilities of the case, and issues it in great and constantly increasing quantity. Then

[1] See Moses, "Legal Tender Notes in California," *Quarterly Journal of Economics*, Vol. VII, p. 1.

the stage may be reached when no one will longer accept the paper, and when the bottom completely drops out of it. Its value then falls not only because its quantity is very great, but because people are no longer willing to accept it in exchange for goods. Its supply is increased; and at the same time the demand for it (the offer of goods for money) declines, — may even cease entirely. Such was the case with the notes which the Scotch schemer and adventurer, Law, persuaded the French government to issue in 1720. They were put forth in such enormous and unceasing amounts that they completely lost acceptability and depreciated to nothing.[1] Such was the case with the paper money issued by the American Congress during the Revolution. Continental money was printed in amounts so vast that it became utterly distrusted, and depreciated much more than in proportion to its quantity (whence the saying, "not worth a Continental"). Such, too, was the case with the assignats of the French Revolution in 1790–1796, when the French government put out notes which at first were redeemable in land, but soon were poured forth without pretense of any redemption, and in such unlimited quantities that they became quite worthless. Still later, in 1864–1865, the same was the fate of the paper money of the Southern Confederacy.

But no such extremity of depreciation has been reached in more recent instances. During the nineteenth century many countries resorted to issues of paper money, and depreciation commonly ensued. Yet, with the exception of the hapless South-

[1] The breakdown of confidence in the paper seems to have taken place in this case with dramatic suddenness. An effort by the government to put a limit to depreciation caused an unexpected and utter collapse. During the first stages of depreciation, "strange as it may appear, the deterioration of the notes in value does not appear to have affected their circulation. All that people looked to was nominal value, and while the notes were called livres, nobody inquired what a livre meant. But the instant the denomination was altered; the instant government declared that a note for ten livres should be worth only five, — the baselessness of the paper fabric was detected. The terror was as universal and as blind as the confidence had been. To use Sir James Steuart's words, on the 22d of May, a man with one hundred millions of bank notes might have starved in the street." SENIOR, *Three Lectures on the Cost of Obtaining Money*, p. 76. The reference is to Sir James Steuart's *Principles of Political Economy*, Part II, Chapter 59 (Vol. III, p. 52, edition of 1770).

ern Confederacy during our Civil War, no important country in the nineteenth century carried the process so far that confidence in the paper was completely lost. Very considerable issues have been made, under conditions which enabled the paper to maintain its circulation and to depend for its value on its quantity. This sort of situation, less extreme but in many ways less simple than the kind already illustrated, will be mainly discussed in the following sections.

§ 2. Paper money, whether convertible or inconvertible, tends to drive out specie. The expulsion takes place through the operations of international trade. The newly issued paper enlarges the quantity in circulation, and sooner or later raises prices. The rise in prices causes imports to be greater, exports to be less; and specie flows out in payment of the imports. Paper money, of course, does not flow out; it cannot circulate in foreign countries. The mechanism is not usually so simple as this; sundry complications in its working will appear when the subject of foreign trade is reached for detailed consideration. But in essentials the process is here stated correctly. Specie disappears through the channels of international trade, in proportion as paper money is issued. If half as much paper is put out as the specie previously in circulation, the medium of exchange will become half paper, half specie. If exactly as much paper is put out, all the specie will disappear, and only paper will remain. And *a fortiori* this will be the case if the paper exceeds in quantity the specie previously used.[1]

This last stage is that of "overissue"; that is, of issue beyond the point where prices remain the same as under a specie régime. Any added quantity of paper, beyond this point, is no longer offset by an equivalent expulsion of specie, but creates an abnormal level of prices. All the consequences of such a rise show themselves. Creditors lose, debtors gain. Prices of com-

[1] Theoretically, these statements require a correction, because the outflow of specie will raise prices in foreign countries, and so affect the whole international level and therefore the relation of paper to specie in the issuing country. But this correction is of no real importance in the experience of countries that have resorted to paper.

modities rise faster than do ordinary wages, and faster than those incomes which are called "fixed," because strongly affected by custom. Business men make money. The rate of interest rises. An exhilaration is felt in the industrial world, precisely as when prices rise from added supplies of specie.

The exhilaration lasts so long, and only so long, as the process is kept up. It is the result not of higher prices, but of rising prices. When once the higher level is reached all around, quiescence comes; nay, as a rule, lethargy. The effect is like that of a drug; when the stimulus no longer acts, a reaction sets in. One of the recurring phenomena of periods of rising prices, whether from specie or paper, is the complaint that there is not enough money. However much the quantity of money may have been increased, people aver there is not enough "to do the business," or not enough "to finance prosperity." This simply means that prices have been adjusted to the increased supply, that the upward movement has reached its term, and that the pleasant stage of apparently advancing prosperity has come to an end.

Hence there always springs up a plentiful crop of persons who advocate still further additions to the monetary supply. Most people have only vague notions of what money is, what are its functions, how it affects prosperity. Their instinctive attitude is almost always that of welcoming an increase in the money supply. Especially during and after periods of rising prices, the panacea of ever plentiful money has many ardent advocates. Sober sense sooner or later returns to the great mass of the community, and the projects of fiat-money advocates are brushed aside. But one of the greatest objections to paper issues is the unsettlement which they cause in people's ideas on the nature and effects of money. Absurd notions emerge, and the simplest lessons of economics must be retaught. The right adjustment of the monetary system — intrinsically a task of no small difficulty — has to be undertaken in face of a tumult of ignorance, passion, and dishonesty.

When paper has been issued in such amounts as to cause a

rise in prices above the level at which they would have stood under a specie standard, specie ceases to circulate and becomes itself a commodity. Paper becomes the sole medium of exchange, and gold (or silver, as the case may be) is bought and sold at prices in paper, like other things. In precisely the same way, after the gold standard established itself in the civilized countries, silver, being no longer a full money metal, was bought and sold in terms of gold. Under a régime of overissued paper gold sells at a premium in paper, and paper is depreciated in terms of gold. The paper is a nominal promise to pay in gold, but is not equal in value to the gold which it purports to represent. Hence the price of gold is commonly stated, not in terms of so much per ounce or pound, but in terms of itself, so to speak, — how many paper "dollars" are needed to buy one gold dollar.

Gold never disappears entirely from such a country, even though it ceases to be the medium of exchange and disappears from ordinary circulation. Some gold is always wanted for use in the arts; and for these uses it is bought and sold, like copper or nickel. Some is commonly wanted also for transactions which are by special stipulations to be carried out in gold. A class of dealers in gold usually appears, who make it a business to buy and sell this metal, as other dealers do with the commoner metals.

The premium on gold roughly measures the depreciation of the paper, but measures it no more than roughly. The real depreciation of the paper is the rise in prices. That could be measured, more or less accurately, by the index-number method. But any rise in prices is, as we have seen, irregular. Some commodities advance more than others, some not at all, some decline. The change in any one may or may not be such as to indicate the general change. So it is with the price of gold, or the specie premium. It is subject to influences of its own, among the most important of which is the demand for remittances abroad, — the necessary use of gold in transactions with foreign countries. Sometimes these special influences cause the premium to be in advance of the general rise in price, sometimes to lag behind.

Yet the divergencies between the specie premium and the real depreciation of the paper, though sometimes very pronounced, are not likely to endure long on a considerable scale. The premium usually indicates with fair accuracy the real depreciation of paper money. If the premium on the average is about 100 (*i.e.* if 200 of paper are needed to buy 100 of gold), we may infer that paper prices are about double what gold prices would be. If the premium is somewhere between 10 and 20, as it was in the United States during the years from 1870 to 1876, which preceded the return to a specie standard, we may be sure that prices in general are somewhat higher, but not greatly higher, than they would be in gold. And when the premium steadily declines over a period of years, we may infer that paper prices are coming nearer to what gold prices would have been,— that they either are falling, or are failing to rise as gold prices elsewhere are rising.

One of the factors which lead to special fluctuations in the gold premium is the prospect of the redemption of the paper in gold. Paper money is rarely issued with the intention or expectation that it will depreciate. The issue commonly takes place under stress, as a supposedly temporary expedient, with little time for deliberation, and with a desire to return as soon as possible to a specie basis. Any event which makes early redemption in specie probable, lowers the premium; any untoward event raises it. When Napoleon broke loose from Elba in 1814, the premium on gold in England rose; when the news of Waterloo came, it fell sharply. In the United States, the premium fell at once after the battle of Gettysburg, and rose high during the anxious summer of 1864. Such abrupt turns have led to the statement that confidence in the paper money governs its value, or at least greatly affects its value. It is more legitimate to say that confidence in redemption affects the value of the specie. General prices do not move up and down under the influence of military or political fortunes. It is the price of specie that is affected; for dealers and speculators discount at once the consequences for the financial stability of the government and for the possible resumption of specie payments.

§ 3. Of the various phenomena connected with paper money, no better illustration can be found than in the experience of the United States from 1862 to 1879, to which references have already been made. During the Civil War, in 1862–1865, great quantities of inconvertible paper were issued, far in excess of the specie previously in circulation. Prices rose rapidly, and at the close of 1864 were at least double what they had been in 1861. The specie premium rose in the same degree, and at one time (in July, 1864) was at the extraordinary height of 185; that is, a dollar of gold sold for $2.85 in paper. Immediately after the close of the war, in 1865, some parts of the paper money issues were withdrawn; prices fell sharply, and the price of gold dropped to about 150, *i.e.* the gold premium sank to 50. Throughout all these stirring and anxious years, the paper continued to circulate readily (except in distant California), and with no such loss of confidence as comes from complete discredit of the issues. The quantity, though reduced in 1865, still remained redundant, and depreciation lasted for many years, until finally in 1879 specie payments were resumed. The process by which prices were brought to the gold level and by which the real depreciation of the paper was ended, was rather that of growing demand for money, because of the increase of population and wealth, than of lessening the supply of money through retirement of a large part of the paper. It was a process not inaptly called "growing up to the currency."

The course of events is illustrated by the chart, which shows the range of prices during the period from 1860 to 1880. The index number which best indicates the course of prices is the median, not the arithmetic mean; because, for some of the years of greatest fluctuation, the arithmetic mean was unduly affected by the extreme prices of a few commodities. Nothing could show better the evils of excessive paper money than the soaring line of 1862–1865, and the sinking line of later years; the inequities between debtor and creditor, the instability of pecuniary relations, the slow and painful process of return to the normal standard.[1]

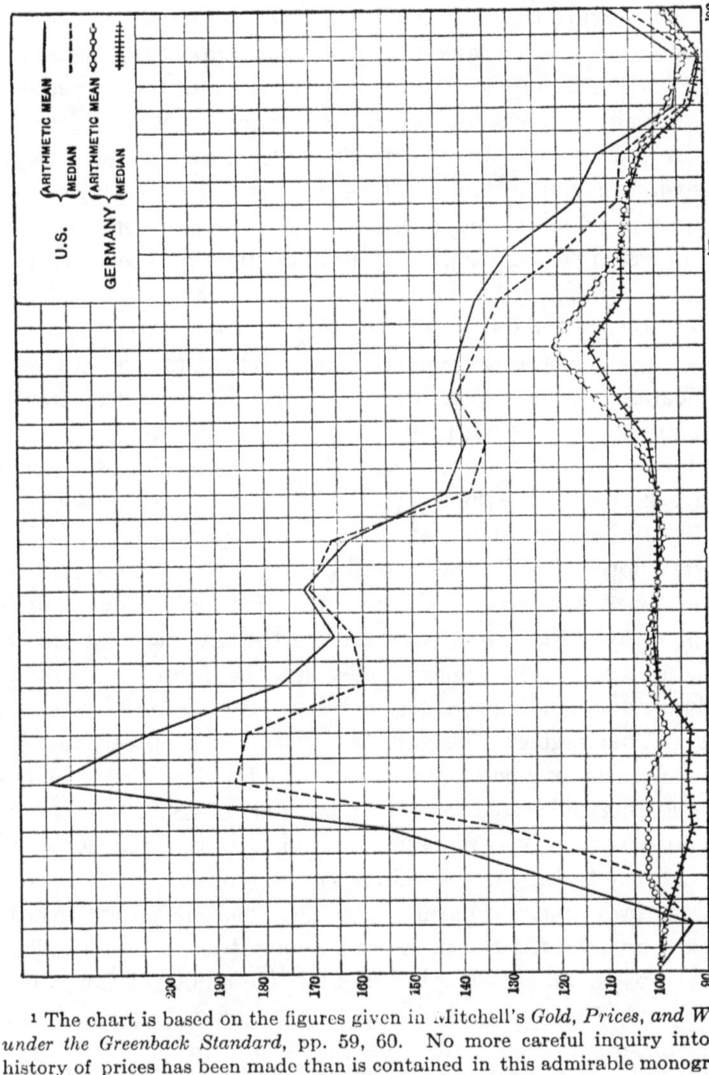

[1] The chart is based on the figures given in Mitchell's *Gold, Prices, and Wages under the Greenback Standard*, pp. 59, 60. No more careful inquiry into the history of prices has been made than is contained in this admirable monograph. None the less, some of the phenomena of the period are not yet fully understood, especially the great rise in prices in 1864–1865.

For comparison, the chart shows the course of prices in Germany as well as in the United States; the index numbers for Germany being calculated from the prices of precisely the same articles as for the United States. For each country, both the arithmetic means and the medians are shown. The divergence of the two sets of lines indicates unmistakeably the effect of the American paper issues.

It was during the ten years, more or less, preceding the resumption of specie payments, that the paper money advocates had their opportunity. Then all sorts of fallacies about the blessings of plentiful money had vogue. The controversy led, as is inevitable in a democratic community, to a long succession of compromises. One of these was the act for the resumption of specie payments itself. Still another result of this unsettled period was the injection of silver into the currency under the acts of 1878 and 1890.[1]

§ 4. History shows that overissue, always threatened by paper money, has rarely been avoided. Resort to this easy way of meeting public expenditures has usually been the consequence of war. Though Law's notes of 1720 in France were not due directly to military needs, the other well-known cases of notes utterly discredited, — the assignats of the French Revolution, the Continental money of our own War of Independence, the Confederate notes of 1862–1865, — all arose from the stress of war. Other issues which reached the stage of depreciation, though not of complete collapse, were due to the same sort of stress. England resorted to paper money (in the form of Bank of England notes, made inconvertible by law) during the Napoleonic wars. Prussia, during the same period, turned to direct state issues. Austria long had a much discredited paper money. Notwithstanding endeavors to resume, the wars of 1853, 1859, 1866, kept Austria to a paper money régime, until, in very recent times, she has succeeded in regaining specie equivalence. Russia, until our own time, has hardly known what specie money means. Spain, Portugal, the South American countries, all have fallen into the paper money slough, and most have not yet extricated themselves. The United States, as we have seen, had her trying experience during and after the Civil War. It deserves to be noted, too, that the War of 1812–1815 brought the United States to the verge of government issues. Had that war lasted a little longer, the final step toward a paper régime would probably have been taken. The cases of resort to paper, without en-

[1] Cf. Chapter 21, § 4.

suing depreciation and unsettlement, can be counted on the fingers of one hand. The most notable is that of France in the War of 1870–1871. The notes of the Bank of France (which were made virtually government paper, not exchangeable for specie), were issued in large amounts to aid the government in its financial exigencies during and after that great struggle. Yet the situation was handled with such caution and skill that only a slight specie premium appeared, lasting a short time only. The possible gain from a resort to paper was secured in this case without any serious drawback.[1]

The probability of overissue, with all its disturbing consequences, is the main ground for condemning paper money. To this must be added the corresponding disturbance of the reverse process, — the return to specie payments. So unsettling is a paper money régime that no community has willingly retained it, and every advanced country which has fallen into it has sooner or later extricated itself. Though paper money may do all the work of a circulating medium, it does so with a constant prospect of backsliding. Whether there is enough of it, or too much, or too little, is always a matter in the discretion of the government for the time being. The value of specie is deeply rooted in the established ways of mankind. For any one country, its value is not within the control of legislation at all. Its international acceptance gives it a basis on which the currency system of a country can rest securely. Hence every capable and ambitious community which has resorted to paper money resolves in the end, even at great sacrifice, to get back to specie.

A difficult problem sometimes presents itself as to the way in which the return to a specie basis shall take place; whether by redeeming the paper at its face value in specie, or at its market value. The first course has the bracing effect of recognizing a promise to pay as really a promise, and of meeting it to the letter. The second, however, may be more substantially equitable where the paper money has been depreciated for a long time.

[1] Cf. Chapter 26, § 2.

Then the injustice caused between debtors and creditors can no longer be undone. A new generation has come on the scene, and has made its engagements on the basis of paper. To shift these into specie engagements, with a transition to prices presumably lower, is to injure present debtors as much as past creditors were injured. Hence if the paper is depreciated, say one third (the price of gold being 150 in paper), and if it has been depreciated to this extent for many years, the most equitable plan is to redeem it in gold at two thirds of its nominal value. This is done most simply by creating a new coin having two thirds of the gold content of the former coin. The existing paper standard, and the existing range of prices and incomes, are thereby recognized once for all, but are anchored for the future to a firm specie basis. This is substantially what Austria and Russia have done in their resumption operations of recent years.[1]

But where the paper money is not of long standing; where the community has not become habituated to any sustained and fairly constant depreciation; where return to a specie standard has been steadily expected, and has been borne in mind as at least a possibility by all lenders and borrowers, — there the sound policy is to resume at par. Redeem the paper at its full nominal value, and maintain the good tradition that a dollar is a dollar. Doubtless it is a half-illusory tradition. The gold dollar is not necessarily a stable dollar. But it is a dollar more stable than any which the legislation of a particular country is likely to devise by itself. In this matter, as in so many others, it is well that sound rules of general expediency should crystallize into moral precepts. The doctrine that it is honest to redeem a paper dollar in gold at its face value, no doubt implies more as to the nature of "honesty" than the average man will understand, but is not to be caviled at unless there be very seri-

[1] This, too, is what Japan did when she changed from a silver to a gold basis in 1897. It is true that Japan did not have paper money; her currency was based on silver, which had been depreciating, with reference to gold, as the price of silver fell after 1873. Determined to adopt the ways of advanced countries, Japan turned to the gold standard, and established a new coin, the gold *yen*, equal in value to the silver yen as it stood at the time.

ous grounds for questioning the substantial balance of equity in favor of specie in general and gold in particular.

At all events, the return to specie payments has commonly taken place by resumption at par. This was the case in England after the Napoleonic wars; it was the case in Italy, in the resumption of 1883 (then half-hearted and unsuccessful, and only in recent years really accomplished). It was the case in the United States in 1879. Austria and Russia, which have just been referred to as changing from paper to gold on the basis of the market value of their paper, had the excuse that "specie" for them might have meant either silver or gold. Their paper had been issued at a time when silver was the familiar and accepted monetary metal in most parts of the world and in their own boundaries. They returned to specie at a time when gold had become the accepted metal, and when silver had much depreciated in terms of gold. The establishment of a new gold standard took place, reasonably enough, on the basis, not of depreciated silver, but of new gold coins representing the market value of the paper in the period of resumption.

§ 5. An interesting case, illustrating in another way how the quantity of money acts on its value, is that of what may be called inconvertible specie. The conspicuous instance is the rupee of British India. It is a silver coin, having about the same content of fine silver (165 grains) as forty-four cents of the American silver dollar. Formerly it was freely coined at the mints of British India; that great region had the single silver standard. When the fall in the price of silver set in after 1873, the rupee began to depreciate in terms of gold. The fall of silver had important effects. It necessarily influenced the foreign trade of India; it influenced also the finances of the Indian government. That government has large payments to make in England, almost always in gold. It collects its revenue in silver in India. The lower the price of silver in terms of gold, the farther will the Indian revenues fall short of meeting gold payment in England. When silver sold in London at about 61*d.* per ounce (*i.e.* when the ratio of silver to gold was about 15½ to 1), the rupee was worth 23*d.* in English money. At the lowest price which silver touched until 1892 (40*d.* in that year), the rupee was worth only 15*d.* In 1893, when the United States at last ceased its purchases of silver, the government of British India took the bold step of closing its mints to the free coinage of the rupees. Since that date, the rupee has been inconvertible specie. It is not freely coined, and its value no longer fluctuates with that of silver bullion. The Indian government does not undertake to redeem it in gold, but is willing, conversely, to give rupees for gold at the rate of one rupee for 16*d.* in gold. Hence the rupee cannot be worth more than 16*d.* in gold. The hope of the Indian government was to make it worth as much as 16*d.*, and thus to secure stability in the gold value of the rupee. That hope has been fulfilled. Though there was a period of some years after 1893 when the rupee was not maintained at the price of 16*d.*, since 1898 this has been accomplished. The limitation of quantity has given the rupee an artificial value, just as limitation of quantity gives paper an artificial value. The bullion in the rupee has been worth, at the lowest quoted price of silver in recent years, only 8*d.* (in 1902), or one half of the value which the rupee has maintained as coin. The essential cause of this maintenance of an artificial value has been a demand for the rupees which is great compared to their limited quantity.[1]

An interesting case of a similar sort, though one closely connected with inconvertible paper, is that of Austria from 1879 to about 1892. Austria had paper money after 1848, depreciated with reference to specie. By specie only silver was meant; for Austria had had a silver standard, and the paper gulden (or florin, as it was often called in English) was a promise to pay a gulden in silver. The depreciation of the paper during the earlier part of the decade 1870–1880 was roughly 10 per cent. But after 1873 silver itself began to depreciate, gradually

[1] Since 1899 the Indian government has redeemed the rupee in gold at 16*d.*, but without assuming a formal obligation to do so.

dropping toward the point where, in terms of gold, the silver gulden was worth no more than the paper gulden. In 1879, when this point was actually reached, silver was presented at the Austrian mints for coinage, because it was profitable to carry bullion to the mint, and to use the silver coin in Austria at the ruling prices of goods. Had this situation continued, more and more silver would have found its way into Austria, paper and silver would have circulated side by side, and the paper (whether or no convertible at the government agencies into silver) would have been worth as much as the silver, and no more. Prices would have accommodated themselves to the combined quantity of the two sorts of money. But to the Austrian government this intrusion of silver was not agreeable; the desirability of the metal was in question. Accordingly, in 1879 it stopped the free coinage of silver. Thereafter the circulating medium consisted in part of inconvertible paper, but in part also of silver gulden coins, of which some had been left over from old days, some had been struck just before the suspension of 1879. Both sorts of money were equally legal tender; they circulated side by side; both had an artificial value, due to the limitation of the total quantity. The silver gulden coins had a value greater than that of the silver bullion contained in them. No better illustration could be found of the way in which mere limitation of quantity maintains the value of money.

The final outcome from this curious situation has already been indicated. Austria determined to go over to the gold standard, and adopted a new coinage system, in which the crown was the unit. The amount of gold put into the crown made it equal to one half the market value of the existing paper or silver gulden. All debts payable in guldens could be liquidated at the rate of two crowns for each gulden, and the guldens were to be gradually replaced by coins (and paper convertible into coins) of the crown standard. In other words, the inconvertible paper and silver were both to be transformed into gold-standard money at the existing rate of depreciation,

— if the term "depreciation" can be accurately applied to this peculiar state of things. The process of change, it may be remarked, took longer in Austria than had been expected, and though the first legislative steps were taken as early as 1892, the plan has even now (1910) not been completely carried out.

§ 6. There have been suggestions or dreams of international paper money,—some sort of universally accepted token which should circulate between nations and within any one nation, should be regulated in quantity and presumably in value on a systematic plan, and should enable specie to be dispensed with as money. Then such labor as mankind would still devote to mining gold and silver would be directed solely to procuring them for use in the arts. That labor which is now given to procuring the bullion used as money would be set free, and money would be got in the much cheaper fashion of printing strips of paper.

The change is not unthinkable, and it appeals to those who like abstract speculation and ideal construction. As a proposal of anything practicable, it is not worth discussion. The nations of the earth find it hard to come to agreement on much simpler matters, and no international compact of this sort is now within the range of possibility. The solid basis of an actual physical scarcity, of a high cost resulting from scarcity, of wide general acceptability and serviceableness,— these circumstances underlie the universal use of specie, and make it certain that, for as long a time as we can consider in present economic arrangements, gold and silver, and mainly gold, will be the basis of the world's circulating medium. Gold is not a perfect monetary medium, but it is the best which the fallibility of human nature and the present degree of civilization enable us to devise.

§ 7. Convertible government paper may be a promise to pay, with some limited stock of specie provided for payments; or it may be simply a certificate of deposit. The latter is perhaps hardly government paper; it is simply a device for facilitating the use of specie; yet it is also in outward form a promise to pay.

The best example, and in modern times almost the only example of the certificate of deposit, is found in the familiar gold and silver certificate of the United States. For every such promise to pay that is outstanding, the full amount of gold or silver is kept in the vaults of the United States Treasury. In this case there is no difference whatever between the paper and the specie, except in the convenience of handling. The specie simply circulates in the form of the paper substitute. For silver this substitution has proved of great importance. The silver dollars are bulky and inconvenient when carried in quantities. The certificates enable the silver to circulate much more freely and in larger volume than would be possible for the coins. This reason for resorting to certificates does not exist for gold coins. The wide use of gold certificates in the United States is due partly to our custom of not redeeming worn gold coins at their face value, partly to habit. Our people have long been accustomed to paper money. Throughout the earlier part of the nineteenth century, bank notes were the chief medium for everyday purchases; later, during the period following the Civil War, inconvertible paper completely displaced gold. Although specie payments were resumed in 1879, much current money is still in the form of paper, such as the bank notes and the United States notes; and in that form the large volume of silver money is much more convenient. Purses and pocket books are all adapted to paper money, hence gold certificates are usually preferred to gold coin.

Of a different type are government notes proper, these being strict promises to pay, not mere certificates of deposits. The most conspicuous example of this sort of convertible of money is again in this country. The "United States notes" just referred to, commonly spoken of as "greenbacks," are reissues of the inconvertible paper issued during the Civil War. When specie payments were resumed, these notes were not paid off and destroyed, but simply made convertible. The amount then outstanding, $346,000,000, still remains. The United States

Treasury will redeem the notes on demand in gold coin; but it does not reserve dollar for dollar toward redeeming them. Indeed, for many years after 1879, no special supply of specie was set aside to redeem them; they were simply to be paid out of any surplus money the Treasury happened to have on hand. In 1900 a special fund of $150,000,000 of gold was created, to be held solely for the redemption of these notes when presented, with provisions for replenishing the fund by the sale of government bonds in case it should be depleted. Since that date no doubt has arisen, and none is likely to arise, of the likelihood of their redemption in specie. During the decade preceding 1900, there had been on several occasions serious doubts; for then the total volume of paper outstanding (including the silver money) was very large, and the situation was so disturbed as to lead to the presentation of notes for gold. Since 1900 the various forms of paper and silver money, while not absolutely diminished, have become less as compared with the extraordinary increase in the demand for money, due to rapid growth in population and in production. The United States notes, though redeemable, are in fact rarely presented for redemption. They circulate side by side with gold, are a complete legal tender for debts, are sufficiently limited in quantity, and exert in every respect precisely the same influence on prices as would the same quantity of gold coin or gold certificates.

Essentially similar are the *Reichskassenscheine* of Germany, — promissory notes of the German Empire, payable on demand. These are not, like our United States notes, a legal tender for debts; but they are receivable at par in all payments to the empire and to the several states. No special fund is provided for their redemption. But the issue is so small (only 120,000,000 marks, or about $30,000,000) that their easy circulation side by side with gold is assured. The Canadian government also has outstanding an amount of convertible notes ($29,000,000) not inconsiderable for that country; they are legal tender, and are protected by a specified reserve of gold.

The questions of principle concerning convertible government paper are simple. So long as convertibility is really maintained, the value of paper necessarily is the same as that of specie. Within the country of issue, it serves as money precisely as specie does. It presents none of the peculiar questions presented by inconvertible paper. It can affect the general range of prices only indirectly. By releasing so much specie, and presumably causing it to be exported, it virtually adds to the world's stock of specie, and thereby tends to raise the world level of prices; and this tendency will affect the issuing country as well as other countries. An effect of this sort, it is obvious, may come from inconvertible paper also; for that, too, in driving specie out of the country of issue, increases by so much the total amount circulating elsewhere in the world.

More complex are the questions of expediency. Government convertible paper is a dangerous tool; not so dangerous as inconvertible paper, yet far from safe. There is the same difficulty in keeping within the bounds of prudence. A small and strictly limited issue, like that of Germany, causes no difficulties. A comparatively large one, like that of Canada, especially when combined with a free use of bank notes (as in that country) causes the margin of specie in the circulating medium to be unduly narrow. In the United States, as in Canada, the margin of gold is none too broad; for, in addition to the United States notes, we have the silver certificates and the national bank notes, all depending for their solidity on the concurrent circulation of an additional quantity of gold. It cannot be said that the United States notes now are a serious source of danger; but they have been so in the past, and they may be so again in the future.

A strong objection to government paper, even though it be convertible, is in its effect on the *morale* of the circulating medium. It is a mere promise to pay; true, one that it is proposed to keep, but one kept at the will of the debtor. A government cannot be sued and compelled to pay. In the end, the creditor must rely simply on its good will. Some element of fiat thus attaches necessarily to government money. On the other hand, all the economies and advantages from the use of paper money can be secured through banks, public or private. These, being not the state itself, but agencies of the state, can be held to their obligations. The trend in all the advanced countries is toward the use of bank notes, not of government paper, as a means of economizing the use of specie. To this topic we turn in the chapters to follow.

CHAPTER 24

Banking and the Medium of Exchange

§ 1. Banks perform two functions, equally important, yet very different. They act as agencies for the collection of savings and for investment; they create a part of the medium of exchange. The two functions are often performed by the same institution, but not infrequently are separated. A savings bank has to do with investment only; and this is the case with many banks of Continental Europe. A strictly commercial bank is not concerned with the sort of "investment" to which the term is commonly limited, — that which looks to the creation of permanent plant. But such a bank supplies, in English-speaking communities especially, a highly important part of the circulating medium. In this chapter and the chapters following we shall have to do chiefly with the monetary aspects of banking operations.

To clear away preliminary matters, something may first be said of those banks by which investment operations alone are carried on. A savings bank accepts deposits; that is, it receives sums of money and promises to repay them. The promise is usually subject to conditions, as, for example, that the bank reserve the right of requiring notice (ten days, or some such period). It is not expected that the depositor, in fact, will wish to have his money back promptly. Ordinarily he leaves it with the bank for a considerable time, and expects to get interest on what he has deposited. The operation is typical of the process by which the saving of money leads to the creation of capital. The money is lent commonly to persons who mean to use it in effective investment, as, for example, in erecting factories, warehouses, dwellings. It goes into circulation again, and repeats its rounds in performing the functions of the medium of exchange. But it has been meanwhile the instrument by which some persons, having procured the command of purchasing power, were enabled to add to the substantive capital of the community. Often the proximate use by the savings bank is in the purchase of securities; that is, of promises to pay, or certificates of ownership, which have been issued by still other persons. In this case the bank is but one link in the chain which connects the savers of money with the makers of capital. The same process of collecting surplus means and attending to their investment is carried on by government postal savings banks, except that here the money deposited is commonly used in buying government securities, and the effect in adding to the real capital of the community — its apparatus of production — is more doubtful.[1]

Many banking institutions, both public and private, are concerned solely or mainly with such operations. The bankers and brokers who deal in so-called investment securities act as middlemen for the prosperous, just as the savings banks do for persons of smaller means. The so-called mortgage banks of Continental Europe, organized as public or semi-public institutions, perform the same function. Many of the great corporate banks of Germany, France, Austria, systematically conduct extensive operations in placing investments. They accept deposits in sums large or small, and either sell securities directly to the investor, or undertake, as does a savings bank, to pay him a stipulated rate of interest. The great historic private banking houses of England and the United States, and of the Continent also, — the Barings, the Morgans, the Rothschilds, and their numberless rivals and associates — carry on chiefly investment operations. They further and promote new enterprises. Commonly, they advance largely from their own means in the early stages of such enterprises. In due time, when the stage of settled business and accruing profits has been reached, they sell the enterprises or, more often, the securities based on them, to the saving and investing public. Each

[1] See Book I, Chapter 5, § 9.

banking house of this sort usually has its circle of customers and friends, who have faith in its judgment and honor, and are guided by its advice.

But all these operations have little to do with monetary questions proper. It is the operations of the commercial banks that are chiefly associated with the problems of money, — banks which do not undertake to manage permanent investments, but to lend on short time to the active business community. Such banks receive deposits, but primarily for the convenience of the depositor in the safeguarding of cash, and with an obligation to repay at any time on demand the whole sum deposited. In many cases, also, such banks issue notes. By their use of notes and of deposits they affect very greatly the medium of exchange.

In unfolding this subject, the same method will be followed as in preceding chapters. The simplest cases, illustrating the main principles, will first be considered, even at the risk of apparently losing touch with actual conditions. The complications and qualifications will then be introduced step by step.

§ 2. The simplest operation is note issue. A bank note is a promise to pay a specified sum to the bearer on demand. In law it is like any other promissory note payable to bearer. Title to it passes in full by delivery, and each successive holder has the same rights against the bank. If the institution which issues it is well known, the note may pass from hand to hand for an indefinite time, and perform the essential functions of money. Even if the institution is not well known, the note may remain long in circulation if people have become accustomed to the use of such paper substitutes, and if there is no special ground for distrusting the particular bank that issues it. Money is to a very great degree a matter of custom; what one person offers in payment, and the next person is likely to accept in payment, passes readily from hand to hand. Experience has amply proved that not only notes issued by responsible institutions, but notes issued by others that assume the outward show of responsibility, pass into the channels of circulation with surprising ease.

The bank, none the less, is under a strict legal obligation to pay every note, whenever presented, in that money which is legal tender for debts in general. We may assume specie, or gold, to be the only legal tender. The bank must keep at all times some gold wherewith to repay (or, as it is said, redeem) notes that are presented. If it keeps just as much specie as it has notes outstanding, its note issue obviously can be no source of profit; for the expense of printing the notes and of maintaining the bank office there is no compensation. But if it keeps less gold than the notes outstanding, there is the chance of profit. The excess of notes issued over and above the specie kept on hand is often called the "uncovered" issue. The larger the uncovered issue, the greater the opportunity for gain. Every bank which is left to follow its course without legislative restriction, tends to keep as little specie as possible, and to have as large an uncovered issue as possible.

The more secure a bank note is, — the more certain is payment in full whenever demand is made, — the less probably will notes in fact be presented for payment. They are then likely to circulate continuously as money. This condition is virtually reached under most modern legislation upon bank notes. They are usually issued (as will be more fully explained below) either by great public institutions or by private banks held to infallible payment. Consequently, the holder has no inducement to present them, and the bank is under no pressure from him to maintain a fund for their redemption. It has followed, as a further consequence, that additional legislation, or custom equivalent in binding force to legislation, is needed in order that there shall be kept on hand a considerable supply of specie for note redemption.

Bank notes thus take the place of specie very much as inconvertible paper does. An extreme case may even be imagined in which they would entirely displace specie. That extreme can never be reached, so long as the banks are held to their obligation to pay on demand. Some specie must always be kept. But where banks are allowed to issue without restraint, a near approach to the extreme may be reached. So it was in the United States before 1860, when a multitude of banks, chartered by the several states, issued notes, and each was under the temptation to put out its notes as freely as possible. The everyday circulating medium consisted of these notes, and only a narrow margin of specie was held in the bank vaults. In some parts of the country, especially in what were then the new regions of the West (Illinois and Wisconsin, for example), redemption of the notes in specie was not insisted on by law and business custom, and they were virtually inconvertible paper. In New England, New York, and the Eastern seaboard generally, and in Ohio and Indiana, the notes were really convertible into specie, yet their specie basis was small as compared with all the demand obligations of the banks.

A simple and effective device for preventing bank notes, even though freely issued, from completely displacing specie, is to prohibit notes of small denominations. This is now the common practise in European countries. Bank of England notes cannot be issued under five pounds, Bank of France notes under fifty francs, German bank notes under twenty marks.[1] Where this is done, and where no other form of paper is issued in small denominations, a considerable circulation of specie is assured. If the banks were to issue an undue quantity of large notes, and if these were to displace specie, people would feel inconvenience from a lack of money fitted for everyday minor transactions, and would present the large notes at the banks' counters, not necessarily from any sense of uneasiness, or from any wish to enforce redemption, but simply for the convenience of having the notes "broken" into convenient denominations. If the banks can issue small notes, this demand will of course be satisfied without resort to specie; and then it is

[1] Both the German and the French notes of the smaller denominations are in fact issued sparingly, with the express design of preventing the displacement of specie.

possible that bank notes will almost entirely displace specie. This was the common situation in the United States before the Civil War, when almost all of the states permitted small issues, and the everyday circulation was made up almost wholly of bank notes. Under the national banking system, banks may not issue notes in smaller denominations than $5, and recent legislation (of 1900) has provided that only one third of their issues can be in notes of this amount.[1] But restriction of this sort achieves little so long as the government itself issues notes of small denominations, as our government does with its own convertible notes (greenbacks) and its over-valued silver dollars and certificates. A substantial gain from such legislation is secured only when its effect is to bring about a large circulation of full-value specie, — that is, of gold.

§ 3. In modern times, especially in English-speaking countries, notes do not stand alone. Beside them, and of much greater volume and effect in a country like the United States, are the deposits. Though there are important differences between notes and deposits, as will appear presently, a fundamental similarity exists, long noted by careful observers, yet little understood by many writers on banking, and, oddly enough, often not understood by the very bankers concerned with the daily management of notes and deposits.

Most persons think of a deposit as cash left with a bank. This the word signifies; and this the transaction originally was. Historically, deposits began as specie left with trusted persons. This was the case with the bankers of Venice and Florence in the early period of the Renaissance, and with the goldsmiths of London during the second half of the seventeenth century. Where the banker or goldsmith kept intact the specie so left, he evidently made no gain; nay, he would probably demand a fee from the depositor for the care of the gold or silver. When next a depositor had a payment to make, it

[1] Until the resumption of specie payments in 1879, national banks were allowed to have one sixth of their notes in denominations of less than $5. There was no occasion for restricting them so long as specie did not circulate in any case.

was a natural process to give to the payee an order on the banker, or to deliver to him the banker's receipt. It was an equally natural process for this third person, if he had no immediate need of the money, to continue to leave it in the banker's charge, simply getting another receipt or having his name inscribed, instead of his debtor's, on the banker's records as a depositor. If many persons did this, having faith in the banker's honesty and solidity, he might use part of the specie in his own ventures, or lend it out to others. In the earliest times, the persons to whom such deposits were intrusted were commonly engaged in active business, and they used the funds in their current operations. Later, they developed the safer practise of lending the funds, on short time and on good security. Only as they so became systematic lenders, did they come to be bankers in the modern sense. Specie was then kept on hand merely in such quantities as were supposed necessary to meet the demands of persons actually calling for it; and the deposits became a source of profit.

This sort of depositing still plays a considerable part in contemporary banking operations. In the United States and England, many persons keep bank accounts merely for the convenience of not handling and safeguarding large sums of cash. Such are salaried persons, and those of the leisure class who have considerable means. These take to the bank and deposit at once whatever money or rights to money may come into their hands, making most payments by checks on the bank and drawing cash only for petty expenses. They habitually leave most of their current funds on deposit. The banker knows by experience that only a certain fraction (and a surprisingly small fraction) will be called for at any one time. A very great part of what is deposited can be lent out again by him for profit.

But the larger part of the deposits in the commercial banks of a country like the United States or England do not arise in this way. The deposits are in the main *created* by these banks.

It is easy to see in what manner bank notes are created.

A bank's main business is to lend, and to lend not its money or its capital, but its credit. This is what it does when it puts out bank notes. We usually say that a bank "issues" its notes. In fact, it lends them. It turns over to the borrower instruments which he can use in purchases, and these instruments circulate because the credit of the bank is good. The bank lends him, in other words, *its* credit, which in that form serves as well as money.

Essentially the same thing is done when a bank lends in the form of a deposit. The common and typical operation is that of the discount of a note. The borrower brings to the bank his promissory note, perhaps signed only by himself, perhaps fortified by the indorsement (*i.e.* guarantee) of others. The bank then credits him with a "deposit" of the amount of his note, less the agreed interest.[1] He has the right to draw on the bank as if he had actually deposited money. That right he may exercise either by demanding cash directly at its counters, or (more probably) through a check, which directs the bank to make payments to others. The first step in the ordinary commercial loan is the creation of such a depositor's relation with the bank.

But it is obvious that this first step will have no special consequences if the depositor exercises his right at once. If he draws out immediately the full amount credited to him, the result is the same as if he had carried off cash without the intermediate step. And it may appear that this is what he is likely to do; for he borrows with the purpose of using money means in business operations. But any depositor who did this, and who had no other relation with the bank, would be an unprofitable customer, and not one to whom the bank would habitually extend "accommodation." All banks, and

[1] The interest in case of bank discount is usually calculated on the face of the note, not on the amount lent or credited. Thus if a note for $1000 is discounted for three months at 6 per cent, the interest (1½ per cent for the quarter year) is calculated on the $1000, and the depositor is credited with $985. When the discount proceeds in this way at 6 per cent, the borrower in fact pays a slightly higher rate of interest on the amount lent to him or put to his credit.

especially the commercial banks of deposit, deal chiefly with their own circle of customers. These are both borrowers and depositors, both creditors and debtors. They keep their account with the bank, and there is a tacit understanding, not infrequently an explicit bargain, that the amount of loan accommodation extended to them shall be in proportion to the balance which is on the average to their credit as depositors.

It is possible, even probable, that very soon after a loan is made, the borrower will draw heavily against it. He is not likely to draw out the full amount; for every man, and especially every business man, wishes to keep some balance at the bank as a reserve for contingencies. But even if he draws out the larger part, his bank balance does not long remain depleted. Payments to him from his customers and debtors flow in from day to day, and are deposited in the bank as they come in. Meanwhile, as the days and weeks pass, he must prepare for the maturity of the note with which the transaction began. He does so by accumulating deposits, and toward the end of the period during which the note runs he has larger amounts to his credit. When his note becomes due, he pays it by drawing against the accumulated deposits; that is, essentially he offsets the debt which he owes on his note against the debt which the bank owes him on deposit account. Therewith the transaction is wound up.

But this transaction does not stand alone, and this business man does not stand alone. He will resort to the bank again for loans, and others will also resort to it; for all men in active business are borrowers, in order to carry on their operations continuously and on a larger scale than their own means permit. Their transactions with the banks are repeated in an endless series. Suppose now that a number of such persons are dealing with a bank as borrowers and depositors. While some are discounting and are drawing heavily on the deposits created for them, others are preparing to meet their maturing notes and are depositing heavily. Some happen to have made large payments in the ordinary course of business, and their deposits are scant; others have been receiving large payments, and their deposits are heavy. At any given time, the bank has a volume of deposits, large or small according to the business it has built up, and has corresponding resources in the way of notes discounted. Probably it has also some deposits of the non-business kind, independent of its lending operations; and probably it has also some loans not related to its deposits. But it has continuously a volume of resources (debts to it) closely related to a corresponding volume of deposits (debts due by it).

These continuing deposits are like money; or, to be more accurate, they are essentially like bank notes, and they serve as part of the medium of exchange just as any other circulating medium does. It may seem odd to speak of a deposit as part of the circulating medium. Most persons would accede to the statement that a check serves to effect payments as well as does a gold coin or a paper note; but they would say that the check, not the deposit, is the equivalent of money. Yet a moment's reflection will show that the check bears the same relation to the deposit which the coin used in making payments bears to the coin carried in the pocket. Not all the coin (taking coin as typical of the money that passes from hand to hand by delivery) is buying commodities all the time. Part of it is carried in pockets or kept in tills, by way of reserve, to be used at convenience. The portion of it actually used in purchases is determined by what we have called the rapidity of circulation of the money. Deposits similarly are a reserve, a potential means of payment, drawn upon at convenience. Just as, in reckoning the total quantity of specie in a community, we count the whole supply on hand, not merely that which happens to be making purchases at a given moment; so, in reckoning this form of the circulating medium, we must count up the total volume of deposits, not that part which happens to be in immediate use in the form of checks. The check is simply the deposit in actual use, and the proportion of checks to deposits represents the rapidity of circulation of deposits.

Rapidity of circulation is high, in the case of commercial banks and business men's deposits. Checks are drawn against such deposits daily, and fresh deposits are made daily. In the language of the commercial world, these are "active" accounts; their turnover is rapid. The deposits of persons of the leisure class are much less active. Coin and everyday pocket money — whether coin or bank notes or government paper — probably have in all cases a much less rapidity of circulation than a commercial bank's deposits.

§ 4. All use of money could be done away with, if there were but a single bank, if all deposits were kept at it alone, and if all payments were made by checks on it. The payee of a check ordinarily "deposits" it. Thereupon this single bank would deduct so much from the amount credited to him who drew the check, and add so much to the amount credited to the payee. No money would pass, and the payments would be effected simply by substituting one person for another as the bank's creditor (*i.e.* depositor).

Suppose now that there are two banks, having different sets of customers. Some customers and depositors of bank A will draw checks payable to those of bank B; and on the other hand customers and depositors of bank B will draw checks payable to those of bank A. Each bank will receive daily checks drawn on the other bank, deposited with it for collection. The banks can readily offset claims, and arrange to pay only such differences as may be due to one or the other. It is conceivable that they may even arrange not to pay the differences at all, but to keep a running account, the balance being one day in favor of bank A, the next in favor of bank B, with a tendency to equalization in the end. At all events, the amount of specie or money that will have to pass between them from time to time will be small as compared with the transactions concluded by mere offsetting.

Next, instead of two banks, imagine a dozen, twenty, any number; the same process can be carried on. Daily each bank receives checks drawn against the other banks. Daily each has to meet the checks drawn by its own customers, and deposited by the several payees with the other banks. Though a few checks may be disposed of within each bank (when the payee happens to keep his account in the same bank as the drawer), most of them are not settled quite so easily. Yet they are disposed of in practically the same way. They go through the clearing house, where the process of offsetting checks against each other is carried to its farthest limits.

A clearing house is a general organization of the banks of a given place, having for its main purpose the offsetting of cross obligations in the form of checks. Every bank sends to the clearing house all checks it has received against other banks, and each has to meet the checks drawn against it. The totals, of course, exactly offset each other. Any one bank may have a debit or a credit balance, and is in strictness bound to pay in cash, or entitled to receive in cash, the balance due. In practise, the balances are often settled in other ways. Sometimes they are paid by checks on another large bank. In London, clearing-house balances are settled by checks on the Bank of England, with which each of the associated banks keeps a deposit account; and then all the payments are finally effected by mere offsetting, without the use of any cash at all. In the interior parts of the United States, clearing-house balances are often settled in New York exchange; that is, by checks (commonly called "drafts," when drawn by one bank on another) on large banks in New York, with one or another of which each interior bank keeps an account. The final settlement of the transactions then takes place through the New York clearing house, with a minimum use of cash. Sometimes clearing-house balances are simply left to go from day to day, as debts due by one bank to another, subject to payments of interest by the debtor bank. A bank which is debtor at the clearing house one day may expect to be creditor another day, and, unless it happens to have an unusual supply of cash in its own coffers, may let any daily balance against it stand as a debt due the creditor banks. This practise of course depends on the willingness of the creditor banks to let the debt stand, and also upon the rules agreed on by the banks in general for clearing-house operations. The healthier practise is to maintain payments of balances in cash once for all; but the same reasons which induce all deposit banks to reduce their cash to the minimum lead them to mitigate by postponement the strict obligation to settle clearing-house balances in cash.

At all events, most of the checks are disposed of by being balanced against each other. The larger the banks, and the greater their number, the more likely it is that any one will have at the clearing house about as much to its credit as to its debit. In a comparatively small city it is more likely that the offsetting will not be complete, and that any one bank will have a considerable balance in proportion to the total transactions to receive or pay. In a large city the offsetting process is achieved with extraordinary completeness. In New York and London 95 per cent or more of the clearing house exchanges are settled by offset, and the balances payable and receivable by individual banks amount to less than 5 per cent of the total. Practically the same proportion is found in cities like Philadelphia, Boston, Chicago, Liverpool, and Manchester.

Clearing houses develop *pari passu* with deposit banking. Deposit banking, again, has developed most in English-speaking countries, and most of all in the United States. The London clearing house was established in 1775; this early date is conclusive proof that deposit banking was then carried on in large volume by a considerable number of banks. The New York clearing house was established in 1853; a date somewhat late in view of the early and rapid development of deposit banking in New York. Every considerable city in the United States now has its clearing house, and not a few cities that are inconsiderable. In 1908 there were 115 cities having clearing houses.

§ 5. Deposits in their operation as a circulating medium are among the most marvelous of economic phenomena. Like the division of labor which they serve to facilitate, they have developed by no intention, and have had little restraint or guidance from legislation. They work out their results by processes which are but half understood by the very persons who manage them. In countries where deposit banking is largely resorted to, like

England and the United States, all wholesale transactions, and a large and growing volume of retail transactions, are carried on by them. They combine in a remarkable degree safety and convenience. They are safe because a check is payable to a specified person, and the bank is answerable for making payment to that person only or to his endorsee.[1] They are convenient because a few strokes of the pen serve to remit any sum, however large, and to remit that sum precisely to the last cent. The mechanism is wonderfully smooth in its working, and effective.

Two things are essential for the development of deposit banking; or rather two phases of one thing, — confidence. Checks cannot pass from one person to another unless there is confidence in the probity of the drawer. Business custom has supplied substantial ground for this confidence. Quite apart from criminal penalty, he who draws a check without having credits at the bank to meet it commits industrial suicide. More important is confidence in the bank itself. The basis of the entire system is the repute and good standing of the bank. It can endure, for any individual bank, or for the banks as a whole, only so long as people think the bank's obligation to pay money to be equally good with the money itself. For the highest development of the system, moreover, it seems to be necessary that the custom of loans through deposits — the creation of deposits — should be widespread; for this is essential to the greatest quantitative growth.

Given these conditions, the vast but frail mechanism maintains itself in unceasing round: loans are made, deposits created, checks drawn, deposits maintained, loans again made, and so on. It consists of a mere mass of debts, contracted without any formality, and evidenced only by a few figures on bank ledgers and pass books. It is a sort of phantom circulating medium, ever appearing and disappearing, never substantial, always in danger

[1] In England checks are commonly "crossed"; that is, the drawer, knowing what is the payee's bank, writes the name of that bank across the face, indicating at what bank the check is to be deposited by the payee. But experience in the United States, where checks are not crossed, indicates that this precaution against fraud can be dispensed with.

of melting away from a breath of suspicion, yet so serviceable as to be renewed after every collapse and to be maintained notwithstanding every danger.

§ 6. The wide use of deposits has important effects on the rest of the circulating medium, and therefore on the mode in which notes are dealt with by the banks.

A bank's liability for its deposits is more likely to be forced upon its attention than that for notes. Both are alike demand obligations. But the note, which passes from hand to hand by delivery, may remain outstanding a long time, and its presentation for redemption may become almost a remote contingency. On the other hand, when a deposit goes into active circulation, — that is, when a check is drawn, — the bank is likely soon to hear from it. True, a check may read "Pay to the bearer" and so may pass from hand to hand by delivery, like a note; but such checks are little used, if for no other reason than that they lack safety for transmission. Again, a check may be indorsed by the payee to another person, by him may be further indorsed to still others, and so again and again. In each transfer it may serve to effect payments as well as a bank note or a coin. But this use of checks is also of no considerable consequence; since the precise sum for which a check drawn is not likely to be wanted in a number of successive transactions. As a rule a check soon travels back to the bank on which it is drawn, commonly *via* another bank and through the clearing house. Thus the demand obligations of the deposit has constantly to be faced. This, obviously, is the case especially with the active deposits of commercial banks.

Against the steady presentation of checks a bank has the funds which are steadily being put into its care by its customers, — that is, the checks on other banks and the spare cash deposited with it. The maintenance of its unfailing volume of resources depends on that foundation of confidence just described, — the habitual putting in its charge of all free resources not needed by its customers for immediate payments. Given this, and it cannot only create deposits, but maintain them by constant renewal; always subject, however, to a daily presentation of demands against deposits.

When, however, the use of banks as repositories of all spare funds, and so the use of deposits as currency, has become highly developed, the rest of the circulating medium becomes involved in the all-pervading operations of the banks. "Cash" or "money," — including bank notes and government notes, such as pass by mere delivery, — all this comes to be used chiefly in retail transactions. When so used it is likely to find its way regularly to the bank counters, since most retail dealers keep a bank account, and send in their daily receipts for deposit. The cash is drawn out again by an entirely different set of persons: by other merchants, by employers for use in pay rolls, and by all depositors for pocket-money use. Hence cash is constantly passing in and out of the banks.

This situation, for example, has an influence on the mode of circulation of bank notes. When the note is the only form of bank currency, it may remain afloat a considerable time without being presented at the bank of issue. But when notes and deposits are freely used side by side, the notes are constantly getting into the hands of some bank or other. To the receiving bank two courses are then open. It may pay the note out again over its counter, indiscriminately with other cash; or it may send it for redemption, like a check, to the bank of issue. The former course is likely to be adopted where the notes have been issued by a great public bank, or, as in the case of our national bank notes, by private banks held to very rigid limitations upon the amount of issue. The latter course is likely to be adopted when there is free opportunity for the receiving bank to issue its own notes.[1] The note of the other bank which it has received on deposit represents for it the equivalent of cash; the note can be sent to the issuing bank for redemption. The bank's own notes,

[1] Where, however, there are many small banks, the likelihood is less; because of the trouble of sorting many notes and sending them off to distant places in petty batches. This fact is often forgotten in discussions of schemes of banking reform for the United States.

when paid out over the counter, represent only its credit. They cost nothing so long as they remain outstanding. The bank, therefore, will use its own notes for counter payments, or for "till money." Notes of other banks will be treated like checks; both notes and checks will be sent to the clearing house for redemption. In New England this was the common practise before 1860, when there were many banks both of deposit and issue, and each had the wish and the liberty to extend its own credit as much as possible. A clearing house for notes may, for convenience, be separate from that for deposits. So it was in New England, where the Suffolk Bank was the agency through which notes were cleared, and where the system hence came to be known as the Suffolk Bank system. Whether through the same clearing house or a different one, notes then return to the banks as regularly as checks do. They may then be re-issued, as deposits may be re-created. In both cases the maintenance of their circulation depends on the continuing repute of the bank and the unfailing confidence of its customers.

But, as has already been noted, and as will be more fully explained in the next chapter, notes are not now commonly dealt with by banks as deposits are: they are rather treated like ordinary cash. In most countries they are both fortified and restricted by legislation, and for most purposes are used like any other "money." Hence they are paid out indiscriminately by banks, as well as by individuals. In that case the process of redemption is slow. One of the most difficult problems of principle in banking legislation is whether this system is good, — whether notes should be hedged in, made absolutely safe, amalgamated as completely as possible with coin; or whether they should be kept strictly separate from legal tender money, treated as simple demand obligations, freely issued, and subject to constant redemption and re-issue by the banks.

CHAPTER 25

Banking Operations

§ 1. Against their demand liabilities in the form of notes and deposits, banks must have cash, or assets readily convertible into cash.

Cash in a bank's vaults is "idle" money; it is earning nothing. Whether the bank be one of deposit or issue, it is under constant temptation to reduce to the lowest terms its holdings of specie or other legal tender money. Some cash it needs to hold, in order to meet demands at the counter and balances at the clearing house (unless, indeed, the latter can be met in other ways). Some cash more it may hold against the contingency of a "run," — sudden demands by depositors resulting from a distrust in the bank. But this possibility is little regarded, as a rule, unless under compulsion by the law. Why not invest "idle" cash, put it out in loans or purchases of securities, and get an income? Hence the actual holding of legal tender money tends to be reduced to the minimum which experience shows to be needed in the ordinary course of business. That minimum is surprisingly slender. Five per cent of the demand obligations seems to be ample. The English banks of deposit, which issue no notes, and (for reasons to be explained in the next chapter) do not trouble themselves about any reserve against runs, rarely keep more than this proportion against their deposits, and often do not keep so much. American banks also, unless compelled by law to keep more (as they commonly are) find that they get along comfortably with five per cent.

None the less, the other resources of a bank must be of a sort to enable it to face the fact of demand obligations. It must have quick assets. Its loans are on short time, and in a well-managed bank are marshaled in such a way that some of them are maturing week by week and day by day. Recurrently, at short intervals, the bank becomes entitled to repayment of loans, and thus is in a position quickly to increase its cash or diminish its demand liabilities (*i.e.* its deposits).

The typical form of the short-time loan, as has already been said, is discounted commercial paper. All manufacturers and all wholesale dealers, and most retail dealers, give credit to purchasers, and in turn borrow from the banks. Loans to them, on short time, and in connection with their current dealings, are to a high degree secure; for to meet them is the first condition of a man's standing in the mercantile community and so of the very possibility of maintaining himself in business. By the older tradition, the banker was the confidential friend and adviser of the business men who were his customers; well-informed upon their affairs, and disposed to aid them with credit according to their pecuniary deserts. This sort of relation, with discount of commercial paper based on it, still plays a very large part in ordinary banking operations.

Side by side with these intimate relations there have always been, and of late have grown in volume and importance (at least in the United States) transactions of a more cold-blooded sort. Loans are made with collateral; that is, on the pledge of property that can be sold by the bank if the loan is not promptly paid. Securities — stocks and bonds of all sorts — are the most welcome form of collateral, because the stock exchanges give the most perfect facilities for disposing of them. Every bank has a certain proportion of loans, commonly secured by stock exchange collateral, and payable on demand, which it is expected at once to convert into cash if there should be any sudden large presentation of demands against the bank by depositors.

Other assets of a quickly realizable sort are also found in a bank's resources. Familiar and easily salable securities are often held, such as can be turned into cash at a moment's notice in case of need. Every English bank parades on the published balance sheet its consols, and treats these as if they were the same thing as cash. The United States bonds, and the state and municipal bonds, which our trust companies are apt to enumerate first in their published statements, are of the same sort. When a bank, after it holds as much of such securities as are desirable for general safety and repute, still finds that it has more cash than is needed for its current operations, it will "go into the market" and buy with the surplus anything that seems safe and profitable. It may buy ordinary "good" securities, even though its usual course of business is not to buy and sell stocks and bonds. It may buy "outside paper"; that is, the promissory notes of business firms which are not its own customers and depositors. This is done through the bill brokers of England, and the note brokers in the United States, — a set of middlemen who have lately become of growing importance in American banking. The note brokers peddle the commercial paper of well-known firms among banks whose resources are temporarily, sometimes permanently, greater than they can utilize among their own clientele. The practise of buying such notes of course increases the range of the banker's cold-blooded operations. Its advantages and disadvantages have been much debated. It is said to distribute the banker's risks better; he is not so much bound up with the fortunes of the particular clique or trade that makes up his regular customers. On the other hand, it makes him deal with persons whose affairs he knows with little certainty; and it brings possibilities of overexpansion by the borrowers, and of unexpected loss to the bankers.

A purely commercial bank confines itself to such operations as these. But a bank may be more than purely commercial. It may have large deposits from persons not in active business; and then, of course, is most likely to buy general securities or outside paper. More important is the tendency to combine general financing and investment operations with commercial banking, a tendency which on the whole seems to be growing. The national banks of the United States and the joint stock banks of England are traditionally separate from promoting and investment, and restrict themselves to commercial business. On the other hand, as was pointed out in the last chapter, the great private banking houses have been mainly investment agencies, nursing new enterprises and enlisting a clientele of well-to-do customers who look to them for advice and guidance in placing their accumulations. Many large institutions of modern times combine all these kinds of banking, as, for example, the great banking companies of Germany and France.[1] A similar wide range of operations is carried by many of the so-called trust companies of the United States. Some of these do strictly what their name implies, — act simply as trustees, administrators, executors, fiduciary agents. But most of them combine promoting and investment with banking of the traditional sort. Even our national banks have been led by competition and the search for profit to enter on promoting and financing operations to a greater degree than in former times.

The combination of different operations by a single institution, in close connection with deposit banking, brings dangers. The due balancing of demand liabilities with quick assets is not easy to maintain where other operations are undertaken which look to permanent investment. The danger of a commercial crisis is more imminent and more serious when the deposits which are payable on demand and are interlocked with the effective circulating medium, are closely connected with new ventures that tie up resources for a long time and necessarily entail large risks. None the less, it is probable that this sort of financial combination will be undertaken in the future more rather than less. It opens the prospect of larger profits than routine commercial banking offers. It is not easy to restrict by legislation, even if restriction were clearly desirable. It is in accord with the general trend to consolidation and large-scale management; and its growth must be watched with the same uneasy interest as all the extensions of capitalist enterprise into larger and more complex aggregations.

[1] Cp. what is said in Chapter 26, § 4, of the German banks. The Crédit Lyonnais, a remarkable institution, is the largest of the French banks.

§ 2. It is the business of banks to lend. They lend more freely in proportion as their cash holdings or reserves are large. Hence there is a close connection between the rate of which bank loans are made, that is, the rate of discount, and the quantity of money held by the banks.

A common notion is that the rate of interest depends on the quantity of money, rising when that is plentiful, falling when it is scarce. The notion, thus broadly stated, is absurd. The abundance of money affects its exchange value, that is, the general range of prices. Advocates of paper money have often supposed that a greater quantity of money would lower the rate of interest. In fact, as we have seen, the period during which prices are rising is one not of lower interest, but of higher. When once the definitive stage of higher prices has been reached, there is nothing in the nature of the situation to make interest higher or lower; though, under a régime of inconvertible paper, it often happens that the general unsettlement causes the risks of lending to be deemed higher and so raises the rate of interest by a sort of insurance premium. But all this does not modify in any essential the general proposition that the rate of interest depends, not on the supply of money, but on the relations between savings and their utilization in production.[1]

But, though the rate of interest does not depend on the quantity of money circulating in the community at large, the bank rate for loans is affected by the quantity of money which is held in the banks' vaults. The commercial world is constantly speaking of the value of money and the plentifulness of money; and it uses both phrases in a special sense, referring to the banking situation. By value of money it means primarily the rate of interest or discount on short-time business loans. By plentifulness of money it means a relative abundance of cash in the banks, leading to a free offering of loans. Relative abundance, be it noted: a large or small supply relatively to the demand obligations of the banks. When they have more cash than seems needed for daily calls and for safety or pru-

[1] See Book V, Chapters 38, 39.

dence, they lend freely. Thereby they either add to their demand obligations (by increase of deposits or notes) or part with some of their cash in the direct purchase of commercial paper or securities. In either case the relation of cash to liabilities is altered, until something like the normal situation, or supposed normal situation, is reached. Conversely, when the cash is scant as compared with the demand reasonably to be expected, banks draw in. They refuse to make new loans, or to renew old ones; or at least, they "take care" of their steady customers only, and turn a deaf ear to others. Hence the rate of discount varies according to the plentifulness of cash held by the banks. Large cash holdings lead to "easy money" and free lending, small holdings to "tight money" and restricted lending.

These tendencies, and the fluctuations in interest rates which result, appear most conspicuously in the case of demand loans. On these the rates of interest may vary widely. A demand loan, it must be remembered, is subject to call by either party: the debtor can be called on to repay at any time, but he also has the option of making repayment at any time. When banks have plenty of cash, they lend freely, and at very low rates, on demand; for, if other more profitable ways of using their funds should present themselves, they can at once call for payment of the demand loans and turn to those more profitable. Hence one hears of call money in New York, where these fluctuations are most striking, quoted as low as one per cent a year. On the other hand, a trader who is in stress for means to meet immediate liabilities will pay a high rate for a demand loan, knowing that he can repay at any time and hoping to do so in a few days. One hears also of call money quoted in New York at 100, even at 200 per cent a year. Of course no one would borrow at this ruinous rate through a year; but it might be done for a few days in order to tide over an emergency.

Demand loans are usually cold-blooded, made to any one on the deposit of collateral. The debtor must pay without mercy when called on, and if he fails to do so, the collateral which he has given is sold at once.[1] The loans are commonly connected with transactions on the exchange, especially on the stock exchange, and are an important part of the mechanism by which speculation is facilitated. From the point of view of the bank, they are a highly convenient part of its business. A profit is certain, sometimes large, sometimes small, but always appreciable; and yet the bank's resources are not tied up and cash can be called back — at least by the individual bank — if there is more profitable use for it elsewhere, or if there is a sign of danger. And from the point of view of public advantage, there is also some gain. For sundry useful business transactions funds are wanted over short but uncertain periods, and for these demand loans are adapted.

But there are also grave public disadvantages from such transactions. They facilitate gambling speculation, not only in stocks, but in grain, cotton, and other standardized commodities. All the real and serious evils of speculation are made greater, or at least are made more easily possible, by the willingness of banks to lend funds on call to any one who will pledge sufficient security. Naturally, with the tendency toward specialization in all modern industry, there are some banks which turn more freely than others to this sort of lending; and indeed in every great financial center there are a few banks which make this almost their exclusive business. Such lending, too, is closely connected with the tendency to accumulate all spare bank cash in the financial centers, like New York and London; a tendency which is more particularly connected with the development of deposit banking and with

[1] Many loans which are nominally on demand, are in reality not subject to this sort of drastic treatment. Loans in this form are made more than in previous times to merchants, taking the place of sixty-day or ninety-day paper, yet not essentially different from it. It is understood that the bank will not in fact "sell out" the borrower. And even stock exchange call loans, when made to brokers who are regular customers, are payable on demand more in name than in fact. Banks like to parade on their published accounts a large volume of demand loans, as if their promptly realizable resources were abundant. In fact, the convertibility into cash is often more nominal than real.

some of the dangers in that system, of which more will be said elsewhere.

The rate of interest on ordinary commercial loans — time money for thirty days, sixty days, ninety days — of course shows much less fluctuation than that on demand loans. For regular customers and depositors of banks, the rate of discount often varies very little, even though cash in the banks may be more or less abundant; there being an understanding that they shall have "reasonable" accommodation at a "fair" rate, that is, at the customary or current rate. The rate on advances of this sort goes up and down somewhat, and oscillates about the general rate of return on permanent investments. Discounts for less regular customers fluctuate more sharply according as the cash holdings of the banks are larger or smaller. In times of stress such loans may be very hard to get, and may be made at high rates, — 8, 10, 12 per cent; while regular customers may still be taken care of at the traditional rate, say 6 per cent or 5 per cent. Conversely, when money is "easy," the banks may buy "outside paper" on terms which yield them less than the usual rate. The business man, in arranging his banking connections, often has a choice between these two ways of securing his credit. He may deal steadily with one bank, very likely a conservative one, paying to it a fairly steady rate of interest through good times and bad, and sure of support in periods of stress. Or he may float his paper through note brokers, and borrow here and there at varying rates. Then he takes his chances as to support in the periods when no bank has much free money and when all business men are demanding loans. The former course is that which conduces to the safe and steady conduct of industry; the latter is that which promotes the recurrence of commercial crises. Yet the latter often seems immediately the more profitable, and, under skillful as well as venturesome management, may be in fact the more profitable. In every community there will be found the two types of banks and the two types of business men. The fluctuations in the rate of interest naturally appear most sharply in the dealings between the venturesome banks and the venturesome business men.

§ 3. A successful banker or bank manager must have above all qualities that of judgment. He must be a good judge of men and a good judge of enterprises. He must be well informed on what is going on in the community about him. In a strictly commercial bank he must have besides these qualities a measure of caution. The management of a commercial bank is not on the whole very difficult. It calls for prudence, probity, adherence to routine and system, large acquaintance in the business community. In all forms of banking, the good business repute of the individuals in charge is a *sine qua non.* The more complex operations of a financing and promoting institution calls for rarer qualities; not only for judgment and caution, but for some venturesomeness also, and for managing ability. Risks must be taken, heavy commitments made to new enterprises, forecasts made with accuracy for a comparatively distant future, the right men selected for the conduct of difficult operations. Here the born captain of industry often finds his richest opportunities.

The profits of banking may be great; and, as with any industry where good will plays an important part, they seem little subject to the leveling influence of competition, even though there be no approach to monopoly. The essential element in a successful bank is high repute, attained by a long course of prudent and well-conducted business. Once the good will is built up, the bank may maintain itself for an indefinite time by mere size and momentum. It can make new loans, create new deposits, maintain its hold on its customers, and enlarge almost without limit. Though its profits may be great, rivals will find difficulty in competing with it, not to speak of supplanting it. True, like all good will, this cannot be maintained indefinitely without some effort. New banks will find ways of accommodating or enticing customers, new blood will appear in the business community, old banks may become fossilized and may slowly lose their clientele. But some great banks in all the important cities hold their own from generation to generation, partly no doubt by continued good management, but to no small degree from mere sustained good will.

§ 4. It is often said that a bank supplies capital and by so doing adds to the productive resources of a community. In the strict sense of capital (capital goods) a bank obviously does nothing of the kind. Tools, machinery, building materials, are created by labor, not by saving or lending. But a bank, though it does not create capital, is a most important instrument in regulating the command of capital and in promoting the effective use of capital.

So far as savings banks, investment banks, and similar financial institutions are concerned, nothing needs to be added to what has already been said.[1] They are intermediaries in the process by which saving furthers investment and the making of capital.

Commercial banks have often been described as performing the same functions in the same way. They are said to gather rills of savings — money means not immediately needed by the owners and deposited by them in the bank — and to lend them to producers, very much as savings banks lend the accumulations which are more deliberately set aside. So far as deposits arise by the actual putting into banks of spare cash, this description fits. But so far as deposits are created by the banks, and so far as notes are issued by them — these being the peculiar operations of commercial banks — the description does not fit. Here command of capital is supplied by the banks without that sort of saving which is ordinarily associated with the process of investment. Money means are created, and the command of capital is supplied, without cost or sacrifice on the part of any saver.

The social utility of commercial banking with its costless supply of funds is somewhat different from that of other forms of banking. It arises from the fact that the commercial banks facilitate primarily the operations of the active business men.

[1] See Book I, Chapter 5, § 4.

In so doing, they bring about one clearly advantageous result: they promote the continuity of industry. The merchant or manufacturer who has completed one stage in his operations need not wait, before beginning again, until he has disposed of the salable product, or received the proceeds of a sale. The bank enables him to anticipate what is due him, or is reasonably certain to come to him, and so enables him to enter forthwith on another stage. At least equally important, but not so obvious, is the influence which banks exercise on the make-up of the business world. As will appear in later chapters, something like a process of natural selection determines who shall come to the lead in the conduct of business.[1] In that selective process the commercial banks play a dominant part. They lend freely to the men of whom they think well; they turn a deaf ear to him whose projects seem unpromising. Their willingness to give credit makes it possible for the capable man to extend his operations, even though he start with little or no means of his own. No doubt they sometimes make mistakes, and enable empty pretenders or reckless speculators to get command of large resources. But bankers, to repeat, need be above all things good judges of men. On the whole, they put the control of the industrial forces into the hands of those likely to turn them into profitable channels. They are the leaders among the leaders in the industrial world.

Obviously, bankers judge borrowers solely according to pecuniary desert. They lend freely to the man who makes money. How he makes money and how far his money-making conduces to the common good, is none of the banker's concern, no more than it is the lawyer's professional concern to inquire whether his client is doing things for the public ill or good. So long as the borrower's operations are within the pale of the law and of current business morality, the only question is whether he is "safe" and is likely to be a profitable customer in the present and future. If money is commonly made by efficient guidance of the forces of production, banking con-

[1] See Book V, Chapter 49.

tributes to that guidance. If money is commonly made by overreaching others, by fraud or gambling, by taking advantage of necessitous laborers, banking contributes to such misdirection of energy. Investment of every sort through the mediation of financial institutions stands or falls, as to its social utility, with the working of the whole institution of private ownership of capital. Commercial banking particularly stands or falls, as to its social utility, with the merits or demerits of the business man's doings. On these general problems, — the crucial ones of economics, — the last word cannot be said until the very close of our discussion.

CHAPTER 26

CENTRALIZED BANKING SYSTEMS

§ 1. The intimate connection of banking operations with the circulating medium led early to their regulation by law. While legislation has covered a wide field, it has yet been directed mainly to the monetary aspects of banking. Partly under its influence, partly under the more elusive influence of national custom, very different banking systems have grown up in the various countries. To describe these in detail would far transgress the scope of a book like the present. Yet some account both of the laws and of the banking habits of leading nations is essential for an understanding of the general situation, and particularly of the relation of banking to monetary phenomena and to the general movements of prices.

The need of the regulation of note issues was seen almost as soon as the use of bank notes began. It became clear at a very early date that notes could get into circulation easily; that a bank's obligation to redeem in specie was often postponed by the continued circulation of the notes from hand to hand; that this obligation could be evaded by a private bank even when the notes were presented for payment; and that unregulated issue was sure to bring, in a considerable proportion of cases, recklessness and eventual collapse. The English-speaking countries particularly, such as England, Scotland, and the United States, were confronted recurrently with heavy bank failures, entailing loss or even disaster for persons by whom the notes had been received in the ordinary course of dealings. In the first half of the nineteenth century such catastrophes were all too common in the three countries named. On the continent of Europe note issue by banks had from the first been regarded as a public function, and had been permitted only to institutions closely connected with the government and supervised by it. During the nineteenth century two fundamentally different modes of regulation developed: the one through a great central bank, having a monopoly of note issue and possessing in large degree the character of a government institution; the other through systematic supervision of scattered and separate banks. Centralization and public or quasi-public note issue are on the whole winning their way. Most of the continental countries, as just remarked, have followed this principle from the outset. England adopted it in her famous Bank Act of 1844. Switzerland has very recently (1905) changed from a decentralized system to one of a public bank with sole right of issue. The United States is by far the most important of the countries which still maintains manifold note issue; with her are Scotland and Canada.

§ 2. Of central banks three important and typical examples are found in the Bank of France, the Bank of England, and the Imperial Bank of Germany.

The Bank of France is the simplest of all the great banks, and indeed among the simplest of all banks, great or small. It has a monopoly of note issue, — no other bank in France may put out notes; and it is virtually under government management. But there is no special regulation of its banking operations, no separate provision looking to the safety of its notes, virtually no limitation on the amount of notes it may issue.

The Bank of France is a corporation, with stockholders, directors, and all the paraphernalia of a private institution. It pays dividends to its stockholders. But the manager is appointed by the government, and, though there are consulting committees through which the stockholders have some powers, its direction is virtually in the hands of the government. The bank is the fiscal agent of the government, being the custodian of the public funds. It has the administration and recording of the public debt of France, — a simple bookkeeping task, but one of great magnitude inasmuch as the amount of the debt is enormous. Much more important is its relation to the government as lender. When the French treasury needs funds, it turns to the Bank of France for advances. Its services to the country in the trying period during and after the war of 1870–1871 can hardly be overestimated. The government turned to it for heavy advances, which largely took the form of note issues. The notes were made inconvertible, — the Bank was not only allowed to refuse payment in specie, but was inhibited from such payment. Virtually, the Bank became the agent of the government for issuing inconvertible paper money. But the issues took the form of loans to the government, on which interest was paid to the Bank; and the redemption of the notes in specie was ultimately to be undertaken (and in fact was undertaken in 1878) by the Bank. It has already been pointed out that this is one of the very few cases in which inconvertible paper has been issued without leading to depreciation, and the only case in which this has been done on a large scale. That such great aid was furnished to the French government and people, without the demoralizing effects which usually flow from paper money, is to be ascribed in no small measure to the fact that the issue was not made directly by the government, but through a bank which was financially separate and which could be called on without friction or controversy to resume specie payments when the time was ripe.

The Bank of France has a monopoly of note issue; it may do quite as it pleases with regard to the specie held in its vaults for the payment of the notes and its other obligations. As a matter of fact, it has held during the last generation a great and increasing stock of specie, — needlessly large, if one looks merely at the safety and solidity of the notes. That stock is partly gold, partly silver. The silver consists chiefly of the overvalued five-franc pieces; and these, though legal tender and completely available for the Bank in meeting its obligations, are yet dependent for their current value on the gold coin in use side by side with them.[1] But the stock of gold coin —

[1] See above, Chapter 21, § 2.

both that held by the Bank and that in circulation in the community — is so large as to prevent the silver from being a source of weakness. In recent years the Bank of France has held in specie — gold and silver together — nearly as much as the total notes outstanding. Until about 1890, this specie consisted in nearly equal parts of gold and silver; but after that date the amount of gold grew to be double and triple that of silver, and the holdings of gold have become more than ample for security.

The deposit obligations of the Bank of France are comparatively small. The habit of deposit banking and of payments by check has taken little root in France. It has established itself only in Paris and in a few other large centers, and even in these only for a limited circle of large wholesale dealers and private bankers. Most transactions, large as well as small, are settled in specie or in Bank of France notes. Hence the demand liabilities of the Bank take chiefly the form of notes; and the deposits are so moderate that, even when they are added to the notes, the specie holdings are still very large.

These specie holdings are large, undoubtedly, by intention. The Bank being virtually a government institution, its affairs are managed, not indeed without regard to profit for the stockholders, but very largely with regard to the real or supposed needs of the community. Its great stock of specie, which to a money-making banker would mean so much of needlessly idle funds, has been heaped up partly for economic reasons, partly for political. On economic grounds it is thought safe to have a very broad basis of specie and a central bank of impregnable strength. On political grounds it is desired to have a great stock of coin, and especially of gold, to which the government can turn in case of need. Though the Bank of France has not deliberately set to work to hoard gold, it has welcomed the accumulation in its coffers of the gold which growing prosperity has brought into the country, and which has found its way to the Bank because notes proved more convenient for larger transactions than coin itself.

Bank of France notes can be issued only in denominations

of fifty francs and over; in practise few notes of less than one hundred francs are issued. The restriction insures a large everyday use of gold, and a saturation of the general circulating medium with gold. This important limitation on the use of paper, the slight use of deposits and checks, and habits of deliberation and caution in the people which make the rapidity of circulation probably low for all forms of the medium of exchange, have brought about a large supply of money per head of population. France not only is a rich and populous country, but has a supply of specie large in proportion to her riches and population. This brings, no doubt, a safe and solid monetary system; but it betokens also some deficiency in industrial vigor and enterprise.

The Bank of France supplies a perfect instance of elasticity in the use of bank money. Whether through notes or deposits, it is entirely free to extend its operations as fast and as far as it sees fit. In fact, its note issue fluctuates very readily, enlarging and contracting from week to week according to the calls on it by the public. Yet it cannot be said that the Bank does for its public everything which can be expected of an ideal banking system. The monopoly of note issue, and management by government officials, prevent it from feeling the driving force of competition and of immediate profit, and so from extending its operations in such a way as to promote business enterprise to the maximum. It is mainly a banker's bank. It lends to bankers, who in turn lend to the commercial public; or rather, it rediscounts the paper which the private bankers and banking companies have already discounted. These other bankers cannot use notes of their own issue, being prohibited therefrom by law; and they cannot use deposits, except on a limited scale in Paris and the great cities. Hence the French banking system has serious drawbacks. French bankers are restricted, and of necessity to some degree cautious. There is little opportunity for profit in strictly commercial banking, and no temptation to take risks for the sake of gains. Hence there is not quick patronage of new men and new enterprises, and little stimulus for the bold and adventurous.

§ 3. A very different type is presented by the Bank of England. The organization of this, the earliest and most famous of the great modern public banks, is regulated by the Bank Act of 1844. But, like almost all British institutions, the Bank of England is regulated not only by statute, but by a body of customs and traditions which are no less binding than statutes, and which are in this case of at least as great economic consequence.

The salient feature of the Bank's organization is the complete separation of note issue and deposit. Notes are put out by the Issue Department, having the function of issue and that only. Deposits are managed, and the real business, or at least the main business, is conducted by the Banking Department. To all intents and purposes the two departments are separate institutions.

The operations of the Issue Department are very strictly limited. Up to a specified amount it may put out notes, holding as security for them government obligations, but not coin. For every note beyond this amount it must hold pound for pound in gold. The specified uncovered amount was fixed in 1844 at £14,000,000. It was provided that, according as other banks then having the privilege of note issue (all of them country banks) should withdraw from business, or for any reason should cease their issues, the Bank of England might enlarge its uncovered limit by two thirds the amount of notes previously permitted to these country banks. The expectation was that the other banks would gradually cease their issues, and that the Bank of England would secure a complete monopoly of notes. Under this provision the Bank's uncovered issue has slowly risen, until in 1907 it amounted to £18,450,000. The process of extinction for other notes has gone on steadily, and their amount has become comparatively small (less than £2,000,000).

The principle underlying this regulation of the Issue Department was that a certain volume of notes would find ready circulation and use, and could be issued without danger of causing inflation or of completely expelling specie. This volume was represented by the fixed limit of uncovered issue. Notes issued over and above this limit were to be really in the nature of certificates of deposit. In so far, the theory of the Bank Act was sound, and its application has proved wholly within the bounds of moderation. The limit set to the uncovered issue in 1844 was such as to prevent the notes from being then a cause of danger to the stability of the monetary system. With the increase of population and wealth since that date, the limit has become superlatively safe.

The total amount in circulation is much beyond the limit; but the excess represents notes which are, in essentials, certificates of deposit, and are used simply because more convenient than coin. No Bank of England note can be issued for less than £5,—a restriction which causes gold coin to be required for a great number of transactions, and probably limits very much the extension of the coin-covered note issue. The business of the Issue Department is now mainly that of the exchange of coin for notes and notes for coin according to the convenience of one or the other to the holder. Bank of England notes have long been synonymous with gold; they pass the world over as equal to the coin. They are legal tender in Great Britain, except, of course, in payments by the Bank itself, which must redeem them in gold. But their legal tender quality adds nothing to their ready circulation or international repute.

Entirely different is the position of the Banking Department. This is a pure bank of deposit, — the most important bank of deposit in the world. It is entirely unregulated by law; yet it is so regulated by custom as to be no less safeguarded than the Issue Department.

The Banking Department is the center of a great system of deposit banking. Deposit banking in the modern sense was practised on a considerable scale in England in the eighteenth century (the London Clearing House dates from 1775), and since then has had a continuous development. England and Scotland, and to a large extent Ireland also, are permeated by numerous banks of deposit, extending credit freely in that form, having vast deposit liabilities, and utilizing to the full the machinery of checks and clearing houses. Some of these banks are the historical private banks, which usually carry on also a financing and investment business. Others are great joint-stock banks, more likely to confine themselves to commercial business. On the whole, the joint-stock banks have gained on the private banks, and many of the latter have changed to the joint-stock form. All of these, however, sail close to the wind so far as cash holdings are concerned. They keep as much cash as is needed for current demands, but little in the way of extra reserve. Part of their resources, often a considerable amount, is invested in consols, which are readily salable; and they have a good deal of "money on call," that is, demand loans. But their actual cash is usually at the minimum needed for ordinary demands at the counter,—not often five per cent of the deposits.[1] But they do keep, in addition, a certain amount on deposit in the Bank of England, and this they regard as perfectly equivalent to cash on hand. We have already noted, in describing the clearing-house system, that the Bank of England (which means its Banking Department) serves as the agency for settling balances between banks; clearing-house settlements being made, not in cash, but by checks on the Bank. Hence every important bank keeps an account with the great central institution,—an account which fluctuates from time to time, according to debit or credit at the clearing house, but which is steadily maintained at a substantial amount. It serves to meet clearing-house debts; it serves also as a resource in case of general uneasiness or of any unusual demands by the particular bank's creditors.

The Bank of England thus has in its Banking Department great deposits due to other banking institutions. It has also

[1] The English banks (other than the Bank of England and a single large joint-stock bank) do not state their cash separately; they lump together, as resources immediately available, their cash, money on call, and deposits in other banks, and often include consols in this same lump sum. Their cash holdings can only be inferred.

deposits due to its own mercantile customers, — usually firms conducting large-scale operations, — and to financial and investing brokers and middlemen at large. Against this mass of demand liabilities it is under no legal obligation to keep any specified holding of cash. Yet by tradition and custom it is bound to keep a "reserve," or, rather, *the* reserve, — the store of cash on which the business community looks as the stay and prop of the entire banking system. That cash is expected to be between forty and fifty per cent of the demand liabilities, — vastly more than is necessary for ordinary demands. The Bank is not managed in this regard solely for profit, or even primarily for profit. It is managed as a public institution. In its Banking Department by custom, as in its Issue Department by law, it is the guardian of the solidity of the English monetary system.

The large reserve of the Bank, and its consequent freedom and strength, enable it to give support in two ways. It can pay out cash to any depositor who wants it, and it can make loans freely to any person who needs them. Making loans means creating deposits, and creating deposits means that the borrower is put in a position of security, — he can have cash if he needs it, and he is assured of meeting his liabilities if they press heavily or unexpectedly upon him. This sort of aid the Bank can extend to the other banks if they are in straits and yet are solvent. It can extend the aid also to the general mercantile public, though it is less likely to aid the general public directly, than indirectly by enabling the other banks to do so.

To maintain its reserve, the Bank adjusts its rate of discount, raising the rate when the reserve is undesirably small, lowering it when the reserve is needlessly large. Such is the natural policy of any bank; but this policy is followed most steadily and with most conscious intent by the great public institution of which the Bank is the type. The movements of the Bank rate of discount are closely connected with the mechanism of foreign trade and the flow of specie from country to country, of which more will be said when the subject of foreign trade is reached.

The working of all this mechanism in times of crisis is curious;

and, although the full consideration of crises must be postponed, the peculiar relation of the Issue and Banking departments at such times may be described here. It is an odd relation: the very device which was adopted to prevent crises is used for allaying them by being set aside. When the present system was established in 1844, it was expected that the rigid restriction of note issues would prevent crises, their cause being supposed to lie in unregulated note issue. Experience soon showed that this expectation was without ground. Crises recurred, and no less severely. But it appeared also that pressure during a crisis was directed on the Banking Department. To this the depositing banks looked for cash; to this uneasy and hard-pressed bankers and mercantile firms looked for loans. In the crisis of 1847, very shortly after the passage of the act in 1844, the Bank, being confronted in its Banking Department by a double demand for providing cash and loans, secured from the government a suspension of the act of 1844. That is, it secured authority to put out more uncovered notes from the Issue Department than the fixed sum specified in the act. The Banking Department, it must be remembered, is normally in the same relation to the Issue Department as the general public is. It holds notes which the Issue Department must redeem in specie, the bulk of its cash being usually in the form of notes. But when the act was suspended, the Banking Department could take to the Issue Department government securities and get notes in exchange. The Issue Department, by handing out additional notes covered by these securities, enlarged by so much the holdings of cash in the Banking Department. No breath of suspicion or uneasiness has ever attached to the Issue Department. Bank of England notes have retained, and indeed had attained even before 1844, their sterling repute. The suspension of the act thus operates as a means to supply the Banking Department with additional cash in times of great emergency.

This mere possibility of getting additional cash has served to dispel uneasiness and allay a panic. It is security, the certainty of finding support if needed, that is really wanted in such times.

People do not want cash; they wish to be sure of getting it if wanted. The suspension of the act puts additional supplies of cash, potentially unlimited, at the disposal of the Banking Department. The mere knowledge of the existence of this resource restores confidence. In fact, the Bank has never called for additional uncovered issues to any considerable extent. The act was first suspended in 1847, and again in 1857 and in 1866. In later times of panic its suspension has been under consideration, but has not in fact been resorted to. It is to be added, moreover, that the Bank has learned during the last half century both to appreciate more fully its own public responsibility, and to deal more promptly and effectively with the conditions of incipient panic.

The present public position of the Bank of England is the more striking because it is not only a private corporation, like the Bank of France, but, unlike its great rival, is managed quite without government intervention. It is not even managed by bankers. It has a board of directors, who by long custom must not be bankers;[1] they elect from their number a governor and a deputy governor, each of whom holds office for but two years. If one were to plan deliberately the organization of a great public bank, nothing of this sort would possibly be hit on; indeed, *a priori*, one would think it the worst possible arrangement. Yet, like so many British institutions, developed tentatively and incrusted with a mass of binding traditions, it works very well indeed.

§ 4. The Imperial Bank of Germany, or Reichsbank, is modeled somewhat on the Bank of England. But the model is improved in some respects, while its actual working is much affected by the great differences in business habits between the two countries.

The Imperial Bank was established in 1875, and, as in England, was expected to become eventually the sole note-issuing

[1] This statement should be qualified. Certain classes of persons whom the English dub "merchants," but whose business operations are largely of a banking kind, may be directors.

institution. As in England, banks of issue previously existing were allowed to continue their notes, subject however to considerable restriction.[1] Whatever note issue is given up by them falls to the Reichsbank. By this process the Reichsbank also has gradually come to possess to all intents and purposes a monopoly of the right of issue, the total issues by other banks hardly exceeding one tenth of its notes. For the Reichsbank (and for each of the smaller banks also) the principle of a limited uncovered issue was established. The Bank may issue notes (1909) up to a total of 550,000,000 marks, without having them covered by cash; for every sum beyond this limit mark for mark must be held in specie.

The further regulation of this uncovered issue, however, proceeds in a way very different from the English. In the first place, the securities to be held for the uncovered issue must not necessarily be government securities as in England; they may be ordinary discounted paper. More significant is the absence of any separate holding of specie against the notes. The cash held against the covered notes is not impounded in an Issue Department and held specifically for the redemption of notes; it is simply the general cash held by the Bank against all its liabilities. If these liabilities were solely, or almost solely, in the form of notes, this difference would not be important. If, on the other hand, the Reichsbank were, like the Bank of England, the center of an all-pervading deposit system, it would be of very great importance. In fact, the situation is midway. The Reichsbank has considerable deposits; but the main form in which it extends credit is that of notes, and the greater part of its liabilities is in notes. Though its cash must protect the deposits as well as the notes, the amount held is superlatively ample to protect both forms of liability. Like the Bank of France, the Reichsbank has

[1] The only other note-issuing banks in Germany are the state banks of Bavaria, Saxony, Wurttemberg, and Baden. Their total uncovered issue was, in 1909, 68,700,000 marks. They are often spoken of by the Germans as "private" banks, by way of distinguishing them from the Reichsbank. In the text, when speaking of German "private" banks, I refer not to these, but to the great mass of non-public institutions having no note issue at all.

added very much to its stock of specie (most of it gold) during the last thirty years, and has been able to put out an increasing quantity of notes covered by cash, — a growth due partly to the increase of population and wealth, partly to a growing habit of using paper representatives for specie.

Still another peculiarity of the Reichsbank is the elastic limit, so-called, of its note issue. The limitation of the uncovered issue, whether by the Reichsbank or by the minor banks, is not absolute. They may issue beyond the limit, but must pay a tax at the rate of five per cent a year on the excess.[1] This provision, unique when adopted, was clearly suggested by the awkward English expedient of suspending the Bank Act. Recognizing that there would be times when a freer issue might be to a high degree desirable, the Germans allowed it, yet with a handicap, in the form of the tax, so heavy as to prevent recourse to it unless really called for. This extra tax-weighted issue may be regarded as an emergency issue. But its working in a country like Germany, where deposit banking has so moderate a development, takes place under conditions very different from those in England. The extra issue has in fact been used not infrequently by the Reichsbank, and has served a good purpose, at times when the community was in need of more abundant banking accommodation. But its use has not been, like the suspension or threatened suspension of the English Act, the symptom or the remedy for panics.

The relation of the Reichsbank to the general banking system of the country is more like that of the Bank of France than that of the Bank of England, though in many respects it follows ways of its own. As has already been said, there is in Germany no such use of deposits and checks as in England, and no such vast volume of deposit liabilities. There is, indeed, greater use of deposits than in France. Both the Reichsbank and the great

[1] In the case of the Reichsbank, however, recent legislation (1909) has permitted the issue, without payment of tax, of an additional 200,000,000 of marks at the end of the months of March, June, September, and December; the intent being to provide currency at those dates for the heavy quarterly payments then customary.

private banks have encouraged this form of bank operations, and with some results; yet after all with nothing like what has developed spontaneously in English-speaking countries. The private banks, being debarred by national custom from any wide use of deposits and by law from the use of notes, turn to the Reichsbank for aid in the extension of current commercial credit. As much as one half of the total commercial paper discounted in Germany finds its way, chiefly through rediscount by other banks, into the hands of the Reichsbank. The Reichsbank has very greatly facilitated payments within Germany, by its widely ramifying system of branches, through which it effects payments freely between one part of the country and another. Its services to industry have been great, and have been rendered with an energy and a conscious purpose characteristic of the Germans of the present generation. Like the Bank of France, though a private corporation, it is managed by government-appointed officials, and, like all the great public banks, with a steady view to public advantage rather than private profit.

Among the striking industrial changes in Germany since 1870 (no country has shown changes more striking) has been the growth of the great banking corporations, especially the noted trio, — the Deutsche Bank, the Dresdner Bank, the Diskonto-Gesellschaft. In the extent of their operations, these are strong rivals to the Reichsbank; but their operations are of a different character. They combine all sorts of banking operations. They do the business of ordinary commercial banks, partly by some use of deposits in the large centers, partly by rediscounting at the Reichsbank. They do also a very great investing and promoting business, by no means limited to Germany, but extended with remarkable enterprise and skill to all parts of the world. Their deposits are in the main what most people think of as "deposits," — not credits created by them, but funds left with them for temporary or permanent investment. They have built up a great business of many kinds, with large commitments, large liabilities on time and on demand, upon a very narrow basis of cash. They rely on the Reichsbank for support in case of stress, very much as the English banks rely on the Bank of England. The Reichsbank itself, closely connected in its current dealings with the other institutions, yet stands aloof from them. It has great cash reserves, almost unlimited potential resources, an unshakable prestige. For every solvent institution, and for the business community at large, it promises unfailing and adequate support in times of trouble. Its great service to Germany has been to supply a firm foundation, not only for the circulating medium, but for the whole structure of industrial credit.

CHAPTER 27

Decentralized Banking Systems

§ 1. By far the largest and most important example of a decentralized system of banking is found in the United States. In the usual description of our American conditions, most attention is given to the national banks and to the regulation of note issue. But the other banks are hardly less important; and for both kinds of banks, deposits play a great and unusual part, and are subject to regulation in an unusual way.

Note issue is limited to the national banks. The limitation is accomplished by a tax on other issues so heavy as to be prohibitory. The national banks may issue notes on depositing government bonds as security at the Treasury of the United States. These bonds remain the property of the several banks, which receive the interest on them. Notes may be issued up to the par value of the bonds, but not exceeding the market value. The bonds serve to insure the payment of notes if a bank should fail, or if it should withdraw from business. In that case, the Treasury sells the bonds, repaying to the bank any premium they may bring over par; or the bank itself (directly or through its winding-up agent if bankrupt) may turn over to the Treasury cash enough to pay all its notes outstanding, and then resume possession of the bonds, and do as it will with them. In addition to this security for eventual repayment, each bank must keep at the Treasury a cash fund of five per cent of its circulating notes, to provide for their immediate redemption if presented. The system has a certain resemblance to that of the Bank of England, in that a specific portion of the bank's property is set aside for the security of the notes, and held solely for that purpose. This segregated property is, for the national banks, chiefly in securities, and only a little is in cash; for the Bank of England, under present conditions, it is preponderantly in cash, and only a moderate proportion is in securities. There is, too, a certain resemblance, in that no limit is imposed upon the total amount of notes that may be issued. Each individual national bank is indeed restricted; it may issue notes only up to the amount of the bonds deposited, and in any case only up to its capital as a maximum. But the amount issuable by the banks as a whole has no limit. There is, of course, the fundamental difference between centralized and decentralized issue; and there is the difference, no less fundamental, that in England the bank note is meant, after the uncovered issue is passed, to be covered by precisely the same amount in specie, whereas the national bank note is designed to bring in every instance an addition to the monetary supply.

Through this strict regulation national bank notes are made secure beyond any question. Their redemption in legal tender money is no less assured than that of Bank of England notes. Hence they circulate as freely as these, and with as little likelihood of being presented by the public at the issuing bank. This favorable outcome is inevitable when bank notes are made good beyond peradventure. Every person accepts them unhesitatingly as money, and passes them to the next person in making payments. Not only every individual, but every bank, treats them once for all as money, and pays them out in the ordinary course of transactions. National banks, it is true, sometimes exercise discrimination in paying them out over the counter. By preference they pay out national bank notes (those of other banks as well as their own) rather than legal tender notes or specie, because the latter count as reserve against deposits, whereas national bank notes do not. But presentation of a national bank note for redemption at the counter of the issuing bank never takes place. Nor does presentation take place with regularity at the National Treasury, where the five per cent fund for redemption is required to be kept. National bank notes, once set afloat, remain in circulation indefinitely, quite regardless of the credit of the banks whose name they bear, and in large measure regardless of the continuance of the conditions which brought about their original issue.

§ 2. By far the most important feature of the banking system of the United States is the use it makes of deposits. What has been said of banking in the preceding chapter is here strikingly exemplified in a system ramifying far into our economic structure. And the regulation of that system by law is unique. No other country has grappled by direct legislation with the problems presented by deposit banking.

National banks are required by law to keep a stated proportion of cash — specie or legal tender notes — against their deposits. The requirement is different for banks in different sorts of places, the general principle being that more shall be held in the large financial centers, and less in small places. For this purpose the banks are divided into three groups. In the first group are the banks of three "central reserve cities," — New York, Chicago, and St. Louis, — where the reserve must be 25 per cent at least. Of the three, New York is so far the most important that it is common to think of it alone as the central reserve city. The second group contains the banks of other "reserve cities," some forty or fifty in number.[1] These also are required to hold a reserve of 25 per cent. But only one half of this (12½ per cent of the deposits) must be in cash; the other half may consist of a deposit in a central reserve city bank. Finally, the third group includes all others, called "country banks," which are obliged to keep a reserve of 15 per cent. But their reserve, again, need not be entirely in cash; only two fifths (6 per cent of the deposits) must be actually in the vaults, the remaining three fifths (9 per cent of the deposits) being permissibly in the shape of deposits in banks of the first or second group.

Obviously, it is not compulsory to hold cash to the full stated percentage of reserve. Only the banks of the three central

[1] Forty-three in 1908.

reserve cities must have fully 25 per cent of cash. That reserve which takes the form of deposits elsewhere is something very different. The reserve city banks in which it is deposited do not keep dollar for dollar in cash against it. They treat it, in the main, like any other deposit, and keep little more than the reserve required for deposits in general, — 25 per cent. Some cautious bank managers in the reserve cities believe that against deposits by other banks a reserve of 50 per cent should be held. But this represents what the banking world in general would call excess of caution. Much less than 50 per cent is commonly held; as a rule, probably little more than the legal minimum. Whether the cash in such cases be a trifle more or less, the requirement as to "reserve" is evidently very different from a requirement for holding the stated proportion in cash. And when a country bank keeps part of its reserve in a reserve city, and the reserve city bank keeps part of its reserve again in New York (or possibly in Chicago or St. Louis), there is a double attenuation. The final result, for the national banks as a whole, has been that the total cash held against total deposits, notwithstanding the 25 per cent requirement for reserve cities, has been 15 per cent or less.

As already noted, the national banks by no means occupy the whole field. Side by side with them are the banks authorized by the several states. These are sometimes *eo nomine* "banks," and sometimes are "trust companies." The latter are as a rule simply banks of deposit, differing from the others only in that their business is less restricted by law and is combined to a greater degree with general investment operations. In addition there are innumerable private banking firms. Most of those which call themselves "brokers and bankers" are as a rule brokerage firms acting mainly as financial middlemen, and often acting solely as agents for speculators. Though some among them maintain a considerable deposit business, and thus are bankers in the strict sense, deposit banking tends on the whole to be confined to the incorporated banks and trust companies. A similar tendency appears in England, although it develops more slowly in that land of rooted custom. There, also, the great private banks are either changing to the joint-stock form, or else confining themselves more and more to fiduciary and investment business.

The state banks in the United States — meaning by that term all the banking institutions outside the national system — do a business very nearly equal in volume to that done by the national banks. The total deposits of the two groups during the first decade of the present century were practically the same. But the state banks are under much less restriction than the national banks concerning the amount of cash which they must hold against their deposits. There are, indeed, some provisions on this subject in the laws of several of the important states. But the requirement is usually for such a small amount of cash as to be meaningless, — so little would be held in any case.[1] The state banks are virtually allowed to manage their holdings of cash in whatever way they find most profitable. This means, of course, that they reduce their holdings to the minimum which seems needed for current calls. Therein they act as do the English joint-stock banks. Like these, again, they keep deposits elsewhere, to which they turn in case of stress. The national banks of the reserve cities, especially those of New York, serve as the holders of reserve, not only for the national banks, but for the state banks also.

The whole American system of deposit banking thus brings a great concentration of responsibility on the national banks of the central reserve cities, and, above all, on the New York banks. They occupy a position similar to that of the Bank of England; they are the depositaries of the really available stock of free cash, hence the nerve center of the whole sensitive system. The provisions of the national bank law which allow part of the required reserve to be kept in reserve cities no doubt add to this concentration. These pro-

[1] New York and Massachusetts present exceptions to this statement. They have recently (especially by laws of 1908) required their trust companies and state banks to hold substantial stores of cash.

visions have been condemned as a defect in the system. But their influence in shaping the general banking relations is not so great as is often supposed. A similar concentration would probably develop in any case. In all countries, and especially in those where deposit banking is highly developed, every outlying institution must keep in touch with the financial center and must be prepared to effect payments through it. Every institution finds it advantageous, nay necessary, to keep an account at the center, and ordinarily to have a balance to its credit there.

The peculiarities of the American situation are the lack of a strong sense of public obligation among the New York banks, and the absence of an ample store — or at least, any sufficiently available store — of cash to which the banks in general can turn in emergency. It is not to be expected that a number of competing banks, each managed with the object of securing as much profit as possible, should steadily follow such a policy of restraint as that of the Bank of England. In great emergencies, the banks of New York, like any associated body, will show high public spirit; as they did, for example, in their advances to the national government at the outset of the Civil War, and as they have done in some acute panics. But this is very different from the settled pursuit, year in and out, of a policy that would lessen their earnings. They keep the reserve required by law, but of their own free will keep no more. They try to come to the assistance of other banks when these are in difficulties, but chiefly from a consciousness that their own prestige and prosperity are also involved. They do not regularly husband their resources in order to be prepared to give such aid.

The funds which reach the New York banks as the deposit of "reserve" by other banks, they use, and indeed are compelled to use, in such manner as to extract what profit they can get. These bankers' deposits are peculiarly subject to large and sudden drafts; hence each New York bank holding them tries to keep a large volume of assets within instant command. The resort is mainly to demand loans secured by stock exchange collateral. It is true that in every great financial center floating funds accumulate. Money at call is freely offered in London, Paris, Berlin, as well as in New York. But loans of this sort play an unusually large and conspicuous part in the American center. The fluctuations in interest rates are greater and more abrupt than in the European money markets, and the connection with stock speculation is closer. What is more important, the demand loans are deceptive as regards their real availability for the lending banks. Though any one bank may call them, and so strengthen its position when pressed by demands from depositors, the loans are no real resource to the banks as a whole. There is no cash to be had by calling them. The only cash which in the last instance is available is that already in the vaults of the banks. A huge superstructure of deposits in the country at large thus has a foundation in New York much narrower than is indicated by the apparently available resources of the individual banks.

The American banking system, decentralized as to note issue, may seem to be centralized as to deposits. In some respects it is, but in other respects it is decentralized for deposits as well. In most of the advanced countries, general banking operations are carried on chiefly by a comparatively small number of banks, each of them large and each having many branches. This is particularly true of the deposit banks of Great Britain and Canada. In the United States branch banking is virtually unknown. Thousands of banks, scattered all over the country, go their ways independently. This situation is due in part to legislation prohibiting or restricting branches; but the legislation itself reflects deep-seated habits and traditions. A prejudice against large-scale institutions, as tending to monopoly, also in part accounts for it. Still other important factors are the federated political system and the strength of local feeling. It is difficult to say whether the absence of branch banking is or is not an advantage. The ease of establishing small institutions and the competition between the innumerable banks has led to a great permeation of the country with credit facilities, especially since the great improvement during the last generation in transportation and the postal system. On the other hand, there results a situation which may fairly be described as in some respects anarchical, — a failure to work together, a vast helplessness in times of stress. Such as it is, this marked decentralization is part of the established order of things, very difficult to change, and necessarily to be reckoned with in schemes for legislation.

§ 3. Two other existing decentralized bank systems may be briefly described.

The Scotch banks, like those of England, were subjected to some rigid restrictions in the middle of the nineteenth century. An act of 1845 allowed note issue to those banks only which then carried it on, and to an amount equal to the notes then outstanding; with the further provision that additional notes must not exceed the specie actually held by each bank. In this sort of restriction there is resemblance to the English act of 1844. But none of the other striking features of the English legislation were applied in Scotland. No one bank was given a commanding position, or put in the way of securing eventually a monopoly of issue. And as to the several banks which were allowed to put out notes, the provision for their holding of specie was not accompanied by any such sharp separation of "issue" and "banking" operations as in the case of the Bank of England. While specie was required to be held pound for pound against every note outstanding, this specie was not pledged specifically for paying the notes, but was available also for paying deposits. What specie was held as reserve against deposits served also to authorize the issue of notes. In practise the effective limitation has been the fixed maximum of notes; the total permitted being, in 1907, for the existing ten banks, £2,676,350. The ready circulation of this moderate volume was made the more easy by allowing the issue of notes of a denomination as low as £1.

The Scotch banks, as just noted, are few in number, — only

ten. They are large institutions, each with many branches; the total number of banking offices is near one thousand. In other words, though Scotland has few banks, the banking system permeates all parts of the country. This wide-reaching extension is facilitated by decentralized note issue; for at the smaller branches the notes, especially the one-pound notes, serve as till money, and enable a banking office to be maintained without locking up in it any considerable amount of specie. By far the larger part of the business of the Scotch banks, like the business of English and American banks, is carried on by the use of deposits, with all the mechanism of checks and clearing houses. In their deposit and clearing house operations, the Scotch banks make the same use of the Bank of England as do all the banks of Great Britain, and in the same way rely on the great central institution for holding the ultimate free banking reserve. But in their local operations the use of notes plays a part of some importance.

Scotch notes, thus issued with comparative freedom by competing banks, illustrate what was said in a preceding chapter[1] of the way in which notes circulate under a banking system making wide use of deposits. They come back constantly to the bank of issue. Each bank pays out over its counter its own notes. Whatever notes of other Scotch banks come into its hands, are presented at the clearing house with the checks on those other banks. Notes do not remain afloat indefinitely; their average period of circulation after each issue is but a few days. But they are constantly reissued, because there is steady need in the community for such a circulating medium, and because there is steady retention by each individual bank of its customers' confidence.

§ 4. A situation similar in some respects is found in Canada, where the business community is largely Scotch by descent, and has developed a banking system based on the Scotch example, but reshaped in very important particulars. The number of banks, twenty-nine in 1910, though greater than in Scotland,

[1] See Chapter 24, § 6.

is very much smaller than in the United States. The individual banks, on the other hand, are large as compared with the average American bank. The minimum capital allowed by law is $500,000, and the average capital is $1,500,000; whereas, under our national banking system, banks with a capital as small as $25,000 are permitted, and the average capital is less than $150,000. But figures of this sort indicate the capital and size per bank, not per banking office. The Canadian banks, like those of most countries (the United States presents the only great exception), have many branches, which ramify all over Canada, and raise the number of banking offices to more than two thousand. Hence the Canadian system brings about a permeation of the country by banking facilities not less than in the United States.

The issue of notes is more free than that of any other country of considerable size, yet is subjected to precautions which insure their solidity. A bank may not ordinarily issue notes in excess of its paid-in capital, nor notes of lower denomination than five dollars; otherwise it is unrestricted. But the notes are secured by a prior lien on all the assets of the bank in case of failure,—a provision made more effective by the fact that stockholders (as in our national banks) are then liable for double their original subscription to capital. More significant, though hardly more important in securing solidity, is the provision for a safety fund in government hands. This fund amounts to 5 per cent of the notes outstanding, and is used to pay the notes of banks that fail. Finally, it is provided that, in case of failure, notes bear interest at 5 per cent from the date of the act of bankruptcy. Hence all other (going) banks are ready to take such notes from the holders at par, because the notes are certain of redemption at an early date, with interest, from the safety fund.

Though notes are issued freely, they are also freely redeemed. Every bank must redeem notes at the office where they are issued, and also (what is more important) at redemption offices in the trade centers. A bank pays out over its counters its own notes, but sends to the redemption agencies the notes of other banks that come into its hands. In Canada, as in Scotland, notes take their place in bank clearings precisely as checks do. Hence they have the same elasticity as deposits, created as needs arise in the local community and extinguished by redemption as those needs cease. This elasticity is of special importance in connection with seasonal variations in production and exchange, such as take place, above all, in a predominantly agricultural community,—a matter to which further reference is made in the next chapter.

Like most other countries, Canada makes no legislative provision for the safety of deposits. Every bank is required to make monthly reports of its condition to government officers, and the publicity thus secured may be a sort of safeguard for depositors. But there is no requirement for reserves; the amount of cash held is left to the judgment and self-interest of the bank managers.

The Canadian system, so far as notes are concerned, combines freedom with safety. The notes are secure beyond question. There is no danger that a holder of the everyday circulating medium may suddenly find on his hands a depreciated or worthless piece of paper. The freedom with which notes can be issued facilitates the wide extension of branches, especially in the outlying agricultural districts. In turn, this facilitates note issue, and also brings about a tendency toward equality in the rates for loans in different parts of the Dominion. The system may not be an ideal one, but it has important points of superiority over that of the United States.

CHAPTER 28

PROBLEMS OF LEGISLATION ON BANKING

§ 1. Some of the more important problems as to legislation may now be considered, in the light of the preceding discussion of the theory of banking and the characteristics of leading banking systems.

It is clear that there is universally provision of some sort for the special security of bank notes. This is strikingly the case in the legislation of England and of the United States; hardly less so in Canada. On the Continent the general prevalence of monopoly issue has in practice the same effect. Notes may be issued only by central banks, backed by the state and no less solvent than the state itself. On the other hand, special provision for the security of deposits is rare. The legislation of the United States stands almost alone in its requirements as to reserves and the like; and even here the protection of the depositors is safeguarded much less rigidly than that of the note holders. Is this difference in the treatment of the two sorts of obligation reasonable?

No doubt, the difference has rested historically on the fact that the similarity between notes and deposits has not been perceived. Though deposits subject to check form part of the circulating medium quite as much as notes do, and indeed are quantitatively much more important in countries like Great Britain, the United States, and Canada, they are not commonly regarded as "money"; yet notes are so regarded. But though the special protection to note holders is explained in this way, it must be justified, if at all, on other grounds.

The grounds for giving special security to note holders are two. In the first place, notes are more likely to be held by the poorer and dependent classes. Deposits are used chiefly by the well-to-do. Notes circulate among all classes, and notes of the smaller denominations are likely to be in the hands of workmen and others of slender means. Next, and not less important, is the difference in the way in which a person becomes creditor of the bank. A depositor almost always becomes creditor by his own choice; a note holder commonly becomes so without any volition of his own, and, moreover, by a process of whose legal import he usually knows nothing. A note circulates from hand to hand as "money." The person to whom it is offered in payment would commonly find difficulty in refusing it. Ordinarily he is quite unaware that, in taking it thus freely, he is simply, in the eye of the law, replacing another person as creditor of the issuing bank.[1] Who are the note-holding creditors at any given time is a matter of accident; since each person receiving a note keeps it until he has occasion to use it in a purchase. Depositors, on the other hand, select their bank with some deliberation. No doubt, they are often influenced by the bank's mere propinquity or by its general reputation. None the less, the initiative comes from them, and the first responsibility is theirs.

These distinctions, however, must not be pressed too far, nor permitted to obscure the fundamental point of resemblance, — that deposits, like notes, constitute part of the *de facto* circulating medium. The same fundamental reasons which make it important that notes should be secure, make it important that deposits should be secure. The essential question concerns the expedient ways of promoting security.

[1] The legal position of the payee of a check is different from that of the holder of a bank note. The payee of the check does not, like the note receiver, become at once a creditor of the bank. The bank's liability is only to the drawer of the check (the depositor). If the bank refuses to pay the check when presented, the depositor only, not the payee, has a right of action against it. On the other hand, the sending of a check in payment of a debt does not at once liquidate the debt. Should the bank fail, or for any reason refuse to pay the check, the debtor who has sent it is still liable. If, indeed, the payee of a check fails to take steps with reasonable diligence for its presentation at the bank on which drawn, the legal situation becomes different. If he puts the check away, and waits unduly before presenting it, he substitutes himself for the drawer as creditor of the bank. Failure of the bank in the interval then means loss to him, not to the bank's original creditor (depositor). Hence the business practise of always sending all checks received for immediate "deposit," *i.e.* for collection at the clearing house, through one's own bank. By this process the receiver of a check makes himself as promptly as possible a creditor of his own bank.

In the legislation of the United States, at least, the principle of providing in some way for the protection of depositors is too firmly established to be open to question. It shows itself not only in those requirements as to reserves which have already been noticed, but in a whole code of banking legislation. The nature of the loans which a national bank may make is rigidly defined. Not only in the national bank laws, but in those of the states, there is regulation of the extent of loans to any one individual, of loans to directors, and, not least, provision for publicity of accounts and periodical examination. The Comptroller of the Currency at Washington has a staff of examiners, and large powers over the national banks; the several states either have similar bureaus for their own banks, or are moving toward such supervision.

All this regulation is unique in the United States. Just as the requirement as to cash reserves for deposits is unknown elsewhere, so is all the detailed regulation of loans, reports, and special liabilities of officers and directors. The situation is a curious one. In a country where the general tradition has been to let capitalistic industry pursue its course unfettered, the very center of capitalist operations has been subjected to a degree of control undreamed of in other countries. The cause of this remarkable extension of state interference is to be found partly in the early development and wonderful spread of deposit banking, but still more in an underlying dim consciousness that here was really a most important and far-reaching part of the circulating medium. Once the system is fully established, no individual can keep out of it. It is indispensable that he have his bank of deposit and his bank account. And though he may choose his own bank, and may be supposed to be on the watch as to its character and solvency, his means of getting information are necessarily uncertain. The public concern in banking, which at first was chiefly for the security of notes, has come to be no less for their equally pervasive and far more powerful successors, the deposits.

Hence the proposal that deposits should be made absolutely

safe, like notes, is not an illogical or revolutionary one. Obviously, no method of segregation of particular assets (such as is used in regard to notes by the national banking system) can suffice for the purpose; since the only possible security for all deposits would be the solidity of all assets. The only feasible method is one of insurance, — compulsory contribution by every bank to a public (or publicly supervised) guarantee organization, out of which the deposits of a collapsed bank would be met; an application to deposits, in other words, of a system like that of Canada for notes. The main objection to this proposal is that one great safeguard — perhaps the greatest safeguard — against reckless banking would be removed. This is the banker's fear of the depositor. Though his legal obligation to meet deposit liabilities on demand would indeed remain, the probability of the presentation of demands would be greatly diminished. If every depositor knew that his "money" was sure to be forthcoming in any case, being guaranteed by the state or other adequate organization, pressure on a bank from uneasy depositors would be less likely to follow suspicious doings. A bank might pursue a reckless course for an indefinite time, or at least for a longer time than if the confidence of the depositor needed to be constantly nurtured.

This objection, though strong, is not necessarily conclusive. Reckless banking takes place now, even under the eye of the unguaranteed depositor. If the guarantee were one not of immediate payment, but only of ultimate payment, — if the depositor, though secured from eventual loss, were still subject to the possible inconvenience of having his funds "tied up" for a time in a liquidating bank, — it would still be to his interest to be watchful and, when suspicious, to withdraw his account. The strong interest which stockholders have in prudent management would continue to be a check on recklessness. The course of legislation on this matter, as on others, is likely to be much affected by actual experience. A succession of conspicuous bank failures, bringing great loss to depositors, would immensely strengthen the movement for deposit guarantee. Then measures which now seem beyond the range of practicability might be found feasible after all.

§ 2. Much has been said in recent discussion in the United States about the need of elasticity in the currency, and especially in the bank notes.

Most persons who speak and write on this topic have very confused notions of the grounds on which elasticity is desirable. They think, as a rule, only of elasticity upwards, — of a system under which the money supply will expand freely and indefinitely. Most business men and most financial writers of the daily and weekly press are (unconsciously) inflationists. Though usually opposed to such inflation as brings obvious depreciation, they welcome plentifulness of money and rising prices; this "makes business good."

The general feeling in favor of easy expansion is promoted by failure to distinguish between an elastic currency and an "emergency" currency. As will appear presently,[1] there are times of crisis when a potential increase in the money supply may be of high service, such as, for example, the possible increase of Bank of England notes after a suspension of the Bank Act. But the need for this sort of expansion is infrequent and usually of short duration; indeed, under a well-devised and well-tested banking system, such a need hardly exists. At all events, the concern of the community in emergency issues is very different from that which it has in a currency elastic with reference to the recurring ordinary fluctuations of industry.

An elastic currency is really desirable on two grounds: first, adaptation to normal variations in transactions; second, completer supply of credit facilities to those likely to make good use of capital.

The typical case of normal variation in the demand for money appears in harvest times, — the inevitable compressing of transactions when the crops are garnered. The farmers must then pay extra laborers, and later must themselves be paid by merchants and middlemen. In almost all countries there is an

[1] See Chapter 30, on Financial Crises.

autumnal drain on the money market; the available supplies of cash, held chiefly by banks, are more heavily drawn on at this season. In a country predominantly agricultural, as the United States still is, the drain is especially marked. The flow of money to the West and South, "to move the crops," is a familiar annual phenomenon. There is occasion for an expansion of money in proportion to this seasonal increase of transactions, and for contraction afterward. Freely issued bank notes might meet the need, being put out as loans to dealers and farmers at the harvest season, and returned to the banks of issue, through a quasi-automatic process, at the close of the season.

The second gain from an elastic note issue, that of wider extension of credit facilities, is important in proportion as the extension of banking in general is dependent on the use of notes. This gain alone justifies our modern practise of leaving to private hands the supply of so important a constituent of the circulating medium. Were it not that commercial banking promotes the extension of credit and of capital to capable managers of the productive forces, both note issue and deposit banking would rightly be public operations once for all. In countries where notes are the main form of bank credit, elastic issue is of prime importance in promoting greater continuity and more ready enterprise in business operations. These advantages are likely to be secured to a greater degree by competing banks than by a monopoly bank; but they are in either case secured more readily from elastic issue than from rigidly regulated issue.

Neither gain from elasticity of issue is secured by our national banking system. The banks do not accommodate their issues to seasonal variations, because the issue of notes depends, in the first instance, on the profit obtainable by buying government bonds and issuing notes against them. It is often said that the issue of national bank notes has no relation whatever to the community's monetary needs, and depends solely on the current price and current interest return of government bonds. This is, in my judgment, an overstatement of the case; on the whole, and in the long run, the volume of national bank notes does adapt itself to the changing extent of the needs for circulation. But it is true that these issues have no elasticity over short periods.

The national bank system never proved suited to the conditions of the strictly agricultural parts of the United States, and never brought about any adequate extension of credit facilities for them. Some part of this failure was due to the industrial conditions of newer regions; no system of cautious banking is adapted to places of undeveloped industries and uncertain future. The problem of agricultural credit is a peculiar and difficult one, above all in the United States, and it is not easy to say what sort of banking system best meets our needs. Needs there are, as is shown by the extraordinary number of small state banks in the Mississippi and Missouri valleys; and this development of banks out ide the national system shows also that the system itself is inadequate. There is ground for saying that a more elastic sort of issue, if properly safeguarded, would have promoted the extension of good credit facilities.

But these considerations, both as to adaptability and permeation, have come to be in recent years of much less importance in the United States, because of the steady extension of deposit banking. Deposits are ideally elastic. They expand and contract under the very influences that lead to expansion and contraction in the volume of transactions. It cannot be said that they vary in precise proportion to transactions, — if they did, fluctuations in the general level of prices would be less than in fact they are. They seem to expand more sharply and to contract more sharply than the transactions with which they show general sympathy. But elastic they certainly are, — it is their great virtue, though also their great potential evil. They promote in the highest degree activity, continuity, flexibility, in business operations.

It follows that in deposit-using countries the question of elasticity with reference to bank notes by themselves is not of the first importance. People lay undue stress on note issue, partly because of the confusion with emergency issues, partly because they fail to understand that deposits stand side by side with notes as part of "bank money." In a thickly settled manufacturing country like Great Britain, deposits give all the elasticity needed; hence the rigid note system of England causes no appreciable inconvenience. Though the case is different in agricultural regions like Canada and our Western states, yet in almost all parts of the United States, including the great farming districts, deposit banking has shown an extraordinary growth in recent years, and a remarkable capacity for meeting the needs of a scattered population with pulsating industries. There are still, and will always be, variations in the demand for hand-to-hand money in the form of specie or notes; and there are therefore grounds for advocating conditions of note issue essentially different from those of the national bank system. But the need is not so imperative as is often supposed. A certain degree of elasticity — of accommodation to varying demands — is inherent in any highly developed medium of exchange, even though it be specie alone. Elasticity of note issue in the United States is desirable, but is not of the first importance; least of all is it a panacea for monetary and industrial disturbances.

§ 3. What is to be said, finally, of the advantages of centralized note issue compared with decentralized, and what conclusion can be stated? To these questions, no unqualified answer can be given. Much depends on historical and political conditions, on tradition, habit, and economic development, in the several countries. The English system works well in Great Britain, the French in France, the Canadian in Canada. It does not follow that any of them, if transplanted to the United States, would work well here.

So far as security is concerned, there is no ground for preferring centralized to decentralized issue. This at least is the case where notes are issued by banks which also carry on other banking operations and more particularly conduct a deposit business. By giving notes a prior lien on the assets, and by a guarantee fund (as in the Canadian system), the security of the notes can be made absolute, and their holders protected infallibly from loss. Where, indeed, a bank carries on the function of issue solely, and where virtually all of its liabilities are thus in the form of notes, such safeguarding is more difficult, — it involves provision for the solidity of all the assets of the bank. In English-speaking countries, however, note issue always forms a minor part of the credit operations of a commercial bank. Hence notes can be made safe without the state's undertaking minute supervision of all the bank's operations.

None the less, centralized issue under government management (direct or indirect) means more certain and unquestionable safety, — safety as great as that of the government itself. No doubt, there is the danger that public banks will be made agents for the issue of inconvertible paper money. But this danger is not greater than that of the direct issue of such money by the government itself; and the prospects of the eventual resumption of specie payments are at least as good for bank notes as for government notes.

The pecuniary profit which the public can secure from monopolized issue is a minor matter. That profit may be either direct, as when the government shares in all dividends on capital above a certain amount (for example, in Germany and Switzerland), or indirect, as when the bank gives its services gratis for managing the public debt and the public finances (for example, in England and France). But the profit is never a considerable item in the public budget, and, such as it is, might be secured in even greater amount through the simple device of convertible money issued directly by the government. The stability and serviceability of the circulating medium, and the effects which its mode of issue has upon the industries of the community, are mainly to be considered. Compared with these vital matters, the profit to a government from one way or another of dealing with the money supply, whether specie or paper, is a negligible matter.

The deciding considerations (at least, those of a strictly economic character) would seem to refer on the one hand to the mitigation of crises, and on the other to the services which banking institutions render in ordinary times. It happens that these considerations tell in opposite directions. A central bank is the better agent for dealing with crises. A decentralized system promotes more effectively the wide extension of banking facilities.

The mode in which a central bank can give support in times of panic will be more fully explained in the second following chapter.[1] Its services on such occasions constitute probably its greatest economic advantage, at least for a country like England or the United States. Though it cannot prevent alternations of industrial excitement and lethargy, of good times and bad times, it may mitigate the range of the oscillations, and give inestimable aid at the critical stage of an acute panic. At just this point the present decentralized banking system of the United States is most open to criticism. It has broken down completely in times of stress, not once, but repeatedly, — so often that a remedy of some sort is imperative. Whether a remedy can be found in some modification of existing arrangements is not clear; but unless so, this consideration alone would be almost decisive in favor of a central bank.

In favor of decentralized issue is the likelihood of a more active and abundant provision of banking facilities, and so of a more effective utilization of the community's resources. Competing banks, actuated by the motive of profit, are more effective agents to this end than a monopoly bank; they have the advantages which private management commonly has over public. They reach out to get business instead of waiting for business to come to them. The more enterprising the management of a monopoly bank, the less does this argument tell in favor of decentralization. Both the Bank of France and the Reichsbank have proceeded with energy during the last thirty years in adding to the number of their branches and in extend-

[1] Chapter 30.

ing their operations. None the less, they still remain chiefly banker's banks. They use the private bankers as middlemen for ascertaining the needs of borrowers, for scrutinizing their projects and business ability, for guaranteeing their solvency. Such middlemen's services are not to be had gratis; they are paid for in the rates of discount charged to the borrowing public.

The argument that non-monopoly issue conduces to the flexible extension of credit facilities, is important according to the degree in which the facilities are dependent on this form of bank credit. It has already been pointed out that in the United States, where banking is most decentralized, note issue is declining in importance. The extraordinary spread of deposit banking has relegated it to a minor place in banking operations. Country districts, thinly settled and not in quick communication with financial centers, have been supposed the best field for credit extension in the form of notes. Hence it is often thought that the great agricultural regions of the United States would benefit most from free and flexible issue. But the perfection of mail arrangements has conduced to the use of deposits and checks in every nook and cranny. The whole problem of banking, in its connection with the ready extension of credit for industrial operations, has become very different from what it was fifty years ago. The national banking system, even in its best days, was not well devised for meeting the needs of the agricultural parts of the United States. The wonderful growth of state banks in the West, having no right of issue, indicates that this right is not essential to a permeation of the country by banking facilities. Regulation of note issue, whether through a central bank or through supervision of scattered banks, is now much less important than the strengthening of the vast and top-heavy structure of deposits.

§ 4. Like all questions which are chiefly of an economic sort, this one has its other aspects also, — fiscal and political; and these often are difficult to separate from the purely economic aspects.

A central bank has obvious fiscal advantages for the government. It may be of great service in the course of ordinary financial operations, of even greater service in times of public stress. It acts, in the countries where the system is established, as the regular custodian of the public funds. In times of war or other emergency, it can afford powerful aid, putting all its resources in the extreme case at the disposal of the government. Both of these advantages have strongly influenced the establishment of the great public banks of Europe. So far as concerns the United States, the relations between a central bank and the central government would present administrative and fiscal problems of unusual complexity, because of the extraordinary irregularity of our government's receipts and disbursements. To enter on this intricate matter is beyond the scope of the present book; suffice it to say that the possible services and the possible difficulties of a central bank are, from a fiscal point of view, equally great, and that the attainment of a balance of clear gain would depend on the unpredictable element of management at once skillful and high-minded.

On the purely political side, there are unquestionably grave possibilities of harm. The character of the management is of the utmost importance; and this depends not only on formal organization, — on the powers which the government and the stockholders have in selecting the managers, — but on political and industrial traditions.

The first and second Banks of the United States (1791–1811 and 1817–1837) became entangled in the political controversies of their times, and so became impossible as controllers of credit and industry. The lesson was long supposed to show conclusively that we in the United States cannot keep such an institution "out of politics," and therefore must forego the advantages which it may offer. To many men of the business class this objection still appears insuperable; just as it does with regard to government ownership of telegraphs, railways, and other so-called public industries. The trend of opinion, however, is unmistakably toward public control in many directions, and toward experiments in the direction of public ownership. A central bank does not appear as impossible as it did a generation ago. Obviously, no lasting benefits to the community could be got unless it were in the hands of a staff of trained and capable officials, independent of current political movements, aloof from popular clamor, having permanent tenures and dignified positions. Their posts must be such as to enlist ability of the first order. Here is the gravest problem of democracy. Administrative efficiency is the *sine qua non* of any extension of government functions. No one is entitled to speak with assurance of the way in which the American people will meet this need.[1] Yet efficient management can perhaps be expected in a bank more confidently than in other directions, since the operations directly touch the business class alone. How far complete divorce from political influence can be secured, is impossible of prediction.

Not less important than the question of political pressure is that of business pressure. To serve its purposes, a bank should be conservative as well as powerful. It should offer aid freely to the business community in times of danger and panic, but should hold aloof in times of speculation and inflation. That which would probably be its greatest service in the United States — to mitigate the oscillations of industry and the effects of crises — could be rendered only if it refused to foster the conditions which engender crises. And here it would be sure to meet with criticism and attack. The business community likes a "boom." Not only the arrant speculators, but the "solid men" also, would clamor for loans to help trade, to support business, to finance prosperity. Unless the managers of a central bank could say no firmly, they would simply add fuel to the fire, make the eventual collapse more severe, the inevitable readjustment more painful. Coolness, independence, courage; close connection with business affairs and yet aloofness from them, — this is a policy not easy to follow,

[1] Compare what is said below, Book VII, Chapter 62, on the prospects of public management.

yet essential for a great bank which has in mind not the largest pecuniary gain, but the permanent public good.

To repeat, no one can predict just how a central bank would work in the United States. It would have to establish gradually its own place and its special functions. It would have to meet not only the difficulties arising from political and business pressure, but others due to the decentralization of all banking.[1] The final outcome of its operations, even if it kept clear of all entanglements with party leaders and business magnates, might be very different from what its advocates expected. The Bank of England has come to be what it is by a process of slow growth in unforeseen ways. The Reichsbank has proved to influence German business much less by its note issue than was expected, and much more by its other business. An immense bank of deposit as well as of issue, such as a United States central bank must be, has possibilities for both evil and good, all depending on its management and on the way in which the rest of the country's banking system might develop under its influence.

[1] The absence of branch banking, and the existence of thousands of separate and independent banks of deposit, make the American situation peculiar. The public banks of Europe have to deal, in the main, with a comparatively small number of large banks, and exert their influence mainly through them.

CHAPTER 29

CRISES

§ 1. Two great sets of phenomena will be considered in this chapter and in that which follows,—industrial crises and financial crises. It would perhaps be more accurate to say, not that two sets of phenomena will be considered, but that two phases of one and the same phenomenon will be. The industrial and financial collapses are closely connected. Yet, if only for convenience in exposition, they may be analyzed separately. On the one hand, there are the depressions of industry over whole countries, often international in their range, taking years to run their course, and connected with far-reaching social problems. On the other hand, there are the financial panics, which affect most directly the banking and mercantile community, run their course in a few weeks or months, and are associated with problems of money, banking, and credit. The present chapter will deal chiefly with the industrial phases; the chapter following, chiefly with the financial.

Both sets of phenomena show a certain periodicity. Financial panics occur with curious regularity, and each is likely to be followed by a long-continued stage of industrial depression. Something like a ten-year period has long been observed. In the United States, for example, financial crises appeared in 1818, 1825, 1837, 1847, 1857. Then came a break in the apparently regular sequence; but beginning with 1873, the ten-year cycle seemed to appear again, there being well-marked crises in 1873, 1884, 1893, 1903. A double pulsation in the cycles seems also to have occurred. The crises of 1818, 1837, 1857, were severe, those of the intervening periods comparatively mild. Those of 1873 and 1893 were again severe; those of 1884 and 1903, mild. Hence some writers have inferred a twenty-year period for great crises, with others of less severity about halfway between. In England a similar periodicity appears. Industrial crises have come in the main at the same time as in the United States, though not always with the same intensity. Thus the crises of 1818 and 1837 were much more severe in the United States, those of 1825 and 1847 more severe in England. There have been some disturbances, to be sure, not common to both countries. For example, a sharp crisis occurred in England in 1866, to which there was no obvious counterpart in the United States; and a sharp crisis occurred in the United States in 1907, to which there was no obvious counterpart in England. It would be more accurate, probably, to say that there was a lower intensity of disturbance in the United States in 1866 and in England in 1907, than to say that there was no counterpart; for every crisis has in modern times some international spread, and the extent of its effects is only a question of degree. Some of the greatest crises have been sharply felt the world over, such as those of 1857, 1873, 1893. Others have been severe in one country only, as those of 1866 for England, and of 1907 for the United States, or 1899 for Germany.

The regularity of the disturbances led to Jevons's striking sun spot theory, which holds that the observed recurrence of sun spots every ten or eleven years explains the recurrence of crises. Though this seems at first blush absurdly far-fetched, it is not beyond the bounds of possible truth. Jevons maintained that the sun spots indicate variations in the heat from the sun; this affects vegetation and crops on the earth, which in turn affects the course of industry. The theory, none the less, has never had acceptance. A similar explanation has been sought in fluctuations in precipitation over decades, which again operate by their influence on crops.

All explanations of this sort rest on an exaggeration of the regularity of the fluctuations. For some periods the ten-year cycles have indeed been curiously regular, as from 1818 to 1857, and again (in the United States at least) from 1873 to 1903.

But the regularity has not been that of a well-defined natural phenomenon. After the crisis of 1837 in the United States, there was another in 1839. There was a break in the apparent ten-year sequence, as we have noted, from 1866 to 1873; another from 1903 to 1907. There have been disturbances in intermediate years, not so often noted, but not less well-marked. So in England in 1890, when something very near to a crisis developed in the United States also; again in Germany in 1899. France has been singularly little affected by some of the world-wide crises. The crash of 1873, for example, brought hardly a ripple in that country; whereas she has had some marked revulsions of her own, as in the failure of the Comptoir d'Escompte in 1889.

None the less, unmistakable repetition and some periodicity we do find. Periods of activity recur, followed by periods of depression, with an acute breakdown to mark the revulsion from one extreme to the other. The symptoms throughout are familiar. During the stage of activity, new enterprises are freely launched, old ones find a ready market for their products, business men are confident and even optimistic, labor finds regular and well-paid employment. Credit is easily expanded, prices rise, rates of interest and discount tend gradually to go up. Toward the latter part of such a stage, there is apt to be a period of halt and uncertainty, — something like a premonitory chill. Then new enterprises find unexpected obstacles, while those half-launched must bid high in order to get the funds they wish. Rates of discount rise, and scarcity of money is complained of. Suddenly there comes an overturn, usually precipitated by the failure of some well-known banking establishment. Thus in 1857 came the collapse in the United States of the Ohio Life Insurance and Trust Company; in 1866 in England, that of Overend, Gurney and Company, a great firm of bankers and brokers; in 1873, that of Jay Cooke and Company, a famous American banking house. In 1884 three large national banks failed in New York; in 1907 the Knickerbocker Trust Company failed in the same city, with other banking institutions dragging in its train. Then follows the acute stage, — the monetary crisis. Banks are confronted by sudden great demands; they are pressed both to enlarge their loans and to pay out their cash; business houses fail; in the worst cases, as in 1857 and 1873, even in 1907, a complete paralysis of industry sets in. With the more or less rapid subsidence of this acute phase, the period of industrial depression begins. No new enterprises are launched, old ones contract their operations, employment is comparatively scant and uncertain. Cash accumulates in the banks, reserves are high, rates of interest and discount low, prices tend to fall. Then, after a few years, bottom is touched, revival sets in slowly, and the old round is repeated.

§ 2. The causes of the larger oscillations, — the industrial phenomena, — are to be found partly in the division of labor and the time-using or capitalistic method of production; and partly in some elemental traits of human nature. They are partly economic, partly psychological.

We have already noted the successive division of labor: the marshaling of different stages in the processes of production. Thence ensues an interval, often long, between the first stages of production and the final emergence of the consumable commodity. Thence comes the possibility of mistake and maladjustment, and also the possibility that the maladjustment will not be promptly ascertained. Here is one great cause of the industrial crisis, — ill-adjusted production.

This cause acts most strongly when rapid changes are taking place in the arts. Crises have appeared on the largest scale and with the widest effects during the period since the Industrial Revolution, and in the countries whose progress has been most rapid. When there are heavy investments of capital in new enterprises, then the chances of error are greatest, and at the same time a course of error can be persisted in for the longest time without retribution. The railways, so far-reaching in all their industrial effects, have been of the first consequence here also. Many of the crises of the nineteenth century were closely associated with excessive or unprofitable railway building. Such were the crises of 1837 in the United States, of 1847 in England, and again of 1857 and 1873 and 1884 in the United States. A railway takes a long time to build, and calls for very large investment. While it is being built, and for some time after it is completed, there is uncertainty as to how far it will prove profitable, — and profit is usually the test of serviceability. The railway opens up new territory, or rearranges the geographical division of labor in old territory. Not until it has been in operation for some years can it be definitively known whether the final increase in enjoyable goods, or human satisfactions, has been such as to justify the huge investment. Railways have sometimes been built into regions where no advantageous development at all proved to follow. More often they have been built faster than the rest of the industrial structure could be adjusted to their transforming effects; hence there has been a long interval during which they were not yet profitable.

The same possibility of miscalculation and maladjustment appears in all making of plant. It shows itself most in those industries which supply the materials used in fixed capital and machinery, — those which stand at the very beginning of the processes of production and farthest removed from final fruition in enjoyable goods. Such are the industries supplying iron, timber, stone, and the like. Iron is in modern times the most important of these materials and feels more than any other the fluctuations of industrial activity. Iron and steel are in demand chiefly for investment. The millions of tons which are turned out annually mean new instruments of production, new railways, new structures, new appliances. These added instruments bring eventually more consumable goods; but whether of the kind which will be in demand, or so adjusted to the demand as to be sold at a profit, is very difficult to predict.

§ 3. Here the psychological factor comes into play. A pervading spirit of optimism fills most business men in times of activity, as a spirit of pessimism does in times of depression. A few very sagacious and sober persons may indeed remain unaffected. These hold off when others press on, and venture freely when others hesitate. But they are as rare as the persons who remain rational in a mob or quiet in a cheering crowd. Most business men respond to the influences that surround them. They enter on new enterprises or enlarge old ones when all the world about them is doing likewise.

This contagion is not merely contagion; it rests on a real interdependence. Business men are chiefly buying and selling with each other. Only the retail tradesmen, and such industries (essentially retail in character) as street railways, are dealing with the final consuming public. The maker of iron and steel sells to the maker of machinery, he to the manufacturer, he to the wholesale agent or jobber, he to the retailer. Every one of these, unless possessed of almost unlimited capital or credit on his own account, necessarily depends on what others will buy of him. Whatever be his own opinion of the source or extent of ultimate demand, the direct influence on him comes from those who stand next in the long chain of apparently separate, yet essentially interdependent, operations.

A curious part, and one too much neglected in discussion about the course of crises, is played by the distributing middlemen, — the wholesalers and jobbers and retailers. These constitute the immediate purchasing public for the "producers." When they buy freely, business is brisk; when they hold off, business is dull. They are not only subject to the psychological contagion; they are also moved by very simple calculations of profit and loss. Their operations are almost exclusively in the simple purchase and sale of goods, and their success depends almost solely on prices. They buy freely when they think that prices will rise, and cut down purchases when they think that prices will fall. The very fact that they so think, and accordingly act, accelerates the rise of prices in the one case, and accelerates the fall in the other. During an up-swing period, they add to their stocks, thinking to sell them at an advance, or at least to protect themselves against a later rise in the prices of what they buy. Then comes the shock, — a bad failure, a financial panic. They jump to the conclusion that "things are going down," countermand old orders as far as possible, give no new ones, live from hand to mouth in their purchases and sales, and wait until they think that prices have touched bottom. Sooner or later a good crop, the unexpected profitableness of some new venture, a turn in foreign trade, — some such event gives the start to a new upward movement. The middlemen reach the conclusion that it is time to buy again, and to take advantage of low prices. Business becomes more active, optimism returns. Prices go up, and go up the more certainly and quickly because all the dealers now think they will go up, and buy in consequence. There is thus an accumulation of extra stocks in their hands in times of rising prices, and a depletion in times of low prices; some really increased flow to consumers at the one stage, some really lessened flow at the other; but also an alternate excess and deficiency of the supplies held in the middlemen's reservoirs.

§ 4. During a stage of depression, the industrial machine seems to be half-stalled. The different parts do not act together. The dealers and middlemen perform their functions haltingly. They do not buy the accustomed or normal supplies, because they are uncertain of what the future will bring. The very fact that they curtail purchases, causes the manufacturing employers to cut down production. Workmen are thrown out of employment, and in turn do not buy of the retailers. During the brief but acute phase of the financial crisis, there is sometimes a universal collapse. Nobody buys, nobody can sell; nobody employs, nobody can find work. This phase rarely lasts more than a week or two; but it is likely to be followed by a prolonged period of halting purchases, lessened production, uncertain employment. The intricate machinery of production and exchange is first thrown violently out of gear by the financial collapse; and though this may be short-lived, and the mechanism may be got at work again, it shows the effects of the shock for a long time, and does its work ineffectively.

The period of hesitancy and "poor business" lasts a longer or a shorter time, according as there has been during the preceding active period more or less of real maladjustment in the industrial arrangements. If, for example, there have been really too many railways built for present needs, too many electric enterprises launched, too much iron and steel made, too many factories put up, — then there must be a wait until some of these appliances (the older and poorer) have been abandoned, or until the growth of population and of other industries has restored the due equilibrium in the division of labor. Thus in the years before the great crisis of 1873 there had been very rapid railway building in the United States, while the fundamental industry of the land — agriculture — had been neglected. During the long years of depression that followed, railway construction stood still; but a great increase took place gradually in the population and resources of the agricultural states of the Middle West. Then in 1879–1880 there came a sudden turn, the first impulse being given by a change in foreign trade; large crops had been reaped and good prices were got for them. All was ready for a revival; the industrial readjustment had really been carried out; the business community (in this case suddenly) woke up to the fact, and a new period set in, with all its concomitants of general hopefulness, free purchases, active speculation, new enterprises of all sorts, and the consequent incubation of a new crisis and a new era of depression.

Since the psychological factor is of such central importance, the extent and duration of the so-called good and poor times, and the particular occasion of the turn one way or the other, seem to rest on accident, — that is, on irregular and unpredictable causes. An unexpected great failure may precipitate a crisis. Unexpected good crops sold at high prices (a combination which the United States have been fortunate in enjoying sundry times) may, on the other hand, postpone one that is fairly due. This last seems to have been the case in 1890–1891. Then all the materials for a revulsion were present; but a turn in agricultural prosperity put the day of reckoning off for a year or two, and the crisis finally came, with special severity, in 1893. This crisis and the ensuing period of depression were intensified and complicated by the political struggle in regard to the silver question,—should the money of the country rest on a gold or a silver basis? — a question which necessarily made many business operations uncertain, and which, in its psychological effects, created even more uncertainty and hesitancy than the monetary question *per se* made inevitable. The revival which set in after 1896 was promoted, again, by all sorts of causes: the Republican victory at the polls, which promised the maintenance of a secure gold standard, and another favorable turn in foreign trade. In view of the frequent appearance of irregular causes of this sort, the degree of regularity which still persists in the recurrence of crises is surprising.

It is probable that depression is less prolonged, and revival more easy, when the underlying conditions are favorable to rising prices; when, for example, the supply of specie is increasing markedly. It is possible, on the other hand, that these very conditions increase the speculative and uncalculating activity of the period of incubation, and make the collapse more disastrous when it comes. Thus the crisis of 1857came after the Californian and Australian gold discoveries had given for years the basis of rising prices. It was very severe, and yet was short-lived in its course; within a year or two its effects seem to have worn away. The crisis of 1873, on the other hand, was followed by a period of general falling prices, especially in the United States, where a decline from a régime of inflated paper prices was gradually and painfully taking its course; and the period of depression after 1873 was unusually long.

§ 5. Still a further factor is to be noted in connection with industrial crises, the increase of capital and its relation to savings and to banking operations.

New enterprises mean on the one hand the creation of real capital, and on the other hand the accumulation of fresh savings, — the double process by which, under the régime of private property, the capital of the community is added to. The employing capitalists borrow from the investors, or in other ways enlist their savings. Though the bankers and active business men invest some accumulations of their own, they secure funds very largely from the inactive investors. In any case, whether using their own means or those of others, they cannot invest more than the available savings of the community make possible. But this limitation is a long-period one. It does not operate directly, but through a series of middlemen.

The development of corporations and the consequent growth of opportunities for investment by inactive investors have greatly enlarged and complicated all this mechanism. New enterprises nowadays are usually launched in corporate form, and the money means for carrying them on are procured by putting stocks and bonds on the market. The stocks and bonds are first sold mainly to banking and investment houses, and by these are retailed to investors. The banking and investment house, while it does not guarantee the solidity of the securities which it puts on the market, yet feels a responsibility for them. Its prestige and permanent prosperity are involved in promoting only successful ventures. The most important and useful function of such firms and institutions is the exercise of judgment regarding new enterprises; and here, too, is the main source of their profit. But they have no way, beyond shrewd guesswork, of estimating the total amount of securities which the investing public can buy. In times of buoyancy and hope, the various investment firms go ahead without hesitation, and take the securities of all promising enterprises. They advance their own means, and borrow more on short time from the strictly commercial banks. The whole banking and brokerage and stock-jobbing fraternity is borrowing and lending, and buying and selling securities. Many of the smaller fry and the "outside" speculators exercise no independent judgment at all, but simply buy or sell with the crowd, swallow all sorts of exaggerated statements or rumors, think only of the prices of securities from day to day, and, in the contagion of the moment, are singularly inattentive to the fundamental forces on which their doings are based. The psychological factor plays a large part.

When this has gone on awhile, it begins to appear that more has been undertaken than the accruing savings of the community make possible. The mass of securities offered to investors is greater than these have the means to buy. The rate of interest on long investments rises, as does the rate of discount on bank loans. New enterprises now find it difficult to get support; while those already launched find it harder and harder to procure the additional funds needed for completing their outfit. The commercial banks demur at renewing loans to the corporations and individuals who have borrowed of them under pledge of new or old securities as collateral. Simultaneously there is likely to be a check in mercantile expansion, a halt in the general upward movement. On all sides it appears that the means for additional investment operations have been overtaxed.

The beginning of a revulsion usually comes, as has been said, with a financial failure. Some banking house which has exceeded its own resources and that of its clientele, or which has exercised bad judgment upon a new venture, goes to the wall, and precipitates a general collapse. Thus the firm of Jay Cooke and Company, whose failure marked the beginning of the crisis of 1873, had promoted the building of the Northern Pacific Railway, — a great undertaking, and one eventually successful, but then far ahead of the population and industries of the region traversed. With the general ensuing collapse, it became clear that there had been many such premature enterprises, as well as not a few ill-judged ones, and that more of new capital had been planned than the available savings made possible. This was indeed the case the world over before the crisis of 1873. It seems to have been again the case the world over in the opening years of the present century, leading to the breakdown of 1907.

In sum, the causes of industrial depression seem to be reducible to various kinds of maladjustment, all connected with the intricate division of labor and the long stretch from production to consumption. There is likely to be maladjustment in the planning of some particular kind of capital, — railways, or electric enterprises, or textile mills. There is likely to be maladjustment in a greater addition to the total of the community's capital than is justified by the total of its available savings. There is excess or deficiency in the stocks of dealers and middlemen. There is accentuation of the whole series of misfits because of the psychological factor. The greater the maladjustment of all sorts, the more prolonged and painful will be the ensuing process of readjustment and recovery.

CHAPTER 30

FINANCIAL PANICS

§ 1. The financial panic which commonly appears as the acute stage of a crisis affects both the general business and mercantile firms, and the banks and financial institutions. Though these two groups are affected together, their fortunes being always interlaced, it will conduce to clearness if they are considered, so far as possible, separately. We will begin with the general business community.

All business men conduct their affairs on the basis of giving and taking credit. Each individual is both creditor and debtor, has his bills payable and his bills receivable. In the ordinary course of things, these obligations are met punctiliously. Failure to meet them means that the delinquent loses his standing in the business world; he is no longer in the game. It is on this severe ground of expediency that the discount of mercantile paper is so secure a banking investment. And the commercial banks, it need hardly be said again, find their main reason for existence in taking over the loans and discounting the paper of active business men.

Anything which unsettles the expectation that mercantile debts will be promptly met, may cause a panic among business men. Each knows that his paper is coming due, and that to enable him to meet it he must receive payment of what is coming due to himself. If he fails to pay his own obligations, he gets poor comfort from the fact that his own failure is due to the failure of his debtors to pay; his standing is broken none the less. Now all obligations are likely to be greater, and more dependent each on the other, during an upward industrial movement. Where there has been some really serious maladjustment, some failures are inevitable. But then it becomes also possible that one failure will entail another, and this still another, until business firms topple over in succession like a row of bricks. Of this sort of collapse a dramatic example occurred in the great crisis of 1857, when, both in England and the United States, an extraordinary number of firms collapsed.

When the storm is brewing, the one thing needed in the business community is assurance against indiscriminate ruin. This can be given by the banks, if they are themselves in a position to render aid. What merchants and manufacturers want at such times is "accommodation." They do not want cash. As will presently appear, when we take up the banking phase of the crisis, there may be at the same time a run on the banks for cash, especially in the deposit-using countries. But while some business men may join in the run, it rarely touches the mercantile community at large. What is needed for its peace of mind is primarily the assurance that support will be afforded against possible temporary embarrassment. Loans are wanted, not cash; or rather, assurance that loans can be had if needed. Business men want to be "taken care of." In deposit-using countries, they want the banks to make them advances — to credit them with deposits — which can be used in meeting their accruing obligations, even though the debts due to themselves fail to be met promptly.

§ 2. The banks (to proceed to the other phase of the situation) are thus confronted with an intensified demand for loans. At the same time they are likely to be confronted with a demand for additional cash. The two are in conflict with each other; for a drain of cash means a lessening of the resources on which depends an increase of loans. None the less, in times of panic, the only sound policy for banks, in their own interest as well as in that of the community, is to lend freely. Toward carrying out that policy, a great central institution can give unmistakable aid. The central public bank has a conscious duty toward the public, and, rightly conducted, is prepared for the performance of its duty in times of stress. By providing cash from its own ample holdings; by making loans itself; not least by bolstering up the banks at large so that each of them is encouraged to take care of its own customers, — the great central bank can certainly mitigate a panic, and can probably prevent the stage of general collapse from being reached. The Bank of England has learned by long and hard experience, but has thoroughly learned, that free offering of accommodation of all sorts is the way to meet a panic. The rate of discount is indeed advanced by the Bank, perhaps sharply; and it is advanced by other banking institutions also. But all solvent business firms have the assurance that loans can be had if wanted. The same assurance is given by the great public banks of the Continent, which, different though they are in their constitution and in their methods from the Bank of England, have learned with comparative ease, from the trying history of the great English institution, that bold generosity is the proper policy in a panic.

Such is the policy which the banks of the United States should adopt, — boldness and liberality. This policy, it is fair to say, they do largely follow. The strong and carefully managed banks of the larger cities have faced crises with courage, and have permitted none of their solvent customers to go by default. But the maintenance of a bold stand is very difficult for scattered and independent banks, without any acknowledged and responsible head. And there are peculiar difficulties from the unusual development of deposit banking in this country. The banks themselves are likely to be in peril during a panic, and thus not in a position to give vigorous support to others.

The policy of bold lending necessarily involves risk. Lend freely to solvent persons, — but who is solvent? The emergency usually comes after a period of active expansion, when many new ventures have been started and when prices have been raised by credit expansion. How will half-finished operations or newly completed plants turn out? How far will mercantile engagements stand the strain of lower prices? These must be matters of uncertainty. At one extreme there will be many business houses of unquestionable solidity, subject only to possible temporary embarrassment. These should clearly be supported. At the other extreme will be some of unquestionable insolvency, — the agents or the victims of ill-judged and unsuccessful investments. These must succumb to the inevitable. Between will stand not a few firms with large commitments, large liabilities, more or less uncertain assets. How far to go in supporting these, calls for the exercise of the banker's highest faculties of judgment. Here, again, the great public bank can take some risks which the private bank, however large and however strong, must regard with hesitation. Thus in 1890 the Bank of England took the lead in committing itself heavily in guaranteeing the liabilities of the Barings when that famous banking firm was in danger. In 1889 the Bank of France did substantially the same thing for a large Paris banking institution, the Comptoir d'Escompte, whose impending failure would have shaken the French business community; and in 1900 the Reichsbank of Germany took the risk of bolstering up the threatened Dresdner Bank. These, as it happens, are all cases in which the public banks extended aid to other banking institutions; but the latter were in difficulties because of their advances in support of miscellaneous business enterprises. The same sort of aid to seriously endangered banks and firms has been given by the associated banks of the American cities; but with reluctance and sometimes with a possibility of eventual loss, and only under the persuasion that even greater loss would come from the precipitation of a general panic. The right line is not easily drawn in such circumstances between deserved retribution for individual offenders and undeserved harm to the business community at large.

In Continental countries, where deposit banking is less developed, some of the phenomena of crises are different from those in England and the United States. But to the degree to which their industry is active and progressive, they are subject to mercantile crises as well as to the larger oscillations of activity and depression. There is the same interlacing of business men's obligations, the same probability of general expansion of business and general enlargement of obligations, the same possibility of panic and collapse.

§ 3. There are some phases of the general disturbance which specially affect the banks of deposit-using countries, and most of all those of the United States.

Deposit banking implies that the banks have a great volume of demand liabilities, and a comparatively small amount of cash with which to meet them. If there is a general and sustained run on all the banks, the cash almost inevitably proves insufficient. There is then nothing left except a general suspension of cash payments. To prevent such a general run, to maintain the confidence of depositors, to keep in working order this intricate part of the machinery of exchange, — this is the object which legislation and the policy of banks strive for.

When any one bank is beset by a run — caused perhaps by some unfounded rumor, some unreasoning fright among its depositors — it appeals for aid to the other banks. These have the strongest motive for granting aid, by supplying cash from their own holdings; since fright is contagious, and the failure of any one bank is likely to precipitate a general run. But the condition on which aid is granted usually is, and always ought to be, that the bank in straits be solvent; that its loans and other assets prove on examination to be sound, and sufficient in the ordinary course of events to meet its liabilities. The possibility of a run, and the necessity in that case of exposing its whole situation to critical professional eyes, are the strongest forces for preventing reckless and dishonest banking. A bank which is once fairly going, even though it be really insolvent, can keep going for a long time. It can carry on its books, as if good, loans or securities which are bad. So long as depositors continue their daily round of deposits, loans, checks, there is little to reveal the true situation. But once there is a run, the bank must show its hand. Where there is an organized clearing house, a committee representing this institution (that is, the combined banks of the place) examines the threatened member, and learns whether aid is deserved. If it is, the reserves of all the banks are massed at the point of danger. Every depositor in the imperiled institution is told he can have his cash if he wishes it; and at the same time public assurance is given by the clearing house committee that the bank is solvent. And if it is not solvent, and must be wound up with possible loss to depositors, the combined banks face the situation boldly, "take care" of the embarrassed depositors, and endeavor to quiet general apprehension. By such means an incipient panic may be averted.[1]

But when there is a general panic and a general run — when, moreover, some banks are really insolvent, and others are in an uncertain condition — the situation is more difficult to handle. Here again it is unquestionably a vast advantage if there be some one great strong institution with ample cash holdings and unshakable prestige. For the banking institutions of the United Kingdom, the Bank of England is in such times the citadel of refuge. It can undertake to supply cash when needed, and to guarantee solvency if there be real solvency. Thus in the striking case already referred to, in 1890, when the threatened suspension of the Barings might have caused a calamitous panic, the Bank not only took the lead in guaranteeing that firm's liabilities, but prepared to strengthen the whole credit structure of the country. It secured an extra store of cash from the Bank of France, and it made ready for a possible suspension of the Bank Act of 1844, — the maneuver already described[2] for getting additional cash resources. These measures sufficed; there was no acute panic. So strongly intrenched is the Bank of England nowadays, so conscious of its obligations to the public, so effectively secured by its form of management against being itself entangled in dangerous ventures, that it is probably in a position hereafter to cope with any financial panic in its

[1] Precisely this was accomplished at Chicago in 1906, when the failure of the Walsh banks (several banks controlled by a promoter of that name) might have caused a panic, which was staved off in the manner described.

[2] Chapter 26, § 3.

own country. It is not indeed able to control the periodic oscillations of industry, and the painful revulsions from activity to depression; but it has learned how to deal with the acute stage which hitherto has so commonly marked the transition, and which has intensified so much its ill effects. To prophecy that acute financial distress will never recur in England, would be unsafe; but the unreasoning, moblike panic has become highly improbable.

§ 4. In the United States, the other great deposit banking country, there is nothing in the experience of the last generation to indicate that the financial panic is a thing of the past. The situation is in many ways different from that in England, and in many ways contains greater elements of danger.

The national banks of the reserve cities, and especially those of New York, occupy, it is true, a position analogous to that of the Bank of England. But the analogy does not reach far. They are many in number, and, though combined for some purposes in the Clearing House Associations, they cannot act with the energy and promptness of a single institution. Even if they were organized to act unhesitatingly, they are not in a position to give all the assurance and support that are needed. Their reserves of cash are only such as the national banking laws compel; sometimes a little more, but, at the times when panics are likely, seldom appreciably more. Not least, they are themselves not above suspicion. Most of them, it is true, are always found to be solvent and even super-solvent. But there are commonly some black sheep, with rumors and suspicions of more. Most of the banks, solvent or not, are uneasily conscious that they have not an invulnerable position: it necessarily ceases to be so when general confidence begins to be shaken.

To these causes of danger is added the fact that deposit banking is extraordinarily widespread. Not only is the total volume of deposits in the United States very great, but the number of individual banks and of individual depositors is enormous. There is a larger proportion than in England of persons who are likely to be affected by unreasoning panic. Deposit accounts are kept not only by those doing business on a considerable scale and by persons of large means, but by petty retail tradesmen, farmers, women. These easily get into a fright when some great bank fails and rumors are flying thick as to others. An overt run, or a silent steady withdrawal of cash, may then be precipitated. The banks, on the other hand, are scattered, are sensitive to the possibility of sudden demands, and are themselves by no means free from panicky feeling. Many of them are small; many, large and small, conduct their operations in ordinary times with a minimum of cash. When danger threatens, they telegraph for cash to the reserve city bank in which they keep a deposit. They do so not only to meet real drains by their own depositors, but to provide against possible or anticipated drains. Among the banks, as among their individual depositors, a spirit of *sauve qui peut* may develop; and then a full-fledged panic bears forth.

The provision in the national banking laws by which country banks may count as reserve for themselves what they keep on deposit in reserve cities probably increases the dangers of the situation. As has already been said, this provision is by no means the sole cause or the main cause of the concentration of cash holdings and of final responsibility. Some concentration of this sort is inevitable, and indeed makes for the more economical and efficient working of deposit banking. But the reserve regulations under the national banking system operate as an additional inducement to the scattered banks to keep deposits (on interest) in the central cities, and thus intensify the drain on these in times of stress.

The device to which the banks of the United States, especially those of the large cities, and above all those of New York City, have turned at such times, is that of combining their reserves by resorting to clearing house certificates. These are a sort of currency, issued under the supervision of the clearing house organization to the individual banks and used for settlements among themselves. A bank which finds itself pressed goes to the authority constituted for the emergency (usually a small committee representing the clearing house banks), and pledges some of its assets, — securities or mercantile paper. It then receives certificates in convenient (large) denominations,[1] which can be used in settling balances at the clearing house. On these certificates interest is paid by the bank which takes them out, usually at a high rate (seven per cent, or thereabouts); the interest being paid directly to the clearing house committee, and through this to the bank receiving the certificates in settlement. The effect is to leave the cash held by the banks free for use in paying depositors, — whether local depositors or banks in other places. Its effect is also to facilitate defense for any one bank exposed to a run. Other banks can turn over to it, by way of loan, some of their cash, and this can be paid out freely to frightened depositors. Quite as often, however, the defensive effect is indirect. A depositor, even though uneasy, often hesitates to go to the counter and demand cash directly. He draws a check in favor of a friend, and has the sum deposited by the friend in some other more trusted bank. Such a check, then, is met at the clearing house by certificates; that is, it is met virtually by a pledge of the bank's assets other than cash.

The clearing house certificate plan, however, has proved quite inadequate to prevent a breakdown of the American deposit system. It has mitigated or prevented some minor disturbances; but on three conspicuous occasions, in 1873, in 1893, in 1907, complete collapse ensued, notwithstanding its use. In each of these great panics the banks of the country virtually suspended payments. Thereby they committed acts of bankruptcy, and under the strict letter of the law could have been forced into liquidation. The fact that the suspension was universal and well-nigh inevitable, caused its strict legal consequences to be ignored; and after a few weeks or months the usual course of payments was resumed. But during these weeks and months, on all three occasions, legal obligations

[1] The amount of clearing house certificates is usually less (80 per cent or thereabouts) than the face value of the commercial paper or the market value of the securities.

were put aside. Neither individual depositors nor outside banks could get the cash which they had the right to demand. No doubt their demands were in one sense unreasonable. Individuals called for cash because they wished to hoard it, by tucking it away in drawers or in safe deposit boxes. Outside banks wanted it partly because their own depositors made similar demands, partly because they themselves were in a fright lest such demand should come. Whatever the cause, the breakdown was well-nigh complete. A depositor in 1893 or 1907 was allowed to draw pocket money — a few dollars — by his bank; but any demand for considerable sums was met, in most cities and by most banks, with flat refusal.

To describe the various further consequences of these banking collapses would carry us beyond the limits of the present book. In the crises of 1873, 1893 and 1907, there was the curious phenomenon, at the height of the disturbance, of a "premium on currency"; perhaps described more accurately as a depreciation of deposits. Persons in need of cash, or very solicitous to procure cash, were willing to give, for cash, checks on solvent banks (checks which were available, however, only through the clearing house) at an advance of as much as two, three, or four per cent. Even more striking was the large resort to various substitute media of exchange, in the form of checks payable to bearer and of clearing house certificates in smaller denominations. There was a literal scarcity of cash, and those who needed it, such as employers having large pay rolls, had to turn to these cumbrous substitutes. Of all the incidents of an acute financial crisis, that of 1907 gave conspicuous illustrations, — failures of some large banking houses, shock to confidence in others, demands for cash from frightened depositors and frightened banks, virtual suspension of cash payments in most cities, a so-called premium on currency, sharp fall in the prices of securities and staple commodities. The events of 1907, repeating as they did in unusual severity those of 1873 and 1893, made it clear that no effective way had been devised in the United States to meet the financial panic.

The generic feature of an acute crisis, whether in mercantile community or as regards the banks, is loss of confidence. Business men lose confidence in the punctual meeting of their mutual obligations; the public and the depositing banks themselves lose confidence in the punctual payment by banks of their obligations. The scarcity of cash and the high rates of discount are a result and a symptom, not a cause. The remedy must be one that will restore confidence. Only so far as an increase in the supply of cash does this is it a remedy. More effective than anything else is a bold and liberal policy by the banks: free offering of loans and free offering of cash to all who want it. To pursue that policy, the banks must not only be strong, but must have an ample reserve of strength, and the ability to convince the public that they have it. The suspension of the Bank Act by the Bank of England — the classic example of a specific remedy for panics — led on only one occasion to the actual issue of more notes. The mere knowledge that more could be got, and as many more as might be needed, has sufficed to restore confidence; or, more accurately, has contributed to allay the general uneasiness which might have precipitated a full-fledged panic.

The unhappy experiences of 1907 in the United States led in 1908 to some legislation, expected to be helpful, for an "emergency currency." An act of that year authorized the issue of additional notes by national banks in times of stress, under the approval of the Comptroller of the Currency: either against the deposit of additional securities (not necessarily United States bonds) or against ordinary bank assets, such as commercial paper. But it is not clear how far this sort of device will prove effective. An emergency currency will be of little avail unless there be prompt and resolute action by the associated banks of the various cities, and especially of New York, in regard to all the other procedure called for in a crisis. Other remedies — a central bank, or a complete overhauling of the national banking system — are also under consideration. But the whole subject is in the melting pot, and the only thing certain is that the need of recasting the banking and currency system is urgent.

§ 5. The acute stage of a crisis does not last long. A few weeks of excitement and anxiety, of banking and mercantile collapses, of pressing demand for "money" (*i.e.* loans) at high rates of discount, are followed by rapid subsidence and quiescence. Almost invariably, cash accumulates in bankers' vaults within a few months of a panic, and the rate of discount falls to a low figure. These conditions hold for a considerable period, longer or shorter according as the revival of activity comes late or early. During this period the banks, though willing and able to extend advances, find the business community unresponsive, and an abundance of cash in their hands goes hand in hand with low and falling prices.

It might seem that the panic proper, which is brief, must be of concern chiefly to the business and banking classes. But it is often followed by long-continued and widespread effects; and these effects, though not due solely or even chiefly to the panic, are aggravated by it. The confidence which is restored, after a few weeks or at most months, is a slow and sluggish feeling, very different from that buoyancy which marks the period of activity. When, as is commonly the case, the acute crisis comes as the climax of such a period of activity, the reverse period of depression is doubtless inevitable. But the depression is greater and lasts longer if the panic has been severe. The psychological factor again tells. Business men, after such a serious trial, hesitate to engage in new enterprises, and are cautious in the conduct of the old. Dealers and middlemen curtail purchases, waiting for better times, — partly from cold calculation of lowering prices, but largely from the mere contagion of depression. Hence there is less real production of wealth. The process of advances by capitalists to laborers, on which the wages of hired workmen proximately depend, takes place less actively, and there is less employment of labor. Hard times are in reality hard, and the more so if the panic which precipitates them has been violent.

The period of depression is often a healthy one, or at least is essential for industrial health. Sometimes it is complicated by other than the ordinary or normal causes, and brings to end real evils and real difficulties of a different origin. Thus, in the United States, inflation of the currency through irredeemable or quasi-irredeemable paper has intensified some periods of expansion, and the return to a sound currency has been a part of the subsequent periods of depression. The sharp crises of 1818 and 1837 came as the climax, not only of general speculative activity, but of excessive issues of notes by scattered and ill-regulated banks. The return to a stable currency was essential to restored industrial health, but, coming as it did with the general readjustment of a period of depression, was inevitably trying. Something of the same sort is true (for the United States) of the crisis of 1873. The collapse after 1873 and the severe fall of prices were part of the process by which the return to specie payments was brought about. And even without these extraneous circumstances, the period of depression which follows a crisis is often in reality invigorating. It restores the proper balance of the different parts of the industrial organism. The period of activity, on the other hand, is often one of prosperity in appearance more than in reality. It means a false start, a pace which cannot be maintained. And through all these ups and downs, the fundamental forces which make for material advancement continue to have their steady and half-unperceived effects: the progress of invention and the increase of capital, the accumulation of savings, the industrial, intellectual, and moral advancement of the workers. Too much attention is commonly given to the more obvious phenomena of superficial prosperity, to good times and hard times, and too little to the great factors on which in the long run depends the improvement of the condition of mankind.

None the less, it is true that panics are bad in themselves, and bad in their after effects. A violent crisis prolongs the subsequent period of depression, or at least makes it more severe. The worse the shock, the harder the recovery. Anything which can be done to mitigate the financial panic contributes to mitigate the depression of the industrial crisis.

§ 6. Remedies or at least palliatives for the financial panic are easier to find than those for the larger cycles of industrial depression. A currency anchored securely to a specie bottom, and a well-devised banking system, with effective provision for meeting emergencies, — these are the best means for coping with the financial panic. They have been reasonably perfected in the leading European countries; and it is possible at least to indicate the general measures which should be devised for the United States.

For the grave evils which flow from the industrial aspects of crises it is much harder to find a remedy. Something may be gained by diffusion of better education among the classes from whom business men are recruited. The excitement and demoralization, the psychological factors, which play so considerable a part, rest largely on ignorance. Business men, though well informed of what goes on in the circle of their immediate operations, are often singularly ignorant on the wider aspects of industry and on the economic history which records the warning experience of the past. Something may be gained, too, by direct government action. It has been suggested that large public works, in the way of roads, buildings, harbor works, parks, public improvements of all sorts, should be undertaken most actively in periods of depression, and held back during periods of activity, thus counteracting to some degree the alternations of private investment. Public activity has tended in the past to proceed just the other way, it has accelerated or slackened its pace sympathetically with private activity. Where great industries, such as the railways, are under public management, the opportunities for some kind of check-weighing may seem to be present to a special degree. But it is by no means clear how far public action of this sort can be made an efficient palliative: for public works undertaken not with an eye to clearly perceived needs, but with a view to general effects on industry and employment, are likely to be ill-conducted, and so in the end unsuccessful and themselves irregular.

In the main, oscillations of industry must be accepted as inevitable concomitants of the régime of private property. They may be mitigated, but they are not likely to cease. They are part of the price which must be paid for that progress which private ownership and employing capitalism secure. No doubt they are among the black features of the existing system. Helpless embarrassment, halting production, hardship and suffering for the unemployed laborers — these are held up by the socialist critics, not without show of reason, as damning facts. A systematically organized scheme of production would preclude these evils. But deliberate planning of industry, carried out universally — and this means socialism — would lack also the vigor, the elasticity, the forward movement which mark existing industry. Here, as in all things human, and certainly in all economic arrangements, no ideal perfection can be looked for. Good must be balanced against ill, and that mode of conducting industry must be accepted which brings the greatest attainable gain, even though it bring in its train also no small amount of loss.

CHAPTER 31

The Theory of Prices Once More

§ 1. We return now to the main topic of monetary theory: the relation of the quantity of money to prices, and the causes that determine the general level prices. It was explained at the beginning of the present Book [1] that, under the simplest conditions, prices vary exactly with the quantity of money; but it was said that this proposition required great qualifications under any except the simplest conditions. The nature of these qualifications and the more refined general formulation of the theory we are now prepared to consider.

At the outset, something must be said of the relation of credit to prices. This again, we may analyze by taking up first the simplest conditions.

A purchase on credit has the same immediate effect on prices as a purchase with cash. If, in addition to a given number of purchasers offering money, there are as many more, whose credit is good, offering to buy on time, the effect on the seller is the same as if the entire number offered money. With a fixed supply of commodities, prices would double in either case.

But this is only the proximate effect. Sooner or later, the goods bought on credit must be paid for. When they are paid for, money must be used. Credit *per se* does not permanently dispense with the use of money in payments; it only postpones the use of money. At the later date, when the debt comes to be paid, money will be used, and what money is so used will not be available for other sorts of transactions. To the extent that money is dispensed with at the outset, to that extent more of it is called for in the end. In the long run, therefore, credit stands for no independent factor in the determination of prices,

[1] See above, Book III, Chapter 18.

and is no real substitute for money, — no real cause of addition to the monetary demand for commodities. It simply affects the time when the money shall pass.

For a period, however, an extension of credit may have the same effect on prices as a corresponding increase in the quantity of money. In the great pendulum swings of modern industry, there are apt to be intervals of considerable length — a year or two, perhaps more — when new purchases on credit are made more freely than payments on account of earlier purchases take place. During such a period credit operations act to raise prices, by the difference between the volumes of the two sets of transactions. In times of depression there is the reverse situation, — hesitancy in purchases and contraction of credit dealings. Then the payments of old debts exceed the new purchases on credit, and the balance sinks the other way. Shifts like these, though probably not of great consequence, play some part in bringing about the oscillating tendency of price movements.

§ 2. The extension of credit, however, may cause not merely a postponement of the use of money. It may bring into action a train of causes enabling money to be dispensed with. If, for instance, a merchant of high standing buys goods, and gives his promissory note in payment, the transaction *per se* merely puts off the use of money until the maturity of the note. Conceivably, however, the holder of the note may turn it over, with his indorsement, to another person, in payment of goods. If that other person accepts it, the use of money in the second transaction is entirely obviated: yet the effect on prices is precisely the same as if so much money had actually passed. It is further conceivable that the second person may hand over the note in place of money in still another purchase. In the first part of the nineteenth century, this sort of circulation of the promissory notes or acceptances [1] of individuals seems to have been not uncommon in England.

[1] An acceptance of a bill of exchange or draft brings in law the same sort of obligation as the signing of a promissory note. For reasons that root in legal history, acceptance of a bill has been much the more common form in England.

Obviously bank notes supply the most complete instance of this effect of a credit instrument. The note of an individual, given in the ordinary course of transactions, can hardly circulate much, however well known and reputed he may be; for only by an accident can it be of convenient denomination for other dealings. But bank notes, — which may be issued by an individual as well as by a corporation, unless there be legal restriction,[1] — are intentionally made out in denominations for convenient circulation, and pass from hand to hand as money would. The effect of this form of credit is not open to question. Bank notes serve as complete substitutes for money, and affect prices as much (barring some qualifications to be noted presently) as specie would.

Quite a different way in which credit enables money to be dispensed with is in the possibility of enabling transactions to be offset.

If a country dealer sells merchandise on credit to the surrounding farmers, and the farmers in turn bring their produce to the dealer, and hand it over to him on credit; and if periodically the debts are offset, and only the balance is paid (that balance perhaps allowed to stand over as an item for the next succeeding settlement), though little money passes, the transactions are all in terms of money, and prices are affected as if money had passed. Such offsetting transactions were probably common, in many parts of the United States, in the earlier stages of industrial development. In parts of New England eggs are still regularly received by village storekeepers from the country folk, and credited to these against purchases; a sort of barter, but one taking place in terms of money, and with a legal obligation on each side to pay money. But with the specialization of mercantile dealings such practises have almost disappeared. The dealer who buys is rarely the identical person to whom sales are made. The far developed division of labor, here as elsewhere, has caused

[1] It may be noted that in China merchants' notes, payable to bearer, have been in use (apparently for centuries) as a circulating medium. "They are issued by the great houses of business and are accepted in all the principal towns." Huc's *Chinese Empire*, Vol. II, p. 151.

exchanges which are fundamentally simple to be carried on by a divided and complicated mechanism.[1]

The great and effective mechanism which serves to bring scattered exchanges to a single focus, and enables the offsetting of debts to be carried out on a large scale, is that of the clearing house. The checks turned in by a bank are offset by the checks presented against it. In the purchases which have been settled by the checks prices have been affected precisely as if specie had passed at the time of the purchase. At the clearing house the checks are simply exchanged. The transactions are settled in the end without any use of specie or cash, or, to be more accurate, with only a slight use of it, — in that small proportion in which clearing house balances are settled with cash.

The same result, of course, is attained when bank notes go through the clearing house. But bank notes are more likely than checks to perform transactions on the way, passing from hand to hand repeatedly in payments. Checks commonly go at once to some bank of deposit, and thence are sent to the clearing house; and they obviate the use of money almost exclusively through the offsetting process.

§ 3. We may proceed now to the more refined and accurate statement of the relation between quantity of money and prices.

What determines prices in a highly developed community is the relation between the quantity of goods and the quantity of *purchasing power in terms of money.* Formulated in this way, the quantity theory holds good. It is strictly true that the general range of prices depends — the quantity of things on sale being given — on the volume of purchasing power in terms of money. But that volume is by no means the same as the volume of specie or of what is generally termed "money." And

[1] In one case, of no small importance, such direct offsetting of debts does take place on a large scale, namely, through the stock exchange clearings in New York. Here a number of dealers (the stock exchange brokers) buy and sell to each other great amounts of securities, and settle their transactions very largely by a process of offsetting. There is a clearing system on the Chicago Board of Trade also, but it seems to be made use of only to a limited extent. See *Report of the Chicago Board of Trade,* 1907, pp. 111, 112.

the really difficult and controverted question is how far an increase or decrease in the quantity of specie or "money" affects this other quantity, total purchasing power.

Some things are obvious. Certain sorts of paper substitutes for specie operate precisely as specie does. Notes payable to bearer, and government paper pieces whether convertible or inconvertible, add by the amount of their face value to the total purchasing power. Such things are included in common usage under the term "money," and are admitted on all hands to influence prices virtually as specie does. This is obviously the case also with such bank notes as those of the Bank of England. It is very largely the case with our national bank notes, and with other bank notes also; though it is not so clear, in these cases, that there is a net increase of purchasing power by the face value of the note.

Credit also adds to the supply of purchasing power. An offer to buy goods, by a man whose credit is undoubted, acts on their price just as much as an offer by one who proffers cash. But credit, as has just been explained, serves in its ordinary form merely to postpone the use of money. Though it may add to the total of effective purchasing power at a given time, in the long run it brings no increase of the total.

Deposits constitute part of the total purchasing power; and an increase of deposits means an increase in the total. Deposits, be it noted, — not checks; for, as has been said already,[1] checks simply represent this power in actual exercise, not the total available supply. The total supply of purchasing power in terms of money thus consists of various and heterogeneous items; but all forms of it add to that monetary demand for goods which determines the level of prices.

The most intricate question is presented by deposits. A purchase of goods, the discount of commercial paper, the creation of deposits, — all these go together. The very increase in the quantity of goods and in the volume and transactions brings with it an increase in total purchasing power and in the effective

[1] See Book III, Chapter 8, § 3.

machinery of exchange. The statement of a quantity theory in relation to prices assumes two independent variables: total money or total purchasing power on the one hand, total supply of goods or total volume of transactions on the other. But in the case of deposits these two factors seem to be mutually dependent, and the underlying assumption, therefore, seems not to hold.

The same problem arises as to bank notes, where these are issued under condition of freedom and elasticity. They, too, seem not to be an independent variable. They are issued in response to a demand in the form of more commodities to be sold. The issues of the Bank of France, the Bank of Germany, the Scotch and Canadian banks, fluctuate from week to week according as more or less transactions are to be effected.

On the other hand, the volume of deposits (and in some degree of notes), thus affected by the very volume of commodities and of transactions, is not necessarily dependent on the specie or other reserve money held by the banks. One might suppose the extreme case of a community in which all payments were made by check, and all transactions settled through the clearing house. Here there would be no need whatever of specie or "money." Daily or weekly balances at the clearing houses could be allowed to stand over, and sooner or later would be equalized. In such a community, if deposits swelled more rapidly than commodities and transactions, prices might rise indefinitely. Now, where deposits (or notes) are very largely used, is there not an approximation to some such condition? and can there be said to be any dependence of prices on the quantity of specie or of what is usually termed "money"?

§ 4. Though it is true that, where these highly elastic credit instruments are used, the connection between the total purchasing power and the quantity of "money" becomes at any given time very loose, there remains in the long run a real limitation on these instruments in the quantity of specie. This limitation comes in two ways: first, in various links of connection between the volume of deposits (and of notes elastic like deposits) and the quantity of specie; second, in a connection between prices in any one country and prices in the world at large. For the present, we shall give attention chiefly to the first set of factors; the second connect themselves with the theory of international trade, to be considered shortly.

The extent of the superstructure of deposits and notes built upon the foundation of a given supply of cash (meaning by cash, not only specie, but all legal tender paper and other public paper available as reserve) is affected by the following circumstances: (*a*) direct necessity, (*b*) binding custom, (*c*) legal requirement, (*d*) the interaction in the use of deposits, notes, and other constituents of the circulating medium, (*e*) the temper of the business classes. Let these be considered in order.

(*a*) Direct necessity. Some cash every bank must have, even though the amount may be small in proportion to liabilities. The figure of five per cent has been mentioned in the preceding pages. Some such minimum a bank must keep. Even less, four per cent, or three, is occasionally found to serve the purpose; though few banks would wish long to sail so very close to the wind. But somewhere there is a limit.

That limit tends for one reason to be lower for a city bank than for a country bank, for another reason to be higher. A large city bank is less likely to have heavy proportional balances to meet at the clearing house; for its daily deposits from customers are more likely to equal the daily drafts through customers' checks. Similarly, the daily calls for cash over the counter from customers are more likely to be equaled by daily deposits of cash over the counter. The mere fact that its business is large and varied makes it more probable that such items will compensate each other. On the other hand, the city bank is under stronger pressure to hold a safety reserve, — an extra store of cash against emergencies. The great volume of its deposit liabilities makes it sensitive to runs or panics. The display of an extra store of cash may add to its repute, and so may indirectly prove profitable. Yet it does not necessarily conduce to profit: the eventual gain from a high prudential reserve depends on the temper and watchfulness of the business public. It is by no means a universal experience among the banks of the United States that this sort of conservatism is a profitable advertisement.

Where a city bank can turn to a great public institution for support in case of runs, its motive for holding extra cash disappears. It is then like the country bank which relies on the city bank in such contingencies. Hence the English banks, which have the Bank of England to fall back on, have virtually given up holding any safety reserve; the old lady in Threadneedle Street attends to this. But some cash for daily needs, even though it be only a little, they still have to keep on hand.

(*b*) Of the binding force of custom, the Bank of England supplies the most obvious example. Its great reserve of cash, on which rest not only its own deposits, but those of all Great Britain, is fixed by a custom now as strong as law. A similar settled conservatism affects the reserve against note issues held by the Bank of France, the Bank of Germany, and the other public banks of the Continent. The same policy, it may be safely asserted, would be adopted with regard to their deposit liabilities if these should develop on the same scale as those of English-speaking countries.

(*c*) Direct regulation by law is, as we have seen, peculiar to the United States. If all banks were required to keep a cash reserve of twenty-five per cent, as are the national banks of New York City, deposits could grow only in the proportion of four to one of cash. This is far from being the limitation in fact imposed on the national banks as a whole; but there is, none the less, a substantial limitation. The deposits under the national system cannot swell without some proportional increase of cash required for the legal reserve.

The great growth of state banks has very much lessened in recent years the effectiveness of this limitation in the United States. These keep very slender reserves. On the other hand, they use the national banks as depositories, and add very much to the total volume of deposits for which the national banks hold the available cash. The greater profitableness of state banks not hampered by any substantial restrictions as to reserve has caused some national banks to withdraw from the system, and in even greater degree has caused new banks to organize outside that system. The net effect has been to make less strong the foundation of cash on which the superstructure of total deposits rests; or, to put the same thing in other words, to make the same quantity of cash in bank vaults more effective potentially in increasing the total volume of purchasing power. This sort of higher upbuilding of deposits took place very markedly during the great industrial expansion of the opening years of the twentieth century in the United States, and was an important factor in causing the rise of prices which then took place.

§ 5. (*d*) The next cause of limitation is a more intricate one. Deposits and checks cannot serve for all transactions. Cash — that is, specie or notes — must be used for many retail purchases, for payments of wages, for all sorts of everyday payments. It is true that checks are used in the United States to an astonishing degree for transactions of all sorts. Yet pocket money is by no means dispensed with. In England, though checks are used universally for wholesale transactions, they are used for consumers' payments by only a comparatively small number of the well-to-do; coin or notes are needed for most retail dealings and for all wages payments.

Now no one form or denomination of purchasing power is able to exercise an unqualified influence on prices, if it be exchangeable for other forms. Fifty-dollar bills or ten-pound notes, if put out in greater quantity than needed for the convenient disposal of transactions to which they are suited, will flow back to the issuer for exchange into small pieces. If indeed smaller notes are issuable under the same conditions, — if bank notes of all denomination can be issued as freely as large notes or deposits, — this back flow is of no special consequence. But if the only available smaller pieces are gold coins, the consequences are important. Then a given amount of coin must remain afloat somewhere in the community, and the volume of other monetary media has a limitation from the necessary use of that coin. We have seen how effective is a limitation of bank notes to the large denominations; it prevents the expulsion of specie, and limits strictly the field which notes can occupy.[1]

Precisely the same sort of limitation may be effective on deposits. England supplies a simple example. No notes under £5 being issued, and checks being used (by custom) for large transactions only, sovereigns are necessarily in everyday use. If deposits were to swell, and a rise in prices were to take place in consequence, more of gold coin would be called for in everyday transactions. The consequent drain of gold from the banks would put a prompt check on the increase of deposits. The English monetary system as a whole, with its necessary circulation of gold coin, illustrates the interconnection of the different constituents of the circulating medium.

In the United States the same influence shows itself, but in less simple and effective ways. Bank notes under five dollars are prohibited, and the proportion which can be issued even of this size is limited. Moreover, the bond-deposit requirement makes the issue of notes by banks very far from being free. Hence deposits cannot be supplemented in full by bank notes, and to some degree the same sort of force is in operation as in England to compel the circulation of other than bank money. That other money, however, is to a very large degree, not gold, but substitutes for it, — government paper or overvalued silver. All this fiduciary money is maintained at equality with gold, and, so far as its effects on prices go, is in almost every respect the same as so much additional gold. But it prevents the full-value coin from being in circulation in as great quantity as would otherwise be the case. Less of actual gold coin is called for in order to fill the channels of circula-

[1] See Book III, Chapter 24, § 2.

tion with duly apportioned denominations of money, and the supply of gold is consequently a less direct factor in the determination of prices.

This need of specie, or its equivalent, for the common transactions of everyday life helps to explain an odd phenomenon, to which reference has already been made; namely, the common complaint of scarcity of money at the very times when total purchasing power is most abundant and prices are highest. If an expansion of deposits and other credit devices has caused prices to go up, more of everyday money is called for at the banks; for at the higher prices more of the smaller denominations is needed for the convenience of exchanges. Hence banks feel a drain for cash, and they complain, and the business community echoes the complaint, that there is not money enough. The real difficulty is that total purchasing power has increased, and that, therefore, there is occasion for more use of every sort of money; while at the same time the bank reserves on which the swollen credit currency depends have become proportionately smaller, sometimes even absolutely smaller.

§ 6. (*e*) Finally, the temper of the business community affects the volume of deposits. It is not to be supposed that there is an automatic adjustment of deposits to cash in any fixed proportion, — four to one, or ten to one, or twenty to one. What is true is that when the banks have comparatively large reserves, — larger than seem to them worth while, under the influence of all the factors just described,—they lower their rate of discount, welcome every applicant for a loan, and are more than willing to enlarge loans and deposits. But very often they find it impossible to enlarge them. The business community does not respond. A familiar phenomenon, recurring with remarkable regularity, is that in times of depression banks have abundant reserves, that the money market is easy, and that none the less loans are not taken. Conversely, during periods of activity, when every one is optimistic, loans are in demand; and then the banks, though their reserves may be near the minimum and their rate of discount high, not only find it easy to swell loans and deposits, but find it difficult to prevent them from swelling. The psychology of the business community as a whole is an important factor.

There was a long controversy, a couple of generations ago, concerning the mode in which bank notes, if they were allowed to be freely issued, affected business activity and rising prices: whether their free issue had *per se* a stimulating effect, or whether an independent increase of activity was the cause leading to the larger issue. Which, in other words, was cause and which effect? The same question can be raised as to deposits, and it is in this form that the question is now an important one in English-speaking countries. Does an increase of deposits cause greater activity and higher prices, or does greater activity cause an increase of deposits and so bring in its own train the higher prices? The truth seems to be that there is an interaction of causes. When the spirit of hope is pervasive, liberal banking facilities nurture and stimulate it; without general optimism, such facilities lie unused and inoperative.

Hence there is, over short periods, truth in the proposition that the very conditions which bring about an increase in the supply of purchasing power bring about also an increase in the demand; that is, in the volume of commodities or of transactions. In times of activity more goods are produced. Moreover those which are produced pass from hand to hand oftener, — there is more buying and selling between the various middlemen. In other words, the demand for money, or the quantity of goods offered in exchanges, increases. In consequence there is a greater resort to banks for credit facilities, a greater creation of deposits, and so an increase in the supply of purchasing power. This double or sympathetic increase shows itself most strikingly as regards transactions on the great exchanges, — the stock exchange, grain exchange, cotton exchange. Here greater volume of sales goes *pari passu* with an increase of loans and deposits and greater clearings at the clearing houses. Something of the same sort takes place in ordinary mercantile transactions.

All this holds good, however, only for a while. In the long

run, the general relation between deposits and reserves works itself out. The period in which that relation has no immediate effect may indeed be a considerable one. During a stage of depression, and during the early stages of a period of rising activity, the course of prices seems to depend most on the temper of the banks and of the business community. Without some basis of cash reserve the banks could not indeed expand their operations; but whether the basis be broad or narrow seems to matter little. When a period of depression has lasted for a time, hope begins to revive, at first slowly, then more briskly. The low rates of discount at the banks are found tempting, and the banks find it possible to extend their loans. Business gradually becomes more active, more goods are produced, and more are sold. The upward movement, once begun, goes on *crescendo*, until the rush of a full tide of activity is reached. Then deposits are large as compared with reserves, money is tight, the rate of discount is high, and even the rate of interest on permanent investments shows a sympathetic rise. The final halt to the movement commonly comes from a commercial panic, followed by another period of depression, with large bank reserves and low discount.

Thus there is only a rough and uncertain correspondence of bank expansion with bank reserves; much play for ups and downs which have no close relation to the amount of cash in bank vaults, and still less direct relation to the amount of money afloat in the community at large. Where bank media, whether in the form of deposits or notes, are an important part of total purchasing power, the connection between general prices and the quantity of "money" is irregular and uncertain.

§ 7. The second of the general forces which limit the potential effect of credit devices, especially deposits, is found in the working of foreign trade. In the discussion of this topic, something is necessarily anticipated; but the principles important for the present purpose are simple, and need not wait for the full treatment of the theory of international trade.[1]

[1] See the discussion of international trade in the next Book, especially Chapters 33 and 34.

When countries trade with each other, using a common medium of exchange, the level of prices in one is not independent of that in the others. The different countries do not, indeed, have the same prices, — of this, more hereafter. But the price levels maintain themselves in the same relations. If one country's prices rise above its normal range, there is a tendency for imports to flow into it, and for specie to flow out. And if its prices fall below the normal range, its exports increase and specie flows in.

Now, as has been repeatedly pointed out, the wide use of deposits as a medium of exchange is confined to the English-speaking countries. On the continent of Europe this sort of credit machinery is comparatively ineffective. Though notes are largely used, they are by no means put forth under such conditions of freedom, or with such potential effects, as deposits in England and the United States. Hence the connection between total purchasing power and the volume of tangible money — specie and obvious paper substitutes — is much closer on the Continent. The simpler form of the quantity theory comes much nearer to fitting the facts. This is still more true of the outlying industrial regions of South America, Asia, Africa. A rise in prices in England or the United States, due perhaps to one of the periodic bursts of business activity and banking expansion, affects trade with the rest of the world. It stimulates imports, and tends to a drain of specie. The same sort of upward movement may indeed show itself elsewhere; these oscillations have often an international sweep; but none the less a call for specie is likely to come from countries whose credit machinery is less highly developed. Hence a drain of specie to other countries will occur sooner or later as a check on the upward movement of prices in those countries whose credit machinery contains the greatest possibilities of rapid expansion.

This cause acts slowly. Moreover, it seems to operate fitfully, because the currents of international trade are affected by other causes also, among which this fundamental one is often concealed. Yet none the less it is fundamental. Prices cannot rise in one country alone; sooner or later all countries must share in the advance. In most countries of the world, prices cannot rise without a real increase in "money." Hence they cannot rise for any considerable time or to any great extent, in the credit-using countries, unless in all other countries a parallel advance takes place, resting on more copious money.

§ 8. By way of illustrating the principles just stated, let us consider the conditions under which a world-wide advance can take place; in other words, consider the mode in which a marked increase of specie will affect prices. Suppose a greatly enlarged production at the mines, such as has taken place during the last decade or two: through what mechanism will prices be influenced?

The gold from the mines goes first to the mints of the mining countries or of the countries with which they have closest connection. The gold output of the United States goes to the American mints for coinage into eagles and the like; that of Australia to the Australian mints; and that of South Africa chiefly to England. In these countries the gold, after being coined, finds its way first into the vaults of banks, either directly as coin, or in the form of gold certificates or Bank of England notes.[1] If this happens in a period of dull trade, it simply swells bank reserves, and tends to lower even more the market rate of discount. It is very likely to lead to a prompt overflow of the gold to other countries, and especially to the continent of Europe, before the gold can have had any influences whatever on prices or general activity. As will appear more fully hereafter, the money and banking markets of the leading countries are in close connection, and a flow of specie from one to another takes place under slight inducement. None the less, an effect on credit extension and on prices is likely to appear first in the countries to which the gold first goes. It is most likely to appear in them when, for some inscrutable reason, the spirit of commercial adventure has begun to be stirred. If the gold happens to come

[1] In the United States this may take place even without coinage; for gold certificates are issued against the deposit of gold in bars.

in when that spirit has already been aroused; or if, after activity has begun, still further supplies come in, — then all the elements of rapid expansion are present. Then other countries will be affected sooner or later. Some part of the specie will overflow to them, and an expansion take place in them also, more or less rapid according as their monetary and credit machinery is responsive. If new supplies of gold are constantly coming in from the mines, the steady outflow from the mining countries and their immediate connections is made good by the fresh additions, and there is no direct obstacle to the maintenance of the enlarged superstructure of credit. This superstructure will continue to enlarge, under the stimulus of pervading optimism, until at last it becomes top-heavy. More is built up on the basis of the specie, enlarged though it be, than can long be sustained. Reserves become comparatively slender, the rate of discount rises, and, in the language of the financial markets, money becomes scarce and dear. A commercial crisis is apt to ensue; then a period of dullness and superabundant reserves; eventually a new start and the repetition of the old round. As the years go on a general though irregular advance in prices comes about; more rapid in times of expansion, checked in times of depression; earlier in some countries than in others; affecting different commodities to a greater or less degree, according to seasonal conditions, adjustability of production, variations in utility and demand, — yet on the whole unmistakable if the observations extend over some time and cover a wide range of countries and commodities.

Something like this happened in the decade following the Californian and Australian gold discoveries of 1850; something like this happened again during the ten or fifteen years after 1895. In the long run an increase in the supply of specie or gold, greater than in proportion to the increased supply of commodities, works out its effects on general prices.

§ 9. Among schemes for monetary reform which have been proposed is one for an automatic injection and withdrawal of money according as prices fall or rise. For example, it has been proposed that government paper shall be injected into circulation on the basis of officially constructed index numbers. When these index numbers indicate that prices are falling, let more money be put forth; when rising, let some money be retired. The process of impounding an excess might take place by hoarding ordinary receipts for public dues, or by selling securities on terms which would attract investors.

All proposals of this sort rest on the naïve form of the quantity theory. They assume that prices respond promptly and in precise proportion to changes in the quantity of specie or of money equivalent in its mode of action to specie. The truth is that in our complex modern communities the connection between prices and the quantity of money is not a close one or one as to which prediction is easy. An increase in specie may go for some time with falling prices, a diminution with rising prices. An injection of additional money by government fiat might very easily have at one time no effect whatever in stemming falling prices, and at another time might plague its inventors with vastly greater consequences of inflation than they had foreseen. This holds good equally of specie and of inconvertible government paper.

The monetary situation in which the world now finds itself is far from an ideal one. Prices are affected in a seemingly chaotic way; not only by the variations in the supply of specie, in the volume of commodities, in the ways and habits of people in using money and dealing with goods; not only by the more or less spasmodic legislation of the several countries, — but by the ups and downs of credit operations which obey no law but that of inconstancy. Yet it is difficult to see how any far-reaching change can be made, short of a complete revolution of industry. The abolition of private property and the adoption of some form of socialism or collectivism would indeed bring an entirely different mode of carrying on the division of labor and the exchange of commodities. But as long as mankind maintain, rightly or wrongly, the institution of private property, with its essential corollaries of production and investment, and sale and exchange, so long some degree of monetary fluctuation seems unavoidable. Nor does it seem possible to find a better basis for the circulating medium than solid specie,—in our own time, none better than gold. The best check to the irregular fluctuations in the uses of credit devices is that they shall rest securely on specie, and that all forms of them shall be redeemable without fail in specie. So long as this is done, there will be neither very wide fluctuations in the course of any one generation, nor very abrupt fluctuations at any time. For the rest, the drawbacks to the present situation, serious as they are, must be accepted as part of the price to be paid for the general gains from private property and free enterprise.

§ 10. One last topic may be touched briefly: what is "money"? The reader will have noticed that in some previous passages this word has been used in quotation marks, indicating that the sense attaching to it is not certain. What does the word usually mean, and in what sense is it best used?

"Money" usually means whatever passes readily from hand to hand in settlement of transactions. It includes specie, of course; not only full-value specie, but overvalued specie and subsidiary coin. It includes bank notes and government notes convertible into specie. It includes paper, even though not convertible, so long as this in fact passes freely. The term thus does not cover all of that total purchasing power in terms of money which, as we have seen, is the proximate force in making prices. It does not include the great item of deposits. It therefore describes only a part of the circulating medium.

Suggestions have been made for the use of a word or phrase which should connote the whole medium of exchange. It has been proposed that "money" itself should be used in this wider sense. The term "currency" has been used to include everything that passes in effecting transactions, — so including deposits in their active stage of the check. But proposals for deliberate changes in economic terminology have never borne much fruit. The writers who have advanced them have not always acted consistently in accord with their own advice, reverting unconsciously to the use of the familiar words in the familiar senses; still less has there been any general consensus toward a change. Hence the term "money" is most conveniently used in the accepted popular sense. Sometimes what is laid down in regard to money will hold good of all the circulating medium, the context indicating sufficiently the range of application of the word. Sometimes it will mean "cash" only, in the stricter sense. Where it is of importance to discriminate, use may be made of the phrases "circulating medium" or "machinery of exchange," cumbrous though they are.

References on Book III

On money, K. Helfferich, *Das Geld* (2d ed., 1910), is an excellent descriptive and analytical book. On the theory of money and prices, I. Fisher, *The Purchasing Power of Money* (1911), also an excellent book, was published just as the present volume was going to press; I am glad to find its conclusions in essential accord with my own. An entirely different mode of reasoning, and different conclusions, which I find myself unable to accept, are in J. L. Laughlin, *The Principles of Money* (1903). J. F. Johnson, *Money and Currency*, has convenient accounts of the monetary history of various countries, but is of no value on questions of theory.

On banking, C. F. Dunbar, *Chapters on the Theory and History of Banking* (ed. by O. M. W. Sprague, 1900), is a little classic, and contains also abundant references. H. Withers, *The Meaning of Money*, gives a lucid and interesting account of banking conditions in Great Britain. C. A. Conant, *A History of Modern Banks of Issue*, is useful for its descriptive matter. A vast mass of information on the banking problems and experiences of recent years is in the Publications of the National Monetary Commission (1909–1911); ably reviewed by W. C. Mitchell in *Quarterly Journal of Economics*, May, 1911.

On the questions of principle underlying bimetallism, see L. Darwin, *Bimetallism* (1898). The same questions are considered in Helfferich, *Das Geld* (1910), already referred to. Consult, also, J. L. Laughlin, *History of Bimetallism in the United States;* H. P. Willis, *A History of the Latin Monetary Union* (1901); A. P. Andrew, "The End of the Mexican Dollar," in *Quarterly Journal of Economics*, Vol. XVIII, p. 321 (May, 1904).

On index numbers and methods of measuring prices, W. S. Jevons, *Investigations in Currency and Finance* (1884), though of older date, is still to be read, as among the most interesting and stimulating on this topic. See also Professor F. Y. Edgeworth's brilliant memorandum, in *Report of the British Association for the Advancement of Science*,

1887, pp. 247–303; and C. M. Walsh, *The Measurement of General Exchange Value* (1901).

On rising and falling prices in relation to the rate of interest, see I. Fisher, *Appreciation and Interest, Public. Am. Econ. Assoc.*, First Series, Vol. XI (1896), and the same writer's *The Rate of Interest* (1907), Chapters V and XIV. See also two papers by J. B. Clark, in the *Political Science Quarterly*, Vol. X, p. 389, and Vol. XI, p. 259 (1896, 1897), and criticism of these by C. M. Walsh, "The Steadily Appreciating Standard," *Quarterly Journal of Economics*, Vol. XI, p. 280 (1897).

Notwithstanding the abundant literature on crises, there is no good book on the underlying questions of principle. Good historical books are: C. Juglar, *Des crises commerciales et de leur retour périodique en France, en Angleterre, et aux États-Unis* (2d ed., 1889), and O. M. W. Sprague, *A History of Crises under the National Banking System* (1910; published by the National Monetary Commission).

BOOK IV

INTERNATIONAL TRADE

CHAPTER 32

The Foreign Exchanges

§ 1. The mechanism of international trade is not essentially different from that of domestic trade. It is part of the ordinary machinery of exchange; and it is closely connected with the banking operations and monetary phenomena of the several countries. Indeed, the whole theory of international trade presents no fundamental peculiarities: it is but a phase of the general theory of exchange value. But it has been so much debated, is so beset by political and national prejudice, and is so peculiarly tinged by error in popular discussion, that there is advantage from treating it separately.

International trade, like virtually all the trade of modern countries, is carried on in terms of money, and through sales for money by individuals. Like all other trade, it brings in the end the same result as barter — the exchange of goods or services for other goods or services. But proximately it means sales for money. We may advantageously begin our consideration of it by taking up first the money mechanism through which it is carried out.

When a merchant sells goods to a person in the same country, the mode of payment is simple: he receives the money of his own country. But when he sells to one in another country, it is not so simple. Transactions in England are settled in pounds, shillings and pence; those in the United States in dollars and cents. The American who sells in England may sell there in terms of English money; he must then convert the English pounds into American dollars before they are available for him. Or, if he sells in England in terms of American money, he puts the English purchaser under the obligation of converting into dollars the pounds which alone are current in England.

This process of converting the money of one country into its equivalent in the money of other countries is carried out through foreign bills of exchange. Strictly speaking, a bill of exchange is simply an order by one person, addressed to another, directing a payment to be made to a third person. It thus has three parties: the maker or drawer, drawee or acceptor, and the payee. When made out in the precise form settled by the law, it fixes a guarantee on the maker to pay the stated sum, in case the drawee does not do so; and, when accepted by the drawee (he thus becoming the "acceptor") it fixes unconditional obligation upon him to pay it when due. Bills of exchange are freely used in domestic transactions, and are then known as inland bills. A check is but a kind of inland bill of exchange, drawn by a depositor on a bank in favor of a third person. Foreign bills of exchange have no legal peculiarities. Their economic peculiarities (not such as to involve any essential differences) arise only from the differences in the currency systems of the various countries. In the following pages, when bills of exchange are spoken of, foreign bills will be meant. The mechanism of payment in foreign trade through such bills is usually called "the foreign exchanges," — a term which might as appropriately be used to describe exchange between different countries in all its phases, but is limited by custom to the dealings in foreign bills.

For simplicity in exposition, let us suppose that the only transactions leading to the use of bills of exchange are those by which goods are sold. We shall see presently that there are other transactions of no small importance, but the main principles are most easily explained in connection with merchandise transactions.

A merchant in New York who sells goods to a merchant in London has a claim to receive money from the latter; he can draw on the Englishman for the price. He can draw directly or he can transfer his right. That is, an exporter has bills of exchange for sale. On the other hand, a merchant in New York who has bought goods from a merchant in London has an obligation to pay money to this Englishman; he must remit in some way the price. That is, an importer needs to buy bills of exchange. We are supposing here, again for simplicity, that both transactions are carried on in New York; the exporter sells his bill on London in New York, the importer buys his bill on London in New York. Suppose now that the two obligations are for the same amount, say £1000. The importer can buy from the exporter the latter's bill, drawn on his London debtor for that amount. The importer sends the bill to his London creditor; the latter collects the sum from the London debtor. The New York creditor gets his money from the New York debtor, and the London creditor gets his money from the London debtor. By one payment in New York and another in London, the transactions are liquidated without any sending of specie from one country to the other. Through the mechanism of the bill of exchange, the exports serve to pay for the imports.

§ 2. What amount, now, would the New York importer pay, in American money, to the New York exporter? One thousand British sovereigns contain as much pure gold as $4866. Hence, when a bill for £1000 sells for $4866, its precise specie equivalent, exchange is said to be at par. If the American creditor sent to England for his money, brought the gold from London to the United States, and had it coined into American dollars, he would get from the mint this exact number of dollars, $4866.

Suppose, now, a number of exporters and importers in both countries, and a large volume of dealings: the case remains the same. The exporters sell bills, the importers buy them. If the money value of the imports just equals the money value of the exports, the bills of exchange exactly liquidate the transactions. Under such circumstances, exchange will be at par. Foreign trade will be in a state of equilibrium, the exports will just pay for the imports, and no specie will flow from one country to the other.

Suppose, next, that for some reason the exports from the United States exceed the imports in money value. The two sets of transactions — the buying of goods from persons in

England, and the selling of goods to persons in that country — are quite independent. The American exporters may sell goods to a greater money value than that of the goods which the importers have to pay for. They will then offer bills for a greater amount than the importers have occasion to buy. Under these circumstances all the bills cannot be sold to importers. Some will necessarily be left over. The exporters who have the excess on their hands can do nothing but send to England for the specie. This, however, involves expense. The specie must be checked with care, must be boxed, insured, transported by land and water. When it reaches the American creditor, it must be carried to the mint and coined into American dollars, — a process which may take some time. There is the possibility that some of the sovereigns may not be quite full weight, even though not below the limit of tolerance in England. Not least, there is a loss of interest during the period which elapses before the cash is available in the United States. All these circumstances make the American exporter willing to sell a bill for £1000 for a less sum than par, — less than $4866. The amount of reduction to which he will submit, will be only such as offsets the total expense of sending to England for the specie. That expense is surprisingly small, — between England and the United States, somewhere about one half of one per cent. The bill of exchange for £1000 will not sell for less than $4845, or $4.845 to the pound. This is called the specie-importing point. When foreign exchange is at this point, specie begins to come in.

Under these conditions, *all* of the exporters' bills will be at a discount: all will sell for less than their par value. Competition being active between the exporters, no one of them will be willing to sell his bill for a less price than the others. The expense of shipping specie will have to be met by some one or other among them; to each one it is immaterial whether he will sell his bill at a discount or will send for specie. The market rate for all bills, when there is a clear excess of exports, will be at the specie-importing point.

The reverse situation appears when the imports exceed the exports. The importers then need to buy more bills than the exporters can supply. Some of them will have to send out specie, and this involves the same sort of expense as bringing specie in. An importer who has to remit to London can afford to pay more than $4866 for a bill of £1000, rather than send specie. He will pay as much, say, as $4885. If called on to pay more than $4885, he will refuse; for he can ship $4866 to England, and have this coin there converted into sovereigns.[1] Foreign exchange in New York will be at a premium, the extent of that premium being limited by all the expenses involved in transporting specie. The specie-exporting point, determined by these expenses, is about $4.885. When there is a clear excess of imports over exports, exchange will be at this premium; and, in like manner as in the other case, all the importers will have to pay this premium, although most of the transactions are liquidated through bills.

§ 3. These are the simplest supposable conditions. They are rarely met in real life. Here, as in almost all the buying and selling of modern communities, a class of middlemen intervenes. The exporters and importers do not deal directly with each other; neither do they concern themselves with the possibilities of shipping specie in or out. They go to the dealers in foreign exchange. These are sometimes firms which make a specialty of this sort of business, the so-called foreign-exchange houses; sometimes they are banking firms which join it with other business. All these middlemen buy exchange constantly from the exporters, and sell it constantly to the importers. They have their well-known correspondents in foreign countries, either branch houses of their own, or other banking firms; they sell bills on these, and meet bills drawn by these. When the exporters offer more bills than the importers will presum-

[1] Foreign coin, or bullion, when it reaches England, is always taken to the Issue Department of the Bank of England, which is obliged by law to give notes for gold at a fixed rate, involving a very slight charge to the holder of the gold. The Bank of England thus acts as intermediary for the conversion of bullion and foreign coin into English money.

ably take, the dealers none the less buy them; only, calculating that there will be no market for all the bills, and that some will have to be sent abroad and specie got with them, they will buy only at a discount. On the other hand, when the importers demand more bills than the exporters have to offer, the dealers sell to the importers, at a premium, whatever bills the latter want, and themselves send abroad the specie with which to meet these bills when presented. Being in the business and equipped for it, they can ship specie more economically than the importers or exporters. Though they make a profit, it is based on a very narrow margin.

With the presence of dealers comes that process of close bargaining, speculation, equalization, which naturally ensues with the specialization of trade. From the description just given of the simple case, — that of exporters selling directly to importers, — it might be inferred that if there was any discount at all or any premium at all, it would be up to the full limit set by the expense of shipping specie. But with the higgling and speculation among dealers, a discount or premium will appear which may be much within these limits. If, for example, more bills are offered by exporters at a given time than the importers are buying, the dealers may yet anticipate with confidence that before long a turn will come the other way, and that at the later time the importers' demands will be in excess. They will buy the exporters' bills, and wait for the turn. Possibly they will hold the bills in their own hands for a while; possibly they will send the bills to their foreign correspondents, tell these to collect the money from the foreign debtors, and hold the amounts until drawn against later. The current rates of interest on demand loans and short-time loans are important factors in these operations. If "money" is cheap (the rate of interest is low) in the dealer's own country, he will more readily buy exporters' bills, and pay a better price for them. If money, again, is dear in the foreign country, he will also buy such bills more readily, since he can send them to the foreign country and there get a balance to his credit on which interest at a good rate is allowed. To figure out the price at which it is profitable to buy or sell exchange, calls for nice calculation of a number of items each involving a very small fraction, — the direct expense of transportation, the mint charges and delays, the rates of interest in different countries, the probabilities of shifting currents of trade. Competition among the dealers leads to a market rate somewhere between the two specie points.

If, indeed, there is a continued balance of payments to be made one way or the other, — if there is a steady and considerable excess of imports or of exports, — then exchange goes to the shipping point, and specie flows in or out. The operations of dealers may enable the imports and exports to catch up with each other, and so may postpone the shipment of specie; but where there is continuing excess one way or the other, it moves in or out.

In the examples here chosen, we have spoken as if all the transactions in foreign exchange took place in New York, — as if the London merchants were passive, and waited for those in New York to buy and sell exchange, and remit bills to London in settlement of the debts. In fact some of the transactions take place in each country. Which of the trading persons shall take the initiative in any particular case, depends on the bargain between them. It may be arranged that the New York exporter shall draw on his London customer, and so sell in New York exchange on London; or the London customer may assume an obligation to remit to this New York vendor, and so buy in London exchange on New York. Both sorts of transactions are going on all the time, and in both centers exchange between London and New York is constantly being dealt in. When in New York English exchange is at a premium, then in London American exchange is at a discount. All the transactions are under the watchful eyes of the dealers; a remarkably close equalization of rates is brought about; while, at the same time, there is play for profit and speculation in terms of a small fraction of one per cent.

Bankers' bills, so-called, — the bills drawn by dealers and bankers on their foreign correspondents, — naturally sell for a somewhat higher price than most mercantile or trade bills. They contain the names of persons and firms well-known in the business world. Again, sight bills naturally sell for a higher price than time bills. Foreign sales of merchandise, like domestic sales, are usually on time. The exporter who has sold goods is then entitled to receive his money at the end of thirty days, sixty days, or whatever the period for which credit is given. He draws his bill payable after thirty or sixty days, and discounts it at his bank. The bank, if it deals in foreign exchange itself, perhaps holds the bill till maturity, perhaps sends it abroad at once to its foreign correspondent; or sells it to a dealer in foreign exchange, at once or on maturity. The price at which it will sell depends on the length of time it has to run, on the current rate of discount, on the calculations of the probable state of foreign exchange at its maturity. These minutiæ, and others, need not here be entered on. They do not affect the broad questions of principle regarding money, prices, and international trade with which we are chiefly concerned.

§ 4. The rates of foreign exchange are determined, not by the dealings between each separate pair of countries, but by those between a country and all the other countries with which it trades. The exports from the United States to England may much exceed the imports — in fact, they do greatly exceed them every year; but exchange, none the less, may be at par, if the United States imports heavily from other countries.

This situation is illustrated by the state of trade between the United States, England (*i.e.* Great Britain), and Brazil. The United States exports great quantities of cotton and foodstuffs to England; much greater in value than the manufactures which it imports from England. England exports manufactures to Brazil, greater in value than her imports from that country. Brazil, again, exports largely to the United States (chiefly coffee), but imports thence comparatively little. A merchant in New York who has bought coffee from one in Brazil could not easily find an American exporter who had bills of exchange on Rio Janeiro or Bahia to sell. But he could find plenty of exporters who had sold grain and cotton in England, and had bills on London and Liverpool to sell. He buys English exchange and with this pays his debt in Brazil. Bills on London are welcome to the Brazilians, since in that country there are payments to be made for purchases of English goods. All these exchange transactions, of course, do not take place directly between exporters and importers, but through the bankers, who buy and sell the bills, and take keen advantage of every opportunity for equalizing payments without the shipment of specie. Thus by the mechanism of bills of exchange, the exports of grain from the United States to England serve to pay for the imports of coffee from Brazil to the United States; and these same shipments of coffee, viewed as exports from Brazil, serve to pay for Brazil's imports of manufactures from England.

Sterling exchange bills, drawn on London, are the most widely used in international transactions, and especially in settling cross payments between different countries. Great Britain's enormous international trade ramifies into all parts of the world. Many English banks and firms have well-established repute as dealers in foreign exchange. For a century or two England has had great industrial prestige; and the pound sterling is the best-known unit of value for the whole trading world. Hence foreign-exchange transactions are apt to be settled through London, and by bills drawn on London. These are freely used by foreign-exchange houses in settlements among themselves, and enable them to supply bills for the payments which their customers need to make, — either bills on, say, Brazil itself, or bills on London which are freely usable in Brazil.

The total exports of a country are thus to be balanced by its total imports, and the state of the foreign exchanges depends on the whole of its international trade. England exports manufactured goods to all parts of the world, and with these pays for her imports of foodstuffs and raw materials, of which she procures a large part from the United States. The United States, again, buys tea, coffee, cocoa, spices, sugar, and the like, from tropical and semi-tropical countries, and mainly pays for them, not by direct exports to these countries, but by exports of grain, meat products, and cotton, to England and other European countries. If there is a general excess of imports over exports, foreign exchange is at a premium, and specie tends to flow out; while a general excess of exports brings exchange to a discount, and causes an inflow of specie.

§ 5. Suppose, now, that the total exports do not suffice to pay for the total imports. Then they must be paid for in specie. Will that specie flow out for an indefinite time? and what likelihood is there that a balance will permanently remain to be paid in this way?

The accepted answer to these questions, and in essentials the accurate one, is that the flow of specie sets in motion forces which sooner or later stop the flow. When specie leaves a country, prices tend to fall. Hence that country becomes one in which it is advantageous to buy. Lower prices stimulate exports. Conversely, the country to which specie flows tends to have rising prices. It becomes one in which it is advantageous to sell. Higher prices stimulate imports. Hence the flow of specie has an automatic limitation. The greater it is, the more certain is it likely to cease; the longer it has gone on, the sooner is it likely to cease. Merchandise exports and imports on the whole and in the long run balance, in consequence of the effect of the quantity of money on prices.

This is the answer in its simplest form; it is the statement of the fundamental principle. But, like other economic principles, it holds true of the course of industry only in general and in the long run. In details, it needs to be qualified and explained in various ways.

The modern mechanism of banking, currency, and international trade may be said to have an innate repugnance to the flow of gold from country to country. All sorts of devices are resorted to in order to prevent or lessen such a flow.

Most familiar and effective among these devices is regulation through the rate of discount. Gold, like any other form of money, is free capital, or command of capital goods; and it is, moreover, the kind of capital which is in every country equally available. It tends to go to the place where the return on loanable funds is largest. When specie first moves out of a country, it comes ordinarily from the bank reserves; and when it goes into a country, it goes ordinarily into the bank reserves. The rate of discount rises as bank holdings become less, and falls as they become greater. These changes of themselves tend to counteract the movement of specie in large quantities. The great central banks of England, Germany, France, Austria, and other countries systematically raise or lower their rate of discount in order to protect their specie holdings. The same thing happens, though with less direct and conscious intent, in New York.[1]

Often the changes in the rate of discount affect not so much the volume of the flow of gold, as its date and direction. A rise in the rate brings an additional pressure to bear on those foreign-exchange dealers who may be preparing for a shipment of specie. Higher interest on money makes it more profitable to keep the money at home. It tempts bankers to wait until perhaps the currents of foreign trade turn and enable the demand for exchange

[1] The "protection" of specie holdings through the rate of discount is often referred to as one of the advantages of central banks. They are supposed to control the flow better than non-centralized banks. The difference in effectiveness seems to me not considerable, and the argument for centralization on this score of no great weight. Lurking underneath the argument there is often a relic of older notions as to the importance of retaining specie in a country, and the harm from losing specie, — a notion strengthened by the repugnance of the business community toward anything which tends to lower prices. In the main, the flow of specie takes care of itself, and brings neither loss nor gain to a country.

Of course a country whose currency is top-heavy, with a large structure of credit on a slender basis of specie, may be much disturbed by a moderate outflow of specie. This is likely to be the case, above all, in a country which has had inconvertible paper, and has proceeded to resumption of specie payments without having retired a large part of the paper. Compare what is said in Chapter 23, § 4; Chapter 33, § 5.

to be met without the shipment. Or it may lead such persons to arrange for shipment of specie from some other country. If reserves are low and discount rates high in England, and the contrary is the case in Germany, English bankers may buy exchange on Germany, and thereby secure the means of shipping specie from Germany to the United States. Very sharp calculations and very minute fractions in rates (both in rates of discount and rates of exchange) suffice to turn the currents one way or another.

Still another phase of international dealings affects an incipient flow of specie and consequent changes in bank discount, — the movement of securities from one country to another. This is part of the general process of lending and borrowing between nations, of which more will be said in the next chapter. It suffices here to point out that the prices of securities in any one country are usually affected inversely to the rate of discount, rising as this falls, and falling as this rises. Hence securities which have an international market are likely to be sent in place of specie in settling balances. There are brokerage firms which make it a business to watch the fluctuations of such securities in the different markets, — London, Berlin, Paris, New York, — and to buy in the one and sell in the other, on very slight margins of profit; and these dealings are closely dependent on the foreign exchange market and in turn are of prompt effect on that market.

None the less, all devices of whatever sort do not prevent the movement of gold, or its ultimate effect on prices. They serve only to regulate and equalize it, — to prevent it from taking place in a rush or from having sudden and rapidly disturbing effects. When there is a long-continued balance of payments in favor of a country, specie flows into it. Gold, in fact, is constantly moving from country to country. Hardly a month passes without some shipment of it into or out of each of the important countries. This is particularly the case with England, which, being the center of dealings in foreign exchange, is also an international distributing center for gold. Almost every week gold is shipped into England and out of England, — the result being usually a very small net change for England herself, but on frequent occasions a considerable diversion in the flow to or from some other country. When there is a balance of payments to be made to any one country because of a considerable and sustained excess of its exports, the current of gold moves in that direction from England and perhaps from other countries also, and keeps on moving, until gradually equalization is brought about by changes in prices and by a restored balance between the countries.

Sometimes this result is reached without any movement of gold at all, or with a movement that seems not at all in proportion to the result. A country may be issuing paper money, or increasing its bank notes or deposits, — operations which in themselves tend to expel gold. Then what happens is that the country retains both its paper and more or less of its gold, and gets rising prices without any influx of the metal. Again, the country may be one that mines gold. Ordinarily a mining country exports gold in the normal course of its international trade; but when its exports of other things are heavy, it may retain within its own borders the gold which would otherwise go out. The United States is an important gold-mining country, yet for several decades has kept within her borders the whole product of her mines; indeed, has imported a substantial amount of gold in addition. The supply of specie thus gradually accumulated has been the result of a constant excess of exports, and has been the basis of a tendency toward higher prices.

The consequence of all these modifying factors is that the flow of gold from country to country takes place, as a rule, not by large movements at any one time, but by driblets going sometimes one way, sometimes another; often by little-noticed diversions of the fresh supplies from mines. The comparative smallness of the ordinary flow is due mainly to the fact that international trade, long-maintained, has already brought about such a distribution of the precious metals, and such a range of prices in the several countries, that their exchanges balance very closely. It is only when great industrial changes occur that a large movement of specie takes place; and even then it is commonly distributed over a period of several years. Our own country, anomalous in so many of its economic characteristics, presents in this matter also the most marked exceptions to the usual situation. Not infrequently — as, for example, in 1879–1880, immediately after the resumption of specie payments, and again in 1896–1897, after the close of a severe period of depression — a great change in the relations of our imports and exports has caused rapid and heavy inflows of gold, giving the foundation for a rapid and sharp rise in prices.

So insignificant are the ordinary currents of gold from one country to another, so likely to be disguised by eddies and cross currents due to the complexity of international dealings, that some writers have pooh-poohed the whole theory of the equalization of imports and exports by changes in international prices. Yet without this theory it is impossible to explain the facts, and especially the adjustment of the money value of exports and imports. The influence of the quantity of gold on prices, slow-moving as it is, and subject to all sorts of disturbing causes, is the underlying persistent force which determines not only the international distribution of specie, but also, as will appear in the chapters that follow, the variations in the purchasing power of gold in different countries, and the greater or less extent in which those countries share the gains from international trade.

§ 6. The foreign exchanges between most countries rest on the equivalents of different gold coins, — dollars, pounds, marks, francs, and so on. But not all countries are on a gold basis; and where there are monetary systems having different foundations, there is obviously a complication in the foreign exchanges.

British India, for example, was, until 1893, on a silver basis, the monetary unit being the silver rupee. The trade of India was chiefly with Great Britain, whose currency was on a gold basis. The British exporter who sold goods in India had a bill of exchange to sell on that country, — that is, a bill payable in silver. The Indian exporter who sold goods in England had for sale a bill of exchange payable in gold. The price of each bill of exchange was affected, of course, by the ordinary fluctuations in the foreign exchanges, — the relations of imports and exports and the excess or deficiency of bills for making the payments required. But it was affected no less directly by the gold price of silver; and for many years this was the main determining influence. As silver fell in price, the English exporter's bill on India became less valuable in England; it was one for which he could get less sovereigns. Under the same conditions — falling price of silver — the Indian exporter had in India a more valuable bill, one for which he could get more rupees. This situation operated to stimulate exports from India to Great Britain, and to check exports from Great Britain to India. There was something in the nature of a bounty on exports from India, — one which caused bitter complaint among those whose industries were affected by Indian competition.

This situation, instead of leading to readjustment with some promptness, as it would have done between advanced countries, persisted because prices in India did not accommodate themselves to the new relation between gold and silver. Silver flowed into India, and prices did rise in that country. But they rose very slowly in this huge and sluggish population of hundreds of millions, with its semi-medieval conditions and great tenacity of custom. The large use of silver in the arts, especially for ornaments, diverted much of it from monetary channels. Moreover, the fall in the gold price of silver went on year after year; and, though prices of commodities in India might rise a bit, the continuing fall in the price of silver still served to maintain a discrepancy between prices of commodities on the one hand, and the market price of silver and the rates of foreign exchange on the other. Imports and exports were thus affected by an unusual set of forces, — proximately by abnormal foreign exchange, but really by the slow process of adjustment in India to the new price of silver.[1]

§ 7. Similar disturbing effects are produced by inconvertible paper money. Where such money has displaced specie, and where higher prices and a premium on gold have ensued, there are again two sets of influences on the foreign exchanges, — the ordinary shifts in the balance of payments due to exports and imports, and the depreciation of the paper. During the period of paper money in the United States from 1862 to 1879, bills of exchange on London sold in New York at a price determined mainly by the price of gold in our paper money. A bill on London was the equivalent of gold; that is, of gold obtainable at the maturity of the bill and subject to delay until it could be brought over from London. When exports were comparatively heavy, London exchange sold at a premium less than equivalent to the current gold premium; when imports were comparatively heavy, London exchange sold at a premium more than equivalent. Of the causes of fluctuations in foreign exchange under such conditions, those that root in the domestic gold premium are usually more important than those that affect the price of exchange considered by itself; because the limits of fluctuation in exchange proper are narrow, while those of the specie premium are potentially wide. And at such times the price of foreign exchange is a sensitive indication of the state of the paper. A premium on exchange, greater than that of the gold-shipping point, is usually the first sign of depreciation. Even before a premium on gold appears directly, an abnormally high price of exchange points to a difficulty in getting specie and to a beginning of depreciation.

As with silver, so with paper, a discordance between the premium on the paper and the rise in the general prices may

[1] The government of India, as has already been noted (see Book III, Chapter 21, § 5), put an end to this peculiar situation in 1893 by stopping the free coinage of silver and by making the rupee virtually an inconvertible money. Thereafter the artificial price at which the rupee was maintained, and the price of Indian exchange, went together; in fact, the price of exchange on England registered and determined the price of the rupee.

have an effect on international trade. That effect, again, has the appearance of being wrought by the foreign exchanges, yet in truth is due to the discordance between the price of foreign bills (*i.e.* the specie premium) and the range of prices. It has been pointed out [1] that the specie premium does not go up and down in any exact correspondence with general prices. When it is higher than prices, exports are stimulated, since the exporter, selling in a (foreign) gold market, gets more of the current paper money. This same influence, of course, causes the prices of exported commodities to go up, and stimulates exports; they feel the inflation more than most commodities. On the other hand, a specie premium lower than general prices stimulates imports, since the importer finds it easier to pay for his goods; hence imports grow heavier and eventually cheaper. Some writers have supposed that a depreciated paper currency always acts as a stimulus on exports and a check on imports. But there seems to be no ground for saying that it necessarily acts one way or the other. This sort of influence depends on the divergence between the gold premium and the real depreciation of the paper, which may be in either direction.

The relation of imports to exports, again, has a reciprocal influence on the specie premium. If there be an increase of exports, such as may readily occur because of crop changes or altered demand, more bills are offered on foreign countries (presumably specie countries). Then the price of foreign exchange falls, and the premium on specie necessarily falls with it. In the long run the depreciation of the paper and the specie premium will depend on the quantity of the paper in its relation to the quantity of goods. But the state of foreign trade and the relation of imports to exports has a proximate effect on the exchanges and the specie premium. A country which is preparing to return from paper money to a specie basis finds resumption of specie payments easier if the period fixed

[1] See above, Book III, Chapter 23, § 2.

for the transition happens to be one of large exports and low price of exchange.

§ 8. "Domestic exchange," so-called, presents the same phenomena as foreign exchange, only less conspicuously. In Chicago, exchange on New York is sold, just as in New York exchange on London is sold; and the course of exchange and the limits in the fluctuations are determined in precisely the same way. Payments have to be made constantly in New York by Chicago merchants who have bought goods there; they buy exchange (*i.e.* drafts) on New York. Other merchants in Chicago have sold commodities in New York, and draw on their New York creditors. They sell exchange on New York. As in the case of foreign exchange, all these transactions take places through the bankers as middlemen. When the two debts to be settled are equal, exchange is at par. When there are larger payments to be made in New York than to be demanded thence, money must be sent to New York in settlement of the balance. Then New York exchange, or New York "funds," go to a premium in Chicago. That premium is limited by the cost of shipping money, with the loss of interest during the period of shipment. Both items of expense are of course much smaller than in the corresponding case of foreign exchange. The express companies charge forty cents per $1000 for carrying money from New York to Chicago; the cash goes from one place to the other in twenty-four hours. New York funds in Chicago can go a trifle above or below par, but only a trifle.

Just as foreign exchange settlements are made largely through London as the international financial center, so domestic exchange settlements are made in the United States chiefly through New York as the domestic financial center. When a merchant in Memphis wishes to remit to one in Boston, he commonly sends a draft on New York; for such a draft is acceptable in Boston or in any other place. The banks throughout the country are in constant correspondence with those in the metropolis, remitting to them and drawing on them. The closeness of this relation is of course strengthened by the reserve deposit system of our national banks. The clearing house in New York is a clearing house for the entire country. There drafts meet and are exchanged. To or from New York actual shipments of cash are chiefly made.

So small are the premiums and discounts on domestic exchange that they are commonly not paid by the banks to those of their customers who draw on other places, nor are they charged to customers who have remittances to make in other places. The banks deal in domestic exchange among themselves. Sometimes New York funds in a given city, Chicago or Boston, are at a premium among banks, sometimes at a discount. But the banks as a rule do not trouble their customers with these trifling charges, but supply them with New York drafts at par and take their New York drafts at par.

Before the days of railways and of the safe and expeditious shipment of money, domestic exchange was a serious matter in the United States, more serious than foreign exchange now is. In the first third of the nineteenth century, Cincinnati was as far from New York as was London. The shipment of money, moreover, then meant the shipment of bulky silver. Hence exchange was subject to considerable fluctuations, — fluctuations which were often increased by the disordered state of the country's currency, just as fluctuations in foreign exchange are increased by depreciated paper. One of the most profitable parts of the business of banks in those days was the purchase and sale of domestic exchange; while, on the other hand, the uncertainties of domestic remittances were a serious obstacle to the geographical division of labor within the country. During the time when the Bank of the United States (especially the Second Bank, 1817–1837) was in existence, it did much to lessen these fluctuations and uncertainties, and thereby performed one of its most useful functions. In our own day the establishment of a uniform currency throughout the land, and the vast cheapening and expediting of transportation by railways, have brought the fluctuations in domestic exchange within limits so narrow as to make them almost negligible.

CHAPTER 33

The Balance of International Payments

§ 1. In the preceding chapter, foreign trade has been treated as if imports and exports of merchandise were the only items in the balance of foreign payments. But there are other items, often of great importance.

Among the most considerable of these are lending and borrowing between countries, or rather, lending and borrowing between individuals in different countries. Loans contracted by governments play their part, — public borrowings from persons in foreign countries; but much the larger part of these transactions is between individuals. There is a prevalent mode of speech concerning foreign borrowings, and indeed foreign transactions generally, as if they took place between nations, — as if Germany bought goods from France, and the United States borrowed from England. What really happens is that individuals in one country are buying or borrowing from individuals in another. The habit of personifying countries, while often convenient for brevity, promotes or covers up a misunderstanding of the actual situation, and sometimes foments unreasonable prejudice.

Suppose persons in the United States to borrow from persons in England. In the course of such transactions, entered on with a view to investment in the United States, the English lenders are usually bankers, upon whom American borrowers become entitled to draw for the sums lent. The Americans have bills on London to sell. If imports and exports have balanced before, there are now more bills on London offered in New York than the importers wish to buy. Foreign exchange falls in price and specie flows to the United States. If, indeed, these same borrowing Americans happen to make purchases in England; if, for example, they are railway projectors and buy rails at once in England (a common transaction in the second and third quarters of the nineteenth century), — then they may send their London bills directly to the rail makers in that city. In so far, the loan may be effected by the immediate import of commodities and without any flow of specie. But such a combination of borrowing and purchase is by no means universal. Ordinarily, the borrower wants money, or purchasing power; he may use his purchasing power at home, or in the lender's country, or in a third country. The loan is likely to bring in the first instance a fall in foreign exchange in the borrower's country, and a flow of specie into that country.

If this, however, goes on year after year, the same effect is produced on foreign trade as if there were an excess of imports into England. The flow of specie will not go on indefinitely. There will be an effect on prices in England and the United States, such as will stimulate exports from England and imports into the United States. The imports into the United States will not necessarily be from England; there may be greater American purchases in third countries or greater English sales in third countries, or there may be both. The effect is likely to come gradually and almost insensibly, through a little noticed diversion of the usual flow of specie, and through changes in prices that are slight and seem on the surface due to other causes. But experience has abundantly proved that a continuing balance of this kind, like a continuing balance arising from merchandise transactions, is not liquidated in specie. It is settled by an increase of merchandise exports from the lending country. Such a country shows before long an excess of exports, and this supplies the wherewithal for remittances to the borrowing country.

Transactions of this kind are not usually sporadic. They give rise to a steady flow of remittances, to which the merchandise exports and imports accommodate themselves. For a long time England and France have been lending countries, and Germany has recently become one. Such countries, in the earlier stages of lending, show an excess of merchandise exports over imports, and yet no steady discount on foreign exchange and no outflow of specie. The continuing loans are effected by the exportation of goods. The process is one of which neither the lending individuals nor the exporting merchants are conscious. The influence of specie flow and of changing prices is often gradual, silent, and little observed. Sometimes it is accompanied, in the borrowers' country, by rapidly rising prices, extending credit, active business, speculation, general surface prosperity, and in the end a halt to the movement from an industrial and financial crisis. In the United States crises have commonly been accompanied, during the period of incubation, by heavy borrowing from abroad, at first an inflow of specie, then rising prices, and gradually an increase of imports.

Suppose now that the process of borrowing has gone on for a long series of years. Then another factor enters; and in time the situation is inverted. The borrowers have to pay interest on their loans. As more and more loans are made, the annual interest charge swells. The principal of each loan is remitted once for all; but the interest charge to which it gives rise goes on year after year. In time the interest payments that must be made to the creditors' country will equal, and eventually will exceed, the payments on account of new loans which are made to the debtors' country. To this new situation, also, the imports and exports will in time adapt themselves. The lending country, which at the outset had an excess of exports, will in the end have an excess of imports. From England loans have been made for a century to all parts of the world. Though loans continue still to be made, the interest charges on the old loans now much exceed the amounts newly sent out on principal account. Hence the foreign trade of Great Britain shows a large excess of merchandise imports over exports, — an excess, it is true, due partly to other causes, but mainly due to this one.[1]

[1] The capital sums invested by the British people in other lands are put at the enormous total of £2,700,000,000 ($13,500,000,000), and the amount annually payable to persons in Great Britain at £140,000,000 ($700,000,000). *Journal of the Royal Statistical Society*, September, 1909.

The transition in the borrowers' country from an excess of credit charges to one of debit charges — from an excess of merchandise imports to an excess of merchandise exports — may take place slowly and silently, or may be accompanied by a financial crash. The turning point in the United States seems to have come with the crisis of 1873. As will be pointed out presently, the foreign trade of the United States changed in its character after that year; a previous excess of imports was replaced by an excess of exports. Though the shift was not due solely to the new relations of principal and interest in the international lending account, this seems to have been the dominant cause. It is not strange that the transition should be initiated by a crisis, and that the first phase of it should be a period of business depression.

The great lending operations of modern times take place chiefly through the sale of securities. When governments borrow, they sell their evidences of debt. When loans are secured for private enterprises, corporate stocks and bonds are usually sold. The result of long-continued operations of this sort has been that certain securities have an international market, and pass freely from country to country. They are largely used in settlement of international balances, and often obviate a flow of specie. Especially is this the case where a temporary balance of payments has to be met. Then the bankers through whom bills of exchange are bought may send such securities instead of specie. On the other hand, these transactions sometimes cause independent disturbances of foreign trade, and so of banking and financial conditions. If the securities issued by a country's government or its corporations come to be distrusted, they are likely to be sent back to that country for sale, and then to cause a balance of specie to leave that country. Thus in the years from 1890 to 1896, when the contest over the gold and silver standards was going on in the United States, foreign holders of American securities became uneasy and sent the securities to the New York stock exchange for sale, — a movement which contributed to the outflow of specie during those years, and added to the causes of public and private embarrassment.

§ 2. Transactions other than loans affect international trade. One of the simplest is that of payments made to persons living or traveling in a foreign country. American travelers in Europe, and those who have permanently established themselves there, spend annually many millions of dollars, — not less, in recent times, than $100,000,000 a year. What they spend is put at their command in Europe through the mechanism of the foreign exchanges. Usually they have letters of credit, which enable them to draw on bankers. Their drafts appear in the foreign exchange market precisely as do the drafts of persons who have exported goods to the United States. If the merchandise exports and imports of the United States just balanced, then these travelers' drafts would cause exchange on the United States to be regularly at a discount in Europe, and specie would flow from the United States. But to this situation, as to that arising from loans and interest payments, the merchandise trade has adjusted itself. The sums which Americans spend abroad are supplied by an excess of merchandise exports from the United States; an excess which has been brought about gradually and insensibly, in obedience to the same causes which would bring the exports and imports to a precise equality if these alone constituted international dealings. In the same way, British India has an excess of exports; partly because there are interest charges on loans of long standing made by Englishmen to the government of India and to private persons there; partly because there are in England many pensioners from the Indian service, to whom the Indian government must make regular remittances.

A curious and important addition to the payments of this kind has come in the United States, since about 1890, from the remittances of immigrants to their kinsfolk in the old countries. The immigrants newly arrived are frugal; it is the second generation that accepts the more liberal spending ways of the prosperous country. The newly arrived send a good part of their savings to relatives and friends at home, very largely for the purpose of enabling these also to emigrate to the land of plenty. Thereby again a debit item appears in the foreign exchange operations, which adds to the causes bringing an excess of merchandise exports. This item reached surprising size in the first decade of the present century; it was supposed to amount in each year to at least $150,000,000.

Freight charges form another item of the same sort. If the merchandise between two countries is carried solely in the ships of one of them, this one will have in so far a balance due to it. Thus the foreign trade of the United States is now carried on chiefly in the vessels of other countries, England having the largest share. The citizens of the United States make remittances on freight account; and they would have to make them by the shipment of specie if the exports just balanced the imports. England is in the contrary case. Her people are great owners of vessels, and are carriers the world over. By itself, this factor would bring specie into England if her imports just balanced her exports. As a matter of fact, the remittances that must be made from the United States for freight and those that England receives from the United States as well as from other countries, take their place in the general balance of international payments. They also add to the causes which lead in the United States to an excess of merchandise exports, and in England to an excess of merchandise imports.

§ 3. A country which produces specie, and especially in modern times one which produces gold, is in a peculiar situation. If this be the only item (or the dominant item) over and above ordinary merchandise transactions, the country will have regularly an excess of merchandise imports, just as it would have if travelers' expenses or freight charges had to be remitted to it. But it will also have a regular outflow of specie; and therefore foreign exchange will be regularly at a premium. The specie is in this case an ordinary article of export, like wheat or cotton or any other commodity. But it goes out only when the state of the foreign exchanges is such as to warrant its shipment. In the other cases where a country has an excess of merchandise imports, foreign exchange is not ordinarily either high or low; it reaches the shipping points only on the sporadic occasions of balances to be met. But in a mining country the state of the exchanges is normally such as to cause the exportation of specie. This was the case in the gold-mining colonies of Australia, especially Victoria, for many years after the gold discoveries of 1850; and it is still in the main the case in that region. It was the case in Mexico, long the greatest silver-mining country in the world, during the period when silver was specie on the same terms with gold. Since the universal adoption of the gold standard, and its introduction even into Mexico, silver has there become a commodity like any other, and the exchanges are reckoned on a gold basis. For the first decade after the Californian gold discoveries of 1850, the United States was in the same position as Australia.

The more recent experiences of the United States, with regard to the domestic output of gold, illustrate some of the irregularities of international trade, and show in what complex ways the underlying forces work out their results. During the Civil War, the gold in circulation was driven out by the issue of paper money; and thereafter, until the resumption of specie payments in 1879, the annual product of the mines was steadily exported, gold and silver being alike regular articles of export. Since 1879, the United States has accumulated an immense stock of gold. It has done so very largely by the simple retention within her own borders of the output of the domestic mines. In some years, not only has this product been retained, but much gold has flowed in from abroad in addition. Though it has happened, in other years, that not only the yield of the mines has been exported, but even more; yet on the whole, the domestic product, and something more, has accumulated in the country. The course of prices has been affected by these movements, through those processes whose slow, irregular, and half-concealed working has been explained in the preceding pages.

§ 4. A glance at the figures of the imports and exports of the United States during the last hundred years shows that a striking change in the relation of the two items took place in 1873. Up to that date, imports had regularly exceeded the exports; since that date, exports have regularly exceeded the imports. The excess of exports in the early years of the twentieth century was enormous; during the decade ending in 1908 the annual excess was $500,000,000. The reversal in 1873 is easily explicable, from what has been stated in the preceding pages. During the first three quarters of the nineteenth century, the United States had been a borrowing country; and it had been in the early stages of borrowing, — steady recurrences of new loans more than balanced the accruing interest on old loans. Until 1860 the United States, in addition, had been a shipping and freight-carrying country, and its shipowners had been earning freights payable by persons in other countries. After 1873, though borrowing continued, sometimes on a great scale, the annual interest payable to foreigners on the whole offset the remittances into the country on capital account. Freight charges became payable by Americans to foreigners, no longer by foreigners to Americans; for the reason, mainly, that iron steamers displaced wooden sailing vessels and could be built and operated more cheaply by the British and by others in Europe. On the other hand, debit items appeared newly, or rose to dimensions so much greater as to make them substantially new. The traveling expenses of Americans became vastly larger; so did the remittances of immigrants. In some years, repayments of old loans were made, in the form of purchases by Americans of securities which in previous times had been sold abroad. Hence the preponderance of exports after 1873, at first comparatively slight, eventually reaching the remarkable extent just stated. Irregular as the merchandise balances were, influenced as they necessarily were by the accidents of the season and the crops, by monetary legislation, by crises and depressions and "booms," the general trend was unmistakable; the exports advanced more rapidly than the imports, exceeded them in almost every single year, and in most years exceeded them immensely. The flow of specie meanwhile was at some times into the United States, in other times out of the United States; on the whole, as might be expected, more pronouncedly into the United States during the later years of very heavy exports. The redistribution of gold, which was part of the general movement, took place, as has been noted in a preceding paragraph, very largely by the more or less complete retention within the country of the product of its own mines.[1]

§ 5. When the merchandise exports of a country exceed its imports, the country is said to have a "favorable balance" of trade. When its imports exceed its exports, the balance is said to be "unfavorable." The same terms are used when the state of international trade is such as to cause an inflow or outflow of specie; although, as we have seen, such inflow or outflow is by no means a necessary or even a usual consequence of an excess or deficiency of exports. The general notion underlying these terms is that a country gains by having dealings with other countries which are expected to bring specie in, and loses by those which are expected to take specie out.

This notion goes back to the Mercantile writers of the seventeenth and eighteenth centuries, who believed that specie was a peculiarly important part of a country's wealth, and that legislation on international trade should be directed to its accumulation. Any one who has grasped the elementary truths about utility, wealth, exchange, money, will see the absurdity of supposing that the prosperity of a country is bound up

[1] Figures for the merchandise imports and exports and for the flow of gold are given in every edition of the *Statistical Abstract*. Estimates have been made from time to time of the amounts of the various non-merchandise items, such as interest and freight charges, tourists' expenses, immigrants' remittances; for example, by Mr. T. Bacon, in the *Yale Review*, 1900, and for 1909 by Mr. G. Paish, in a monograph on the *Trade Balance of the United States*, a publication of the United States Monetary Commission.

with the inflow or outflow of specie. The astonishing thing is that, notwithstanding the simplicity of those truths and their repeated and widespread exposition, ignorance regarding them should be so common. Many people who think themselves entitled to attention still speak as if an excess of exports promised a profit to a country, and an influx of specie were a realization of that profit.

In part, this way of looking at international trade comes from the habitual attitude of business men and bankers. Plentiful bank reserves, low rates of discount, easy accommodation to borrowers, — these are always welcome to the business community. Conversely, diminishing bank reserves and higher discount are unwelcome. Hence the inflow of specie, which proximately affects bank holdings and short-time interest, is spoken of as a good thing, and the outflow of specie as a bad thing. This outflow, with its consequent pressure on loans, interest rates, and eventually on prices, is often the salutary check on inflation and speculation. But few business men feel it to be salutary. Nearly all would like to see an unending round of rising prices.

There are times, of course, when the balance of international payments — usually resting on the relation between exports and imports — is of real consequence. This is notably the case when a country is trying to extricate itself from a depreciated paper currency. The return to specie payments is possible for such a country only if its foreign trade is in a state which will cause specie to flow in, or will prevent it from flowing out when a fund for resumption purposes has been collected by the government. Though in the long run this inflow or outflow will depend on the state of prices, in any one season the balance of international payments is affected by the seasonal events. If, at the time when a country is preparing to return to a specie basis, financial disturbances or poor crops lead to an "unfavorable" balance, the operation of resumption will be difficult and perhaps unsuccessful. It was an immense aid to the resumption of specie payments by the United States that in the year fixed for it (1879) and in the years immediately following there were unusually heavy exports, due to good crops within the country and poor crops elsewhere; while at the same period improvements in railway transportation greatly facilitated an increase of exports. The consequent inflow of gold, coupled with the retention of the domestic output of the metal, gave an unexpectedly solid basis to the reëstablished specie régime.

In the main, however, the persistence of the Mercantilist attitude is not due to any such considerations of real advantage, but to simple ignorance. People measure their individual incomes in terms of money, profit by an excess of money receipts over money expenses, and fall into the way of regarding money as the important form of wealth. This was indeed the earliest and crudest form of the Mercantilist notion. The same ignorance and fallacy underlie the advocacy of paper money inflation, and the various schemes for making nations prosperous by adding to their stocks of cash.

One curious form of the Mercantilist view appears in the interpretation often given to the state of trade between a country and a single one of its neighbors. Thus the imports from Canada to the United States may be greater than the exports from the United States to Canada; and it is often inferred (for example, in discussion of reciprocity treaties between the two countries) that the trade is one unfavorable or damaging to the United States. Such comparison is meaningless. So far as the relation between imports and exports is a matter of moment at all, this is to be judged by the balance of transactions, not between any one country and a single other, but by its balance with all. That our exports to England exceed our imports thence, or our imports from Brazil exceed our exports thither, — all this signifies nothing. It must be confessed that public men in high station, as well as newspaper scribblers and rabid partisans, fall into loose talk on this subject, and compare the sales and purchases of one pair of countries as if these really gave an indication of their relative gains from trade with each other. The real advantages from international trade, and the relative gains of different countries, are to be gauged in a very different way, as will appear in the chapters to follow.

CHAPTER 34

The Theory of International Trade. Why Particular Goods are Exported or Imported

§ 1. The preceding chapters have considered chiefly the mechanism of international trade. We may proceed now to matters more fundamental: the variations in prices and money incomes in different countries, the causes which determine what commodities a country shall import or export, the real importance of specie movements between countries and of a rise or fall in the value of money, the real gain from international trade. The first topics for consideration will be the mode in which a country's exports and imports are determined, and the cause and significance of variations in prices and incomes.

We shall assume, for simplicity, that trade is free. Duties on imports have important modifying effects, but these can be understood better if the working of unfettered trade is first examined.

Let us begin by calling to mind some familiar but often neglected facts, known to all observers, but rightly interpreted by few. Among the most familiar is that there are differences in the value of money in different countries; that is, differences in the range of prices and of money incomes. It will appear later in our inquiry that the differences in money incomes are the more important, and that prices do not always move with money incomes; but for the present we may assume that prices and money incomes in general move together. Money wages and other money incomes, and most prices also, are higher in the United States than in England, higher in England than in France and Germany, higher in these latter countries than in Italy and Spain; and lowest in countries like Japan, India, China.

While these differences are obvious in money incomes, and in the prices of many goods, it is equally obvious that some commodities differ but little in price in the various countries. These are the commodities which are the objects of international trade, — which move from country to country as imports and exports. These, if we set aside cost of transportation, are the same in price in all the trading countries. Where cost of transportation is considerable, their prices may vary considerably; hence we can only say that the prices tend to be not far from the same. We neglect, for the present, it will be remembered, differences due to duties on imports or exports. Some further qualifications to the general proposition would have to be made if it were attempted to fit it with exactness to all the facts. Sometimes an unfamiliar commodity goes from one country to another, is bought very cheap by traders in the one and sold very dear in the other; there is a serious difference in price. This is likely to happen where discoveries or rapid improvements in communication cause new opportunities for trade to arise. But mercantile competition tends in time to wipe out these differences. Here, as in other directions, the pioneers make money; unusual profits are presently cut away; in the end, only such differences in price persist as are accounted for by cost of transportation and the ordinary business returns. Very few propositions in economics are literally and unfailingly true; they stand for great general tendencies; and among such is the one here stated, — that goods which are the subjects of a constant and considerable foreign trade are sold at nearly the same prices in all the trading countries. Wheat sells at approximately the same price in the United States and England, tea in the United States and Ceylon, coffee in the United States and Brazil, wool in Australia on the one hand, England, France, Germany, on the other.

Nearly the same prices, be it noted. In order that a commodity shall move from one country to another, it must be somewhat cheaper in the exporting country, — cheaper at least by cost of transportation. International trade, like all trade, though it is resolvable at bottom into an exchange of goods for goods, is proximately determined by prices; and prices of the things bought and sold must be somewhat lower in the exporting country.

Money wages, however, are not necessarily lower in the exporting country. Thus they are higher in the United States than in England, yet the United States exports wheat to England. They are higher in England than in China, yet England sends all sorts of manufactured goods to China. They are higher in Australia than in Germany, yet Australia sends wool to Germany. A common notion in regard to international trade is that a country where wages are low is a country that is peculiarly likely to have large exports, and that one with high wages has difficulty in sending out its exports. Yet a moment's consideration of familiar facts such as have just been adduced shows that this cannot be the case. And the preceding chapters have shown that the exports of a country balance in money value its imports (barring those differences one way or the other which are easily explained by payments other than for merchandise). The countries with high money wages have no less exports than those with low money wages. In the trade between the two sets of countries neither can export more than the other; the payments between them balance.

§ 2. These preliminary matters point to the first important proposition with regard to international trade. A country exports the things which are low in price in its borders; these are things in which its labor is applied effectively. Put in words more often used in the literature of economics, a country tends to export those things in which it has a comparative advantage. And, conversely, a country tends to import those things which, if produced within its borders, would be high in price, — those in which its labor would be applied with less effect, those in which it has a comparative disadvantage.

For example, wheat is exported steadily in large quantities

from the United States.[1] The money incomes of those who produce it are high; the farmers and their hired laborers are well remunerated. If the price of wheat is low in the United States, it must be because the labor of those who produce it is effective. That is, the labor is applied to advantage. High wages and high prices do not necessarily go together; high wages are found with low prices if the productiveness of labor is great. We speak now of money wages alone. Regarding real wages, it will appear more fully as we go on that a high rate of wages is the result of general effectiveness or productiveness. But looking at money wages alone, and considering them in relation to international trade, we can see clearly that a high rate is no obstacle to low prices and to exportation if accompanied by great effectiveness. If, on the other hand, there be high money wages without any special effectiveness, then there will be high prices. The employer who must pay high money wages, and whose laborers do not produce abundantly, must sell his product at a high price in order to meet his expenses. In a country of high money wages the producers will continue to export in those branches of industry in which the effectiveness of labor is large. The producers in those branches where the effectiveness is smaller, will find greater and greater difficulty in meeting foreign competition, and may be driven out of business by competing foreign imports.

Again: China exports tea and raw silk; British India exports jute; Brazil, coffee. These are countries in which money wages are low. But they are also countries in which labor in general is ineffective. They import, on the other hand, large quantities

[1] I use wheat for illustration, though the exports are now (1909) declining, and may cease in the course of a decade. The tendency to decline in these once heavy exports is commonly ascribed to the fact that we "need" the domestic product for our rapidly increasing population. This is true, as far as it goes. But the reason why the product fails to keep its former relation to population and "need" is the increasing cost (marginal cost) of wheat; compare Book II, Chapter 13, § 4, and Book V, Chapter 42. That increase in cost means, in other words, lessening effectiveness and lessening comparative advantage; hence lessening exports. The wheat of the Canadian Northwest will probably supply in the future an illustration which will continue to fit the text.

of manufactured goods which are produced more cheaply by effective and highly paid labor in the manufacturing countries. They export those things in which their labor is perhaps ineffective, but is *less* ineffective than it would be in making textiles, hardware, and other manufactures. They export those things in the making of which they have a comparative advantage; that is, those for which, in their own borders, labor is most effective.

Thus we reach, alike for countries with high money incomes and with low money incomes, the same conclusion: those things are comparatively cheap, and those things are likely to figure in the exports, in which the country's labor is the more effective.

It matters not, for the purpose in hand, what are the causes of the effectiveness of labor which constitutes the country's advantage. It may arise from climatic superiority or other natural fitness, or from skill and aptitude due to complex human causes; or it may arise from a combination of these. The advantage of the United States in wheat, and its exports of wheat, rests (or rested) partly on the possession of vast tracts of new and fertile land; but it was much promoted also by the intelligence of its farmers and their large use of agricultural machinery, and by cheap rail transportation from the Western wheat fields to the seaports. All sorts of causes here concur; not only the obviously natural ones, but those connected with land tenure and land ownership, with universal education and universal ambition, with the influence on freight rates of private ownership of railways and hence of unfettered enterprise. However complex these causes, their single outcome is clear: the labor of producing and shipping American wheat is effective. The same complexity of causes lies back of our exports of petroleum and of copper, — great natural resources, but also great enterprise and skill in developing them. In some of our exporting industries, enterprise and skill alone, without unusual resources, suffice to explain effectiveness and cheapness; as in agricultural implements, sewing machines, builders' hardware, electrical equipment. England's large exports of manufactures, which again illustrate the same combination of high money wages, effectiveness of labor, comparative advantage, are due partly to her deposits of coal and iron ore, — the natural foundations of manufactures, — partly perhaps to a favoring climate, very largely to the vigor, enterprise, and skill bred by free industry and free political institutions. China's advantage (or less disadvantage) in tea and raw silk is due partly to climate, partly to skill and experience transmitted from generations to generations of patient workers. That this latter cause of advantage may be precarious is shown by the extent to which, in recent years, some rival countries have deprived China of her former position as almost the sole exporter of these articles. Ceylon has developed large exports of tea, Japan of raw silk, by systematic attention to the best ways of making labor effective in producing these things.

§ 3. Cheapness in price being the proximate element in determining exports, any cause or set of causes which makes a commodity cheap acts as an advantage and so promotes exports. If a particular kind of labor, though not of high effectiveness, can be had at very low wages, the commodities made by it are *pro tanto* likely to be exported.

Interesting questions upon this aspect of the problem are presented by the exports of cotton from the United States. Climate, in its effects on the quality of the fiber, may go far to explain these exports. But social conditions have been supposed also to be an important factor. Before the Civil War, slavery was thought by many to explain the cotton trade of the South; it gave the advantage of very cheap labor. But the great growth of the exports since the war (when once the first years of turbulent transition had passed) shows that slavery in itself was not the controlling cause. It remains true, however, that cotton continues to be grown mainly by negro labor, and that this is cheaper than most American labor. The maintenance of the exports may thus be ascribed to the persistence of social conditions derived from slavery. On the other hand, this very negro labor, cheap though it seems according to American standards, gets higher money wages than are current in Egypt, India, and other countries from which a competing supply of cotton comes to the world's markets. The labor must be at least to some degree effective. Further, much American cotton is grown (in Texas, for example) by white labor which earns the normally high American rates. Here the main explanation of the exports must be found in the effectiveness of the labor, climatic causes being, no doubt, important in contributing to that effectiveness.

Clearer illustration of the influence of specially low wages can be found elsewhere. In Saxony and Bavaria, there are districts where a congested population is willing to work long hours for low wages. Toys, and some sorts of textiles and knit goods, are turned out at very low prices, and are exported in considerable quantities. In England, again, while most exports rest on effectiveness with high wages, there are so-called "parasitic" industries (lace making and chain making are examples) in which wages are especially low, and in which prices are low in consequence. From the social point of view, these are not welcome elements in a country's trade, whether domestic or foreign. But so far as the currents of international trade are concerned, specially low wages and specially productive labor operate in the same direction, — both promote the exports of the commodities affected.

The effect on international trade, in these cases of low wages, depends on their being limited cases. If all wages in a country are equally low, no one commodity will be cheaper than any other, and no effect on exports or imports will ensue. On this subject there is a sort of terror among many persons in countries of high wages like the United States and England, — a fear of universal underselling and wholesale collapse, because wages are lower in some countries from which exports come. The relation between international trade and general low wages deserves a moment's consideration.

Suppose two countries, — say the United States and Japan, — suddenly to open commercial relations, there having been previously no trade between them. Suppose money wages to be lower in all occupations in Japan, and all goods to be cheaper there. Money then has a higher value in that country than in the United States; trade in merchandise moves one way only, goods being sent to the United States; specie alone flows to Japan. Prices and wages will then rise in Japan, and will fall in the United States. As this transition goes on (doubtless a trying one, especially in the United States), the flow of specie will gradually diminish, and will finally cease when equilibrium has been established. But that equilibrium will not necessarily be reached at a stage of equal wages in both countries; still less at a stage of equal prices in both, and consequent cessation of all trade between them. As prices in general move up in Japan, in response to the inflow of specie, it will appear that the prices of certain commodities do not move up to the American prices of the same commodities. These are the commodities in which Japanese labor is effective, or (possibly) in which some sets of Japanese laborers get unusually low wages. Such commodities will continue to be exported from Japan even after wages and prices in general have risen. Conversely, in the United States wages and prices will fall. But as they fall, some things will prove to fall in price below the Japanese level. These are the things in which American labor has an advantage or (possibly) in which it must submit to specially low wages. Such things will begin to be exported to Japan as prices there rise, and they will continue to be steadily exported. In other words, there can hardly be such a thing as continued underselling in all goods. There will almost certainly be an equalization, or an approach toward equalization, of the value of money in the two countries; and thereafter a development of imports and exports, each country exporting those things in which it has an advantage and importing those in which it has a disadvantage.

No such extraordinary case has ever appeared. The adjustment of relative wages and prices in different countries has taken place by a gradual and almost insensible process. Possibly something like an abrupt change took place, in Japan in the last decades of the nineteenth century, when that country, previously sealed to foreigners, was opened to trade with them and entered on her amazing political and industrial transformation. In virtually all cases, the main lines of adjustment were settled long ago. And this general adjustment, it should be noted, has by no means been such as to bring about an equalization of money incomes or of general prices; it has not brought about a uniform value of money the world over. In the supposed trade between the United States and Japan, equilibrium and settled exchange would be reached, — the industrial characteristics of the two countries being as they now are, — while money incomes and most prices were still higher in the United States. What are the causes of the variations in money incomes and in general prices between country and country, we have yet to consider. But it is certain that they do not lead to universal underselling or to a continued trade in which goods move one way only.

§ 4. From the principle of comparative costs, it follows that a country may fail to produce things which it can produce to advantage, — may import things in which its labor is more effective than is labor in the country whence they come. Not all international trade rests on this precise relation; but under it the peculiarities of international trade appear most markedly.

If a country, though under no disadvantage in a commodity, nay, though possessed of an advantage in producing it, has here a *less* advantage than in other commodities, the first sort will be imported. For example, labor in the United States is no less productive in growing hemp than labor in Italy or Russia; it is probably more so; none the less, hemp is imported from those countries. Labor in this country is no less productive in producing flax fiber than labor in Belgium, or in making linens than labor in Germany or Ireland, but flax and linen are still imported, and this in face of a considerable duty (hemp, as it happens, is duty-free). Coarse wool, such as is used in making carpets, could be grown here with as little labor as in China, Asia Minor, Russia, and sundry other backward countries, from which, none the less, it is steadily imported. The everyday explanation of all these phenomena is that labor is too dear in the United States. The explanation is true enough, as far as it goes, — but why is the labor dear? Our high rate of wages does not lead to the importation of all goods, or prevent the exportation of those in which the productivity of labor is large. High general wages are the results of high general productivity. Once established and current, they constitute a difficulty for other possible industries in which productivity is not high. The real explanation of the continued importation of things in which labor is at no disadvantage is that they cannot meet the pace set by those in which the labor of the country is *more* productively applied.

Obviously, it is to the interest of a country to turn its labor into the most advantageous channels; not merely to those industries in which it is at no disadvantage or has only a slight advantage, but to those in which it has the greatest advantage. Similarly, an individual finds it to his advantage to devote himself, once for all, to that occupation in which he is most proficient. The bricklayer does not carry his own bricks, even though he could carry as many as the hodcarrier, perhaps more. He can lay the bricks immeasurably better than the hodcarrier, and gains by confining himself to that. An able business man delegates to clerks and subordinates much routine work, even work involving some responsibility and judgment, which he could do better himself; he confines himself to the still more difficult tasks of management, in which he has peculiar excellence.

By no means all trade between countries, or all division of labor between individuals, is explicable in just this way. Often there is an absolute advantage on both sides. The bricklayer may be skillful without being physically strong; the hodcarrier may be able to carry more bricks. Each can do his own work better than the other. The capable business man may not be able to do clerical work as well as his bookkeeper. A certain impatience and abruptness of temper, characteristic of commanding personalities, may unfit him for monotonous office work. Similarly, a country may be at an absolute disadvantage in one industry, and may have an absolute advantage in another. Such is the relative situation of temperate and of tropical countries as regards the articles they commonly exchange with each other. Brazil produces coffee with absolutely less labor than the United States could, India jute, and so on; the United States produces wheat and makes it into wheat flour, spins and weaves cotton cloth, with less labor than they can.

§ 5. There is a difference in the basis of the gain from international trade, and in its probable extent, according as it rests on differences merely in comparative advantage, or on absolute differences of the sort last described. In the second case, where each country has a clear superiority, exchange between them will be to mutual advantage under any circumstances. Though they may not share equally in the gain (of this more will be said in the next chapter), it will be to their interest to carry on the trade. But where there is only a comparative advantage, the existence of the trade, and the gain from it, rest on the fact that labor does not move freely from country to country. Suppose, for example, that labor in the United States is more productive all around than labor in Italy; it will be none the less to the advantage of Americans to import from Italy those things in which, though they have an advantage, it is a less advantage. But it would also be to the interest of the people of Italy to move *en masse* to the United States. Only because the Italians fail to do so, and prefer to remain in their own country, will that trade be carried on which rests simply on differences in comparative cost.

The indefinite continuance of such trade thus rests on immobility of labor between countries,—on the ties of language, nationality, religion, on the obstacles from ignorance and poverty, which hold people to the land of their birth. Great as is the emigration of modern times, it has not sufficed to put an end to this prevailing immobility. If, in the example just given, all the Italians were to move to the United States, they would be better off than before. So long as they remain at home, they provide the Americans with goods more cheaply than these could be made in the United States. Once in the United States, they would indeed produce the commodities with less labor than before;

but that labor would have to be paid for at the higher American rate, and the commodities would be less cheap. The Americans (let us say, in courtesy, the other Americans) would be less well off. It is conceivable, to be sure, that when the Italians got to the United States, they would not receive the full American rate of wages. They might continue to work for the Americans, as they had done in Italy, at a low rate of wages. And it is true that our newly arrived immigrants, in fact, are in a group by themselves. But their pay shows at least some approach to the American rate. Though they work for wages not up to the level normal in the United States, they do not work for us as cheaply as do their countrymen who remain at home. It happens, also, that often they do not work at the identical things which are imported (or under free trade would be imported) from the old countries. These things it continues to be to our advantage to procure by the way of foreign trade, though our labor may be more efficient in making them than is the foreign labor. In an ideal — and we might call it utopian — distribution of the world's productive forces, the division of labor and of trade which rests solely on comparative differences in costs would not exist. But as men and nations are, no small part is played by the great historical gulfs between nations and races and by the resulting immobility of labor.[1]

§ 6. From the preceding exposition, it might be inferred that a country produces within its own borders no articles which it imports, and that, conversely, whatever articles it exports are supplied *in toto* to the other country or countries. But this does not necessarily follow. More especially it does not follow with regard to the considerable range of commodities which are produced under the conditions of varying costs or diminishing returns.

Take the case of wheat, which the United States exports to England and Germany. Some wheat can be grown to advantage in these countries, — a great deal in Germany, less in humid

[1] This topic connects itself with the general subject of differences of wages and non-competing groups; see below, Book V, Chapter 47, especially §§ 5, 6.

England. They are at a comparative disadvantage only when they force the margin of cultivation and raise wheat on the land less adapted for it. On the better sources of supply, the domestic producers can hold their own, even though imports come in. Hence the national supply comes partly by importation, partly by domestic production. The same is the case in the United States with wool. Some parts of the country have clear advantages for wool growing, and are adapted for little else, — such as the semi-arid plains of Montana. Elsewhere the climate is not so favorable, or (what is more important) the land can more advantageously be put to other uses. Corn and wheat pay better; there is simply a comparative disadvantage in wool growing. The total supply of wool which the country wants at current prices cannot be produced in those regions which are advantageous enough; hence part is imported. This sort of importation — wool into the United States, wheat into Germany — takes place, notwithstanding duties of considerable weight on these products in the two countries. As the better sources of supply in each country have been fully utilized, it has become more costly to procure additional wheat and wool; hence, as the poorer sources are resorted to, the price rises until imports come in over the duty. Most of the supply in each country comes from domestic production; but there is a steady importation.

With manufactured goods the case is somewhat different, since there are not commonly the same limitations set by nature to the increase of supply at constant cost. It is true that some division of the field is likely to take place here also. Not infrequently there are permanent causes of variation of cost between different establishments, — in the iron manufacture, for example, as to supplies of ore and coal. And even when there are not such deeply rooted causes of variation, there are forces of a similar sort in operation for considerable periods. The principle of constant returns, though it works out its results for most manufactures in the long run, is subject to great modification in times of rapid change, such as the modern world has seen in so many cases.[1] At any one time, some establishments in a given industry, say the woolen manufacture, may have such advantages as will enable them to hold their own against foreign competition, and others may not. Part of the supply, but not all of it, will be got by importation.

Nevertheless, division of the field between foreign and domestic manufacturers is less common, and less likely to persist, than such division between foreign and domestic producers in extractive industries. True, it happens occasionally that there is a very even balance between the two, and that minor factors, such as established name and repute, skill in satisfying the tastes and whims of consumers, will determine that some among each set of producers will hold their own in the market. More often, when part of the supply of a manufactured article, and part only, is recorded as coming from abroad, it will be found that the imported article, though it has the same name as the domestic, is of such a different quality as to be virtually a different thing. French and German woolens are imported into England; but they are very different goods from those which the English make and export. The same explanation of an apparently anomalous phenomenon (simultaneous import and export of the same article) applies to some raw materials. Though the United States is a great exporter of cotton, she imports cotton also; but it is not the same as is exported. What comes in is Egyptian cotton, of longer fiber than the ordinary domestic, used for certain knit goods and other fabrics.

[1] See Book III, Chapter 12, § 3, and Book V, Chapter 50, § 2.

CHAPTER 35

THE THEORY OF INTERNATIONAL TRADE, *continued.* WHEREIN THE GAIN CONSISTS

§ 1. In the preceding chapter, the general nature of the gain from international trade, and the causes that determine which among a country's commodities will be exported, have been considered. It remains to examine more carefully the nature of the gain, and the manner in which it is shared by the trading countries.

For this phase of the question, it will be best to turn first to the case where each country has an absolute advantage in the commodities it exports. Such is the nature of most trade between tropical and temperate countries. Such also is the nature of most trade between different parts of the same country.

Within any one country this sort of geographical division of labor does not commonly give rise to any peculiar problems. Exchange takes place between the various sections, but on equal terms. Within a country, there are no very great variations in wages and incomes — for persons of the same capacity and skill — between different districts. Yorkshire is a great woolen manufacturing region, Lancashire is a great cotton goods district; they exchange products; but wages are substantially the same in the two, and they share equally in the advantages of the exchange. Pennsylvania produces iron and coal, the Mississippi Valley wheat and corn, Oregon lumber, California fruits, the South cotton, New England sundry manufactures. Though there is no complete equalization of incomes between different parts of the United States, we find in the country's general industrial conditions an unmistakable homogeneity. Labor flows with much freedom from one part to the other (unless, indeed, it be kept from parts of the South by the race complication), and there is a generally high level of money wages. Not only is the geographical division of labor determined in the main by obvious advantages in production, but the people of all the parts share to about the same degree in the general cheapness and abundance which it promotes.

But between tropical and temperate countries, and between countries civilized and those half civilized, there is no approach to equalization of incomes. India, China, Japan, South America, have very different rates of wages from the United States and Europe. And there are also differences between the United States and European countries, and between the various European countries. Money incomes being different, the gain from international trade is unequally divided. The commodities exchanged are at the same price (barring cost of transportation) in the several trading countries. The English, for example, buy woolen goods and cotton goods and coal, as well as fruits and wines, as cheaply as the Italians. But the English have higher money incomes with which to purchase both sets of commodities, and hence benefit more from the trade with Italy than the Italians do. How explain these differences?

§ 2. Suppose an extreme and simple case, typified by England with exports of coal, Italy with exports of lemons; these exports resulting from obvious advantages in production possessed by the two countries. The quantity of coal which England will send to Italy depends on the conditions of demand in that country. In Italy the coal will sell at the English price, plus cost of transportation, and at this price a certain amount of coal can be disposed of there. In England, on the other hand, lemons will sell at the Italian price plus cost of transportation, and at this price a certain quantity of lemons can be disposed of in England. It is possible that the two amounts will just balance,—the coal exports from England may just equal in money value the lemon imports into England. But if we suppose the two countries to be suddenly brought to trade with each other, no previous process of adjustment having taken place, this would be highly improbable. One or the other sum is likely to be the greater. Suppose the lemons exceed. Then Italy will export to England more (in money value) than she imports. Specie will flow to Italy. Prices will rise there, and money incomes will rise with them. Prices and money incomes, on the other hand, will fall in England. As this process takes place, the export of lemons from Italy will be checked; for lemons rise in price there with other things, while the English consumers who buy them have lessened money incomes. But exports of coal from England will be stimulated. Prices are falling in that country, and the price of coal falls with other things; hence coal can be sent to Italy at a lower price. Its consumption in Italy is stimulated, not only by its lower price, but by the fact that money incomes in Italy are rising. Eventually a stage is reached at which the coal just pays for the lemons. The imports equal the exports in money value, specie no longer flows, equilibrium is established.

Just at what point this stage is reached evidently depends on the nature of the demand for the two articles in the trading countries. If the demand for both is elastic, equilibrium will be quickly reached. If the higher price of lemons quickly checks the English consumption, and if the lower price of coal quickly stimulates the Italian consumption, the money values of the two articles will soon become equal. But if the people of England have a strong demand — that is, an inelastic demand — for lemons, and continue to use very nearly the same quantity of them, even though their price rises somewhat; and if, on the other hand, the people of Italy have an inelastic demand for coal, and do not increase their use of it, even though its price becomes lower, — then a long process of changing prices and changing incomes will ensue. The country whose demand is great for the products of the other country will have comparatively low prices and low money incomes; the country whose exports are in insistent demand in the other country will have comparatively high money wages and money incomes.

The case supposed (imaginary in that it assumes these two

articles to be the only ones exchanged between England and Italy) points to the underlying principle. That country gains most from international trade whose exports are most in demand, and which itself has little demand for the things which it imports, — that is, for the exports of other countries. That country gains least which has the most insistent demand for the products of other countries. In the semi-technical terms which we have used elsewhere, we may say that the extent to which a country shares in the gain from international trade depends on the marginal utility to it of imported goods and the marginal utility to other countries of its exported goods.

This cause operates through that mechanism for the distribution of the world's stocks of specie, and that equalization of international payments, which secures the general equilibrium of exports and imports. It need not again be said how slowly these forces move, how difficult it is to follow their operation in the confused currents of international trade. The imports and exports of the various nations have long accommodated themselves to a scheme (if that word can be applied to something which has grown up without plan or intent) of differences in the value of money in the various countries. Though changes in the scheme take place, they come by slow and half-concealed movements. Many economists of modern times, intent only on those phenomena which are unmistakable and susceptible of exact observation, ignore the less conspicuous underlying forces, and are skeptical concerning the validity of fine-spun theories about them. Yet the broad phenomena are explicable only by reasoning of this kind. As was pointed out at the very beginning of the discussion of international trade, it is obvious that great differences in money incomes exist between the various countries, and that they persist through very long periods. It is obvious, too, that these differences bring inequalities in the gains from foreign trade. The flow of specie, again, is governed by the prices and the consumption of the articles that enter into foreign trade. Notwithstanding that flow, the value of money is not brought to the same level the world over; and notwithstanding the variations in the money incomes and prices, substantial equilibrium in payments between the countries is still reached. All these phenomena are brought into orderly connection by the theory of reciprocal demand.

§ 3. Suppose now another case, nearer to reality. Suppose that, between countries whose trade has previously come to equilibrium, a change in demand sets in; that England, for example, having imported from the United States as much as her exports paid for, now demands more of American goods. Stated more accurately, the supposition is that English consumers buy, at ruling prices, more of the American goods — cotton, wheat, kerosene, or what not — than they bought before. Specie then must flow from England to the United States; or, what amounts in effect to the same thing, new specie from the mines, which would otherwise have gone to England, must be diverted to the United States. If this movement takes place on a considerable scale and for a considerable time, it must affect prices. The same train of consequences will ensue as in the supposed trade between England and Italy. Prices and money incomes will rise in the United States, and will fall in England. Eventually these shifts will again bring equilibrium. The higher American prices will check the increase of exports from the United States, the lower English prices will stimulate an increase of exports from England. Money incomes will reach a somewhat higher level in the United States, a somewhat lower level in England. As consumers of English goods, the Americans will gain; as consumers of American goods, the English will lose. Thus the increase in English demand for American goods will cause the English to gain less from the trade between the countries, the Americans to gain more.

Again, the appearance of a new article of export in a country's foreign trade operates in the same way. Kerosene oil has become an important article of export from the United States during the last forty years (since 1870), — a clear addition to the things which foreign consumers have bought. This had to be paid for. If trade before was at equilibrium, and if no other disturbing factor entered, specie must have been diverted to the United States, as in the case previously supposed. The same consequences must have followed, until, by a gradual stimulus to foreign imports into the United States, and by a gradual check to exports (other than the new article) from the United States, equilibrium was reëstablished, with a new scale of prices in the two countries. The foreign countries indeed gain by having the new article which they did not have before. But they lose by having to pay somewhat higher prices for other American articles, and by having somewhat lower money incomes with which to pay for them.

An obligation to make other payments than those for merchandise has corresponding effects. If a country has remittances to make to other countries, — whether for travelers' expenses, absentees, interest on accumulated debt, freight charges, or the like debit items — it is likely to be in a worse position as regards the gain from its trade with the other countries. The remittances must be made in money, or in money's worth. They must be made in the first instance — international payments having previously balanced — by an outflow of specie. That outflow of specie lowers prices; it stimulates exports and checks imports. In the end the payments are effected by an excess of merchandise exports. But the process which brings these added exports brings also lower prices and lower money incomes in the remitting country, and so lessened advantage from international trade. The need of forcing more exports on the foreign consumers causes the foreigners to get the exports on better terms, and causes domestic consumers to get the foreign imports on worse terms.

§ 4. It is extremely difficult to follow these forces in any concrete case; for it is rare that any one factor operates alone, even rare that several factors combine to operate in the same direction. Nowhere is this difficulty better illustrated than in the experience of the United States during the last thirty or forty years. The play of international demand works out its results over long periods,—it is only thus that the flow of specie affects prices. But during the period mentioned, say since 1873, a multitude of conflicting forces have been at work. We have seen that since that year the foreign trade of the United States in one respect has clearly taken a new turn: the merchandise exports, which previously were less than the imports, have come to exceed the imports.[1] The change is explained by the various additional payments (for interest, travelers' expenses, immigrants' remittances, freight charges, and so on) which Americans have to make to foreigners. This circumstance *per se* would tend to cause an outflow of specie, to lower prices and incomes, to make the terms of international exchange less favorable. But during the same period (since 1873) a great increase in the demand for American exports has set in, — for our cotton, wheat, meat products, and for some manufactures; while new articles of export, such as kerosene and copper, have become important. All this has worked in just the contrary direction. During the same period, moreover, a policy of protective import duties has been applied with great rigor; and such a policy also, as will appear presently,[2] operates in the same favorable direction. Meanwhile gold has been mined on a large scale within the country. Legislation also has been an important factor in the country's monetary supply: consider the resumption of specie payments, the injection of silver money from the acts of 1878 and 1890, the peculiar working of the national bank system. Throughout the period there has been great growth of population and wealth, and therefore a great increase in the demand for money, — an increase which, taken by itself, would tend to lower prices. What a jumble of interacting and conflicting elements! How say whether the forces that made for greater gain from foreign trade outweighed those that made for less gain? How follow in detail the concrete working of any one factor? The difficulty would probably be the same in kind, though less in

[1] See above, Chapter 33, § 4.

[2] See below, Chapter 37, § 1.

degree, if an examination were attempted of the foreign trade over a considerable period of any European country.

The difficulty is one common in economics. A number of forces combine — acting sometimes in the same direction, sometimes in conflict with each other — to bring about a gross result. Being necessarily debarred from deliberate experiment, we must resort to hypothetical reasoning, and must be content with general conclusions confirmed only in part by direct experience. Thus, we reason that an increase in the money supply must raise prices. We find that in the long run, and making due allowance for credit fluctuations, for bank reserves and bank expansion, this is true; and the result is further confirmed by the striking phenomena of paper money inflation. We reason that a flow of specie from one country to another tends automatically to bring its own check, and that payments between countries tend to balance without the movement of specie. We find, in fact, that payments are usually adjusted with a very small use of specie; while those cases in which it moves steadily one way—from specie-mining countries, for example, or from western countries to the sluggish communities of the East—are exceptions of the sort that confirm the rule; they are explicable on grounds of their own. We reason that the stage of equilibrium in payments is reached by a process which involves in the several countries different levels of money incomes and prices; and we find that in fact some countries have markedly higher wages and prices than others. All these verifications of the general reasoning give us confidence in phases of the reasoning which we cannot verify directly. Among the conclusions verified in this indirect way is that reached in the preceding discussion: a country's share in the gains from international trade depends on the play of reciprocal demand. The more insistent is the demand for a country's products in other countries, and the less insistent is its own demand for the products of other countries, the greater then is its gain from international trade.

§ 5. The rise and fall of money incomes and of prices, in

relation to international trade, call for some further discussion. Strictly speaking, it is not the rise or the fall of prices, but that of money incomes alone, which is of consequence.

Differences in the value of money — in the general level of prices and incomes — which result from the play of international demand, are of real and permanent importance only with reference to foreign goods. A general rise of prices and incomes is in the long run immaterial; it means only the use of more counters in exchange. It is true that the process of transition disturbs the relations of debtors and creditors; perhaps true, also, that rising prices bring a certain stimulus to production.[1] But these are transitory effects. It is obvious that in the end people are no better off from having higher money incomes, if prices rise to the same extent. And domestic prices will rise, under the influence of changed conditions of international trade and inflow of specie, as much as wages and other incomes. But prices of foreign (imported) goods are differently affected by these same conditions. They do not rise; they fall. The higher incomes go further in the purchase of foreign goods, and in these purchases only. Conversely, a fall in incomes and prices, due to changes in international trade working in the opposite direction, affects consumers only in their purchases of imported things. As for domestic commodities, the fall in money incomes is offset by the fall in their prices. But foreign goods tend to become dearer, and in buying these there is a real loss.

Changes in the value of money, due to varying currents of international trade, thus bring about not only transitional effects (such as those on debtors and creditors), but permanent effects as well. But these permanent effects are of a different sort from what is implied by the phrases commonly used. They do not arise from the fact that increased exports bring in more money. They arise because foreign goods are secured on easier terms. An increase in the monetary supply, equally distributed over all the world, would benefit no one. But an increase which went to one

[1] Compare what has been said in Book III, Chapter 22, §§ 6, 7.

country alone, or which went in larger proportion to one country than to others, would benefit the people of that country in their dealings with other peoples. And similarly a redistribution of the existing supplies, due to changed conditions of demand in the trade between the different countries, would cause the people of some to secure greater gains from their dealings with others.

One application of this reasoning is obvious. A country gets its gain from international trade only if it takes advantage of the relative cheapness of foreign goods. So long as these are admitted free of duty, and only so long, does it secure in full the real advantage from high money incomes, or from a rise in money incomes. Duties imposed on foreign goods simply cut off that advantage. And if the duties operate to bring about the production within the country of goods which, without the duties, would be imported, the gain from foreign trade entirely disappears. Such, in brief, is the main argument in favor of free trade; and, as far as it goes, it is unanswerable. This is by no means all that is to be said on the controversy between free traders and protectionists, but it is a fundamental truth, much befogged by current fallacies, yet not to be mistaken by any one who has grasped the principles of division of labor, exchange, money, and prices.

§ 6. The extent of a country's gain from international trade depends on two causes: first, the terms of international exchange as just explained; second, the efficiency of its labor in producing exported commodities. Both causes contribute in bringing about a high or a low range of money incomes, as the case may be, and so a greater or a less gain from the purchase of foreign commodities.

The action of the two causes is illustrated by the different positions of the United States and Russia as exporters of wheat. The wheat growers in both countries sell their product at the same price in the world's markets. So far as the play of international demand goes, both gain to the same extent. But so far as the cost of producing wheat goes, — that is, the real cost, measured by the amount of labor needed for producing it, —

they are in very different positions. Wheat is grown with much less labor in the United States, and money wages are higher here. Money wages are lower in Russia, and the wheat growers of Russia, as indeed all Russians, are by so much in a less advantageous position in buying foreign goods. As between any two or more countries competing in the sale of the same article, the extent of their several gains from international trade depends on the relative efficiency of their labor in producing the things exported.

The determining cause of the general rate of money incomes and wages in a country is to be found in the exporting industries. These set the pace; not for real wages, but for money wages. Whatever is yielded by them tends to become, under the influence of competition, the ruling rate in the country at large, — in other industries, as well as in those exporting. In the other industries, this money rate is, to be sure, a matter of comparative indifference, since the prices of commodities will rise and fall with the rise and fall of wages and incomes. The same parallel movement appears in the exporting industries, — the prices of exported commodities go up and down with the money wages of the laborers engaged in producing them. In fact, these money wages are derived from the prices at which the exported commodities are disposed of in the world's markets. The parallel movement does not appear in the case of imported goods; the real gain from higher money incomes, as has been sufficiently explained, is secured from the lower prices of articles of import.

§ 7. A further question arises, in regard to which also there is much misconception. Is a country of higher money incomes — that is, one with advantageous terms of international trade — also a country of higher prices? Most persons would answer the question in the affirmative. But no unqualified answer can be given. It depends.

Commodities may be divided roughly into two classes: those which do enter into foreign trade, and those which do not. The former we may call, for brevity, export commodities; the latter we may call domestic commodities. Under conditions of free exchange, and with due allowance for the expense of transportation, export commodities tend to be at the same price the world over. Domestic commodities, however, may be at varying prices in different countries. The range of domestic commodities remains wide, notwithstanding the cheapening of transportation and the consequent extension of international trade and international competition. Many things are too bulky, in proportion to their value, to be moved far from the place of production; such are brick and stone. Some are so much affected by rooted habit that only the near-by producers can fashion them in the way desired by consumers; such are articles of household furniture. Some are of necessity made on the spot where they are used; house accommodation is an obvious case. The services of physicians, lawyers, actors, musicians, domestic servants are also necessarily rendered on the spot. These utilities are of no small importance, especially for the well-to-do; their price evidently is determined by domestic conditions alone.

Consider now such an item as household furniture, tables, chairs, bedsteads, chests. Will these be dearer in the United States, a country of high money incomes, than in Germany, a country of comparatively low money incomes? The answer depends on the effectiveness of American labor in producing them. If American labor is relatively as effective in this field as it is in export commodities, they will not be dearer. We have seen that American labor is more effective than German labor as regards wheat; otherwise, wheat could not be cheaper in the United States, and could not be sent thence to Germany. But American labor may also be more effective than German as regards tables and chairs; and then tables and chairs, though the laborers who make them get higher wages, will not be dearer in the United States. The principle is simple: those domestic commodities as to which a country's labor has the same degree of effectiveness as it has in making exported articles, will be relatively cheap, just as the exported commodities are relatively cheap. Those domestic commodities in which there is no such advantage will be dearer, and will be dearer to the degree in which the effectiveness of labor is less. The reader can supply for himself the extension of the argument which comes from the fact that some labor in a country, though not effective, is paid at an unusually low rate. Domestic commodities made by such unfortunate laborers will also be cheap.

There is a common impression that the United States, a country of high money incomes, is also a country of high prices. But this impression rests on no certain basis. It is probably due to the fact that many things are really dearer for the well-to-do. Services are almost necessarily dearer in the country of high incomes. Domestic servants, for example, get higher wages than in Europe. Physicians and lawyers get higher fees, teachers higher salaries. There are many things in which personal service, while not the sole element, is yet by far the most important; such are cab service and hotel accommodation. A great part of the income of the prosperous classes is spent on various forms of personal service, and for these classes the "expense of living" (which means the expense of a given conventional mode of life) is high. Therefore, those among them who have fixed incomes find that their incomes go farther if they live abroad; hence their impression that all things are cheaper abroad. But many domestic commodities of general consumption among all classes are probably not dearer. Most food is equally cheap, — not only that which enters into foreign trade, but that which is solely used at home. Fuel is as cheap in the greater part of the country, though not on the Atlantic seaboard, where the expensive anthracite is used. As to the important item of house accommodation (indicated by house rent) it is not easy to make a comparison, because of the difficulty of making allowance for quality. I suspect that, taking into account size, convenience, and attractiveness, prices are not higher in most parts of the United States for the housing accommodations of the masses; though they doubtless are so for the rich, whose houses are built "by the day" and with little use of factory-made frames, doors, and windows. Clothing, and especially woolen clothing, is dearer, — a result due mainly to our policy of high import duties, which prevent us from using our high money incomes to advantage in the purchase of cheaper foreign wool and woolens.[1]

[1] In this chapter and in that preceding, it has been tacitly assumed that within a country (so far as domestic commodities are concerned) exchange takes place, and value is determined, on the basis of labor cost, — that value rests on "cost of production," not on "expenses of production." Elsewhere, however, it has been assumed that supply price, in its relation to value, means expenses of production, not cost (see Book II, Chapter 12, § 1). The explanation of the inconsistency, and the grounds for considering it not repugnant to the general validity of the reasoning upon international trade, must be left for later discussion. See Book V, Chapters 47 and 48, and especially § 5 of Chapter 48, for the further consideration of this difficult subject.

CHAPTER 36

Protection and Free Trade. The Case for Free Trade

§ 1. The main argument in favor of free trade between nations has been already indicated. It is a simple corollary from the principles of the division of labor. Exchange between individuals brings the same gain whether they live in the same village or in widely separated districts. Things are obtained by the exchange more easily and abundantly than they could be obtained by each person's producing for himself. The reasoning which shows that it is advantageous for the farmer to deal with the village blacksmith, for Maine to deal with Florida, for New England with the Mississippi Valley, makes out a strong *prima facie* case in favor of free exchange between the United States and England, between France and Germany. The burden of proof may be fairly said to rest on those who assert there is gain from the contrary policy.

Most of the common arguments in favor of restrictions upon trade, by protective duties or otherwise, are fallacious. Many are crudely Mercantilistic, resting on an assumption that imports are bad *per se* and exports good. The so-called unfavorable balance of trade is made much of. What is expended on imports is deemed so much wasted or lost. It is supposed that a decline in imports or an increase of exports necessarily brings money into the country; and the notion persists that herein there is a gain, which comes directly from the balance of money secured, not through those effects on money incomes and foreign prices which were analyzed in the preceding chapter. Few among those who speak of a gain in exports as profitable ever heard of the last-named process or are able, unprepared, to understand it. They think of exports as bringing in money, and imports as taking money out, and money is the be-all and end-all of their economic thinking. Even if it is pointed out that a continuing excess of exports is due simply to other than merchandise transactions, and does not bring in specie, the notion still persists that exports somehow mean gain and imports loss. The elementary truth that exports are but a means of procuring the imports on easier terms than the same goods could be got by making them at home, — this is rarely grasped, or, if once grasped, is soon let slip.

Mercantilist notions, universally discarded though they are by the well-informed, affect the policy of nations, not only by strengthening the movement toward protection, but in other ways also. The public railways of Prussia and of other German states make special rates for exported goods, on the theory that this sort of movement deserves especially to be fostered. Shipping subsidies are granted by many countries, and colonies acquired and maintained at great expense, with the same object in view. The United States government spends considerable sums in gathering information about opportunities for export, and in promoting otherwise the export market; while various semi-public agencies and museums coöperate for this supposedly praiseworthy object. Underlying almost all activity of this sort is the persistent belief that there is something peculiarly profitable in international trade, and that the profit appears in the sale of the exports, — a belief which exaggerates the importance of the trade, and misconceives the nature of the real gain from it.

Perhaps the ancient association of foreigner with enemy still lingers. People do not worry when New England buys coal from Pennsylvania; but when coal is bought from Nova Scotia, dire consequences are supposed to ensue. Half a century ago (more or less) the region which is now British Columbia was claimed by the United States to be part of its territory. Had the Oregon question been settled at that time in accord with the American claims, no one would have questioned that the resources of British Columbia in lumber, coal, and fisheries were of advantage to Americans. But once a border line is drawn, the situation is supposed to change; and that which would have brought us gain in the way of more abundant and cheaper supplies is fraught with peril precisely because these supplies came from a foreigner.

§ 2. Some of the popular arguments in favor of protection call for brief consideration; for example, that it creates a home market; that it makes employment; and that it raises wages or keeps them high.

When imports are checked, and the things previously imported are made at home, a home market is supposed to be created. It is created; but there is not, as protectionists commonly state or imply, an additional market. Another and different market is substituted. Here again most people's ideas do not get beyond the range of sales and of money dealings. When the linen manufacture (say) is established, those engaged in it buy food and other supplies; and here, it is supposed, is an additional market for food. The real "market"—that is, the real exchange—is of food for linens. That same market existed when linens were imported, and food or other things were exported in payment. To cut off imports means to cut off exports also; it means simply the substitution of exchange within the country for exchange between countries. The real question is whether for a given quantity of food (*i.e.* of labor exerted in producing that quantity) more linen is got in one way than in the other. The very fact that linen can be got cheaper by importation shows *prima facie* that the foreign market is better than the domestic market. The home market argument is most frequently used in the United States with reference to the farmers, who are supposed to get benefit from a greater demand for their products because of the establishment of manufactures. The presumption is, however, that they do not gain, but lose; the "market" which is created offers less in exchange for their products than does the foreign market.

A special form of the home market argument, also much used in the United States, is suggested by the truck farm. Suppose a manufacturing town is established in consequence of protection: the near-by farmers profit by the sale of milk, vegetables, and the like. These farmers do in fact profit, but simply because, while they sell all their produce in the town, they purchase a very small share, if any, of the particular things which are made in it. If they had previously exported all their vegetables and dairy products, and if the manufacturing town, after the duty, supplied precisely the goods which they had previously procured by importation, they would lose, not gain. The truck farmers, in truth, are ordinarily within the limited circle of real beneficiaries from protection. They gain, however, not as farmers, but as landowners. They are like the lucky holder of urban sites in a newly established town. The great mass of farmers do not gain, but lose, — those who supply most of the needs of the manufacturing population and who buy most of its products. The non-landholding people of the manufacturing town also fail to gain. As will appear more fully in the sequel, neither employers nor workmen are, under conditions of free competition, permanently better off. Only those gain in the end whose sites, whether agricultural or urban, are more advantageously situated under the new distribution of the population.

Closely connected with the home market argument is that in regard to employment. That protective duties add to the demand for labor seems patent to the everyday man, and especially to the workingman. When imports are kept out, is it not clear that more employment exists for the workmen who make at home the things formerly imported? Here, again, people see only the first and most obvious results, and do not stop to think what other results must follow. If there are less imports, there will be less exports; and labor, if employed more in the new way, is employed less in the old. One of the most persistent of economic errors is the notion that employment is an end, not a means; and one of the hardest things to fasten in the average person's thinking is that the end to which employment should be directed is the increase of the national income, — the total flow of consumable goods and of services which constitutes the real revenue of the community.

Most workingmen, for reasons which are stated elsewhere,[1] oppose labor-saving appliances, and welcome arrangements which seem to increase the demand for labor. Most of them are instinctively protectionists, since the same fallacies are current in arguments for protection as in arguments for increasing the employment of labor. The workmen of any one group or set are concerned solely with their own share of the national income. Anything which adds, or seems to add, to the demand for their particular kind of labor is of course welcomed; and then, by an easy transition from the particular to the general, it is inferred that all labor is more in demand because of the circumstances which increase the demand in this particular direction.

One form of the creating-employment argument is that there is always unemployed labor and always unemployed capital. Put on a duty, bring this labor and capital together for making an article previously imported, — and is there not a gain? Obviously, the same question could be asked if the labor and capital were brought together in making an article previously exported, — is there not (on protectionist principles of the mercantile kind) even a greater gain? The truth is, that this problem is far removed from the protective controversy. Unemployed labor is a grave social evil; unemployed capital is a real waste. Some proportion of unemployment, no doubt, is inevitable both for labor and for capital; it results from progress in industry, from shifts between occupations, from the processes of change and transition. To minimize it is among the most important of public tasks. It is also among the most difficult. There is no ground for supposing that a system of protection would affect it one way or the other.

If a new industry is stimulated in a country by a protective duty, it by no means follows that the labor which is unemployed is adapted to that particular industry, or is in a place

[1] See Book V, Chapter 51, § 3. The discussion of this topic, as of others in the protective controversy, has a wide range, and more particularly touches the field of the distribution of wealth, covered in Book V.

where it can take advantage of the new opportunities. It takes time for adaptation and removal. Given time, however, all the forces of spontaneous activity tend to bring together unemployed labor and unemployed capital in any case. And even supposing the wildly improbable outcome that the unemployed forces were really brought together in an industry created by protection, — the solution of the problem would be but temporary. Inventions and improvements, redistribution of industries and of population, crises with all their dislocating effects, would ere long cause the problem to present itself again. A country quite without international trade, shut within its own borders, would be confronted with unemployment, as with other ills, so long as its industry rested on private property, complex division of labor, free movement of labor and capital, hopes, fears, and mistakes in the business world.

§ 3. In the United States, by far the most common and most effective argument in favor of protection is that it makes wages high, or enables wages to be high. With many persons it is an accepted article of faith that American wages can be kept high, and the American standard of living can be maintained, only if there is protection against the goods made by the cheaper labor of other countries. Yet I conceive that no argument in favor of protection is more fallacious than that of pauper-labor competition.

Evidently the argument is not of universal application. How could there be any exports at all, if lower wages always gave the foreigner an advantage? As much is exported (virtually as much) as is imported. The exported goods are made by laborers who get high wages in the United States; yet these goods, so far from being undersold in foreign countries, are themselves underselling those of the foreigners. The explanation is simple: the efficiency of labor in the exporting industries is great, and therefore high wages and low prices coexist. And that effectiveness is the *cause* of the high money wages; and these wages, again, may or may not be accompanied by high prices of the domestic commodities which are outside the realm of international trade. This whole subject cannot be understood except in connection with the principle of comparative costs. In those industries in which the United States has a comparative advantage in effectiveness, high wages can be paid, and yet low prices accepted, with profit to the employing capitalists. In those in which there is no such advantage, the current high wages cannot be afforded. In this latter class, though labor be as effective as in competing foreign countries, and though the industries in that sense are well adapted to the country, they encounter the difficulty that other industries are still better adapted, yield still larger returns, and set up a prevalent high rate of wages which these less advantageous industries cannot sustain.

Of course it is true that, when once industries which possess no sufficient advantage have been established under the shelter of protective duties, high wages can be maintained, *in those industries*, only by the continuance of the duties. This sort of situation — the existence of industries dependent on duties — was historically the occasion of the protectionist argument about wages. Wages have always been higher in the United States than in other countries. Before a protective system was adopted, it would have been absurd to say that they were due to any such system. When new industries are called into existence by protection, they must, of course, in order to secure their workmen, pay the same wages as are generally prevalent; and once they are established, it can be maintained with reason that high wages to their workmen are dependent on protection. As long as the workmen remain in those industries, the high wages they receive are so dependent.

The free trader argues that if the duties were given up and the protected industries pushed out of the field by foreign competitors, the workmen engaged in them would find no less well-paid employment elsewhere. Presumably they would betake themselves to the exporting industries, in which labor is advantageously applied. The protectionist answers that there would then be "overproduction" in those industries, —

that more goods would be produced, prices would be lower, and then wages lower. No, replies the free trader, — there would be more goods, but not lower prices or lower wages. For there is a new demand for these exportable goods, *pari passu* with the new supply. Goods are imported which were formerly made by protected industries. The new exports must be paid for by imports; there is a new foreign "market," replacing the last domestic "market." The eventual result, says the free trader, is that more workmen will be turned to the advantageous industries, and more goods will be exported in exchange for more imports; there will be higher wages (in terms of commodities) all around within the country, resulting from the more productive direction of its labor.

In all this reasoning, the free trader is right. There are some further questions concerning the effect of the supposed change on money wages, which will be presently considered;[1] but these do not affect the essentials of the argument. Of course the reasoning applies only to the long-run course of events. It assumes that labor (and capital, too) will shift from a less profitable to a more profitable industry; that when a protected industry is deprived of support, and those engaged in it are confronted with the alternative of either accepting lower wages or quitting, they will quit and go to better-paid occupations. Any such process of transition is difficult and trying. When carried out on a very large scale, — say by the sudden abandonment of a protective system under whose shelter many industries have grown up, — it may cause for a time something like disaster. The extent to which existing industries are in fact dependent on protection, is commonly exaggerated by both its advocates and its opponents; but, none the less, the question of vested interests is a very troublesome one. It may be deemed better, on the whole, to let things stand, or change them very slowly and cautiously, rather than incur the disturbance and damage of a radical change. But all this does not affect the question of principle, which is not

[1] See Chapter 37, § 1.

squarely presented unless we ask what would have been the best policy from the outset.

The question of wages — to anticipate for a moment — is at bottom one of productivity.[1] The greater the productivity of industry at large, the higher will be general wages. There are very intricate problems as to the precise nature of this connection, and as to the deductions from the general product, or the shares in the general product, on account of interest, rent, employer's gains. Under certain contingencies, it is conceivable that protective duties will affect the various processes of deduction or sharing, and so will influence wages otherwise than through their effect on product. But these are rare contingencies, and are negligible for the discussion of the main problem. *Prima facie,* protection restricts the geographical division of labor, causes industry to turn to less advantageous channels, lessens the productivity of labor, and so tends to lower the general rate of wages.

§ 4. One phase of the wages argument appears in the proposition, much heard in the United States of late years, that duties should be so adjusted as to "equalize cost of production" between this country and foreign countries. This has been propounded as a "scientific" solution of the tariff problem. When the labor cost of a commodity, it is said, is higher in the United States, let a duty be imposed sufficient to enable the domestic producer to meet his foreign competitor on terms of equality, — and then let them fight it out. It needs little reflection to show that such a policy, consistently followed, means the complete wiping out of all the advantages from international trade, nay, the wiping out of international trade altogether. The greater the disadvantage of a country in producing a given commodity, the more labor must be given to producing it, and the higher will be the expenses of the employers. In proportion as the efficiency or productivity of labor is less, more must be paid out in wages to secure the greater amount of labor required per unit of output; then

[1] See below, Book V, Chapter 51.

"labor cost" is so much higher; and duties must be made correspondingly high if the labor cost is to be equalized. Any commodity, however unsuited to the industrial aptitudes of a country, can be produced in it if only its price is made high enough; and by keeping out foreign competitors, there is no limit (short of the possible extinction of demand) to the rise in price. If the principle of equalizing cost were consistently carried out, we should exert ourselves most strenuously to promote by high duties the domestic production of an article according as we gain most from its importation. No doubt, the persons who propose the principle would probably refrain from pushing it to its logical conclusion. They would shrink from clapping on duties high enough to cause lemons to be grown in Maine, or (to use Adam Smith's familiar illustration) grapes in Scotland; though all this could be done if labor costs were unflinchingly equalized. They think of the commodities for which the domestic disadvantages are not glaring. But the difference is only one of degree. There is no rational reason for saying that a disadvantage in labor cost — that is, a disadvantage in industrial effectiveness — of twenty per cent should be offset by a protective duty, but that one of fifty, one hundred, two hundred per cent should not be so offset.

One thing is to be said in favor of the notion: duties should certainly not *exceed* the rates necessary to "equalize labor cost." If they so exceed, there is the possibility that a domestic monopoly may levy additional burdens on the consumers. This possibility arises if competition among the domestic producers is not free. As will presently appear, no special benefits to the protected producers accrue, and no monopoly profits are derived, if domestic competition keeps prices down to the level of expenses of production. But where there is a possibility of monopoly and of abnormal profit to the protected capitalists, it is not unreasonable to say that, if they must have protective duties, these should not be greater than suffice to enable the industry to be carried on. But it is absurd to urge that the proposal, even in this form, is a "scientific" solution of the protective question. It simply amounts to saying that protection should not be carried to the point where it may foster monopoly.

§ 5. The strength of the general presumption against protection will be made clearer by a consideration of the working of protective duties in greater detail.

When a duty is imposed on a commodity, its price usually rises by the amount of the duty. Usually it does so, but not necessarily; and not always at once, but often only in the end, even in those cases where this normal result is to be looked for. Strictly, the result is to be expected only if the commodity is produced under free competition and under the conditions of constant return.[1] Ordinarily a duty, like any tax on a commodity, increases by so much the expense of getting the article to market. The amount of the tax or duty must be added to the price charged the consumer if the producer is to get his usual return. But a rise in price has its effect on demand. Very likely the same quantity cannot be sold at the higher price. The producer, none the less, may not be able to lessen the supply with any promptness; he may have a large

[1] If a commodity is produced under the conditions of diminishing or of increasing return, the case is obviously different. Under diminishing return, a tax per unit of quantity tends to check consumption, lessen production, lower marginal cost, and so increase price by less than the amount of the tax. Conversely, under increasing return, a tax, by lessening consumption, tends to raise marginal cost and so to increase price by more than the amount of the tax. A tax on a monopolized article works out its results through the principles of monopoly value; and it is quite conceivable that such a tax, in the case of an article for which the demand is highly elastic, will cause little rise in price, and will be borne chiefly by the monopoly producer. All these possibilities, however, appear in the case of internal taxes quite as much as in that of import duties. They present no special problems in international trade; they are part of the theory of value. Moreover, they are not often of much practical consequence. As intimated in the text, the usual case is, in the long run, that of constant return. The most important qualification of the general reasoning probably is to be made for articles subject to a quasi monopoly of good will or trademark, where the producers, though they have no permanent or unqualified monopoly, make unusual profits for a considerable time, and can possibly be deprived of a part of these profits through the operation of a tax. Compare what is said below, Book VIII, Chapter 70.

plant committed to making the particular thing. For a while, therefore, price may be raised by less than the amount of the tax; conceivably it may not be raised at all. Only as supply is slowly adjusted to the new situation will normal conditions be regained and the price raised so as to recoup the producers and dealers for their increased expenses of production. Hence it is true that a duty on imports, and indeed any tax on a commodity, may fall for a while on the producer, foreign or domestic; while yet in the end, it falls with its full weight on the consumer.

So long as the commodity continues to be imported, this rise in price brings a tax, but no national loss. It is true that the consumers are in effect deprived of so much of their incomes; but what they lose, the public treasury gains. Taxes are presumably levied for useful public purposes. They do not stand for waste. If the needed revenue had not been got by customs duties, it would have been got in some other way, and the same tax would have been levied on the public.

Suppose, however, that after the duty has been imposed, domestic producers supplant the foreigners. They charge higher prices than the foreigners did; they *must* charge higher prices, in order to get a profit. If they could bring the commodity to market at the same price as the foreigner, there never would have been any importation. The fact that the domestic producers did not enter the field before the duty was imposed, shows that they are under a disadvantage.[1] When they are stimulated by the duty to enter the field, and sell their article at a higher price than the imported one had previously cost, the consumer pays the tax in precisely the same way as if the article continued to be imported, — that is, in the shape of higher prices. Only, there is in this case no revenue to the public treasury. The extra price stands for so much bonus to the domestic producers, to enable them to maintain themselves in a disadvantageous industry. And it represents so much national loss. In most discussion of protective duties,

[1] But see what is said in Chapter 37, § 2, on protection to young industries.

at least in the United States, the common assumption is that the creation of a domestic industry, supplying a commodity which was previously imported, represents so much gain. Strictly, the reverse is the case. The payment of duties on continued imports brings no loss; the loss arises from the domestic supply.

Hence, where the principle of free trade is consistently followed, a customs duty on an article is accompanied by an internal tax of the same amount on the domestic product. Then the combined taxes operate solely to bring in revenue, and have no effect on the direction of industry within the country. Such is the present (1910) system in Great Britain. Her customs duties are limited to a few articles of general consumption, such as tea, coffee, cocoa, sugar, beer, spirits, tobacco. On such articles as beer and spirits, an internal tax is imposed at the same rate as the customs duty. Tea, coffee, cocoa, sugar, and the like will not be produced within the country under any circumstances, or at least not under any such moderate duties as are, in fact, levied; the duties on them are of a purely revenue sort.[1] Sometimes, in popular discussion, it is said that the imposition of any duties whatever is inconsistent with the principle of free trade. Obviously, this is a mistake; it is only the imposition of duties that cause a substitution of domestic products for imported that conflicts with the principle.

When a customs duty operates to bring into existence a domestic industry, the domestic producers do not make unusual gains; that is, not if the commodity be brought to market under competitive conditions. Very likely those who take the initiative in producing the article make unusual profits on the first im-

[1] Tobacco is in the same class with tea and coffee; all of it is imported. Its cultivation in the United Kingdom is prohibited, on the assumption (a reasonable one) that only sporadic cases of its cultivation would appear in any case, and that the supervision and taxation of these would cost more than any internal revenue would justify. The most convenient way to collect the British tax on tobacco is to levy a customs duty on the imports, and prevent once for all domestic production.

position of a duty. In time, however, profits will fall to the normal level, and at that normal level prices will be higher than foreign prices only if a real disadvantage handicaps the domestic producers. In other words, nobody gains, and the community loses, — the loss consisting in its paying more for the protected article than it would have had to pay without the protection.

Where there are not competitive conditions, — where there is a monopoly, complete or partial, permanent or temporary, — the domestic producers may make unusual gains. To the extent that they do so, another item enters into the account. There may not only be some national loss, but in addition a shift of revenue from one set of persons to another set. The commodity may be produced at higher expense within the country, and may have to sell on that ground for a higher price than if imported. It may sell for a price still higher, because the domestic producers are in a position to keep out competition and make unusual gains. It may even happen that the imposition of a duty enables domestic producers who are under no disadvantage at all, and who could bring the article to market as cheaply as the foreigners, to form a combination and exact a price higher than the competitive one. In such a case there is no national loss at all.

Naturally enough, this last-mentioned case is precisely that in which protection is most unpopular, though in a sense least harmful. Where the protected producers make no unusual gains, the system is supposed to work not unfairly. The vague and distant consequences on general industrial efficiency which strict economic analysis brings out are within the ken of comparatively few persons. The direct consequence of robbing Peter to pay Paul, which appears in case of monopoly, strikes the popular imagination at once and leads to indignation, even though, on cool consideration, it appears that Paul gains what Peter loses, and that the community as a whole is no worse off.

The ease with which popular feeling can be roused against a monopoly has led to the frequent statements that protection breeds monopoly. The former head of the American Sugar Refining Company — a "trust" or would-be monopoly — once remarked to a congressional committee of investigation that "the tariff is the mother of all trusts," and the aphorism became the text of many free trade sermons. Its truth is limited. The causes of combination are deeply rooted in the industries of modern times. They are found mainly in the development of production on a great scale; and it is superficial to ascribe a tendency so far-reaching to a single external cause.

It is true that protective duties sometimes bring combination more easily and at an earlier date, and sometimes increase the gains from it. This is particularly the case where the situation is ripe for consolidation within the country, but not ripe for international consolidation, — a stage of development not uncommon, especially in the United States during recent years. It is not to be supposed that the tendency to combination, strong and far-reaching though it is, works out its results automatically, irrespective of favoring causes or legislative influences. Protective duties have been in the United States during the last generation a favoring cause. Though the trust problem is in its essence very different from that of protection, — a graver problem, and of far larger social consequence, — the two interlace in some industries.

Just as protective duties may bring unusual gains to some capitalists, if these can keep out competitors, so they may bring exceptionally high wages to some workmen, on the same condition of keeping out competition. This is commonly less easy for the workmen, but it is not impossible, at least for considerable stretches of time. It is most feasible in occupations of the handicraft sort, calling for special acquired skill, and not subjected to the machine processes. Such is, or at least has been until very recent times, glass blowing. Certain kinds of glass, especially window glass, have called for the services of the blowers, whose trade is not easily learned. They have had a tight union, have restricted entrance to the trade, and have maintained exceptionally high wages. The employers in this industry have also combined; so that there has been a double monopoly of capitalists and workmen, promoted by very high import duties. The two favored sets have alternately quarreled and joined forces, with the advantage in the end, as usual in such cases, to the employers. Here, as elsewhere, new inventions have come in, and the application of machinery has tended to deprive the handicraft workmen of their special advantage. But so long as the old conditions remained (and the transition to machinery is by no means completed in this industry) the tariff system may be said really to have kept up wages, — not wages of workmen in general, but those of a limited group. And here, as in the case of government industries,[1] workmen in general are likely to regard with approval this advantage to the small group, even though it may mean higher charges to consumers and to the great body of the workmen as consumers. Anything that means high wages to any set of manual laborers finds favor with the labor leaders and doubtless with the dumb rank and file also; partly from mere clannish sympathy, but mainly from inability to distinguish between the causes that bring real advantage to all and those that bring advantage to a favored few only.

[1] Compare what is said in Book VII, Chapter 62, § 5.

CHAPTER 37

PROTECTION AND FREE TRADE, *continued.* SOME ARGUMENTS FOR PROTECTION

§ 1. The simpler aspects of the protective controversy have been considered in the preceding chapter, — those which bring out most strongly the case for free trade. They tend to show that the increase in price due to a protective duty represents a net loss. But there are ways in which the loss may be offset. The consideration of the various possible modes of offset brings out those arguments for protection which have some degree of validity.

First there is a possible effect on the terms of international exchange.[1] The first influence of a duty is almost necessarily to lessen imports. Even if it be a purely revenue duty, it will lessen them; the rise in price will cause a decline in consumption, unless demand happens to be quite inelastic. If the duty is protective, and operates to stimulate domestic production, the decline in imports will be more certain and greater. Hence, the movement of specie will be into the country. Then will ensue the train of consequences (always supposing the flow of specie to be considerable and continued) already familiar to the reader. Prices and incomes rise within the country, and fall in foreign countries. Exports in time begin to be checked, as the prices of exported articles rise; imports are stimulated, as the prices of imported articles fall. The length of this period of transition, and the extent of the change before it comes to an end, depend on the play of reciprocal demand. If the commodities exported from a country are of a sort insistently demanded in foreign countries; and if, on the other hand, the commodities which it imports are not such as to be consumed more largely as their prices fall, —

[1] In the sense in which that phrase was used and explained in Chapter 35.

then the change may be considerable. Eventually equilibrium is reëstablished; exports diminish and imports increase until payments again balance. When this stage is finally reached, the country that imposed the duty will have higher money incomes and higher prices. The higher incomes will be of no benefit so far as domestic purchases go, since within the country prices have risen in the same proportion. But they will be of advantage in the purchase of things imported.

In such a case, there is a balance of loss against gain. The consumers lose as purchasers of the protected articles, that is, of those made at home under the influence of the duties; but they gain as purchasers of things that continue to be imported. Even if the particular articles subjected to the duties are completely shut out, there will remain imports of other articles. Thus, in the United States, protective duties during the last generation have served to prohibit completely the importation of many manufactures; but tea, coffee, sugar, tropical articles of all sorts, sundry raw materials, some finer manufactures, have continued to come in. All these, if the reasoning of the preceding paragraph holds good, are got in reality more cheaply because of the duties. It is true that some of the things imported, being still subject to duty, are absolutely raised in price; but for this advance there is a full recompense in the revenue received by the public treasury, and in the relief (presumably) from other taxes. But even these imports are not raised in price by the full amount of the duties, — there is some offset because foreign prices in general have fallen, and domestic money incomes have risen.

How far is reasoning of this sort applicable to the concrete facts? Precisely to the same extent as the general reasoning on the distribution of the gains from international trade. How difficult it is to verify this in detail has already been shown. Take the case of the United States during the last thirty or forty years, when a system of high protective duties has been steadily maintained. Throughout the period a whole series of other factors has been influencing international trade in opposing ways. The protective system, in so far as it has restricted imports, has been among the factors making for gain in the terms of exchange. The high tariff has contributed something toward a higher range of money incomes. How far the gain from this source has served to offset the loss from the domestic commodities produced and sold at higher cost, is impossible of calculation. It is a gain, at best, little reckoned with in the popular controversy. Most people who try to persuade the public to their opinions on one or another side of the tariff question reason only about what is "good for business," about employing labor, higher prices to consumers, extortionate monopolies. Even the simpler questions really involved, as to the general effects of the geographical division of labor, they perceive but vaguely; the more intricate ones here considered are quite beyond the understanding not only of the average man, but of the average writer on protection.

It is obvious that all countries could not play this game. No one of them has a monopoly of imposing import duties. A condition of mutual grasping and recrimination may be imagined, in which each country tries to get from the other all it can, with the eventual result of some advantage to one among them in the form of higher money incomes, and of considerable loss to that country and to the rest from the curtailment of the advantageous division of labor. Commercial strife has come perilously near this state in modern times; but the immediate object held in view by the combatants has never been that of getting some of the imports cheaper. The motives and objects have invariably been of a semi-mercantilist sort: to check imports generally, to market more and more exports. Reciprocity movements are a compromise resulting from this familiar sort of contest.

§ 2. The argument for protection to young industries points to another way in which the *prima facie* case in favor of free trade may be fairly met, and the initial loss from protection offset. The gist of it is that an industry really advantageous for a country may be prevented from arising because of ignorance, lack of experience, and all the obstacles that impede success in unfamiliar undertakings. Stated in another way, the argument is that while the price of the protected article is temporarily raised by the duty, eventually it is lowered. Competition sets in, it is said, and brings a lower price in the end. The free trader asks, why any need of a duty, if the domestic producer is really able to sell at a lower price than the foreigner? The answer is that this reduction in domestic price comes only with the lapse of time. At the outset the domestic producer has difficulties, and cannot meet foreign competition. In the end he learns how to produce to best advantage, and then can bring the article to market as cheaply as the foreigner, even more cheaply. Most persons who use this second form of the argument (as to the eventual lowering of domestic prices) are but dimly aware of its identity with that for protection to young industries. But the two arguments are one and the same, resting on the premises of temporary obstacles and eventual success.

The theoretical validity of this argument has been admitted by almost all economists. The question is how far and under what circumstances there is ground for applying protection with prospect of this good result. The argument was first used (in such a way as really to make an impression) in the United States during the earlier part of the nineteenth century, when this country was in the transition from dominantly agricultural and commercial conditions to the stage of modern manufacturing. It was carried from the United States to Germany by its best-known advocate, Friedrich List, who applied it to Germany in her transition during the middle of that century from semi-medieval to modern conditions. The United States was then a "young" country, and Germany, though an old country, had manufacturing industries young so far as modern ways were concerned. There was force, as to both countries, in the contention that manufactures with machinery, power, large-scale operation, were certain to arise in any case, or at least had an advantageous opportunity; and that the process of transition and growth could be made easier, and a beneficial result could be reached at an earlier date, by a temporary handicap on the developed competitors of older countries. England, of course, was the country then in the van, against which such shelter was sought.

List and the other more moderate advocates of nurturing protection said that duties for this purpose should be moderate and should be temporary. They should be moderate — not to exceed say twenty-five per cent — because, if the domestic industry was at a great disadvantage in the beginning, there was little prospect that it would ever reach independence. They should be temporary — not to endure more than twenty or thirty years — because in the end, by supposition, the domestic industry would not need them, and ought to be able and willing to face foreign competition. It was further added that agricultural commodities and raw materials give no field for this sort of protection. Their geographical distribution is determined chiefly by unalterable physical conditions. Only in manufacturing industries can the legislator have a prospect of encouraging young industries with good results.

These limitations on the argument are reasonable; more particularly the exclusion of agricultural articles. The government can do much to promote efficiency in agriculture; but chiefly by diffusing education, improving the conditions of tenure, promoting science. There are respectable arguments, as will presently appear, for duties on such articles; but they are of a very different kind from this one, which looks to promoting eventual cheapness. The United States has long levied protective duties on wool, but never with any prospect of getting wool cheaper thereby, and with less prospect now (1910) than ever. Germany and France levy duties on grain, as England did until 1846; but there was not for England in the earlier time, nor is there for the Continental countries to-day, any outlook for securing domestic supplies at once more abundantly and cheaply.

The other limitations seem also reasonable; but in actual experience it is not so clear that they must be observed in order to secure the desired result. Not only moderate duties, but very heavy ones, may set things going, and eventually lead to an independent domestic industry. Of this possibility the recent history of the silk manufacture in the United States supplies an illustration. A duty of sixty per cent on silks was imposed during the Civil War (1864). The object at first was revenue. Then a domestic industry grew up; and the duty was maintained, even increased (especially in 1897). Competition became active, and great improvements were introduced. The silk manufacture has indeed been the last of the textile industries to be adjusted to the machine processes; but this development seems to have been promoted in the United States by the establishment of the industry under the shelter of protection. It is certain that advances in manufacturing methods have taken place; it is probable that some branches of the industry, though not all, have reached the stage where the fabrics can be put on the market as cheaply as they can be imported. Nor is it inconsistent with this outcome that the domestic producers still clamor for protection. They are simply in the habit of doing so. Most business men know very little outside the immediate range of their business. If foreign competition has been long shut off by a high duty, they are ignorant of its possible effects; and if there is a proposal to permit it again, they object on general principles, even though they are quite able to hold their own. The protective system, especially when exaggerated stress is laid on it through party politics, begets an abject fear of all foreign competition. Notwithstanding this common attitude of the domestic producers, it is quite possible that the object of protection to young industries has been, in fact, attained; though, no doubt, the only certain way to ascertain this is to remove the duties and let the domestic producers meet the foreigners on even terms.

While it is possible that protection to young industries may be successfully applied where advantages in production rest not on natural grounds, but on acquired skill, it is extremely difficult to say how far there is a probability of such success. The question is part of one much wider, — the general causes of the advance of the arts. Economic history shows that the spread of the various trades and manufactures in different countries has taken place by no "natural" process, and that "artificial" factors, such as governmental encouragement, the emigration of skilled artisans, the social and political organization of a country, have been of large, often dominant, effect. It would be absurd to apply to the conditions of medieval and early modern times a theory of natural advantages and of settled differences in comparative costs. On the other hand, the lesson of history seems to be that other modes of encouragement have been more effective than protective duties; such as rational education, free industry, abatement of social barriers, promotion of invention by patents and trademarks. In very modern times, with the wide diffusion of industrial education, the ease of communication, the technical press, the eager search for all ways of investing capital at a profit, — the argument for protection to young industries would seem to have lost much of its force. None the less, possibilities still exist, as in the case of the silk manufacture just cited. Unfortunately the decisive test — eventual removal of duties — is one which domestic producers are likely always to oppose; and hence it is difficult to ascertain in any concrete case whether the community ultimately gets a real gain sufficient to offset the initial loss.

§ 3. Political considerations are often urged in favor of protective duties.

The most conspicuous illustration is afforded by shipping. In the days of wooden vessels, a merchantman was not so very different from a man-of-war, and at all events training in handling the two was the same. Moreover, a merchant marine was an effective auxiliary in times of war. The first of these reasons is less important in our day, when steel battleships have intricate and highly specialized machinery of their own. The second is perhaps as important as in former days. A modern navy needs an elaborate complement of scout ships, supply ships, colliers, not to mention transports. A large mercantile marine supplies these, or at least aids mightily in supplying the suddenly increased need of them which arises in time of war. If, to use Adam Smith's phrase, defense [or aggression?] is more important than opulence, it will be worth while to promote a mercantile marine, even though it cannot do its work so cheaply as foreign shipping. It might even be economical to subsidize a merchant marine, under conditions which assure the availability of the merchant ships in time of war; this course being very possibly cheaper than that of hurriedly creating an auxiliary fleet when war breaks out.

Viewed simply as a matter of the adjustment of a country's productive forces, the protection of shipping presents no new question of principle. If foreign ships can carry goods more cheaply than domestic ships, let them do it, says the free trader. There is no wonder-working magic in having your own ships. They exist simply to carry goods; and the same grounds which hold for letting the foreigner produce and sell goods to you, if he can do it more cheaply, hold for letting him transport goods for you, if he can do it more cheaply.

The only economic peculiarity in the shipping situation is that the same method of protection, by duties, is not here available; at least not for shipping engaged in foreign trade. Though a system of preferential taxes can be elaborated, it is peculiarly open to retaliation. Tonnage duties may be made higher on foreign ships than on domestic; or duties on goods imported in foreign bottoms may be made higher. But this sort of discrimination invites easy retaliation. The domestic ships so favored must in due time go to foreign ports, and in those ports they in turn may meet the same sort of hostile treatment. Not only may they do so, but they certainly will. Retaliation of this sort has been universally applied. Hence all countries have found themselves compelled to enter on reciprocity arrangements for vessels engaged in the direct trade between them, and have agreed to treat domestic and foreign vessels on the same terms. Coastwise shipping — from one port to another in the same country (including colonies) — is of course not subject to this limitation, and here protection can be applied without hindrance. Most countries which maintain protection in any form apply it to the coasting trade, usually by excluding foreigners once for all.

For shipping in the foreign trade, the only available protective policy is that of direct subsidy. The difference between this and protection through duties is one of method only. In the case of subsidy the community is called on to pay money directly in order to promote a particular industry. In the case of protective duties it is called on to pay indirectly, in the form of higher prices to those engaged in a particular industry. The subsidy or bounty method has been applied in other cases than shipping; frequently in older times, more sparingly in our own day. For example, it was applied in 1890 in this country, when the duty on sugar was abolished, and the domestic producers, who had previously had the benefit of higher prices because of an import tax, were given a direct bounty of the same amount (two cents a pound) on the domestic product.[1] A bounty, or subsidy, however, is a much less insinuating method, and much more likely to become unpopular. Import duties, though they come in essentials to the same thing as bounties, can be defended by a host of persuasive though fallacious arguments; but the direct payment of money to a favored industry presents in unmistakable form the question whether it is really worth while thus to tax the community. From the free traders' point of view, this very simplicity is an argument in favor of using in all cases bounties and subsidies rather than import duties.

National pride and prejudice have been important factors in promoting the growth of protective feeling, and have been particularly so in regard to shipping. The Stars and Stripes have disappeared from the seas: here is the most effective popular argument in favor of shipping subsidies. Vaguely associated with this are the arguments in favor of a merchant marine as a means of supplementing a fighting navy. This combination of sentiment, military glory, and serious political considerations belongs outside the strict scope of economics. But the drift of all rational economic thinking is against subsidies to shipping,

[1] That bounty was abolished in 1894, when the sugar duty was reimposed. The only industry for which a bounty has been advocated of late in this country is shipping.

as indeed it is against all jingoism. Soberly considered, merchant ships are but implements for promoting the division of labor, and the Stars and Stripes on them are cause for pride only if the ships are made and handled to the real advantage of the community. Soberly considered, battleships are *prima facie* a waste; if a necessity, a sad one; and not to be built one iota beyond the limits of clear necessity.

§ 4. Considerations as to general social soundness are supposed by some to strengthen the case for free trade, by others that for protection. But it is doubtful whether a strong case can be made out on such grounds either way. It is said by the protectionists that diversified industry has social and educational advantages, and that a community whose occupations have a very narrow range will be deficient in intelligence and adaptability. In view of the degree of industrial diversity which is certain to appear under any circumstances in a modern country of advanced civilization, this sort of vague allegation has no probative force. Possibly more can be found in the free traders' argument that a diversity of industries secured by the promotion of manufactures at the expense of agriculture brings social and political drawbacks. Manufactures mean large-scale production, concentration in comparatively few hands of management and probably of ownership, dependence of workmen on wages by hire, increasing inequality. They mean, too, crowding in cities, and the temptation to employ women and children. In the earlier part of the nineteenth century arguments of this sort were much used in the United States against protection. They were not without weight; they are not without weight even now. The soundest parts of our American nation are in those regions of the North where agriculture is still the dominant industry. But, after all, the mode in which an industry is conducted, and the character of the people engaged in it, are more important than the nature of the industry itself. The workingmen of the English manufacturing districts in Lancashire, Yorkshire, and Scotland are better social stuff than the agricultural laborers of eastern Germany and probably even than most of the peasant proprietors of

France. Protection and free trade are minor factors as compared with the diffusion of education, the general range of intelligence, the distribution of wealth and income, the demarcations of social classes, political and industrial freedom.

A special application of social and political arguments has recently been made in Germany, combined, however, with reasoning of a strictly economic sort. There the controversy has been between the advocates of the *Agrarstaat* and of the *Industriestaat*,[1] the former being in favor of duties on grain and other agricultural products, the latter opposed to them. To the former — the protectionists — dependence on foreign countries for indispensable foodstuffs seems to bring evils and dangers. An agricultural population, or at least one with a due proportion settled on the land, is thought to be better social material than one mainly engaged in manufactures. A great development of manufactures, moreover, and a dependence on foreign markets for disposing of the products, bring uncertainty. Hostile tariffs, or the loss of the advantage in production on which the exportation rests, may put an end to the trade and endanger the established industries. Finally — and here the crux of the arguments is reached — the present relations between the European manufacturing countries and the oversea countries from which they get food are essentially temporary, — temporary, that is, compared with a nation's life history. The supply of food, and especially of wheat, from the United States, Argentina, Canada, rests on predatory cultivation.[2] The continuous cropping of the soil can be maintained only so long as new land is still available. Sooner or later — and it will be soon, say these protectionists — the virgin lands will all be occupied; and then a conserving cultivation, with varied crops, must come. Meanwhile, population in these new countries increases rapidly, their own consumption of foodstuffs becomes greater, their economic situation becomes steadily less favorable to the expor-

[1] The German word "Industrie" means "manufactures." It is often misunderstood and mistranslated to mean "industry."

[2] See what is said in Book V, Chapter 42, § 5, on predatory cultivation.

tation of grain and the like. This transition has already begun in the United States, hitherto the greatest exporter of agricultural produce. It must set in, with time, in other such countries also.

Hence those old countries in which great manufactures develop, based on an exchange of the manufactured products with imported food, must face the possibility, nay the probability, of an eventual revulsion. Food will no longer be obtainable by importation. The manufacturing population must then go back, in part, to the land. But this population, under the stimulus of plentiful employment and cheap food, will have become large, and an endeavor to support it at home will meet all the obstacles of diminishing returns from land. The example of England is held up as a warning. Her great population, which the country's own resources cannot possibly supply with food and materials, is necessarily dependent on foreign trade, and must be constantly uneasy lest the process of exchange with other countries may fail.

There is much validity in this train of reasoning. As put forth by careful thinkers, it admits the *prima facie* loss from protection. It would seem plain that in the present generation food is got cheaper by foreign trade, and that the exchange of manufactures for food is for the time being advantageous. True, some of the ardent protectionists hesitate in this sort of admission, as people commonly hesitate and minimize in concessions to their opponents; but the admission must be made. It must be admitted, also, that the process of checking the growth of manufactures by making foodstuffs dear is a trying one. It is a sacrifice to the apparently distant future, which in the present generation must be unpopular. But where the sentiment of nationality is strong, and the welfare of coming generations is prized, such sacrifice may be called for.

To go into all the details of the controversy on *Agrarstaat* and *Industriestaat* would pass the limits of this book. The free traders aver that in a country of great extent and diversified climate like Germany, no such extreme development of manufactures as in England is to be looked for; that the probability of failure of supplies from food-exporting countries is exaggerated; that if there comes eventually a check to the exchange of manufactures for food, it will be by no sudden disastrous halt, but by a gradual process to which industry and population can adjust themselves; and finally that, in the present, the burden of import duties is heavy, and that the chief beneficiaries are a small knot of large landed proprietors. The main economic argument of the protectionists, as to the future failure of food supplies, raises a question difficult in many directions, — namely, how far it is wise to go in the restriction of immediate satisfactions for the sake of a distant and more or less uncertain future. Shall we now husband our coal supplies, which we know to be limited? Or shall we use them freely according to present needs, partly indifferent to the future, partly trusting to possible discoveries and improvements for other sources of heat and power? Shall the Germans (and English, too) persist in a policy of free trade and of dependence on foreign countries for food and materials needed now, without speculating too anxiously upon the continuance of these supplies in the uncertain future? It is easy to err in endeavoring to provide too carefully for coming generations. Such are some of the large problems which the protective controversy now presents in a country like Germany, — problems which give fair ground for differences of opinion, and involve considerations much weightier than those usually put forward by protectionists in the United States.

§ 5. A somewhat different phase of the tariff controversy has appeared in England. There the steps towards a manufacturing nation (*Industriestaat*) have been irrevocably taken, and the question is as to the best means of remaining with safety and prosperity in this far-developed stage. It would seem at first sight that here a policy of free trade alone is tenable. Yet the reaction against it has appeared in England also, and not without the support of effective arguments. These arguments, so far as they are really of weight, all turn on the expediency of reciprocity arrangements.

In the preceding pages it has been said more than once that exaggerated importance is commonly attached to a country's exports. For a country in England's situation, however, there is substantial ground for watching the exports with special care, and perhaps with some anxiety. They are the means for obtaining indispensable imports. The alternative of producing the imports at home — of turning the labor and capital from making the things exported to making those now imported — hardly exists. England must import; and in order to import, she must export. Hence every event which lessens the market for exports must cause concern. Among those events is the imposition of protective duties elsewhere. It is a matter of large consequence for England to maintain in other countries an open market for herself. Hence the advocacy of imperial federation, or imperial preference duties, as a means of inducing the colonies to relax, if not to give up, their duties on English goods; and hence the advocacy of duties on foreign goods in England, as a means of chaffering with other countries in negotiations for the reciprocal reduction of tariff barriers. In England, as in Germany, and indeed in all countries, the vulgar fallacious arguments in favor of protection play a large part in the popular controversy: increased employment for home labor, support of domestic industry, tribute to foreigners in payments for imports, and so on. But these arguments are more insidiously dangerous in England than anywhere else. That country depends for its very existence on manufacturing industries which are able to face the competition of the world. If once her own industries really lean on protection against foreigners, her knell is sounded. The only solid ground for advocating duties is to enable the diplomatists to higgle for lowered duties elsewhere. And the only ground for preferential arrangements with the colonies is to induce them to admit English goods with no duties or with lowered duties.

In its direct economic effects, the levy of duties on imports in retaliation for duties elsewhere on a country's exports, makes the situation not better, but worse. If Germany levies duties on English goods, the advantages from the division of labor between the two countries are lessened by so much. If England then levies duties on German goods, those advantages are lessened by so much more. If, indeed, one takes a Mercantilist view of foreign trade, and assumes that its chief object is to procure a market for the exports, then retaliation and reciprocity assume a different aspect. Then a country becomes always intent on increasing its exports, and always uneasy at increasing its imports; and then it will perhaps consent to admit the imports more freely only if tempted by a bait of selling exports more freely. So long as this state of mind exists, there is at least a possibility of securing an eventual relaxation of restrictions by first imposing restrictions.

What may be the substantial grounds for expecting, in the case of England, a real extension of international trade by this process, it is difficult to say. Adam Smith remarked that this matter was not for the economist, but for that crafty and insidious animal called the statesman or politician. The stanch free traders aver that other countries, and the English colonies also, will go their way undisturbed by retaliatory duties or preferential offers, or will make concessions that are only nominal; and that England herself will suffer, and in no way gain, from her own restrictions. On the other hand, it must be admitted that the Mercantilist notions persist with extraordinary tenacity. The immense majority of persons think of a reduction of duties, not as a gain to their own country, but as a favor shown to the foreigner; and conversely they think of tariff reductions by foreigners as the opportunity to sell more goods abroad and profit thereby.

§ 6. The growth of protection during the last generation has been a remarkable phenomenon, in view of the weight of rational opinion against most of the arguments commonly advanced for it. Half a century ago, — that is, during the generation following the repeal of the English corn laws in 1846, — the indications seemed to be that free trade, or at least a great relaxation of customs barriers, would extend over the civilized world. But in the decade 1870–1880 the current began to turn the other way. Country after country has set toward protection, and England is the only one that has held consistently to unrestricted trade. The protectionist reaction is explicable on various grounds. The growth of nationalist feeling is one important cause. Protection seems, to most people, a "national" policy, and in fact is so, in the sense of causing exchanges to be made within a country rather than between countries. The principle of free trade has a certain cosmopolitan flavor, and assumes (as well as promotes) a spirit of peace and good will among the nations. Another cause has been the breakdown of the British school of political economy, and the admitted need of a thorough reconstruction of economic theory. This has promoted skepticism as to free trade, which was one of the cardinal doctrines of that school; although no part of the system of the older economists has stood the test of time and criticism better than their reasoning about international trade. Still another cause has been the competition of oversea countries with the agricultural producers of the Continent. The landed interest there, formerly indifferent or hostile to duties, has joined in the demand for protection against underselling foreigners. At all events, during the last generation a wave of protection has succeeded the previous one of free trade.

There are some indications of a movement the other way, — a reaction toward lower duties again. The game of obstructing imports has been played by the various countries, each against the other, to such an extent that they seem to be getting weary of it. They have resorted to reciprocity arrangements as a method of reaching a more liberal policy; and this is likely to be the method of the immediate future. Whatever the grounds on which this new movement rests, and whatever the methods used, almost all economists regard it with favor. The rampant protectionism which has taken such hold in France, Germany, Russia, above all in the United States, has the support of few sober thinkers; though there are many economists to whom unqualified free trade seems to bring difficulties of its own. Whether England, in a general movement toward reciprocity, would profit more by holding aloof, and accepting only the results of lower duties as arranged by the other countries; or whether she would gain by threatening to impose duties of her own and thus entering actively into the bargaining process, — these are questions to which, to repeat, no certain answers can be given, and which must be left for the English people and statesmen to decide as best they can.

§ 7. In the United States, a severely protective tariff has been maintained since the Civil War. The financial exigencies of the war caused high duties to be levied, especially in 1864; and in the successive tariff acts passed since that time, these duties have been retained, and in many directions raised further. No country now (1910) has a more rigid or all-inclusive tariff system than the United States.

The economic effects of this system it is impossible to follow empirically. We have seen that its effects on the terms of international exchange are so interwoven with those of other factors that no unraveling is possible. Even more baffling is the task of following or measuring its effects on general prosperity. The protectionists, on this subject, as on the rate of wages, have preached and protested that all good things come from their tariff. Such talk results naturally from the exigencies of partisan conflicts and the need of simple arguments for the mass of voters. So loud and persistent has been the talk that for many persons not unintelligent it has become an article of faith that the prosperity of this country rests on the protective tariff. Yet there is no greater delusion. A multitude of factors explain our general welfare, — vast resources, a far-spread division of labor within the country, a free, active, and intelligent population. Has not this North American region been for centuries, under all sorts of economic and political conditions, the envy of the world? But to trace in detail the part played by any one factor in promoting or retarding the enviable outcome, is well-nigh impossible. Certain it is that, so far as the tariff is concerned, we must rely chiefly on general reasoning. The first and obvious effect of protection is to turn industry into less advantageous channels; and there is, in my judgment, no good case to rebut this *prima facie* conclusion, and to establish a balance of gain, from such a tariff system as the United States has had since the Civil War.

The protective duties have caused a real burden of taxation for the community, — a burden alike as to the things imported and as to those whose domestic production has been brought about. True, the duties on imports have yielded revenue. But they have led to public extravagance. The persistence in maintaining high duties, and the inflow of many imports over the barrier of the tariff, have resulted in greater revenues than was expected or desired, and have promoted wasteful expenditure. The main burden, none the less, certainly the burden specially due to protection, has appeared in the higher prices of the things made at home. That burden has in many cases been increased for the consumer, or at least kept heavy for him, by monopoly, temporary or permanent, among the domestic producers. It is small comfort that, in case of monopoly, the consumer's burden may represent, not national loss, but diversion of gain to favored persons.

Yet it should be said that on many articles the duties have been but nominal. These articles have been made as cheaply within the country, and (competition being active) sold as cheaply. The mere imposition of a duty does not raise prices. It does so only if a foreign supply is cut off, and a more expensive domestic supply is thereby induced, or a domestic monopoly fostered. The extent to which manufacturing industry in the United States is dependent on the tariff system is vastly exaggerated by the protectionists. One would suppose, from their doleful predictions, that not a chimney would smoke but for the tariff. In fact, the United States is certain to be a great manufacturing country under any conditions. So much is assured by its wonderful resources of coal and minerals and by the ingenuity and enterprise of its people. Its comparative advantage is by no means confined to agriculture. But this same consideration indicates that the free traders have gone too far in ascribing ill effects to all the parts of the protective system. It has not changed the course of industry as far as their charges imply. The country would be prosperous, and would have greatly diversified industries, without a high tariff as certainly as with it.

§ 8. The conditions on which depends the maintenance of manufactures in a country like the United States deserve a moment's consideration. Agriculture still remains the dominant industry, though not as pronouncedly so as in former times. Some manufactures always have existed, side by side with agriculture, from the very necessities of the case. These produce what we have called domestic commodities, — those not subject to foreign competition in any event. The manufactures whose products could conceivably be supplied by importation are those which alone present the tariff problems. With the cheapening of transportation and the crumbling away of special national ways and prejudices, the range of these potentially competitive manufactures is probably widening. They can maintain themselves, in a state of freedom, only if they have as great a comparative advantage as agriculture. They can hold their own against foreigners if their labor is more effective in the same degree as labor in agriculture is, or if they can get labor on unusually cheap terms. Labor may be more effective (and these are obviously the kinds of advantage which are really to be desired), either if the natural conditions are advantageous, or if the labor is intelligently directed and applied. Both these causes of advantage — natural resources and intelligence in applying labor — tell in giving the United States an advantage in agriculture. Both tell, also, in manufactures.

The exportation of wheat, cotton, corn products, from the United States, though in large part the result of favoring conditions of climate and soil, depends also on agricultural machinery, well-selected seeds, cheap transportation to the railway and by the railway. The exportation of some manufactures (or things classed in our statistics as manufactures), such as copper and kerosene oil, depends on the same combination,—natural resources and skill. But in many manufactures which are exported the advantage seems to be in skill only. Such are sewing machines, agricultural implements, electrical apparatus, locomotives. These are simply made better, or are made more cheaply through better machinery, because of Yankee ingenuity. And there are many manufactures which, while they do not export heavily, have complete possession of the domestic field, and are not in danger of competition from imports, for the same reason; such as boots and shoes, pressed glassware, the commoner grades of cotton goods. These various manufactures, quite able to face foreign competition, are the ones which it is really profitable for the people of the United States to have; and their range, as already stated, is wider than would be supposed from the common assertions of both protectionists and free traders.

The usual cause of advantage in manufactures is better machinery and methods. Take the case of the shoe manufacture, which has been cited as one of our efficient and independent industries. Shoes are not imported; they are beginning to be exported in considerable quantities. The Americans have taken the lead in the invention and perfection of machinery for making them. But machinery can be bought or copied. The Germans, perhaps, can copy it, and then, working it with cheaper labor, can undersell the Americans. This is, or at least was, often true of the Germans; they have been good imitators, though slow originators. It is said that American steel skates, devised and perfected in the United States, were copied to the smallest detail in Germany, and then, being made there with cheaper labor, were imported into this country again. This sort of imitation is not always possible; since, for working machinery, a force of intelligent and skillful mechanics is often as necessary as the machinery itself, and is much more difficult to copy. But the thing is possible, if not always, at least in many cases; and the more so if machinery becomes automatic. The salvation of the industry then is, in a country like the United States, incessantly to improve machinery. Constant progress is the condition of maintaining the comparative advantage. Once the same methods — that is, the same efficiency of labor — prevail the world over, and the country where wages are lower can sell cheaper.[1]

It is commonly said that the United States is likely to have an advantage in those manufactures where machinery is much used. This is true; but the real explanation is not often given. The mere use of labor-saving machinery does not give an advantage. Machinery represents only one way of applying labor. It is the use of labor-saving machinery to a greater degree or in a more ingenious way that enables the output to be comparatively cheap, even though the wages of laborers be high. In those industries which are adapted to the machine processes, American labor is *likely* to be more efficient. Which those industries are, cannot be settled by any rule. The march of invention is irregular. Sometimes Americans take the lead, sometimes Englishmen, sometimes Germans or Frenchmen. It is proverbial that Americans have a more than creditable record in this sort of competition; and the economic corollary is that they do well to confine their manufacturing activity to those industries in which they seem able to keep in the van.

In some cases in the recent history of manufacturing industry in the United States, it is to be admitted that this process of getting the lead seems to have been promoted by protection. That is, protection to young industries has been successfully applied. The object has been attained by a rude, blundering, expensive method; but in fairness we must grant that attained it has been. The silk manufacture has already been cited as an example. Possibly the iron and steel manufacture presents

[1] This holds true, that is, of any one industry. If *all* industries had the same methods and the same efficiency the world over, there would presumably be no differences in wages, and hence no trading advantage for any one country because of cheaper labor. International trade would then cease. Cp. Chapter 34, § 3.

another. But this latter case is more doubtful, because the question always arises whether such an industry, not really new to the country (as was the silk manufacture), would not probably have grown to independence under any circumstances. The steady increase and thickening of population, and the growing scarcity of free land, tend in any event to bring about a development of other than agricultural industry. The great stream of immigration, and the altered conditions of labor supply thereby brought about, strengthen still more this tendency. The tariff system, even where it may seem to have acted in the way of protection to young industries, has often but quickened slightly development which would have come soon enough without it.

§ 9. Making all possible allowances for the various ways in which the initial burden has been offset in the United States, there probably remains a heavy debit balance against protection, through the creation of industries dependent upon it. These present the problem, always difficult, of the claims of vested interests. No one would propose that persons who had in good faith made great investments in plant, on the reasonable supposition of the continuance of the protective policy, should be deprived of the protection suddenly and without notice. It is true that their own statements regarding the rates of duty which they "need" are always exaggerated, and that a much greater reduction is usually feasible, without real breakage, than they are willing to admit. None the less breakage is to be avoided. The reaction against protection, if it should come, ought to proceed by gradual and tentative steps. This sort of consideration, however, need not be shown with regard to many raw materials, in producing which no considerable plant is needed. Such, for instance, is wool, on which the United States long maintained a heavy duty, not defensible on any solid economic ground. The tariff act of 1894 was wisely framed so far as it abolished once for all the wool duty; this was the one bold step taken in that unfortunate and short-lived measure. The duties on timber, hemp, coal, are similarly indefensible, and could be done away with at short notice.

Nothing has been said, in this review of the tariff problem in our own country, of some of its more obvious bad aspects, — the pressure of interested producers to obtain measures favorable to themselves, the contributions of a semi-corrupt character to party chests, the log rolling by which each legislator strives to secure in the general scramble duties that will be of benefit, or at least will be thought of benefit, to his own constituents. The tendency, in popular government, for each representative to press the real or supposed interests of his special constituents is the greatest evil of democracy. It has been experienced to the full in our tariff legislation. But it appears in many directions, in things good as well as in things doubtful, — in education, harbor improvements, the postal service, public control of railways and other industries. Something of the sort must be faced whenever the state undertakes to direct and regulate matters of economic consequence. We must keep in mind chiefly the general outcome, under such working conditions as the existing state of political machinery makes possible; and from this point of view the question of protection also must be judged.

References on Book IV

On the foreign exchanges, see G. J. Goschen, *The Theory of the Foreign Exchanges* (last ed., 1901), and G. Clare, *The A B C of the Foreign Exchanges* (1895). On international trade, the chapters in J. S. Mill, *Principles of Political Economy* (last ed., 1871), Book III, Chapters 17 *seq.*, though in some parts unduly elaborated, are still unsurpassed. A good modern statement, almost too compact, is in C. F. Bastable, *The Theory of International Trade* (4th ed., 1903). A mathematical treatment is in three papers by F. Y. Edgeworth, "The Theory of International Values," in the *Economic Journal*, Vol. IV (1894). I venture to refer also to my own paper on "Wages and Prices in Relation to International Trade," *Quarterly Journal of Economics*, Vol. XX, August, 1906.

Notwithstanding the mass of literature on free trade and protection, no book covers the controversy satisfactorily. H. Fawcett, *Free*

Trade and Protection (1885), states the simpler reasoning in favor of free trade and refutes the cruder protectionist fallacies. A. C. Pigou, *Protective and Preferential Import Duties* (1906), is able and discriminating, but written with reference chiefly to the contemporary controversy (1895–1905) in Great Britain. On this, see also W. J. Ashley, *The Tariff Problem* (1903). On the German debates, see, among others, L. Pohle, *Deutschland am Scheidewege* (1902), and A. Wagner, *Agrar- und Industriestaat* (1902), both in favor of protection for agriculture; and on the other side, L. Brentano, *Die Schrecken des Industriestaates* (1901), and H. Dietzel, *Weltwirthschaft und Volkswirtschaft* (1900). On the tariff history of the United States, E. Stanwood, *American Tariff Controversies in the Nineteenth Century* (1903), a narrative account of legislation and discussion by a protectionist; and F. W. Taussig, *The Tariff History of the United States* (ed. of 1909).

www.ingramcontent.com/pod-product-compliance
Lightning Source LLC
LaVergne TN
LVHW101452200926
848483LV00001B/108